ANIMAL MODELS IN PSYCHOPATHOLOGY

ANIMAL MODELS IN PSYCHOPATHOLOGY

Edited by
Nigel W. Bond
Macquarie University, Sydney, Australia

ACADEMIC PRESS   **1984**
(Harcourt Brace Jovanovich, Publishers)

Sydney   Orlando   San Diego   Petaluma   New York
London   Toronto   Montreal   Tokyo

ACADEMIC PRESS AUSTRALIA
Centrecourt, 25–27 Paul Street North
North Ryde, N.S.W. 2113

United States Edition published by
ACADEMIC PRESS INC.
Orlando, Florida 32887

United Kingdom Edition published by
ACADEMIC PRESS, INC. (LONDON) LTD.
24/28 Oval Road, London NW1 7DX

Printed in Australia

National Library of Australia Cataloguing-in-Publication Data

Animal models in psychopathology.

Includes index.
ISBN 0 12 114180 2.

1. Psychology, Pathological – Animal models. 2. Animal
psychopathology. 3. Psychiatry, Comparative.
I. Bond, N. W. (Nigel William), 1949– .

616.89'07'0724

Library of Congress Catalog Card Number: 84-70401

CONTENTS

CONTRIBUTORS

Dale M. Atrens, Department of Psychology, The University of Sydney, NSW Australia, 2006.

J. R. Bassett, School of Biological Sciences, Macquarie University, North Ryde, NSW Australia, 2113.

P. J. V. Beumont, Department of Psychiatry, The University of Sydney, NSW Australia, 2006.

Nigel W. Bond, School of Behavioural Sciences, Macquarie University, North Ryde, NSW Australia, 2113.

K. D. Cairncross, School of Biological Sciences, Macquarie University, North Ryde, NSW Australia, 2113.

David G. Laing, CSIRO Division of Food Research, P.O. Box 52, North Ryde, NSW Australia, 2113.

David H. Overstreet, School of Biological Sciences and the Centre for Neuroscience, The Flinders University of South Australia, Bedford Park, SA Australia, 5042.

Roger W. Russell, School of Biological Sciences and the Centre for Neuroscience, The Flinders University of South Australia, Bedford Park, SA Australia, 5042.

G. Singer, Department of Psychology, La Trobe University, Bundoora, Vic. Australia, 3083.

Leonard H. Storlien, Garvan Institute of Medical Research, St Vincents Hospital, Darlinghurst, NSW Australia, 2010.

M. Wallace, Department of Psychology, La Trobe University, Bundoora, Vic. Australia, 3083.

PREFACE

The present volume is devoted to the general topic of "animal models in psychopathology". It arose out of the idea for a conference, but one which never came to fruition. Nevertheless, it seemed to me that there were enough people with original approaches to various topics covered by the title to make a book on "Animal Models" a viable proposition.

The coverage is selective. I felt that it was important to avoid repeating or updating material covered elsewhere. Instead, I endeavoured to select authors who could focus upon models or disorders that had received little attention in previous volumes on this general topic. Naturally, they had to have received some attention or there was little point in including them! This should be borne in mind as the reader peruses the list of topics and discovers the absence of disorders such as "schizophrenia" or animal models such as the "learned helplessness" model of depression.

It is always a pleasure to record one's "debts" at the completion of a major endeavour. In the present case, thanks are due to Wayne McTegg, who has ensured that my laboratory has run effectively when I was otherwise engaged, and to the various contributors for their hard work and good-humoured acceptance of my "suggestions". Special thanks go to Roger Russell who has never failed to tell me when I got it wrong, and whose advice has been accepted on many occasions. I have appreciated the assistance of the staff at Academic Press: Grant Walker, for his enthusiastic response in setting the project on course to publication; and, more recently,

Jeremy Fisher, whose skills have altered the final contributions in numerous ways, always for the better. Their contributions to this volume have made the process a learning experience for me and one that I have enjoyed immensely. Finally, I have my family to thank, Judith, Emma, Amanda and Catherine. All those Sunday afternoons were not in vain!

1
ANIMAL MODELS IN PSYCHOPATHOLOGY: AN INTRODUCTION

NIGEL W. BOND

I. INTRODUCTION

"We are not just rather like animals; we are animals. Our differences
from other species may be striking, but comparisons with them have always
been, and must be, crucial to our view of ourselves". Thus the philosopher,
Mary Midgley, begins her treatise *Beast and Man* (1979). The purpose of
the present chapter is to examine this basic proposition with reference to
psychopathology. The possibility that empirical studies of infrahuman
animals might shed light on human psychopathology as well as more
"normal" functions has excited many, starting with Pavlov (1927). Indeed,
the history of animal models of psychopathology almost mirrors that of
animal models of learning in both personnel and outlook. Thus, it began
with an initial emphasis upon all-embracing models which gradually became
more and more restricted as it was realised that such imitations were of little
heuristic value in our understanding of the human disorders they were
meant to mirror (Gantt, 1944; Liddell, 1950; Maier, 1949; Masserman,
1964). I shall make no attempt to examine the history of these earlier
attempts and the reader is referred to two excellent articles by Broadhurst
(1960; 1973) for such a coverage.

The present volume is thus the latest seeking to examine a variety of
animal models of human psychopathology. Some of the more recent
include Hanin and Usdin (1977), Keehn (1979), Kimmel (1971), Maser and

ANIMAL MODELS IN PSYCHOPATHOLOGY
ISBN   0 12 114180 2

Seligman (1977) and Serban and Kling (1976). In some respects we begin it with a *faux pas*. The zoologist might ask what is meant by the term "animal" in the title and whose "psychopathology" is being modelled? The short answer is that we are referring to infra-human models of human psychopathology. Herein lies the crux of this introductory chapter. To what extent can we meaningfully "model" human psychopathology in other animals? (This is the question I shall be dealing with but in essence it is part of a broader question concerning the extrapolation of knowledge of one species to any other species.)

To examine this question I shall have recourse to a number of issues. First, we need to examine what we mean by the term "model" and the status of models in psychology. Second, to understand where we locate our particular approach to psychopathology we shall consider the two basic models of man — humanistic and mechanistic. In so doing we shall begin to define the limits of what we can do using animals as "substitutes" for humans. The use of animal models falls very much into the mechanistic tradition and as a result we shall also need to review the status of reductionism in psychology. Third, it is necessary that we discuss psychopathology in some detail. Again, the diversity of approaches to human psychopathology and the transactions involved in the psychiatric process set limits to what we can model employing animals. Fourth, I shall describe what I believe we can do in modelling human disorders. To a certain extent this will lead us into the question of what species are most appropriate as models.

While the above may be academically controversial, it pales beside the vexed question of the ethics of employing animals as models in a context where there is unlikely to be any payoff to the infrahuman species being exploited. Most authors seeking to establish the legitimacy of animal models of human behaviour have provided an ethical justification for their work in the sense that it would be unethical to do certain things to people. It is rare for them to go on and examine whether such things should actually be done to animals. (Of those dealing with psychopathology, the volume by Keehn appears to be the only one to address this issue in a specific chapter.) Given current interest in this topic (for example, the case of Edwin Taub in the United States [Comment, *Science*, 1981] and the bemoaning of many scientists that the public does not seem to understand why they are working with animals) it is appropriate in such a volume to provide a *raison d'être* for such endeavours. I shall complete the present chapter with a section on this topic.

II. MODELS IN PSYCHOLOGY

A. Models and theories

A brief inspection of any reputable dictionary will reveal a plethora of meanings for the word "model". For those interested in working through such lists, the article by Chapanis (1961) is an excellent overview. However, I shall be treating the term as suggested by Underwood (1957): "Scientific or engineering models are representations, or likenesses, of certain aspects of complex events, structures, or systems, made by using symbols or objects which in some way resemble the thing being modelled". There are two basic types of model, the replica model and the symbolic model. The latter are mathematical representations and will not concern us in this volume although they are of considerable interest in modelling aspects of, for example, cognitive functioning employing animals (cf. Grossberg, 1982). We shall be concerned with replica models, which are material representations. However, it is important to note that models are analogies and when we use models we are not making existence claims for them. For example, when we model human cognitive processes using a computer, we are not suggesting that the human brain is itself a collection of micro-chips!

A model is a heuristic device. This is important because in defining a model in the way that we have, we are accepting the fact that a model need not be completely accurate. As noted by Clark (1980), a model is different from a "theory". The latter is a partially interpreted calculus consisting of a syntax relating the terms of the theory and certain semantic rules which give meaning to the terms in the calculus. A theory is a more formal set of propositions and required to withstand tests of it in a more "robust" fashion than a model (Carnap, 1939; Nagel, 1961). Indeed, the relationships between models and theories is such that once one enters existence claims for a model then one is acknowledging that one is no longer working with a model but with a theory and must meet the more stringent requirements set for theories. (At an intuitive level, this distinction is similar to that we might make between the criteria necessary to stablish analogy versus those more stringent criteria necessary to establish homology — see Section IV, B.) Part of the confusion concerning the use of animal models of human psychopathology appears to reside in the fact that people confuse models and theories and demand of the former what they expect of the latter. Although there is no discussion of animal models of schizophrenia in the present volume, many people assume that attempts to produce such models are attempts to produce "schizophrenic" animals. Clearly, they need not be. Unfortunately, many people exploiting animal models do not understand this distinction either, which only compounds the problem.

B. Uses and abuses of models

Given that so much energy has been put into the development of such a large number of animal models of human psychopathology, it is worth spending some time looking at the usefulness of models *per se*. Again, reference to Chapanis (1961) provides us with some insight into the uses and abuses of models. (Since Chapanis is concerned with ergonomic and engineering models, some are of little import for our discussion and have been omitted. The interested reader is referred to the original.)

The first use described by Chapanis is singularly appropriate to our task, in that he discusses models as describing and helping us to understand complex systems or events. This is a typical *raison d'être* of animal models. That is, by resorting to an infrahuman animal stripped of all confounding cultural factors and under the complete control of the experimenter as regards its genetic background and its environment during its often shorter life-span, we may be able to unravel part of the story behind a particular disorder. Examples of such an approach abound in the present volume. Second, Chapanis suggests that models provide us with a framework in which experiments are done. To this extent models differ from theories in that the experiments derived from models would appear to be of the "what if" variety rather than the formal hypothesis testing experiments of the predictions deduced from theories. Third, models help us to see new relationships. An examination of the literature in general psychology provides numerous examples of how we have come to view the nervous system in different ways as a result of the models extant at the time. Thus, the nervous system was once viewed as analogous to a telephone exchange (Broadbent, 1961). With the advent of computers, the predominant model switched, if you will excuse the pun, to viewing the brain as a high speed computer and cognitive processes were viewed in terms of software programming (Newell and Simon, 1972). More recently, with the development of holograms people are starting to produce models of human memory which rely heavily on holography for their analogies (Pribram, 1981). Fourth, Chapanis points out that models amuse us! In an endeavour as highly technical as science, people are often surprised to find that scientists do things because they find them amusing and interesting. A reading of Watson (1968) should put people to rights about that. The motives that lead to scientific endeavour are no different from those of other pursuits and it would be surprising if they were (cf. Mahoney, 1976; Medawar, 1979). Finally, not mentioned by Chapanis but of obvious relevance to the present work, animal models enable us to pursue avenues of research that would be impossible with humans — for example, selectively breeding lines of rats to determine if alcohol preference is under genetic control (Eriksonn, 1972).

If the above are some of the uses of animal models, what are the abuses of such models? Again, we can refer to Chapanis. First, models invite overgeneralization. This is of fundamental importance when we are working with animal models of particularly human concerns and it is a point to which we shall return when discussing the problems of extrapolation from one species to another. Most of Chapanis' other abuses are problems of logic which need not concern us here. However, one final concern he raises is related to the role that models play in scientific endeavours. While it is true that models need not concern themselves as much as theories with contradictory evidence (Clark, 1980), nevertheless this is often taken to the point that model builders seem oblivious to contradictory evidence. One must be wary of falling into this trap.

C. Human models

1. Mechanists and humanists

We have now got some idea of the roles played by models in science, their relationships to more formal theories and their uses and abuses. Given this background, we can move on to examine some current human models to determine the initial context in which we can place our animal models. My major source here is a volume titled *Models of Man* edited by Chapman and Jones (1980) and emanating from a conference held at Cardiff, Wales, in 1979. I do not suggest any primacy for this source except to say that for my purposes it brings into clear focus the fact that we have two distinct human models, in one of which there is a role for animal models and in the other of which there is not.

Stripped of the hyperbole that often surrounds such endeavours, I believe that this conference makes clear that there are currently two traditions in psychology (at least in European psychology), namely phenomenology and empiricism; or, put another way, psychologists can be divided into humanists and mechanists. An examination of these traditions indicates that they talk about totally different things in different ways. The empiricist has difficulty in accepting humanistic theories because they cannot be put to empirical test. The phenomenologist believes that the things that mechanists examine empirically are trivial. There is no need to look further into this schism. However, what should be clearly understood is that the notion of employing animal models falls firmly into the empiricist/mechanist tradition. The concerns of the phenomenologists, focusing as they do on concepts such as "growth" and "essence" and relying heavily on linguistic interaction for their approaches to therapy, cannot be met by such models (cf. Rogers, 1964; Skinner, 1964, for a lucid account of the differences in approach).

Our use of animal models is thus confined to the empiricist/mechanist tradition in psychology. However, even within this tradition, many investigators are unwilling to accept a role for animal models within not only psychopathology, but also in psychology in general. Basically, the problem that arises for many people when encountering animal models is the fact that such models tend to be predicated upon the assumption that many of the disorders encompassed by human psychopathology are physiological in origin. As a result, many psychologists appear to be put on the defensive by the spectre of psychology disappearing as it is reduced to physiology. To overcome this particular prejudice, it is worth spending a short time examining the problem of reduction in psychology.

2. Reductionism in psychology

In this section I have been heavily influenced by Clark (1980). The first point that Clark makes is that when we talk about reduction we are not talking about reducing psychology to physiology, we are taking about reducing a theory in psychology to a theory in physiology. What does this mean practically? Essentially, what Clark is saying is that we can only have a physiological model of a process that we already understand on the basis of an extant psychological theory. To use an example relevant to the present volume, we can only provide a physiological model for those aspects of a psychopathology that we can already describe using a psychological theory. Thus, we can attempt to provide a physiological account for certain features of depression such as the failure of conventional rewards, but we shall have great difficulty in accounting for other features of depression such as the emotional concomitants of the disorder. They must await a psychological explanation before we can presume to produce a physiological model of them.

Second, the reduction of one theory to another does not imply that the characteristics described by the reduced theory are illusory or simply consist of the elements invoked by the reducing theory. Let us take an example posed by Clark to make this point clear. It has been suggested that excitation through the noradrenergic pathways of the median forebrain bundle is the process underlying reward or reinforcement (Stein and Wise, 1973). However, what does such an explanation tell us about the concept of reward? It implies that this process underlies reward and that stimulation of this process will increase the probability of a behaviour that immediately precedes it but it does not clarify the connection between the physical process and the behaviour. To do the latter would require considerably more evidence from a variety of invasive physiological techniques which are simply not necessary for us to accept the psychological explanation. The psychological description is thus more parsimonious and satisfying as an explanation of the behaviour. While we have reduced reward to a particular process occurring within the central nervous system, we have not eliminated the need for a psychological explanation of the behaviour. The point made by Clark is very similar to that made by Skinner (1950).

Finally, our attempts at reduction may be further restricted. If we examine a variety of animals, we may find that for each animal we can map a psychological process, for example, habituation, onto structures in the central nervous system of each animal, whether beast, fish or fowl. However, when we compare across the species we may discover that the underlying structures are different in each case. Thus, we shall have reduced the psychological theory satisfactorily in each case, but it will still have primacy on the grounds of its greater generality.

These propositions form but the bare bones of Clark's treatise. Nevertheless, I think they make the point that reduction will not lead to the disappearance of psychological explanations. Reduction according to Clark will be derivative in nature, not eliminative as has been the uneasy fear of too many psychologists (Fodor, 1968; Sutherland, 1970). Presumably, both psychology and physiology will benefit from this "interactionist" position (cf. Russell, 1972).

III. PSYCHOPATHOLOGY

The terms we have dealt with thus far have been relatively easy to define; however, the same cannot be said of the word "psychopathology". Its usage and what it denotes differ quite considerably depending upon the model of abnormal behaviour held by an individual. Literally, the term means the study of diseases of the mind, which is one reason some people are reluctant to allow for the possibility that animals can tell us anything about the topic. Clearly the area covered is concerned with mental health, although the usage of the term "health" places are discussion within the confines of the medical model, so at this point it might be useful to identify some of the major paradigms in the area of psychopathology.

Inspection reveals at least five major approaches to psychopathology. These are: psychodynamic; biological, including such things as neurobiological and genetic approaches; labelling theory; the behavioural approach; and, finally, cultural. Naturally, these perspectives are not mutually exclusive although a keen student of the history of psychology will already know that the psychodynamic approach falls into the general humanist tradition whereas the behavioural and biological approaches fall into the mechanist tradition. This listing is intended to sensitize the reader to the point that there is no single paradigm in psychopathology. As such, it is unlikely that all those who work in this area will accept the use of animal models as a means of enhancing our understanding of particular disorders. Without delving too deeply at this point it is clear that the biological and behavioural approaches are likely to accept such models given their mechanistic stance to this question and that the psychodynamic approach will eschew such endeavours.

Irrespective of what particular paradigm we work in, we are always faced with questions concerning the processes that lead to someone being labelled as in need of treatment for a disorder. A brief examination of these processes is worthwhile to enable us to understand that there are many things about psychopathology that are beyond the reach of an animal model. The processes that lead to someone seeking or being sent for treatment are essentially social. The sequence in abbreviated form is that persons do, say or think something, in a situation that is deemed inappropriate by the persons themselves or significant others. Practically, this means that there are wide variations in the numbers of people who are labelled as having a psychiatric disorder depending upon such factors as sex, race and social class (Scheff, 1981). There is no need for us to dwell on the sociological aspects of this problem. They are beyond the purview of this volume. The point that needs to be made is that for any group of people who are cited as having a particular mental disorder, there are many other people with similar histories who have not been so labelled and who appear to function quite adequately. Thus, the sample we use to model our disorder is biased at the outset.

If a person seeks or is requested to seek treatment because of some disturbing aspect of his or her behaviour, then he or she will encounter the next step in the psychiatric process which is diagnosis. It is not the intention to deal with the voluminous literature concerned with the accuracy or otherwise of psychiatric diagnosis. There is still considerable debate on this question (Scheff, 1981; Robins, 1981). However, there are two aspects of this process that are instructive for our purposes. First, what symptoms are utilised in a diagnosis and, second, whether particular symptom patterns indicate particular disorders?

To some extent the symptom patterns regarded as important are determined by the conceptual model of the therapist. Thus, psychodynamically-oriented therapists will look for somewhat different symptoms to their behaviourally-oriented counterparts. Nevertheless, if we examine symptoms, then we see immediately that there will be difficulties in providing animal analogues of certain of them. For example, it is puzzling to see how one could model concepts such as "suicidal ideas", "perplexity" and "bizarre ideation" to name but three. It has been embarrassing enough providing an animal model of as overt a symptom as "overdrinking". How much harder will it be to model ideational symptoms that we obtain verbally and not through direct observation?

The second question we need to examine is whether different disorders are associated with distinct symptom patterns? Again, this is an area of some contention but an examination reveals that many of the major psychiatric disorders have somewhat similar symptom patterns. Examples can be found in Zigler and Phillips (1961). The problem this raises is how does one go about modelling a particular disorder if the symptoms associated with the disorder are not specific to it? Abramson and Seligman (1977), in a discussion of the criteria necessary for establishing animal models, argue that one should avoid modelling general features of all psychopathologies, and yet human psychopathologies seem to share a large number of general features. We shall return to an examination of the criteria one might employ in establishing an animal model of a particular disorder. However, the overlap in symptom patterns across disorders has consequences for what we actually try to model.

IV. COMPARATIVE PSYCHOPATHOLOGY: EXTRAPOLATION FROM ANIMALS TO HUMANS

A. Rules and animal models

At the beginning of this chapter I quoted Mary Midgley to indicate the necessity of looking at other animals to gain some understanding of ourselves. However, even if we accept such a premise, we are presented with a problem. How do we determine what is legitimate extrapolation? The point is made neatly by Russell (personal communication) and I quote: "To me this means that the ultimate criterion for our type of models is the validity with which information derived from them can transfer to the human situation. This involves cross-species generalizations, not intra-species. There are problems in making such generalizations. For example, there are no statistics for estimating the validities of such generalizations — nothing equivalent to statistics available for generalizing from samples to populations within a species". This is not to say that there has been no attempt to establish such "rules" and we might begin by examining some of these.

Many of the propositions put forward by previous investigators have already come under scrutiny (Broadhurst, 1960; 1973). Rather than repeat this material I shall devote my attention to the criteria put forward by Abramson and Seligman (1977). They provide four basic rules to be followed in developing an animal model of a particular psychopathology. Similar criteria are put forward by McKinney (1977). These are:

1. Does the model describe the essential features of the causes and cures of the disorder?
2. Is there similarity of symptoms between the model and the actual disorder?
3. Is the underlying physiology similar?
4. Is the model specific to a particular disorder or is it simply modelling the general features of human psychopathology?

It is unlikely that any of the models in this book meet the criteria laid down by Abramson and Seligman. The reader who has followed my arguments thus far will probably agree that these criteria could not be met by any animal model. The first "rule" creates a problem in that we do not know what the causes and cures of most psychopathologies are. To be facetious, that is why we are using models in the first place! This same argument applies to the third "rule". We often exploit animal models to elucidate the physiological mechanisms that underlie particular disorders. With regard to "rule" two, we have already indicated that for most psychopathologies many of the symptoms cannot be modelled in animals. Finally, most psychopathologies share a substantial number of symptoms so that any model that meets the other criteria would almost certainly fall foul of "rule" four because that is the nature of the event being modelled.

The criteria suggested by Abramson and Seligman (1977) seem to be aimed at general models of particular disorders. While this approach has a certain face validity, I do not think that it is the only viable approach. An alternative is to model very specific features of a disorder (for example, the pharmacological basis of the drugs that are effective in allaying the symptoms associated with the disorder). Of course this approach does not negate the pursuit of more general models as suggested by Abramson and Seligman, but in the short term at least it is likely to produce more viable, albeit narrow, "models" of aspects of various disorders. Naturally, at some time researchers have to place their models in the larger context of the "complete" disorder; nevertheless, this alternative avoids controversy, at least initially, as to whether a particular model has all of the general features of the particular human problem. An example of an area where controversy about criteria seems to me to have been a drawback rather than a strength is in the utilisation of animal models in alcohol-related research. In that area there seem to be as many criteria as there are researchers! Despite the narrowness of the approach I have recommended, it still leaves us many questions to answer. Basically, we still have to examine the question posed by Roger Russell at the beginning of this section; how do we know when it is legitimate to extrapolate?

B. Homology and analogy

The most obvious evidence upon which we can rest a case of extrapolation is by demonstrating similarity. Unfortunately, such a demonstration is neither necessary nor is it sufficient. Kornetsky (1977) has made the point that when the medical sciences are dealing with obviously physical problems they at least have the advantage that there is isomorphism or homology between the disorder they observe in humans and what they see in animals; for example, hypertension. Such is unlikely to be the case in the area of psychopathology. Here, we are more likely to be confronted with analogies. An example is Cade's discovery of the use of lithium in the treatment of mania (Cade, 1979). Cade hypothesised that mania was brought about by an excess of urea and injected guinea pigs with lithium urate because it was the most soluble salt. Instead of his guinea pigs becoming excitable, they became lethargic. Following further studies with lithium carbonate, Cade moved on to treat 10 manic patients with lithium and found that it normalised their mood. Clearly, the similarity between activity in guinea pigs and mood in manic humans is analogous at best. This notion of the use of the biological concepts of *analogy* and *homology* to determine the similarity between animal models and their human focus was put forward by Russell (1964) and elaborated upon in the context of models of "normal" behaviour by Von Cranach (1976).

First, we need to establish what we mean by homology and analogy. Homologies are said to be the result of the same organ in different species being subjected to different selection pressures. In contrast, analogies are the result of different organs being subjected to the same selection pressure (Cain, 1976). Of what use are these concepts in advancing our knowledge of the conditions under which we can extrapolate from an animal species to humans? Unfortunately, very little. We can turn to Von Cranach for an explanation of why this is so. Von Cranach notes that the method of homology allows us to answer the question of whether a particular human behaviour is related phylogenetically to its infrahuman counterpart. However, it can only tell us whether the structure of the behaviour is related in the two species, not whether the functions are similar. Thus, if we take the human smile as an example, there is little doubt that a "silent bare-teethed face" can be found in the champanzee (van Hooff, 1972), but it is clear that the chimpanzee does not use this particular facial expression in the myriad ways that humans do in their social interactions. The method of homology is restricted to closely related species and to relatively simple movements. Even given these restrictions it is unlikely to be of much use in helping us establish grounds for extrapolation.

What of analogy? The problem with this term as it has been used to the present is that while it does not restrict the investigator to working with closely related species, it does restrict him to working with species that have been subjected to similar selection pressures. Some might argue that man is unique in that he is a cultural animal and not subject to selection. I do not concur wth this view. Rather, I think our difficulty lies in establishing what the selection pressures were on the human species during the course of its evolution. Inspection reveals a number of different views concerning this question. Thus, one finds proponents of the notion that the social carnivores are the most analogous species since early man was a hunter (Alcock, 1979). Others argue that the savannah primates are the most appropriate since early man was a gatherer (De Vore, 1971). There are almost as many arguments based upon the concept of functional analogy as there are infrahuman species with which humans can be compared! Clearly, the concept of functional analogy provides little foundation upon which to base arguments concerning comparison. Evolutionary theory is a double edged-sword. On the one hand it tells us that there is a continuity to living things; on the other it points to the way that each species is exquisitely adapted to its particular ecological niche (cf. Hinde, 1976).

Homology and analogy illustrate the notion that what we want in an animal model is similarity to the human disorder. This view is exemplified in Abramson and Seligman's rules (1977) and is explicitly stated by Hanin and Usdin in the Foreword to their volume on this topic. Although the pursuit of similarity seems a reasonable goal for a modeller, it brings with it some dangers (Hinde, 1976). Hinde points to three of these. First, we must remember that behaviour is multiply determined and there is likely to be no simple generalization concerning the effects of a particular inter-vention in the one species let alone a generalization that applies to all species. Second, when making comparisons we should take care not to divorce them from the total behavioural repertoire of the species' compared. Two quite similar behaviours may have totally different functions because of the different behavioural contexts in which they occur.

Third, and related to the latter point, Hinde notes that we should always remember that our descriptions of behaviour are abstractions and as such may lead us to oversimplify when we attempt to extrapolate from one species to another.

C. Similarity and difference: The comparative method

Given these caveats we can ask if it is necessary for our animal model to be similar to the human disorder to be viable. The answer is no. Ethology is a discipline that has made a telling contribution to our understanding of behaviour. Modelling, both replica and symbolic, is central to this discipline. Yet, as noted by Immelmann (1980), the replica models that ethologists employ are quite unlike the actual animals they are being used to model, precisely because the ethologist has extracted the important features from the animal and dispensed with the rest. Further, Hinde (1976) makes the point that if we examine the effects of a particular intervention in a variety of species, we can learn as much from those that differ from humans in their reaction to it as from those who react similarly to humans. The range of effects allows us to extract general principles concerning the influences of the intervention. This technique has come to be known as the "comparative" method in animal behaviour (but see Russell, 1952). The comparative method avoids arguments as to which species is the most appropriate as a model for humans as the more species one examines the more robust are the general principles which are likely to emerge. By examining a variety of species a profile of the effects of an intervention can be built up and the possibility of relying too heavily on a species which may be unusual in its reaction to a certain intervention can be avoided. Most of the models in this volume are based upon work with rats. If that were the only evidence upon which such models rested they would indeed suffer from a lack of generality. Happily, other workers around the world are exploiting different species and this fact together with the gains to be made when different laboratories are pursuing the same problem enhances our confidence in the models presented.

While the comparative method is of obvious utility in establishing general principles, it provides us with few clues as to what we can compare initially. How then are we to proceed? First, I think we must ask what the advantages of working with an animal model are. Earlier, I pointed out that an animal model enables aspects of a disorder to be investigated free of confounding cultural factors and with a large degree of control over the animals' environmental and genetic background. This is true, but what is it that we can investigate in animals that we cannot investigate in humans?

Basically, the physiological mechanisms that underpin a disorder (cf. Breese *et al.*, 1978; Warburton, 1983). The vast majority of our knowledge concerning the effects of various aetiological factors in psychopathology, the mechanisms underlying certain symptoms and the physiological changes associated with the administration of therapeutic drugs, comes from work on animals or initiated following animal research. I believe that this is where the utility of an animal model lies. I ask you to recall one of the virtues of a model; that it is heuristic. For example, an animal model is heuristic to the extent that one can take a particular symptom and examine an analogue of that symptom in an animal (preferably several species) to determine the mechanisms that might be involved in producing that symptom in the model animal. To ensure the validity of our extrapolations we shall need to examine where possible the actual human condition. In doing so we are asking whether our model has predictive validity.* The model will not answer our questions directly. What it will do is to provide an economical and efficient way of suggesting hypotheses concerning human disorders. Whether those hypotheses are correct can only be determined by examining the human condition. Used in this way the aninal model does not seek to usurp human experimentation, but to suggest avenues that it may pursue. Of course there will be times when particular hypotheses cannot be followed up in people (for example, where one is employing an animal as a bench-mark in toxicological research). However, the general principles that we can derive using the comparative method enable us to state with greater confidence what the effects on people are likely to be even though we have no formal basis for such extrapolation.

The approach put forward here may seem rather narrow and unambitious in comparison with some earlier endeavours (cf. Gantt, 1944; Liddell, 1980; Maier, 1949; Masserman, 1964; and Pavlov, 1927). However, while this earlier work provided a great deal of information concerning general psychological processes, it told us very little about human psychopathology (Broadhurst, 1973). The value of work carried out in the manner suggested here is that it should not only illuminate the former, but also elucidate the latter.

V. THE ETHICS OF ANIMAL MODELS

There is a continuing controversy over the use of animals in experimentation which will be of benefit to humans alone, if it is of any benefit at all (cf. Regan and Singer, 1976). Stances on this issue range from those

---

* This issue is also discussed by Russell and Overstreet in Chapter 2.

of Singer (1975) and Ryder (1975) who would ban all forms of animal experimentation irrespective of whom it benefits, animals included, through to those who feel that no constraints should be placed upon investigators conducting animal research (White, 1976). The issue is clearly an important one and one that needs addressing in a volume such as this. In so doing I do not propose to go over ground that has been covered previously (cf. Bowd, 1980; Gallup and Suarez, 1980; Magel, 1981; Marcuse and Pear, 1979; Ryder, 1975; Singer, 1975). However, I think it is necessary to examine certain of the tenets of "animal liberation" and their views of what scientific research is about, to determine the arguments behind what some authors see as a moral issue (cf. Singer, 1975).

The first topic that we need to address is the charge made by Singer and Ryder that all exploitation of animals is "speciesism". Speciesism is a term coined by Ryder (1975) and it means "a prejudice or attitude of bias toward the interests of members of one's own species and against those members of another species". In discussing the term Singer points out its similarity to "racism" and "sexism". He implies that to hold such an attitude is as immoral as to hold sexist and racist attitudes. Guilt by association would seem to be the implication. However, to substantiate the meaning of this neologism Singer goes on to attempt to determine the characteristics that set humans apart from other animals. He argues that if we cannot identify such characteristics how can we justify our exploitation of animals? Singer is not alone in this endeavour (cf. Bowd, 1980; Godlovitch et al., 1971; Regan and Singer, 1976). Thus, we must assess whether animals are conscious, whether they suffer, whether they are intelligent, etc. To give the flavour of the reasoning, intelligence does not set humans apart because there are some humans who are retarded and thus less intelligent than, for example, a chimpanzee or even a dog (Singer, 1975). Another favourite is that some chimpanzees may have encroached even upon that exclusively human domain, language (Sebeok and Sebeok, 1980). As exciting as this work is, let us not forget who is doing the teaching! I must confess to being puzzled by this approach. As a biologist, I have no difficulty in defining the characteristics of the human species and I doubt that I could ever confuse a human with a member of another species except perhaps at the fetal stage! I think this listing of characteristics quite misses the point. Animals are not people, as speciesist as it may seem. Indeed, I believe Singer's (1975:24) suggested use of characteristics is quite immoral when he states: "As long as we remember that we should give the same respect to the lives of animals as we give to the lives of those humans at a similar mental level, we shall not go far wrong". I am sorry to say that I am speciesist enough to find an identification of worth based upon the quality of "mental levels" completely unacceptable.

Following on from the discussion of characteristics many authors (Bowd, 1980; Ryder, 1975; Singer, 1975) suggest the following and again I quote from Singer: "So the researcher's dilemma exists in an acute form in psychology: either the animal is not like us, in which case there is no reason for performing the experiment; or else the animal is like us, in which case we ought not to perform an experiment on the animal which would be considered outrageous if performed on one of us". There are logical and empirical problems for this assertion. First, while the statement is set up in the fashion of a logical argument, it fails to convince because of the use of the word "like". The word "like" is defined by the *Shorter Oxford Dictionary* as "similar, resembling"; it says nothing about being the "same as". I would assert that Singer's argument only holds if the word "like" is deleted and replaced by "same as", but clearly Singer cannot do that since elsewhere he admits that obviously people differ from other animals. Empirically, the statement has problems since it is based upon the supposition that animals are only investigated if they are going to behave similarly to people. I have already noted that such is not the case (Section IV, C.).

A claim often made concerning animal experimentation is that it is trivial or not definitive and therefore should not continue since there are few gains to be made from it and considerable suffering involved. Further, since we have an example of a compound that slipped through despite extensive testing on animals (that is, thalidomide) animal experimentation may be downright dangerous. These suppositions deserve some reflection to examine whether they have any basis. To take the last first, while it is true that thalidomide had been extensively tested upon animals, it transpired that it had not been tested upon pregnant animals (Sjostrom and Nilsson, 1972). The fact that subsequent research has shown that not all animals display teratogenesis following *in utero* exposure to thalidomide highlights again my point that we should use several species where possible.

The assertion that much research is trivial and that we should only carry out definitive experiments with animals (if we use them at all) displays an ignorance of the conduct and philosophy of science. An examination of the history of science reveals that there are few if any definitive experiments. True, we see some such experiments written up in textbooks, but textbooks are simply the manifestation of the current paradigm and the "definitive" studies are catalogued to give the flavour of the paradigm (Kuhn, 1962). Often, we discover that the definitive experiment did not work at all (O'Neil, 1969)! To ask animal experimenters to produce definitive experiments is to ask them to do what no one else can do. To answer the charge of triviality and to bring us closer to the topic of this volume, it is interesting to examine the National Institutes of Mental Health (NIMH) volume titled

Research in the Service of Mental Health (1975). This volume had as one of its tasks the study of the processes involved in scientific discovery and technological innovation. To do this it focused upon the tranquillizer chlorpromazine, the development of which was a watershed in the care of the mentally ill. To make the point that there is no such thing as a definitive experiment and to indicate how difficult it is to determine if an experiment is trivial or not I quote Seymour S. Kety: "There are many crucial discoveries, along numerous devious pathways, in ways that could not have been anticipated, to the synthesis of chlorpromazine ... research and applied research, organic chemistry, biochemistry, physiology, pharmacology, surgery, experimental psychology, and eventually psychiatry... The logic of a master plan was completely lacking; in its stead were a multitude of smaller plans, creative and logical but none having as its goal a treatment of mental illnesses... One conclusion, immediately apparent and rather surprising, is that none of the crucial findings or pathways that led, over a century, to the ultimate discovery of chlorpromazine and was essential to it would have been called relevant to the treatment of mental illness even by the most sophisticated judge" (NIMH Report, *Research in the Service of Mental Health*, 1975:147–148).

I think the point is well made. Those who wish only for the definitive experiment or one which will serve a direct or urgent purpose are deluding themselves as to the nature of scientific discovery. How can we say in advance what will be trivial and what will be useful (cf. Gallup and Suarez, 1980)?

I believe the above indicates that the arguments against animal experimentation lack substance. To call someone a speciesist can imply no moral condemnation. What does this mean for the way that we should conduct our experiments? It does not mean, as many animal liberationists would suggest, that we have *carte blanche* to torture our subjects because of our moral turpitude! It means that we should be convinced of the value of the study we are about to pursue, have determined that there is no other way that the information can be obtained, use as few subjects as are necessary to enable reliable conclusions to be drawn and restrict any suffering on the part of our subjects to the absolute minimum. I am the first to agree that, in retrospect, some cruel and useless experiments have been conducted on animal subjects and that we need regulations to determine limits and to guide researchers as to what is deemed reasonable and proper in experimentation upon animals (cf. Report of Working Party on Animal Experimentation, 1979). However, at present, I think the gains to be made from animal studies, in terms of their contribution to the alleviation of human suffering, fully justify our continuing with them. If that makes me a speciesist, so be it!

Clearly, the material I have dealt with only scratches the surface of this particular problem and the interested reader is referred to the references mentioned to obtain a broader view of the pros and cons of animal experimentation.

VI. CONCLUSIONS

In the present chapter I have sought to place the use and utility of animal models within a context where I believe they can make their most telling contribution. In doing so I have noted that the use of animal models is restricted to the mechanist/empiricist tradition in psychology. Their utility takes two forms: first in enabling one to establish general principles concerning various psychological and physiological influences in psychopathology; and second in allowing the direct study of the possible physiological underpinnings of various disorders. At present, there are no rules as to what must be established in order to produce a viable animal model. Similarity is the most obvious feature that most models aspire to and such models do have some face validity. Nevertheless, animals that react in a fashion quite dissimilar to humans can also prove of value in enabling a true comparative study of a phenomenon and in allowing general principles to emerge. However, the ultimate criterion would appear to be whether the model has predictive validity for the human disorder it is modelling: that can only be determined by examining the human condition itself.

REFERENCES

Abramson, L.Y. and Seligman, M.E.P. Modelling psychopathology in the laboratory: History and rationale. In J.D. Maser and M.E.P. Seligman (Eds.), *Psychopathology: Experimental Models*. San Francisco: Freeman, 1977: 1–26.
Alcock, J. *Animal behavior: An evolutionary approach*. Sunderland, Mass.: Sinauer, 1979.
Bowd, A.D. Ethical reservations about psychological research with animals. *The Psychological Record*, 1980, 30: 201–210.
Breese, G.R., Mueller, R.A., Mailman, R.B., Frye, G.D. and Vogel, R.A. An alternative to animal models of central nervous system disorders: Study of drug mechanisms and disease symptoms in animals. *Progress in Neuro-Psychopharmacology*, 1978, 2: 313–325.
Broadbent, D.E. *Behaviour*. London: Eyre & Spottiswoode, 1961.
Broadhurst, P.L. Abnormal animal behaviour. In H.J. Eysenck (Ed.), *Handbook of Abnormal Psychology*, 1st Ed., London: Pitman, 1960: 726–763.
Broadhurst, P.L. Animal studies bearing on abnormal behaviour. In H.J. Eysenck (Ed.), *Handbook of Abnormal Psychology*, 2nd Ed., London: Pitman, 1973: 721–754.
Cade, J.F.J. *Mending the Mind*. Melbourne: Sun Books, 1979.
Cain, A.J. The use of homology and analogy in evolutionary theory. In M. Von Cranach (Ed.), *Methods of Inference from Animal to Human Behaviour*. Chicago: Aldine, 1976: 25–38.

Carnap, R. *Foundations of Logic and Mathematics.* Chicago: University of Chicago Press, 1939.
Chapanis, A. Men, machines and models. *American Psychologist*, 1961, 16: 113–131.
Chapman, A.J. and Jones, D.M. *Models of Man.* Leicester: The British Psychological Society, 1980.
Clark, A. *Psychological Models and Neural Mechanisms.* Oxford: Clarendon Press, 1980.
Comment, Scientist convicted on monkey neglect. *Science*, 1981, 214: 1218–1220.
De Vore, I. The evolution of human society. In J.F. Eisenberg and W.S. Dillon (Eds.), *Man and Beast: Comparative Social Behavior.* Washington, D.C.: Smithsonian Institution Press, 1971: 297–311.
Erikkson, K. Behavioral and physiological differences among rat strains specifically selected for their alcohol consumption. *Annals of the New York Academy of Science*, 1972, 197: 32–41.
Fodor, J.A. *Psychological Explanation.* New York: Random House, 1968.
Gallup, G.G. Jr and Suarez, S.D. On the use of animals in psychological research. *The Psychological Record*, 1980, 30: 211–218.
Gantt, W.H. *Experimental Basis for Neurotic Behavior: Origin and Development of Artificially Produced Disturbances of Behavior in Dogs.* New York: Hoeber, 1944.
Godlovitch, S., Godlovitch, R. and Harris, J. (Eds.), *Animals, Men and Morals.* London: Victor Gollancz, 1971.
Grossberg, S. Processing of expected and unexpected events during conditioning and attention: A psychological theory. *Psychological Review*, 1982, 89: 529–572.
Hanin, I. and Usdin, E. *Animal Models in Psychiatry and Neurology*, New York: Pergamon, 1977.
Hinde, R.A. Differences and similarities in comparative psychopathology. In G. Serban and A. Kling (Eds.), *Animal Models in Human Psychobiology.* New York: Plenum, 1976: 187–202.
Hooff, J.A.R.A.M. van. A comparative approach to the phylogeny of laughter and smiling. In R.A. Hinde (Ed.), *Non-verbal Communication.* Cambridge: Cambridge University Press, 1972: 209–241.
Immelmann, K. *Introduction to Ethology.* New York: Plenum, 1980.
Keehn, J.D. *Psychopathology in Animals: Research and Treatment Implications.* New York: Academic Press, 1979.
Kimmel, H.D. *Experimental Psychopathology.* New York: Academic Press, 1971.
Kornetsky, C. Animal models: Promises and problems. In I. Hanin and E. Usdin (Eds.), *Animal Models in Psychiatry and Neurology.* Oxford: Pergamon, 1977: 1–7.
Kuhn, T.S. *The Structure of Scientific Revolutions.* Chicago: University of Chicago Press, 1962.
Liddell, H.S. The role of vigilance in the development of animal neurosis. In P. Hoch and J. Zubin (Eds.), *Anxiety.* New York: Grune and Stratton, 1950: 183–196.
Magel, C.R. *A Bibliography of Animal Rights and Related Matters.* Washington, D.C.: University of America Press, 1981.
Mahoney, M.J. *Scientist as Subject: The Psychological Imperative.* Cambridge, Mass.: Ballinger, 1976.
Maier, N.R.F. *Frustration: The Study of Behaviour Without a Goal.* New York: McGraw-Hill, 1949.
Marcuse, F.L. and Pear, J.J. Ethics and animal experimentation: Personal views. In J.D. Keehn (Ed.), *Psychopathology in Animals: Research and Treatment Implications.* New York: Academic Press, 1979: 305–329.
Maser, J.D. and Seligman, M.E.P. *Psychopathology: Experimental Models.* San Francisco: Freeman, 1977.
Masserman, J.H. *Behavior and Neurosis: An Experimental and Psychoanalytic Approach to Psychobiologic Principles.* New York: Hafner, 1964.
McKinney, W.J.T. Behavioural models of depression in monkeys. In I. Hanin and E. Usdin (Eds.), *Animal Models in Psychiatry and Neurology.* Oxford: Pergamon, 1977: 17–26.

Medawar, P.B. *Advice to a Young Scientist.* New York: Harper and Row, 1979.

Midgley, M. *Beast and Man: The Roots of Human Nature.* Brighton, U.K.: Harvester Press, 1979.

Nagel, E. *The Structure of Science.* London: Routledge Kegan Paul, 1961.

Newell, A. and Simon, H. *Human Problem Solving.* Englewood Cliffs, N.J.: Prentice-Hall, 1972.

O'Neill, W.M. *Fact and Theory: An Aspect of the Philosophy of Science.* Sydney: Sydney University Press, 1969.

Pavlov, I.P. *Conditioned Reflexes* (translated by G.V. Anrep), London: Oxford University Press, 1927.

Pribram, K.H. The neurobiologic approach. In C. Eisdorfer, D. Cohen, A. Kleinman and P. Maxim (Eds.), *Models For Clinical Psychopathology.* Lancaster: MTP Press, 1981: 121–132.

Regan, T. and Singer, P. (Eds.), *Animal Rights and Human Obligations.* Englewood Cliffs, N.J.: Prentice-Hall, 1976.

Report of working party on animal experimentation. *Bulletin of the British Psychological Society,* 1979, 32: 44–52.

Robins, L.N. Critique of the labelling theory paradigm. In C. Eisdorfer, D. Cohen, A. Kleinman and P. Maxim (Eds.), *Models for Clinical Psychopathology.* Lancaster: MTP Press, 1981: 43–51.

Rogers, C.R. Toward a science of the person. In T.W. Wann (Ed.), *Behaviorism and Phenomenology.* Chicago: The University of Chicago Press, 1964: 109–133.

Russell, R.W. *The Comparative Study of Behaviour.* London: H.K. Lewis, 1952.

Russell, R.W. Extrapolation from animals to man. In H. Steinberg (Ed.), *Animal Behaviour and Drug Action.* London: J.A. Churchill, 1964: 410–418.

Russell, R.W. Neurotoxins: A systems approach. In I. Chubb and L.B. Geffen (Eds.), *Neurotoxins: Fundamental and Clinical Advances.* Adelaide: University of Adelaide Press, 1977.

Ryder, R.D. *Victims of Science.* London: Davis-Poynter, 1975.

Scheff, T. The labelling theory paradigm. In C. Eisdorfer, D. Cohen, A. Kleinman and P. Maxim (Eds.), *Models for Clinical Psychopathology.* Lancaster: MTP Press, 1981: 25–41.

Sebeok, T.A. and Sebeok, J.U. *Speaking of Apes: A Critical Anthology of Two-way Communication with Man.* New York: Plenum Press, 1980.

Serban, G. and Kling, A. *Animal Models in Human Psychobiology.* New York: Plenum, 1976.

Singer, P. *Animal Liberation.* London: Jonathan Cape, 1975.

Sjostrom, H. and Nilsson, R. *Thalidomide and the Power of the Drug Companies.* Harmondsworth: Penguin, 1972.

Skinner, B.F. Are theories of learning necessary? *Psychological Review,* 1950, 57: 193–216.

Skinner, B.F. Behaviorism at fifty. in T.W. Wann (Ed.), *Behaviorism and Phenomenology.* Chicago: The University of Chicago Press, 1964: 79–97.

Stein, L. and Wise, C.D. Amphetamine and noradrenergic reward pathways. In E. Usdin and S.H. Snyder (Eds.), *Frontiers in Catecholamine Research.* Oxford: Pergamon, 1973: 963–968.

Sutherland, N.S. Is the brain a physical system? In R. Borger and F. Cioffi (Eds.), *Explanation in the Behavioural Sciences.* Cambridge: Cambridge University Press, 1970: 97–122.

Underwood, B.J. *Psychological Research.* New York: Appleton-Century-Crofts, 1957.

Von Cranach, M. Inference from human to animal behaviour: Conclusions. In M. Von Cranach (Ed.), *Methods of Inference from Animal to Human Behaviour.* Chicago: Aldine, 1976: 355–389.

Warburton, D.M. Extrapolation in the neurochemistry of behaviour. In G.C.L. Davey (Ed.), *Animal Models of Human Behaviour.* London: Wiley, 1983: 339–353.

Watson, J.D. *The Double Helix: A Personal Account of the Discovery of DNA.* New York: Atheneum, 1968.

White, R.J. A defense of vivisection. In T. Regan and P. Singer (Eds.), *Animal Rights and Human Obligations*. Englewood Cliffs, N.J.: Prentice-Hall, 1976: 163–169.
Zigler, E. and Phillips, L. Psychiatric diagnosis and symptomatology. *Journal of Abnormal and Social Psychology*, 1961, 63: 69–75.

2
ANIMAL MODELS IN NEUROBEHAVIOURAL TOXICOLOGY

ROGER W. RUSSELL AND DAVID H. OVERSTREET

I. INTRODUCTION

A. The nature of toxicology

Technological developments since the start of the industrial revolution have altered significantly the chemical environment in which living organisms had evolved during the millions of preceding years. Even before industrialization, living organisms were exposed to toxic conditions from the physical environment, to toxins generated by biological systems and to adverse effects of substances ingested as food stuffs. Indeed, it does not stretch the definition of toxicity completely beyond bounds to consider that the survival of molecular structures in the primordial "soup" constituting the earth some one to five billion years ago depended upon their resistance to the extremely primitive chemical environment to which they were exposed. Among new structures generated by interaction between those already existing only some survived to become involved in yet more complex forms (Miller and Urey, 1959). This evolution is strikingly illustrated even now in "... an underlying *unity* and economy ... which implied a *biochemical evolution* much more elaborate and much earlier than the *biological evolution* that gave us all the various forms, performances, and behaviours of the plants and animals today" (Bernal, 1962). In this context, it should be remembered that it is the capacity to behave in an appropriate manner in a particular situation which ensures survival of each living

ANIMAL MODELS IN PSYCHOPATHOLOGY
ISBN 0 12 114180 2

Copyright © 1984 by Academic Press Australia.
All rights of reproduction in any form reserved.

organism. The paragraphs which follow are concerned with approaches to studying conditions that threaten adaptive behaviours, with what has come to be known collectively as "neurobehavioural toxicology".

Toxicology is the study of the adverse effects of chemicals on living organisms and the application of knowledge so generated to the prevention and alleviation of conditions which produce such effects (Doull *et al.*, 1980). It is both a science and a technology. It is concerned with both principles and practice. It has evolved as a multidisciplinary field. As its name implies, neurobehavioural toxicology focuses on conditions which exceed the capabilities of living organisms to make adjustive responses, that is, within the limits of normal behavioural plasticities.

Traditionally toxicology has obtained from three general sources the information necessary for the development of a systematic body of knowledge. The precision of the *experimental approach* has been applied to animal models, with the familiar query about the validity of extrapolation to humans. *Field studies*, organized around methods of epidemiology, have been used to study persons or groups exposed adventitiously or occupationally to a suspected toxicant. Significant problems have arisen from difficulties in establishing that the substance in question is the antecedent of effects observed and not other possible variables which are also present. Important information also comes from *clinical observations* of persons who, unfortunately, have had toxic exposures to the extent that diagnosis, therapy and rehabilitation are required. As a very new discipline neurobehavioural toxicology can benefit from all these approaches.

Our present concern is with the first of these means for developing the knowledge necessary not only to understand the effects of toxic conditions on the limits of behavioural plasticities and to treat cases in which the limits have been exceeded, but also to be able to regulate these conditions so as to prevent the occurrence of behavioural abnormalities which endanger the capabilities of individuals to cope with their environments. Behavioural neurotoxicology cannot but be heavily dependent upon experimental studies for information about the mechanisms of action by which exogenous and endogenous chemicals distort normally adaptive behaviour. The logic of the experimental approach enables an investigator to change systematically specific parameters of an exposure to such toxins, to measure concomitant changes in behavioural variables and to control all other conditions. Relatively few experimental studies have been carried out using human subjects. Investigators have come to depend upon the time honoured approach of the biomedical sciences employing animal models. Considerable attention is being given to development of such models and to safeguards in the use of them,* specifications having been established by the

---

* This matter is considered further in Chapter 1.

World Health Organization (WHO — 1975) and by individual research workers (for example, Weiss and Laties, 1975). It is generally accepted that the primary objective in the use of animal models is "... not to find superficial similarities between man and animal, but to abstract principles through study of both similarities and differences" (Hinde, 1976).

B. Behaviours as criteria

Although awareness of the importance of behaviour as a criterion is increasing, mortality and physical morbidity (for example, carcinogenesis) attract major attention when adverse effects of exposure to chemicals are considered. It would be foolish to contest the importance of these criteria. However, human beings live for more than merely avoiding these criteria. WHO has taken the position that health does not mean only the absence of disease but also optimal physical, mental and social well-being; it not only means freedom from pain and disease, but also freedom to develop and maintain functional capabilities. Clearly the behaviours involved in coping with an individual's physical and psychosocial environments are essential among these "functional capabilities". Twenty years ago an article could be written with the title "Functional testing for behavioural toxicity; a missing dimension in experimental environmental toxicology" (Ruffin, 1963). Today attention is being directed with increasing frequency toward the risks of neurobehavioural toxicity. Perhaps this is stimulated in part by aroused public opinion and by the magnitudes of awards by the courts in the judgment of cases where responsibility for exposures to toxic conditions can be established.

C. Environmental management

Prevention of toxic states and the correction of conditions producing such states when they occur is the process of "environmental management". Basically this is a process of *trade-offs* between the *biological limits* within which humans can adjust to changes in their external and internal environments, on the one hand, and, on the other, the social *cost-benefits* which are perceived by them as desirable to the quality of their life. In discussion "health promotion and its environmental base", Michael (1982) has commented: "Probably the most perplexing problem is the difficulty in balancing the priorities between a health economy — the jobs and commerce that sustain our lives — and the goal of achieving the optimal status of positive health and social well-being".

Only relatively recently has governmental regulation of health and safety become the object of major public policy. On *a priori* grounds it would seem that this is a vital area in which science could play a very important role. Decisions leading to regulation should be able to call on scientific evidence to provide realistic estimates of the risks involved and the costs of alternative standards. Is such evidence now available? It is almost a decade since a national research council replied by stating: "All difficult decisions are characterized by inadequate information... Problems of regulating chemicals in the environment are particularly beset with information characterized by a high degree of uncertainty. For some aspects of these problems there exists no information at all" (US National Research Council, 1975). A much more recent conference on "The Scientific Basis of Health and Safety Regulation" concluded that: "In most cases, a complete review of available scientific evidence does not provide clear, definitive answers to the questions regulators must address. Uncertainty inevitably remains, inducing regulators to resort to intuitive judgements" (Crandall and Lane, 1981).

The two preceding paragraphs may appear to be a digression from the main theme of animal models in neurobehavioural toxicology. Because the vast majority of the toxins to which various behaviours are especially sensitive is contained in the external environment, neurobehavioural toxicologists have significant contributions to make to their regulation — and for the neurobehavioural toxicologist animal models are essential to those contributions. First, systematic knowledge arising from research using animal models can help to overcome present uncertainties which influence decision-making in environmental management. Second, animal models can provide the basis of a strategy for assaying the behavioural toxicity of suspect compounds or conditions already existing in the environment (Weiss and Laties, 1979). Third, animal models can be (indeed, for some time have been) used to assess new compounds for risks of behavioural toxicity before they are released for use. And, fourth, animal models can serve as "monitors of environmental pollutants" (Hopper, 1980) once standards have been established, a use to which they will be put in a programme for "Biological Monitoring of the State of the Environment (Bio-Indicators)" established recently by the International Union of Biological Sciences.

II. MODELS IN NEUROBEHAVIOURAL TOXICOLOGY

A. The need

Mathieu Joseph Bonaventura Orfila (1787–1853), a Spanish physician, is often given credit as the founder of a systematic discipline of toxicology.

Orfila based his conclusions on his personal observation of the effects of poisons, as were then known, administered to dogs (Casarett and Bruce, 1980:7). Despite impressions from romantic novels of the period that human life was cheap, systematic observations of the effects of toxins (that is, when the observer was prepared to make them, when independent variables such as dose, route of entry, form of the agent, time of administration, etc., could be controlled, and when dependent variables associated with biological effects could be adequately measured) even then could not readily be made using human subjects. Quite understandably today's scientific ethics require adherence to strict rules for animal, as well as human, experimentation in all fields of the biomedical sciences in which living intact organisms are used as subjects. Alternatives to the use of animal models in toxicology is the study of humans or other species *exposed occupationally* or *adventitiously* to toxic substances or to study effects of toxins on tissue cultures. Certainly both are important, but not sufficient to meet the needs of behavioural toxicology: clinical and epidemiological studies obtain their primary data after subjects have already been exposed; tissue cultures cannot provide information about the total integrated organism. Experimental studies of whole-organism toxicity are essential if the capabilities of human and other animal species to cope with their environments are to be protected against adverse effects of exogenous chemicals and if humans and other animals are to be treated successfully when exposures do occur. The requirements of the experimental approach are such as to encourage research on infrahuman animal models for the purpose of developing principles upon which generalizations to humans may be based. Indeed, the case is being made that there is a need for more sophisticated animal models in neurobehavioural toxicology (Stebbins, 1982).

B. Extrapolation from animal models

The preceding assertion implies certain assumptions about the nature of animal models in the biomedical sciences. The logic underlying the use of the comparative method has been discussed in great detail for many years (for example, Wolf, 1938; Pavlov, 1941; Ivy, 1948; Russell, 1952; Romanes, 1882), and has been reviewed by Bond in Chapter 1. Its relevance to animal models in neurobehavioural toxicology in particular deserves summary here.

Generalization of observations within the biomedical sciences involves two levels of extrapolation: (a) from a finite sample of observations to the general population from which the sample is drawn; and (b) from observations on one species to statements about another species. In neurobehavioural toxicology the uses of animal models as substitutes for human subjects involves reasoning of the second type. There exist statistical techniques for handling generalizations of the first kind, but not for the second. On what basis, then, can the validities of extrapolations from animal models in neurobehavioural toxicology to humans be determined (Tilson *et al.*, 1979)? The general question of validity of behavioural measures is a familiar one in the behavioural sciences.The search for answers has led to a more precise statement of the basic issue: For what decisions is a particular model valid? This in turn has given rise to the classification of "validity" into five major categories.

1. Face validity

A behavioural model may be selected because it "looks good" for a particular purpose. It is analagous, that is, superficially similar, to the human behaviour for which it is a substitute. Experience has given a strong warning against adopting a model solely because it is plausible: ". . . conclusions drawn from other species are considered applicable to man as long as homologous systems are involved" (Bresson, 1976). The term "homology" implies that a behavioural model and its human criterion are alike in origin and in fundamental structure, neither of which can be assessed in terms of superficial similarities (Cranach, 1976; Russell, 1964a).

2. Content validity

Content validity goes somewhat beyond the superficiality of face validity by requiring an examination of the characteristics of an animal model and of the human behaviour it seeks to stimulate. Does the model represent the specific content, that is, behaviours, which the study is designed to measure?

3. Concurrent validity

A third type of validity involves a more empirical approach. Two or more independent sources of information (behavioural measures) from the same subjects, which in terms of the animal model should be indicative of toxic effects, are compared. The hypothesis is that such measures should be highly correlated. They should not be correlated with measures which according to the model are not indicative of actions of the toxins under study. Concurrent validity has also been applied in tests of hypotheses about neurochemical mechanisms underlying behavioural effects of a toxic substance. In such instances behavioural effects of the toxin are compared with effects produced by a chemical agent known to affect the hypothesized mechanism.

4. Construct validity

It is not possible to design an experiment to study effects of a potential toxic substance or even to make systematic observations relevant to them without stating or implying some underlying theoretical model of living organisms and of how they interact with their biospheres. Hypotheses about what may be toxic and what characteristics of an organism may be affected are generated by such models.What shall I look at and where shall I look are basic questions for the neurobehavioural toxicologist which become meaningful within the context of the constructs upon which some theoretical model of the nature of living organisms is based. Empirical observations made during the course of testing hypothesis also gain meaning from their relationships to other observations within the unifying frameworks of some theoretical model.

5. Predictive validity

"... the pharmacologist uses animal subjects in the try-out stages, to the extent that he [sic] finds that animals react somewhat comparable to man [sic]. He rests finally, however, only when he has established his findings on man" (Hilgard, 1948).

"These results, demonstrating concordance between animals and humans in how they behave toward drugs, justify the use of these procedures as a means of predicting the dependence potential of new drugs" (Falk et al., 1982).

Statements of these kinds focus upon a fifth type of validity: can predictions based upon studies of animal models be verified when applied to humans? The objective of predictive validity is to select models that maximize some outcome defined in terms of effects on human beings. The final verification of the validity of an extrapolation from animal models to humans lies in the demonstration that knowledge obtained from the former is related to predictable outcomes in the latter. Expectations may differ as to the level of exactitude anticipated from such predictions. In the best of all worlds one might look for extrapolations describable by precise, quantitative statements. The distributions of individual differences in effects of toxic exposures among humans have variances which place restrictions on such predictions even within the one species. At the opposite extreme "... the animal model would, at the very least, appear to be useful in directing attention toward possible parameters indicative of early and reversible toxicity" (Glick, 1976). For the most part predictions from animal models to humans fall between these extremes, but always their "predictive validity" depends eventually upon comparisons with human criteria.

Although giving due consideration to the first three types of validity discussed above, neurobehavioural toxicology has most to gain from focusing primarily on the latter two. Granted that this is so, a next step in the present evaluation of roles for animal models in neurobehavioural toxicology is to consider a theoretical model in terms of which examples of the uses of animal models may be discussed.

C. A theoretical model

"A scientist ... constructs hypotheses, or systems of theories, and tests them against experience by observation and experiment" (Popper, 1959).

The systematization of knowledge in a discipline of neurobehavioural toxicology can be done most successfully within the framework of a theoretical model of how toxins exert their effects on behaviour. "Whatever effects a drug produces in a biological system must be regarded as ultimate consequences of physiochemical interactions between that drug and functionally important molecules in the living organism" (Goldstein *et al.*, 1974). Read "toxin" for "drug" and the theoretical model upon which the empirical models to be discussed below are based begins to unfold. Toxic agents do not affect behaviour directly. In general terms, they enter the body through one or more of several routes. Once within the body they combine with receptor molecules to produce an agent–receptor complex, a relationship which may be reversible or irreversible. Such interaction with functional macro-molecular components of the organism initiates a series of biochemical and electrophysiological changes which characterize the overall response to the agent, that is, the agent–receptor complex provides a stimulus that sets into motion subsequent effects which are independent of the agent (Stephenson, 1956). Clearly, dynamic biochemical events occurring after exposure to a toxin have significant influence on subsequent behavioural effects. They constitute the "mechanisms of action" underlying those effects. They are essential components of the concept of homology discussed above, essential to the requirement that behavioural effects of toxins in animal models must be similar "in origin" to corresponding effects in humans. They have led to such statements as: "I am convinced that comprehension of the bio-chemical basis of toxic actions offers the only firm basis from which to predict potential toxicity in man" (Paget, 1962).

Hypotheses about the nature of neurobehavioural toxicity are based upon theoretical models of interactions between environmental toxins and the behaviour of living organisms. The most general context within which neurobehavioural toxicology generates more specific theoretical models is the "systems concept". The term, "system", one of the most frequently used terms in science, has been defined as a series of interrelated elements that perform some activity, function or operation (Mesarovic *et al.*, 1968). In neurobehavioural toxicology the total system is conceived as the living organism in its biosphere: inputs are received from the environment which affect the functioning of the organism and produce outputs to the environment (Russell, 1979; Warburton, 1983).

Behaviour, as the term is used here, cannot exist independently of other properties of living organisms: biochemical; electrophysiological; and morphological (structural). Toxins enter the body through various routes and affect biochemical processes, which, in turn, are reflected in changes of behaviour. Animal models in neurobehavioural toxicology must take all these events into consideration. As noted earlier, to do so requires a systematic concept of the living organism in its biosphere as constituting a total *system*. The multivariate and highly integrated organization of living organisms leads to the conceptualization in terms of multilevels, or hierarchies of *subsystems*. These subsystems are self-regulatory and self-correcting, but only within limits. Changes in one may also lead to changes in others. Changes in one direction from a resting state may produce compensatory feedback changes in the opposite direction. Outcome for the total system may be evidenced in changes in the behaviour of the organism, acute or chronic, and to death when the capacities of self-regulating processes are exceeded. In the former instance changes in behaviour may interfere with the organism's capabilities to make normal adjustments to its environment. Plasticities essential for meeting the constantly changing demands of the external physical and psychosocial environments include, in addition to the internal "homeostatic" mechanisms of Claude Bernard, Sherrington and Cannon, substrates for such behavioural processes as habituation, tolerance, learning, and memory, sometimes referred to as "behavioural homeostasis" (Russell, 1964b). This concept of the nature of living organisms has led to the view that some forms of behaviour are linked more directly to their biochemical substrates than others (Russell, 1958). Where the linkage is direct, changes in biochemical events are reflected in specific changes in behaviour. However, when the linkage is diffuse, changes in biochemical events may affect a variety of behaviour patterns and in some instances, the effect may not be observable unless there already exists an abnormal state of the organism (for example, Jenden, 1979).

Extending the concepts of plasticity as developed above, adverse signs may be expected when homeostatic processes can no longer cope with changes in the chemical environment. One of the primary roles of animal models in neurobehavioural toxicology is to provide information about the limits within which behaviour functions normally. Such information becomes one of the major grounds upon which "threshold limit values" may be set in regulations for human safety. The concept of "terminal threshold" is familiar to behavioural biologists and to pharmacologists in their studies of dose–effect relations in drug administration. Increasing magnitudes of exposure to a chemical substance induce proportional changes in behavioural or physiological variables. Eventually a level is reached when malfunctions begin to appear: limits in the plasticities of processes affected have been exceeded. Neurobehavioural toxicology becomes involved when signs of adverse behavioural effects appear.

D. Empirical models

Given that the theoretical model has generated an hypothesis about neurobehavioural effects of some potentially toxic substance, the decision must then be made as to how the hypothesis may best be put to empirical test, in the present case by use of animal models. The complexity of the physical and social environments and their variability from one habitat to another present what from a practical point of view is an insoluble problem until it is reduced to an extent that particular independent variables can be identified for experimental study. This requires selection of specific dependent variables to be measured from among an organism's overall behavioural repetoire.

1. Selection of behaviours to be observed

While investigators cannot be denied the right to select a particular behaviour solely because of their empirical interest in it *per se*, it is reasonable to ask what generalizations they can make from their observations. It is rationally unacceptable to generalize from a single measure of behaviour to "Behaviour" (with a capital B). Consequently preferences have been expressed for the use of "batteries" consisting of multiple behavioural assays and involving sequential analyses.

When little or no information is available about the neurobehavioural toxicity of a substance, the first phase of a sequence may begin with relatively simple measures (Goldstein *et al.*, 1974). For example, systematic observations of gross symptoms "... may provide important information on the toxicological properties of a compound which in turn increases the likelihood of detecting behavioural changes that may otherwise go unnoticed" (Reiter and MacPhail, 1979). This has been referred to as the "primary", "non-specific" or "screening" phase and is followed by a "secondary" phase which focuses on more specific standardized behavioural assays (for example, Tilson *et al.*, 1980; Weiss and Laties, 1975). A third phase may involve study in still further depth, using assays not usually included in a standardized battery and which may be developed *de novo* to measure special behavioural functions.

The research literature shows two general approaches to the systematic selection of assays to be included at these stages. One of these is based upon *a priori* classification of behaviour and involves the selection of behavioural assays which are "representative" of one or more of the classes. For example, "The behavioural and neurological sequelae of human neuro-toxicants may be grouped into categories including sensory, motor, associative or cognitive, affective or emotional, and several other factors such as changes in biological rhythms (feeding, sleeping), alterations in thermo-regulatory control, and signs of systemic toxicity" (Tilson *et al.*, 1980). An *a priori* selection of specific measures to be included in a battery may be based upon a classification established empirically by such statistical procedures as factor analysis.

A second general approach to selection begins with some theoretical model of behaviour such as that discussed above, but with a more detailed description of processes intervening between environmental stimulation and an organism's response(s) to it. A favourite for some time has been derived from communication theory. It analyses behaviour in terms of such processes as sensory input, central fixation and storage, central retrieval or "read out", and motor output. This approach requires an investigator to select measures of behaviour which differentiate among the various processes.

2. Intervening mechanisms

Evidence is accumulating that modelling at the behavioural level can provide information essential to the establishment of basic principles in neurobehavioural toxicology and in their practical applications. However, there also exists ample evidence that behavioural output is not a simple function of environmental input. Living organisms do not behave like push-button slot machines. Conditions intervening between input and output contribute significantly to the overall variance of behaviour. The adjective "neurobehavioural" indicates that such conditions, directly or indirectly, involve the nervous system. These facts imply the importance of modelling of a second kind, that is, the use of models to study biochemical and morphological subsystems which vary concomitantly with behaviour under the same conditions of environmental input. One of the major emphases in the general characterization of toxicity is upon identification of target organs and systems (Egan *et al.*, 1980). In neurobehavioural toxicology this involves primarily the search for and study of functions within the central nervous system (CNS) that constitute "mechanisms of action" by which toxic substances alter normal behavioural plasticities (Overstreet, 1983).

Predictions from animal models to humans may be complicated by the nature or the present state of such mechanisms. There may be species differences in the processes by which toxic agents are metabolized or detoxified once within the body. Some years ago a strong case was made for the view that "... the greatest difficulty in projecting data from animal to man [sic.] arises from species differences in the biotransformation of the drug" (Brodie, 1962). Substances which are not normally toxic may become so when, for example, "genetic lesions" occur which affect the CNS, for example, phenylketonuria.

During the past decade significant developments have occurred in techniques for identifying and studying intervening mechanisms in detail. These include *in vivo* and *in vitro* methods. They involve examination of the whole animal, of tissue preparations, and of synaptosomes taken from neurons of control and affected subjects. They employ such sophisticated techniques as combined gas chromatography/mass spectrometry, micro-wave fixation, and radioligand binding. Without information about mechanisms of action, both basic knowledge and its applications (for example, to patient management and to prevention) are as limited as was the "little black box" period in neuropsychology when lack of knowledge about intervening events prevented understanding of discrepancies in relations between stimulus input and response output.

The suggestion has been made that alternatives to modelling at the level of total organism are to examine "... the mechanism(s) of action of drugs which alter symptoms of disorders of the CNS..." and to study "... underlying neurobiological mechanisms of individual functions which are abnormal in central diseases..." (Breese, *et al.*, 1978). In neurobehavioural toxicology, where behavioural aberrations are consequences of exposure to "drugs", that is, chemical substances, these are not alternatives but are essential to the understanding of the effects of the exposure on the *integrated* organism.

E. Predisposing conditions

The appearance of toxic effects, given similar exposures, varies between individuals: not all organisms are equally susceptible. Efforts to understand the basis for such individual differences have revealed a number of contributing factors, that is, predisposing conditions. Some are characteristics of the organism: sex differences; age; genetically related susceptibility; nutritional condition; and state of biochemical processes, particularly within the nervous system. Other contributing factors relate to characteristics of the agent(s) to which an organism is exposed: chemical structure; extent and frequency or duration of exposure; route of entry into the body; and interaction with other chemicals present in the external environment or already stored in body fluids or tissues. Others arise from the structural integrity of the body, for example, organisms with CNS lesions respond differentially. Still other factors are related to interindividual differences in behavioural states: attenuation of acute effects may be a specific consequence of behaviour in the drug state; tolerance may develop during chronic exposure. Finally, there may be species and populations at special risk because of genotypic differences in susceptibility or because of differences in exposure.

III. MODELS IN NEUROBEHAVIOURAL TERATOLOGY

A. The emergence of experimental teratology

No discussion of neurobehavioural toxicology could be complete without consideration of toxic effects during development, of what has become known as "teratology". The term literally means "the study of monsters". For many years teratological studies were limited to investigations of morphological abnormalities. More recently teratology has come to be defined as the "... science dealing with the causes, mechanisms, and manifestations of developmental deviations of either structural or functional nature" (Spyker, 1975). Experimental teratology emerged during the early years of the present century from the bio-sciences, especially embryology, considerable interest being generated by reports of defects in

pigs resulting from either an absence or an overdose of vitamin A to the sow
(Hale, 1933; 1935). Two major errors of thought became clearly apparent:
first, that the fetus is protected from toxic substances in its amniotic
environment; and, second, that the fetus and newborn have the same
capabilities as the adult to metabolize and detoxify noxious substances.
That even those drugs which have therapeutic values for some purposes may
be among such noxious substances (teratogens) when taken by pregnant
women was brought to world attention by the morphological abnormalities
produced by thalidomide.

B. Guidelines and advantages

It has become quite clear that behaviour is at least as susceptible to
teratogens as are other properties of a developing organism (Collins and
Collins, 1976; Coyle *et al.*, 1976; Werboff, 1978). Adverse behavioural
effects are not as readily recognizable as are physical deformities and
require special assay procedures, for example, psychological tests, to
identify. The underlying hypothesis in behavioural teratology is that
teratogens have special affinities for receptors in particular areas of the
developing fetal brain, giving rise to alterations in development which
produce alterations in normal behaviour. At low exposure levels the
behavioural effects appear in the absence of gross morphological defects.
It is also significant that the risk of a particular teratogenic outcome is
associated with "critical periods" during development, for example,
administration of thalidomide during days 28–43 of human pregnancy.
During such periods a wide variety of teratogens can produce the same
defect.

This very brief outline of developmental neurobehavioural toxicology
is sufficient to indicate both the importance of knowledge in this area and
the impossibility of gaining such knowledge without the experimental study
of animal models to supplement human clinical and epidemiological
research. Indeed, the World Health Organization has established a
Scientific Group on Principles for the Testing of Drugs for Teratogenicity
(WHO, 1967) for the task of recommending "... reliable and practical
methods for the pre-clinical testing of drugs likely to be taken by women
of reproductive age". The recommendations include guidelines for research
with animal models. The guidelines have sufficient flexibility to have
encouraged the use of a wide range of research strategies (Grant, 1976) and
experimental methods. These have been reviewed recently with the conclusion that, despite important contributions to knowledge in teratology "...

the best experimental strategy for the evaluation of potential behavioural teratogens is not yet established'' (Zbinden, 1981).

It is apparent that the primary goal of programmes like those of WHO, and of its counterparts at national levels, is to obtain from animal models information applicable to humans. Successful use of such models is determined by the predictive validity of the knowledge they generate. Accepting this ultimate goal, there are several obvious advantages of developmental studies using animal models. These have been discussed by several authors (for example, Spyker, 1975) and may be summarized as follows: shorter life-spans enable observations of exposures to teratogens to be made from conception to death during relatively brief periods; external environmental conditions can be controlled and thus ruled out as confounding factors; genetic background can also be controlled by selective breeding and the use of inbred lines; influences of the mother and of the maternal environment can be partialled out by such procedures as caesarean section and cross-fostering; and studies may be carried out to discover intervening mechanisms underlying the behavioural effect(s).

C. Some examples

Earlier mention was made of experiments on teratogenic effects of extreme variations of vitamin A. More recent studies have extended knowledge about the effects by showing that behavioural deficits can appear without gross malformation of the central nervous system (CNS). In one such study, proper fostering procedures and other control techniques were applied, rats serving as subjects (Butcher et al., 1972). A water maze was used in order to control for conditions associated with motivation through food and water deprivation or aversive stimulation. Offspring of mothers pretreated with excess administration of vitamin A which did not induce gross structural changes in the CNS performed significantly more poorly than did control subjects. Because measurements established that there were no differences in swimming performance, it was possible to eliminate motor functions as possible confounding factors and to attribute the behavioural consequences of the excess vitamin A to deficits in learning "... caused by functional impairments of the central nervous system" (Butcher et al., 1972). Later experimentation illustrated the importance of critical periods in teratogenicity (Hutchings and Gaston, 1974; Hutchings et al., 1973). In one experiment excess vitamin A was administered on days 14 and 15 of gestation and, in a second study, on days 17 and 18. All subjects were fostered to non-treated mothers at birth. As adults, offspring of mothers in the first experiment were retarded in growth and learned an operant response pattern requiring them to alternately respond and not respond significantly more slowly than control subjects. "The treated rats evidently were less able to inhibit responding to the signal which indicated nonreinforcement" (Hutchings *et al.*, 1973). Rats treated similarly in the second experiment were not retarded in growth, development or brain size and were not impaired in operant learning, although they showed somewhat slower rates of responding.

The kinds of information about teratogenesis that can be generated from studies of animal models are well illustrated in an extensive series of experiments conducted by Spyker and her coworkers to determine effects of methylmercury on the offspring of mothers exposed at various stages of gestation (reviewed by Spyker, 1974). In the methylated form, mercury readily crosses the blood–brain and placental barriers. After birth, 372 apparently normal offspring were selected for long-term study, that is, during their three-year lifespans. Despite the fact that gross signs of abnormalities were not seen, treated offspring were different from control subjects in sensitive behavioural assays at various times throughout post-natal development. "These early indications of trouble were indeed fore-warnings of later, more severe developments: neuromuscular and learning deficits, infections, postural problems, immuno-deficiencies, generalized debilitation, and early aging" (Spyker, 1974).

Groups at special risk as a result of contact with toxic substances are pregnant women, young children and workers occupationally exposed. Neurobehavioural teratology has special concerns for the first two of these. It must use animal models as one of its main thrusts in acquiring the basic knowledge upon which wise decisions can be made about minimizing risks (hopefully to as close to zero as possible). The massive review of GRAS ("generally recognized as safe") food additives by the US Food and Drug Administration is an example of experimental neurobehavioural teratology in action. The protocol for the review was similar to that suggested by WHO as noted earlier. Rabbits, rats, hamsters, and mice constituted the test animals. The results provided one of the major scientific grounds for regulatory action.

IV. ANIMAL MODELS IN ACTION

The paragraphs which follow describe selected examples of the uses to which animal models have been put in neurobehavioural toxicology. There will be no attempt to place the various pieces of each example in their historical sequence. The dates of references to reports of the various investigators will indicate what is apparent in any area of knowledge: there seldom occurs a single *experimentum crucis*; and knowledge accumulates in quantal steps related to the discovery of new concepts or the invention of new techniques. As a recognized discipline, neurobehavioural toxicology is very new, drawing on several older disciplines for the foundations of its systematic body of knowledge.

More than six centuries ago, Paracelsus, historically one of the "great doctors", commented that: "All things are poisons, for there is nothing without poisonous qualities. It is only the dose which makes a thing a poison" (Sigerist, 1958). By "things" Paracelsus was referring to substances in the external environment, to potential exogenous toxins. The number of such possibilities is great indeed. Ten years ago there were more than 10 000 substances on the research toxic substances list of the US National Institute of Occupational Safety and Health (Xintaras *et al.*, 1974). From what has been stated above, it is a lengthy task to investigate even one of these. Potential toxicants in certain areas of risk have received fuller attention than others. The examples which follow have been selected from among these.

A. Animal models of human exposure: Pesticides

The use of chemicals to control invasions of pests is a world-wide practice. These are substances synthesized with the deliberate goal of being toxic — but only to selected organisms. However, occupational and adventitious exposure of humans to these chemicals has been estimated to involve some 500 000 pesticide poisonings each year, about 5000 being fatal. As a result of such statistics, much research has focused on toxicological studies of these compounds.

Among the pesticides in wide usage are the organophosphorous compounds. They are highly specific in their biochemical effects, producing virtually irreversible inactivation of the enzyme cholinesterase (ChE) and certain other esters. Their high lipid solubility results in penetration into the CNS when entering the body by peripheral routes. ChE plays a vital role in inactivating the neurohumoral transmitter acetylcholine (ACh) when the latter is released on stimulation of cholinergic neurons. The significance of ACh to the normal functioning of living organisms has been expressed as follows: "Most impressive is the singular fact that ACh is the only substance that can influence every physiological or behavioural response so far examined" (Myers, 1974). One implication in this statement is that organophosphorus compounds might serve pharmacotherapeutic purposes when malfunctions of the cholinergic neurotransmitter occur in humans, as well as playing the role of toxin in the continuing war against destructive pests. Indeed, they have been used in the treatment of such disorders as glaucoma and myasthenia gravis.*

Early reports of human occupational or adventitious exposures describe general symptoms which include: loss in discrimination performance; involuntary twitching; slurred speech; difficulty in concentration and expressing thoughts; confusion; disorientation; emotional instability; and signs of anxiety and depression (for example, Bowers *et al.*, 1964; Durham and Hays, 1962; Gershon and Shaw, 1961; Grob *et al.*, 1950). Fatalities occur after high levels of acute exposure. Clearly recognizable improvements in symptoms, that is, tolerance, develops during repeated exposures (Summerford *et al.*, 1953). In order to define more clearly the behavioural parameters affected and to relate them to intervening mechanisms, investigators turned to animal models.

From the first of these studies it became apparent that exposure to the organophosphous anti-ChEs produced differential effects on behaviour, some behaviours being affected and others not. From these observations arose the principle that one of the major functions of the cholinergic system in behaviour is a suppressing or inhibiting role, a principle which has since been incorporated into a model of mania and depression in man (Janowsky *et al.*, 1972). The behaviours affected in animal studies were considerably more sensitive to effects of anti-ChEs than were other, pathological signs. This suggests that diagnosis of impairment after human exposure should involve much more finely-tuned behavioural assays than merely to depend upon gross symptomatology, a suggestion which has been accepted in more recent investigations involving human subjects. The fact that tolerance occurred following mild exposures to the organophosphates directed attention toward the search for underlying neurochemical mechanisms, investigations which could not be carried out with human subjects.

The direct neurochemical effect of exposure to the organophosphates is to decrease the activity of ChE. As a consequence ACh is elevated. Both these effects have been demonstrated in a number of animal models. From the behavioural point of view dose-effect analyses have shown a critical brain ChE activity level at about 45% of normal below which behaviour is significantly affected. There are limits when exposures are sufficiently high to exceed the plasticity of the cholinergic system and gross pathological signs, incapacitation and death occur. Within the range of ChE activity where acute effects of the anti-ChEs appear, chronic exposures are characterized by return of behaviours to their pre-exposure levels, that is, tolerance has developed. By what processes does such recovery occur?

---

* Overstreet and Russell provide further information about the role of the cholinergic system in behaviour in Chapter 10.

Again animal models have enabled answers to be sought and found. Direct evidence has come from several laboratories that postsynaptic muscarinic receptors (mAChR) are involved: behavioural tolerance development is associated with a decrease in the number of postsynaptic mAChRs (Schiller, 1979; Ehlert *et al.*, 1980). There is recent evidence from studies of animal models that a second mechanism may also play a role, that is, down-regulation of ACh release from presynaptic neurons (Russell *et al.*, unpublished data).

This very brief overview has shown ways in which animal models provide indispensible means of obtaining information essential to the development of a systematic body of knowledge that may justify the title, "neurobehavioural toxicology". It has indicated how principles discovered during research with animal models may be used in hypotheses about human behaviour and its underlying mechanisms. It has also illustrated the predictive validity of information provided by animal models when human criterion data are available. To emphasize this last point more fully the general observation that exposure to organophosphorus pesticides produces depressant effects on animal behaviour can be compared with results of one of the very few experiments reported when these compounds have been administered to human subjects (Rowntree *et al.*, 1950). Effects of the compound DFP on schizophrenic and manic-depressive patients were compared with effects on normal human volunteers. Behavioural effects on the former were mixed, suggesting multiple neurochemical mechanisms underlying that complex disorder. Major effects among the manic-depressive patients included "... significant mental changes ... which indicated a marked depressant effect of the drug". Normal subjects showed a "... very characteristic mental picture of depression, irritability, lassitude and apathy..." which appeared before the onset of physical symptoms. The concordance between effects of organophosphorous compounds in experiments with animal models, in clinical observations of human reactions and inclusion of the effects in theoretical models of mechanisms underlying behavioural abberations (Jankowsky *et al.*, 1972) illustrates how information from all these sources may be integrated to provide a systematic body of knowledge of value for several purposes.

B. Animal models of human exposure: Industrial solvents

It was stated earlier that one of the three groups at greatest risk of exposure to toxic substances are workers in the occupational environment. Chemical solvents are among the toxic substances used for many industrial processes. For workers exposed to them, the exposure, perhaps, only after a considerable period of time, can result in impairment of the nervous system's functional capacity. Two industrial solvents will serve to illustrate ways in which experiments using animal models can supplement other sources of information about behavioural effects and their underlying mechanisms.

The term "industrial solvent" refers to liquids which dissolve water-insoluble substances such as fats, resins, waxes, forming a homogeneous solution. Industrial organic solvents enter the body primarily in the form of vapour inhaled in normal respiration. From alveoli in the lungs the inhaled chemical diffuses to arterial blood and hence to tissues. Elimination of most of the solvent occurs by diffusion from tissues to venous blood and hence to the lungs where it is expired. Tissues involved en route include the nervous system which, because of its content of fatty substances, is especially sensitive to solvents.

There are numerous reports of carbon disulphide (CS_2) poisoning among workers in the rubber and viscose rayon industries. "Clinically manifested poisoning is characterized by lower vigilance, diminished intellectual activity, diminished rational control, retarded speed, and motor disturbances, whereas traits indicative of depressive mood, slight motor disturbances, and intellectual impairment are characteristic of latent poisoning. This syndrome is probably much more common than was hitherto believed" (Hanninen, 1971). There is evidence for latent effects which may occur in the years subsequent to exposure, being precipitated by later environmental and social stresses (Mancuso and Locke, 1972). These kinds of information have come from clinical and epidemiological studies, some of which have been carried out with expert uses of psychological tests as means of identifying behavioural effects too subtle to discern by less precise methods (Hanninen et al., 1978). Carbon disulphide is soluble in lipids and is deposited in tissues in both free and bound form. In animals it is found in relatively large concentrations in brain and in peripheral nervous tissues, primarily in its bound form which disappears only slowly (Brieger, 1967). Much of the information available about CS_2 has come from clinical and epidemiological studies conducted some time ago, the use of animal models focusing primarily on the nature of internal mechanisms by which CS_2 produces its various effects (see Brieger and Teisinger, 1966, for review). More recent reports illustrate the kinds of information now being generated by neurobehavioural studies. Because of the sparsity of information about behavioural effects of exposure to CS_2 under controlled experimental conditions, behavioural assays in one of the studies (Levine, 1976) were chosen to represent two general categories of behaviour: behaviour maintained by reinforcing only responses emitted after set time intervals (fixed-interval schedules) and behaviour maintained by reinforcing the number of responses emitted (fixed-ratio schedule). Pigeons served as subjects. On some trials they were exposed to a constant level of CS_2 for varying durations and on other trials were injected with varying doses of FLA-63, a dopamine β-hydroxylase (DBH) inhibitor. The latter served as a bench mark for testing the hypothesis that inhibition of DBH is a possible mechanism for the CNS effects of CS_2. Results of the experiments showed that acute exposures to both agents produced marked behavioural effects. Behaviours in all assays remained relatively unaffected after single CS_2 exposures of less than eight hours duration and doses of FLA-63 less than 40 mg kg^{-1}. Successive eight-hour exposures to CS_2 produced cumulative effects, that is, decreases in responding. Behavioural changes after repeated exposures of four hours were similar to, but less marked than, single exposures of eight hours duration. Behaviour maintained on fixed interval schedules was disrupted at lower exposures to both agents than was behaviour reinforced on ratio schedules. The fact that both agents produced qualitatively similar effects suggests that they may have mechanisms of action in common, for example, both involving catecholamines in the central nervous system (CNS). The relative sensitivities of the various behaviours to CS_2 warrants consideration of such behavioral assays as valuable tools for research on other organic solvents. Other investigators have used nonhuman primates in their animal models for studying effects of CS_2 on aversive thresholds, thus providing experimental information relevant to analgesia and nociception, that is, "Pain" (Weiss et al., 1979).

Among other industrial solvents toluene is in wide usage and has long been suspected of having effects on behaviour. Several years ago the Swedish National Board of Occupational Safety and Health sponsored experiments on human subjects exposed to various concentrations of toluene in the inspiratory air and under control conditions the results of which demonstrated that psychophysiological functions, that is, reaction time and perceptual speed, were impaired by the solvent (Gamberale and Hultengren, 1972). The importance to public health of understanding effects of such potentially toxic compounds and limitations of research on human subjects encouraged investigators to turn to animal models for fuller detail about neurobehavioural effects (see Benignus, 1981, for review). These studies have sought information about effects of toluene on diverse animal models ranging from the behaviour of pigeons in complex tasks involving performances controlled by stimuli both external and internal to the subject to transient cognitive deficits and high-frequency hearing loss in weanling rats subchronically exposed to toluene by inhalation (Pryor et al., 1983a; 1983b) to toluene "sniffing" by squirrel monkeys (Weiss et al., 1979). The former model demonstrated differential sensitivity to toluene of performances under the two types of stimuli. The second showed that subtle changes may occur which require detailed behavioural assays to detect. The third provided evidence that toluene can serve as a positive reinforcer in maintaining the behaviour.

C. Animal models of human exposures: Metals

As research on neurotoxins continues to develop, it becomes increasingly clear that there are conditions under which a wide variety of metals may produce adverse neurobehavioural effects. Considerable attention has already been given to the two metals which will serve as examples for our present purposes — lead and mercury. New studies are coming to focus on such others as aluminium, cadmium, magnesium and tin.

That lead (Pb) may have adverse effects on living organisms has been recognized since antiquity. A description of its symptoms, including anaemia, colic, joint pains and central nervous system effects, given in the second century B.C.E. by Nicander is itself based upon still older accounts. Despite accumulating evidence that lead is a potentially toxic substance, it has remained in wide usage during the centuries since then. Lead is not a metal essential in the normal bodily processes of mammalian species (see Singhal and Thomas, 1980, for review). It enters the body through two main routes, the intestines and the lungs. Absorption through skin plays only a minor role for inorganic lead, but is more significant for organic tetraethyl lead. Ingested lead comes mainly from the lead content of food and drink (estimated as 75%–85% v. 15%–25% via the lungs). On entry into the blood stream, lead is rapidly distributed throughout the body. Most of the lead intake is excreted in urine and faeces, the excess being deposited ultimately in bone where it may remain in an inert form for many years. The fact that in young children the proportion of absorption of lead from the intestines is much greater than in adults puts them at greater risk for the development of the neurobehavioural toxicities which constitute major clinical features of excessive exposure. Such exposure may result in encephalopathy and permanent brain damage with impaired intellectual function and behaviour disorders (Milar *et al.*, 1981). There also is evidence that neurobehavioural effects may occur at lower levels of human exposure. The present literature describing neurobehavioural effects of exposure to lead using animal models is more suggestive than conclusive. ''In terms of behavioural neurotoxicity, an appropriate animal model for occupational exposure to lead has not yet been defined'' (Jason and Kellogg, 1980). Other recent reviews of research into effects of exposure to lead on neuro-behavioural variables using animal models have also been critical of both methodology and interpretation of results (for example, Bornschein *et al.*, 1980). Very few experiments have been conducted using chronic low levels of exposure or involving exposure to organic rather than inorganic lead. However, a few general points have emerged. In animal models using adult subjects exposure to lead has been found to have differential effects on behaviour, that is, some behaviours are affected and some are not, before the appearance of incapacitating neuropathies. Spatial learning, passive avoidance, extinction and simple pattern discrimination are reportedly insensitive. By comparison, neuromuscular impairment, size and brightness discrimination and active avoidance appear to be relatively sensitive. In operant conditioning, exposure to lead is followed by increased variability and changes of response rates (increases or decreases depending on the type of schedule involved). Soviet researchers have reported significant disturbance of classical conditioned responses. These effects are clearly dose-dependent, in many cases not appearing until relatively high exposures and high blood lead levels have been reached. Exposure to lead during fetal development or via the lactating mother's milk has been reported to result in increased motor activity in the developing child. Similarity of such effects with epidemiological evidence of hyperkinesis accompanying mild lead intoxication in the human child has suggested that this may be a useful animal model for laboratory studies of risks of lead neurobehavioural toxicity during childhood: "... low level of lead exposure in rats during pre- and neonatal development produced behavioural changes similar to those in lead-exposed hyperactive children" (Gross-Selbeck, 1981). Animal models have been used to study the neurochemistry of lead-induced hyperactivity illustrating the value of such models in the search for mechanisms underlying behavioural abnormalities. These investigations have led to such conclusions as: "the hyperactivity resulting from low-level lead poisoning appears to be associated with inhibition of cholinergic pathways and concomitant enhancement of "noradrenergic pathways" (Silbergeld and Goldberg, 1974). Such relations between inhibition of cholinergic function and hyperactivity take on an even broader significance in the context of the neurobehavioural effects of manipulating the cholinergic neurotransmitter system in which hyperfunction of the system suppressed behaviour and hypofunction had an opposite effect (for further information, see Chapter 11).

The lengthy discussion of neurobehavioural toxicity associated with exposures to lead provided yet another example of ways in which animal models may contribute to a fuller understanding of both the effects and the mechanisms involved in producing them. A briefer consideration of effects of another metal, mercury (Hg), will help to show that lead is not the only metal to produce neurobehavioural toxicity. Dramatic incidents, such as the case of water pollution in Minamata, Japan, and that of contaminated wheat in Iraq, have drawn special attention to mercury toxicity. Mercury is primarily a central nervous system poison. Intoxication in humans is typically clinically revealed by numbness and tingling (paraesthesia) of the lips, tongue and fingertips, followed by the onset of ataxia and incoordination, dysarthria, peripheral visual disturbances and, occasionally, hallucinations. Because of the risks of exposure occupationally or adventitiously, studies of persons exposed to mercury have been carried out in greater detail using standardized physiological and psychometric measures. Conclusions from one of the most recent of these studies (Williamson *et al.*, 1982) were that mercury-exposed subjects showed poorer psychomotor coordination and fatigued sooner than matched control subjects, although simple motor responses were not affected. General levels of arousal were not different. However, unexpectedly, mercury-exposed subjects were superior in sustaining attention, at the same time showing clear deficits in short-term memory. Their results led these investigators to hypothesize that "... homeostatic mechanisms may be upset by increasing mercury levels and so in turn produce the behavioural deficits seen in this study" (Williamson *et al.*, 1982). The search for the nature of such "homeostatic mechanisms" would seem to be a very appropriate opportunity for the use of animal models. Results of research using such models has already shown that relatively low-level mercury exposure may produce impairment of sensory-motor and cognitive functions (for example, Evans *et al.*, 1975; Olson and Boush, 1975; Reuhl and Chang, 1979). Although several species have been used in such experimental research, the generalized outcomes have been similar to neurobehavioural effects of mercury exposures in humans, that is, the comparability of results indicates a high "face validity" for the animal models used. Indeed, one group of investigators who have been major contributors to the research has stated that their experience with methylmercury has made them confident at least in extrapolating from nonhuman primate models to humans: "... these results provide a crucial phylogenetic link in judging the adequacy of extrapolations from subprimates to man" (Evans *et al.*, 1977).

D. Animal models of human exposure: Drugs

The present discussion of animal models at work in neurobehavioural toxicology has so far been concerned with chemical substances from the external environment which are inherently toxic in nature. Warburton

(1978) introduced the concept of "internal pollution": "In the case of internal pollution the chemicals are introduced voluntarily into the internal environment usually in the form of drug medication". His argument is that "... we are the consumers: the internal environments are our bodies, and we are helping the polluting process by demanding and consuming drugs for trivial maladies". There is an offshoot of Warburton's reasoning which has a place in neurobehavioural toxicology. Drugs which are taken for sound therapeutic reasons may also produce unwanted neuroleptic effects. In a very real sense untoward "side effects" which interfere with normal adjustment are instances of neurobehavioural toxicity. Antipsychotic agents in current clinical use produce a variety of extrapyramidal neurological disorders. Some of these are early, acute and reversible. However, others, after many months of treatment with ordinary doses of the drugs, are late in appearing, for example, tardive dyskinesia (Faurbye et al., 1964). Tardive dyskinesia is recognized behaviourally by abnormal oral, facial, and tongue movements, as well as by involuntary quick tic-like and slower, writhing movements of the trunk and extremities; prevalence rates are about 10%–20% of treated patients, the risk increasing with age. The leading hypothesis about the nature of neurochemical mechanisms underlying the disorder is that dopamine may be overactive in its role as neurotransmitter in the basal ganglia or limbic forebrain (Baldessarini and Tarsy, 1980).

Because of the frequency of occurrence and the significance of drug-induced movement disorders a number of animal models have been proposed (Davis et al., 1979; McKinney et al., 1980; Rubovits et al., 1973; Tye et al., 1979). Two main objectives appear to be involved: first, the practical use of the model to predict the risk of new therapeutic agents in producing movement disorders; and, second, the use of the model to test hypotheses about neurochemical mechanisms underlying the disorders (for example, the dopamine hypothesis described above). Two examples of research with animal models will serve to illustrate research being carried out. Chronic administration of various neuroleptics to rodents has been shown to result in behavioural hypersensitivity. Guinea pigs and rats exposed for periods of three weeks showed no supersensitivity at low doses (Klawans et al., 1980). However, chronically administered high doses of chlorpromazine and prochlorperazine produced dose-dependent supersensitivity. This condition was evaluated using apomorphine, a dopamine agonist, and was found to be accompanied by upregulation in numbers of dopamine receptors. Dyskinesias have also been evoked in monkeys by weekly administration of haloperidol (Weiss and Santelli, 1978), with general symptoms analogous to those described above for human patients — that is, the model has high face validity.

Modelling toxic side effects of agents with primary actions which are desirable in pharmacotherapy would appear to have promise for "cleaning up" the molecular structure of the agent and also for adding to basic knowledge of drug actions. It faces, of course, the problems of establishing that the validity of any proposed model extends beyond a simple similarity to behavioural effects.

E. Animal models of human exposure: Genetic faults

Discussion of still other examples of animal models at work will also provide an opportunity to emphasize a concept which is not often perceived as a matter of interest to neurobehavioural toxicology. There are individuals who have toxic reactions to chemical substances which are non-toxic to the majority of the population. Allergic reactions are included among these, reactions which may directly or indirectly affect behaviour (Freedman *et al.*, 1956). However, the example that will best serve present purposes is a well-known genetic fault which has very significant neurobehavioural effects — phenylketonuria (PKU). This is an example of how a genetic fault can alter internal biochemical events in such a way that a normal food substance, phenylalanine, takes on toxic properties.

For many years it has been known that inherited metabolic faults or "lesions" observable in humans are understandable if it is assumed that in each case the body fails to carry out one particular step in a normal series of biochemical events. Such lesions may have very significant effects upon behaviour (Russell, 1958). PKU has been a model for the study of an inborn error of metabolism associated with mental retardation. The mode of transmission appears to be by autosomal recessive inheritance, although one subtype of PKU may be sex-linked. Biochemically, classical PKU is characterized by a deficit in the conversion of the essential amino acid, phenylalanine, to tyrosine due to a missing enzyme, phenylalanine hydroxylase, which is missing because of the genetically determined biochemical fault.

The frequency of occurrence of the disorder and the significance of its effects for humans so afflicted has stimulated the search for animal models which could be used to study in detail the complex chain of events underlying its expression: "... what makes the history of PKU model research noteworthy is the fact that it has confronted so many of the design problems that are an integral part of modern developmental neuroscience research" (Vorhees *et al.*, 1981). Recently, progress in experimental phenylketonuria has been critically reviewed (Vorhees *et al.*, 1981). The early search for an animal model of PKU tended to emphasize single chemical routes to inducing the condition, for example, "*p*-chlorophenylalanine-induced chemical manifestations" of PKU (Lipton *et al.*, 1967). It now appears that recent models using combined administration of phenylalanine and *p*-chlorophenylalanine produce a condition which closely mimics the human disorder. In one such model (Brass *et al.*, 1982), the diets of pregnant animals were supplemented with 0.5% methylphenylalanine and 3% phenylalanine beginning at the twelfth day of gestation. Hyperphenylalaninaemia in the mother was associated with gross elevations in fetal brain phenylalanine content and with the biochemical consequence of this state on the offspring. Inducing PKU in weanling rats has been shown to result in learning deficits at later ages.

The animal models discussed here are experimentally produced, not occurring spontaneously. An increasing number of animal models of inherited human diseases are becoming recognized (Desnick *et al.*, 1982). Among these are some in which a defective enzyme, as in PKU, has been identified with the affected enzyme in the human disease, deficient enzymes usually pointing to defective genes. Such animal models may prove to be particularly valuable for research into the nature of the toxic conditions produced and the mechanisms by which these are eventually reflected in behavioural malfunctions.

Reference to the International Symposium on Animal Models of Inherited Metabolic Disease (Desnick *et al.*, 1982) provides an opportunity to call attention to the fact that human models may also have their place in the neurobehavioural toxicology of animals. In his introductory remarks to the Symposium, Professor Kurt Benirschke, Professor of Pathology and Reproductive Medicine at the University of California, San Diego, described his success with "... the use of a well-understood human genetic error in gaining insight into a disease of lemurs" (Benirschke, 1982).

F. Animal models for biomonitoring

Mention was made earlier of the establishment by the International Union of Biological Sciences (IUBS) of a committee to review past, ongoing, and proposed programmes in biomonitoring and to identify important aspects of biological monitoring requiring attention. Representation has been made by the section of Experimental Psychology and Animal Behaviour of the IUBS that the behaviour of living organisms is often, if not always, more sensitive to changes in environmental conditions than other biological indicators. The need for behavioural markers as elements in biomonitoring systems has become particularly apparent with the growing recognition that human and all other organisms are at risk in the changing chemical environment in which they live and with the development of a discipline of neurobehavioural toxicology. To avoid undesirable consequences of the changing environment, monitoring systems are required to identify and to predict hazardous effects in time to introduce preventive or at least fast remedial procedures. Although chemical assays are a basic requirement in such monitoring systems, biological methods, including biobehavioural, have essential contributions to make. In its statement on biological monitoring the IUBS has commented: "Because living organisms and cell organelles vary in their sensitivity to environmental influences, they can be used as indicators at various levels of integration to assess and to predict environmental changes in a timely manner". Much of what has been discussed in the preceding paragraphs can be viewed as biomonitoring. it has been directed primarily toward experimental laboratory investigation. Biomonitoring needs another essential component, that is, field observations of behaviour as they are probably the earliest and most sensitive indicator of conditions potentially toxic to humans.

However, there is a broader concept for the use of animal models for biomonitoring. It is based upon "Concern with the deterioration of the environment and of man's role in reducing numbers of certain plants and animals, sometimes to zero..." (Baker, 1982). Gaining knowledge about the effects of environmental toxins on species other than human becomes an important activity in its own right. In a recent discussion of "toxic mechanisms in wild life" Bunyan and Stanley (1982) have stated the basic theme: "Since most vertebrates are heavily dependent on their gross behavioural patterns for survival of the species and on their response to their environment for survival of the individual, any aberration in either could be detrimental although clearly the former is more important".

V. ANIMAL MODELS IN NEUROBEHAVIOURAL TOXICOLOGY: PRESENT AND FUTURE

A. Present

Although a formal discipline of neurobehavioural toxicology is only at an early formative stage, there can be no question about the increasing uses to which its concepts and its investigative techniques are being put. Prominent among the techniques is the use of animal models.

"The aim of toxicity studies in experimental animals is to detect the noxious effects of a compound and to decide whether or not it should be tested in humans" (Balazs, 1976). Many by now very familiar reasons are given for the use of animal models as preliminary studies of humans. Some of these are based upon scientific grounds and others on ethical grounds. The only alternatives to research on animals are: to conduct experiments using human subjects, an approach which is not now widely accepted; to study samples of persons exposed occupationally or adventitiously to a potentially toxic substance; or to wait until symptoms are sufficiently severe to demand clinical attention. Recognition that protection of human populations against neurobehavioural toxins requires as early a warning as possible, and that a first step is to study potential risks using animal models, is reflected in guidelines established by international organizations such as WHO and by responsible agencies operating at national levels.

Animal models are also used extensively after substances have been identified as toxic. There is always a need to specify the nature of behavioural effects in detail. Such effects often develop gradually and subtly and cannot readily be specified without the aid of behavioural assay methods applied under controlled conditions. There also is always a need to understand the mechanisms by which toxic substances act. Animal models provide means for searching among the biochemical, electrophysiological and morphological properties which characterize living organisms for the ways in which toxins alter normal conditions.

Animal models are being used in the development of new chemicals which can safely replace those that may cause toxic effects. The field of psychopharmacology has demonstrated its value in helping to develop and to improve drugs which may be used for psychotherapeutic purposes. The elimination of potentially toxic compounds is a most significant part of that discipline's responsibility. Again animal models play key roles.

To overlook the significant contribution studies of animal models in neurobehavioural toxicology are making to basic knowledge about living organisms and their behaviours would be an unfortunate mistake. Quantal steps toward new discoveries and new applications come from the basic understanding of nature — in the present case, of the behaviour of living organisms as they cope with the environments in which they live. Research with animal models is contributing very significantly to the development of such knowledge.

B. Future

It is perhaps more than mere speculation to predict that for most persons, sophisticated or not in the problems of toxic substances in the environment, a choice between the health of a child or research on a mouse would not be difficult. Although this is a *reductio ad absurdum* example, biomedical research is presently facing more realistic choices of this general nature in several parts of the world. The matter has been raised and discussed in Chapter 1. Suffice it to predict at this point that the use of animal models in neurobehavioural toxicology will continue into the future; the risks are too great to do otherwise — and there is no practical alternative.

Given that this prediction is fulfilled, there will still be thorough monitoring of the ways in which animal models are used. In making "some critical remarks and clinical objections" about the use of animal models for human behaviour, Feuerlein *et al.* (1979) have commented: "We look forward to precisely formulated predictions based on a realistic model and carefully designed investigations with the aim of refuting these predictions, instead of outcome studies in which data are embedded in a post-hoc theoretical framework". This blunt statement recognizes the importance of some of the matters of research design and of the validation of animal models discussed in the opening sections of this chapter. More attention to such matters will, hopefully, be a trend of the future as neurobehavioural toxicology continues to develop.

Herein, too, lies another need for the future: the need to develop a systematic discipline characterized by multiple approaches within a general theoretical framework sufficiently flexible to adapt to new concepts and new facts. There have already been several worthy efforts in this direction by individuals who will be seen to have given neurobehavioural toxicology a good start. Both basic and applied research are necessary, the former providing general principles of how toxic substances affect behaviour: ". . . if the past is precedent we can expect that understanding of the principles that govern the effects of drugs and toxicants on . . . [behaviour] . . . will lead to practical and effective technologies" (Heise, 1983). The intermingling of research on humans and on animal models will characterize this developing discipline.

Two other directions for development deserve comment. One is the current interest in biomonitoring of the world's environments. Actions such as those of the International Union of Biological Sciences deserve support. The two facets of biomonitoring should be encouraged: the use of animal models to detect toxic risks; and systematic monitoring for potential dangers to the earth's wildlife.

Finally, actions should be taken to improve communications with those responsible for regulating the chemical environment. It is a sad comment that often little attention is paid to scientific information in decisions about regulation. There are problems which both the regulator and the scientist could help to solve. Often the regulators are confused by the information presented to them. They would wish to have more "one-armed scientists", and fewer advisors who state "on the one hand this, and on the other hand that". Often the scientist does not view this situation from the position of the regulator who must face the fact that environmental management inevitably involves trade-offs between biological limitations and social cost-benefits. Fuller discourse between the two could be enlightening to both — and perhaps make it clear why animal models are indispensable in neuro-behavioural toxicology.

REFERENCES

Baker, F.W.G. *The International Council of Scientific Unions: A brief survey.* Paris: ICSU Secretariat, 1982.
Balazs, T. Assessment of the value of systemic toxicity studies in experimental animals. In M.A. Mehlman, R.E. Shapiro, and H. Blumenthal (Eds.), *Advances in Modern Toxicology: New concepts in Safety Evaluation.* New York: Wiley, 1976: 141-153.
Baldessarini, R.J. and Tarsy, D. Dopamine and the pathophysiology of dyskinesias induced by antipsychotic drugs. *Annual Review of The Neurosciences,* 1980, 3: 23-41.
Benignus, V.A. Neurobehavioral effects of toluene: A Review. *Neurobehavioral Toxicology and Teratology,* 1981, 3: 407-415.
Benirschke, K. Introductory remarks: Symposium on animal models of inherited metabolic diseases. In R.J. Desnick, D.F. Patterson and D.G. Scarpelli (Eds.), *Animal Models of Inherited Metabolic Diseases.* New York: Alan R. Liss, 1982: 1-3.
Bernal, J.D. Biochemical evolution. In M. Kasha and B. Pullman (Eds.), *Horizons in Biochemistry.* New York: Academic Press, 1962.
Bornschein, R., Pearson, D. and Reiter, L. Behavioral effects of moderate lead exposure in children and animal models 2: Animal studies. *Critical Reviews of Toxicology,* 1980, 8: 101-152.
Bowers, M.B. Jr, Goodman, E. and Sim, V.M. Some behavioral changes in man following anticholinesterase administration. *Journal of Nervous and Mental Disorders,* 1964, 138: 383-389.
Brass, C.A., Isaacs, L.E., McChesney, R. and Greengard, O. The effects of hyperphenyl-alaninemia on fetal development: A new animal model of maternal phenylketonuria. *Pediatrics Research,* 1982, 16: 388-394.
Breese, G.R., Mueller, R.A., Mailman, R.B., Frye, G.D. and Vogel, R.A. An alternative to animal models of central nervous system disorders: Study of drug mechanisms and disease symptoms in animals. *Progress in Neuro-Psychopharmacology,* 1978, 2: 313-325.
Bresson, F. Inferences from animals to man: Identifying behavior and identifying functions. In M. von Cranach (Ed.), *Methods of Inference from Animal to Human Behavior.* Chicago: Aldine, 1976: 319-342.
Brieger, H. Carbon disulphide in the living organism: Retention, biotransformation, and pathophysiologic effects. In H. Brieger and J. Teisinger (Eds.), *Toxicology of Carbon Disulphide: An International Symposium.* Amsterdam: Excerpta Medica Foundation, 1967: 27-31.
Brieger, H. and Teisinger, J. (Eds.), *Toxicology of Carbon Disulphide: An International Symposium.* Amsterdam: Excerpta Medica Foundation, 1966: 271.
Brodie, B.B. Difficulties in extrapolating data on metabolism of drugs from animal to man. *Clinical Pharmacology Therapeutics,* 1962, 3: 374-380.
Bunyan, P.J. and Stanley, P.I. Toxic mechanisms in wildlife. *Regulatory Toxicology and Pharmacology,* 1982, 2: 106-145.
Butcher, R.E., Brunner, R.L., Roth, T. and Kimmel, C.A. A learning impairment in rats associated with maternal hyper-vitaminosis-A. *Life Science,* 1972, 11: 141-145.
Casarett, L.J. and Bruce, M.C. Origin and scope of toxicology. In J. Doull, C.V. Klaassen

and M.D. Amdur (Eds.), *Toxicology: The Basic Science of Poisons*, 2nd ed., New York: Macmillan, 1980: 3-10.

Collins, T.F.X. and Collins, E.V. Current methodology in teratology research. in M.A. Mehlman, R.E. Shapiro and H. Blumenthal (Eds.), *Advances in Modern Toxicology: New Concepts in Safety Evaluation*. New York: Wiley, 1976: 155-175.

Coyle, I., Wayner, M.J. and Singer, G. Behavioral teratogenesis: A critical review. *Pharmacology Biochemistry and Behavior*, 1976, 4: 191-200.

Crandall, R.W. and Lave, L.B. (Eds.), *The Scientific Basis of Health and Safety Regulation*. Washington, D.C.: The Brookings Institution, 1981.

Davis, K.L., Hollister, L.E., Vento, A.L., Beilstein, B.A. and Rosekind, G.R. Dimethylaminoethanol (Deanol): Effect on apomorphine-induced stereotypy and an animal model of tardive dyskinesia. *Psychopharmacology*, 1979, 63: 143-146.

Desnick, R.J., Patterson, D.F. and Scarpelli, D.G. (Eds.), *Animal Models of Inherited Metabolic Diseases*. New York: Alan R. Liss, 1982.

Doull, J., Klaassen, C.D. and Amdur, M.O. (Eds.), *Toxicology: The Basic Science of Poisons*. New York: Macmillan, 1980.

Durham, W.F. and Hayes, W.J. Organic phosphorus poisoning and its therapy. *Archives of Environmental Health*, 1962, 5: 21-47.

Egan, G.F., Lewis, S.C. and Scala, R.A. Experimental design for animal toxicity studies. In P.S. Spencer and H.H. Schaumburg (Eds.), *Experimental and Clinical Neurotoxicology*. Baltimore: Williams and Wilkins, 1980: 708-725.

Ehlert, F.J., Kokka, N. and Fairhurst, A.S. Altered [^{3}H]quinuclidinyl benzilate binding in the striatum of rats following chronic cholinesterase inhibition with diisopropylfluorophosphate. *Molecular Pharmacology*, 1980: 17, 24-30.

Evans, H.L., Garman, R.H. and Weiss, B. Methylmercury: Exposure duration and regional distribution as determinants of neurotoxicity in nonhuman primates. *Toxicology and Applied Pharmacology*, 1977, 41: 15-33.

Evans, H.L., Laties, V.G. and Weiss, B. Behavioral effects of mercury and methylmercury. *Federation Proceedings*, 1975, 34: 1858-1867.

Falk, J.L., Schuster, C.R., Bigelow, G.E. and Woods, J.H. Progress and needs in the experimental analysis of drug and alcohol dependence. *American Psychologist*, 1982, 37: 1124-1127.

Faurbye, A., Rasch, P.J., Peterson, P.B., Brandborg, G. and Pakkenberg, H. Neurological symptoms in pharmacotherapy of psychoses. *Acta Psychiatrica Scandinavica*, 1964, 40: 10-27.

Feuerlein, W., Richter, R. and Springer, A. Animal models for human behavior: Some critical remarks and clinical objections. *Drug and Alcohol Dependence*, 1979, 4: 359-363.

Freedman, D.X., Redlich, F.C. and Igersheimer, W.W. Psychosis and allergy: Experimental approach. *American Journal of Psychiatry*, 1956, 112: 873-877.

Gamberale, F. and Hultengren, M. Toluene exposure II. Psychophysiological functions. *Work, Environment, Health*, 1972, 9: 131-139.

Gershon, S. and Shaw, F.H. Psychiatric sequelae of chronic exposure to organophosphorus insecticides. Lancet, 1961, 1: 1371-1374.

Glick, S.D. Screening and therapeutics: Animal models and human problems. In S.D. Glick and J. Goldfarb (Eds.), *Behavioral Pharmacology*. St Louis: C.V. Mosby, 1976.

Goldstein, A., Aronow, L. and Kalman, S.M. *Principles of Drug Action: The Basis of Pharmacology*, 2nd ed., New York: Wiley, 1974.

Grant, L.D. Research strategies for behavioral teratology studies. *Environmental Health Perspectives*, 1976, 18: 85-94.

Grob, D., Garlick, W.L. and Harvey, A.M. The toxic effects in man of the anticholinesterase insecticide parathion (*p*-netrophenyl diethyl thionophosphate). *Johns Hopkins Hospital Bulletin*, 1950, 87: 106-115.

Gross-Selbeck, E. Behavioral screening in lead exposed rats: An animal model to analyze subtle consequences of low level lead exposure in children. *Zeitschrift für Versuckstierkunde*, 1981, 23: 195-198.

Hale, F. Pigs born without eyeballs. *Journal of Heredity*, 1933, 24: 105–106.

Hale, F. The relation of vitamin A to anophthalmos in pigs. *American Journal of Ophthalmology*, 1935, 18: 1087–1093.

Hanninen, H. Psychological picture of manifest and latent carbon disulphide poisoning. *British Journal of Industrial Medicine*, 1971, 28: 374–381.

Hanninen, H., Nurminen, M., Tolonen, M. and Martelin, T. Psychological tests as indicators of excessive exposure to carbon disulfide. *Scandinavian Journal of Psychology*, 1978, 19: 163–174.

Heise, G.A. Toward a behavioral toxicology of learning and memory. In G. Zbinden, C. Vincenzo, G. Racagni and B. Weiss (Eds.), *Application of Behavioral Pharmacology in Toxicology*. New York: Raven Press, 1983: 27–37.

Hilgard, E.R. *Theories of Learning*, 2nd ed., New York: Appleton-Century-Crofts, 1956.

Hinde, R.A. The use of differences and similarities in comparative psychopathology. In G. Serban and A. Kling (Eds.), *Animal Models in Human Psychobiology*. New York: Plenum, 1976: 187–202.

Hopper, D.L. Review of animals as monitors of environmental pollutants. *Laboratory Animal Science*, 1980, 30: 490–491.

Hutchings, D.E. and Gaston, J. The effects of vitamin-A excess administered during the mid-fetal period on learning and development in the rat offspring. *Developmental Psychobiology*, 1974, 7: 222–233.

Hutchings, D.E., Gibbon, J. and Kaufman, M.A. Maternal vitamin-A excess during the early fetal period: Effects on learning and development in the offspring. *Developmental Psychobiology*, 1973, 6: 445–457.

Ivy, A.C. The history and ethics of the use of human subjects in medical experiments. *Science*, 1948, 58: 1–5.

Janowsky, D.S., El-Yousef, M.K., Davis, J.M. and Sekerke, H.J. A cholinergic-adrenergic hypothesis of mania and depression. *Lancet*, 1972, 2: 632–635.

Jason, K.M. and Kellogg, C.K. Behavioral neurotoxicity of lead. In R.L. Singhal and J.A. Thomas (Eds.), *Lead Toxicity*, Baltimore: Urban and Schwarzenberg, 1980: 241–271.

Jenden, D.J. The neurochemical basis of acetylcholine precursor loading as a therapeutic strategy. In K.L. Davis and P.A. Berger (Eds.), *Brain Acetylcholine and Neuropsychiatric Disease*. New York: Plenum, 1979: 483–513.

Klawans, H.L., Carvey, P., Nausieda, P.A., Goetz, C.G. and Weiner, W.J. Effect of dose and type of neuroleptic in an animal model of tardive dyskinesia. *Neurology*, 1980, 30: 383.

Levine, T.E. Effects of carbon disulphide and FLA-63 on operant behavior in pigeons. *Journal of Pharmacology and Experimental Therapeutics*, 1976, 199: 669–678.

Lipton, M.A., Gordon, R., Guroff, G. and Udenfriend, S. *p*-chlorophenylalanine-induced chemical manifestations of phenylketonuria in rats. *Science*, 1967, 156: 248–250.

Mancuso, T.F. and Locke, B.Z. Carbon disulphide as a cause of suicide. *Journal of Occupational medicine*, 1972, 14: 595–606.

McKinney, W.T., Moran, E.C., Kraemer, G.W. and Prange, A.J. Jr. Long-term chlorpromazine in rhesus monkeys: Production of dyskinesias and changes in social behavior. *Psychopharmacology*, 1980, 72: 35–59.

Mesarovic, M.D., Macko, D. and Takahara, Y. *Theory of Hierarchical, Multilevel Systems*. New York: Academic Press, 1968.

Michael, J.M. The second revolution in health: Health promotion and its environmental base. *American Psychologist*, 1982, 37: 936–941.

Milar, K.S., Krigman, M.R. and Grant, L.D. Effects of neonatal lead exposure on memory in rats. *Neurobehavioral Toxicology and Teratology*, 1981, 3: 369–373.

Miller, S.L. and Urey, H.C. Organic compound synthesis on the primative earth. *Science*, 1959, 130: 245–251.

Myers, R.D. *Handbook of Drug and Chemical Stimulation of the Brain*. New York: Van Nostrand, 1974.

Olson, K.L. and Boush, G.M. Decreased learning capacity in rats exposed prenatally and postnatally to low doses of mercury. *Bulletin of Environmental Contamination and Toxicology*, 1975, 13: 73-79.

Overstreet, D.H. Behavioral plasticity and the cholinergic system. *Progress in Neuro-psychopharmacology and Biological Psychiatry*, 1983, 7 (in press).

Paget, G.E. Correlation with potential toxicity to man of toxic effects in animals. *Clinical Pharmacology Therapeutics*, 1962, 2: 381-384.

Pavlov, I.P. *Conditioned Reflexes and Psychiatry.* New York: International Publishers, 1941.

Popper, K.R. *The Logic of Scientific Discovery.* New York: Basic Books, 1959.

Pryor, G.T., Dickinson, J., Howd, R.A. and Rebert, C.S. Neurobehavioral effects of subchronic exposure of weanling rats to toluene or hexane. *Neurobehavioral Toxicology and Teratology*, 1983a, 5: 47-52.

Pryor, G.T.,Dickinson, J., Howd, R.A. and Rebert, C.S. Transient cognitive deficits and high-frequency hearing loss in weanling rats exposed to toluene. *Neurobehavioral Toxicology and Teratology*, 1983b, 5: 53-57.

Reiter, L.W. and MacPhail, R.C. Motor activity: A survey of methods with potential use in toxicity testing. *Neurobehavioral Toxicology*, 1979, 1 (suppl. 1): 53-66.

Reuhl, K.R. and Chang, L.W. Effects of methylmercury on the development of the nervous system: A review. *Neurotoxicology*, 1979, 1: 21-25.

Romanes, G.J. *Animal Intelligence.* London: Kegan, Paul, French, 1882.

Rowntree, D.W., Nevin, S. and Wilson, S. The effects of diisopropylfluorophosphate in schizophrenia and manic depressive psychosis. *Journal of Neurology,. Neurosurgery and Psychiatry*, 1950, 13: 47-59.

Rubovits, R., Patel, B.C. and Klawans, H.L. Effect of prolonged chlorpromazine pretreatment on the threshold for amphetamine stereotypy: A model for tardive dyskinesias. *Advances in Neurology*, 1973, 1: 671-679.

Ruffin, J.B. Functional testing for behavioral toxicity: A missing dimension in experimental environmental toxicology. *Journal of Occupational Medicine*, 1963, 5: 117-121.

Russell, R.W. *The Comparative Study of Behaviour.* London: H.K. Lewis, 1952.

Russell, R.W. Effects of "biochemical lesions" on behavior. *Acta Psychologia*, 1958, 14: 281-294.

Russell, R.W. Extrapolation from animals to man. In H. Steinberg (Ed.), *Animal Behaviour and Drug Action.* London: J. & A. Churchill, 1964a: 410-421.

Russell, R.W. Psychopharmacology *Annual Review of Psychology*, 1964b, 15: 87-114.

Russell, R.W. Neurotoxins: A "systems" approach. In I. Chubb and L.B. Geffen (Eds.), *Neurotoxins: Fundamental and Clinical Advances.* Adelaide: University of Adelaide Press, 1979: 1-7.

Russell, R.W., Booth, R.A. and Jenden, D.J. Suppression of presynaptic release of acetylcholine in development of tolerance to the anticholinesterase, DFP. Unpublished data.

Schiller, G.D. Reduced binding of [^{3}H]-quinuclidinyl benzilate associated with chronically low acetylcholinesterase activity. *Life Sciences*, 1979, 24: 1159-1164.

Sigerist, H.E. *The Great Doctors.* New York: Doubleday, 1958.

Silbergeld, E.K. and Goldberg, A.M. Lead induced behavioral dysfunction: An animal model of hyperactivity. *Experimental Neurology*, 1974, 42: 146-157.

Singhal, R.L. and Thomas, J.A. (Eds.), *Lead Toxicity.* Baltimore: Urban and Schwarzenberg, 1980.

Spyker, J.M. Occupational hazards and the pregnant worker. In C. Xintaras, B.L. Johnson and I. deGroot (Eds.), *Behavioral Toxicology.* Washington, D.C.: US Department of Health Education and Welfare Publication Number (N10SH) 74-126, 1974.

Spyker, J.M. Assessing the impact of low level chemicals and latent effects. *Federation Proceedings*, 1975, 34: 1835-1844.

Stavinoha, W.B., Reiger, J.A.,Ryan, L.C. and Smith, P.W. Effects of chronic poisoning by an organophosphorous cholinesterase inhibitor on acetylcholine and norepinephrine content of the brain. *Advances in Chemistry Series*, 1966, 60: 79-88.

Stebbins, W.C. Concerning the need for more sophisticated animal models in sensory behavioral toxicology. *Environmental Health Perspectives*, 1982, 44: 75-85.

Stephenson, R.P. A modification of receptor theory. *British Journal of Pharmacology*, 1956, 11: 379-393.

Summerford, W.T., Hayes, W.J., Johnston, J.M., Walter, K. and Spillane, J. Cholinesterase response and symptomatology from exposure to organic phosphorus insecticides. *AMA Archives of Industrial Hygiene*, 1953, 7: 383-398.

Tilson, H.A., Cabe, P.A. and Burne, T.A. Behavioral procedures for the assessment of neurotoxicity. in P.S. Spencer and H.H. Schaumburg (Eds.), *Experimental and Clinical Neurotoxicology*. Baltimore: Williams and Wilkins, 1980: 758-774.

Tilson, H.A., Mitchell, C.L. and Cabe, P.A. Screening for neurobehavioral toxicity: The need for and examples of validation of testing procedures. *Neurobehavioral Toxicology* 1979, 1 (Suppl. 1): 137-148.

Tye, N.C., Horsman, L., Wright, F.C. and Pullar, I.A. Differential enhancement of locomotor activity by dopamine agonists following chronic neuroleptic treatment: An animal model of tardive dyskinesia. *European Journal of Pharmacology*, 1979, 55: 103-107.

US National Research Council. *Decision Making for Regulating Chemicals in the Environment*. Washington, D.C.: National Academy of Sciences, 1975.

Von Cranach, M. (Ed.), *Methods of Inference from Animal to Human Behavior*. Chicago: Aldine, 1976.

Vorhees, C.V., Butcher, R.E. and Berry, H.K. Progress in experimental phenylketonuria: A critical review. *Neuroscience and Biobehavioral Reviews*, 1981, 5: 177-190.

Warburton, D.M. Internal pollution. *Journal of Biosocial Sciences*, 1978, 10: 309-319.

Warburton, D.M. Extrapolation in the neurochemistry of behaviour. In G.C.L. Davey (Ed.), *Animal Models of Human Behaviour*. London: Wiley, 1983: 339-353.

Weiss, B. and Laties, V.G. (Eds.), *Behavioral Toxicology*. New York: Plenum Press, 1975.

Weiss, B. and Laties, V.G. Assays for behavioral toxicity: A strategy for the Environmental Protection Agency. *Neurobehavioral Toxicology*, 1979, 1 (Suppl. 1): 213-215.

Weiss, B. and Santelli, S. Dyskinesias evoked in monkeys by weekly administration of haloperidol. *Science*, 1978, 200: 799-801.

Weiss, B., Wood, R.W. and Macys, D.A. Behavioral toxicology of carbon disulphide and toluene. *Environmental Health Perspectives*, 1979, 30: 39-45.

Werboff, J. Developmental psychopharmacology. In W.C. Clark and J. del Guidice (Eds.), *Principles of Psychopharmacology*. New York: Academic Press, 1978: 395-407.

WHO Scientific Group on Principles for the Testing of Drugs for Teratogenicity. *Report*. Geneva: World Health Organization Technical Report Series No. 364, 1967.

Williamson, A.M., Teo, R.K.C. and Sanderson, J. Occupational mercury exposure and its consequences for behaviour. *International Archives of Occupational and Environmental Health*, 1982, 50: 273-286.

Wolf, A. *Textbook of Logic*, 2nd ed., London: Allen and Unwin, 1938.

World Health Organization. *Early Detection of Health Impairment in Occupational Exposure to Health Hazards*. Geneva: World Health Organization Technical Report Series No. 571, 1975.

Xintaras, C., Johnson, B.L. and De Groot, I. (Eds.), *Behavioral Toxicology*. Washington, D.C.: US Department of Health, Education and Welfare Publication Number (N10SH) 74-126, 1974.

Zbinden, G. Experimental methods in behavioral teratology. *Archives of Toxicology*, 1981, 48: 69-88.

3
THE EFFECT OF ENVIRONMENTAL ODOURS ON THE SENSE OF SMELL

DAVID G. LAING

I. INTRODUCTION

Humans encounter odours from a variety of sources during their daily activities. Inside the home, there are aromas from cooking, toiletries and air fresheners; outside it are fragrances from the garden, aromas from shops, and odours from cars and factories. Exposure to these stimuli can vary widely — from fleeting experiences as we pass gardens or perfumed ladies, to many hours of contact in the workplace or home.

Although odorants are chemicals, they are generally viewed as annoyances rather than health hazards, because they are usually present in low concentrations in the air we breathe. This view is also reflected by the numerous toxicological studies of odorous chemicals, which usually are concerned with the effects of exposure to the very high levels found in some work environments. The deleterious effects on health of a wide range of environmental chemicals were reviewed recently by Damstra (1978).

However, complaints by the general public over the past decade have prompted health authorities to investigate the effects of odorous air pollutants. The level of intrusion of odours into our environment is well illustrated by the fact that as much as half of all complaints about air pollutants in some regions of the United States have been concerned with odorants (Copley International Corporation, 1973). Common sources of odours are pulp mills, livestock, food processors, rendering plants and chemical industries. The offending odorants include mercaptans, amines,

ANIMAL MODELS IN PSYCHOPATHOLOGY
ISBN 0 12 114180 2

and aldehydes, many of which can be detected in very small quantities by humans (National Research Council, 1979: 182–183). It is not uncommon, therefore, for odorants to be detected many miles from their source, thus increasing the area from which complaints arise.

Unfavourable responses to odours now include nausea, vomiting and headache, shallow breathing and coughing; disturbances of sleep, stomach and appetite; and irritation of eyes, nose and throat (National Research Council, 1979: 62–63). Odours have also been reported to affect the enjoyment of food, home, and the external environment. Such effects, interestingly, can be caused by pleasant or unpleasant odours. However, apart from causing annoyance in the workplace, environmental odours have not been implicated in chronic physiological or psychological conditions in humans. A tenuous status quo therefore exists about the effects of odours on humans, with both health and pollution authorities generally concerned with the reduction in levels of pollutants to low annoyance levels, rather than their elimination.

Recent experiments with animals (Døving and Pinching, 1973; Pinching and Døving, 1974) indicate that prolonged exposure to low levels of odorants can lead to changes in the morphology of olfactory cells in the forebrain, and alter the ability of an animal to smell (Laing and Panhuber, 1978). Different olfactory cells were reported to be affected by different odours (Pinching and Døving, 1974). This has raised the possibility that the patterns of normal and altered cells resulting from exposure are related to the coding of odours. Since these reports suggest brain cells are vulnerable to low concentrations of odorants in the environment, and the effects may well have significance for olfactory coding, the aim of this chapter is to discuss the evidence for the effects of exposure, their relevance to olfactory coding, and how they could affect olfactory dependent behaviour of humans.

First, however, an outline of the anatomy and physiology of those parts of the olfactory system that are relevant to this chapter is given to provide a background for the discussion that follows.

II. ANATOMY AND PHYSIOLOGY

A. Olfactory epithelium

Odour receptor neurones reside in the olfactory epithelium in the *regio olfactoria* of the nasal cavity in most vertebrates. Each neurone is character-ized by a single dendrite (Fig. 3.1) which penetrates to the surface of the epithelium where it can contact odour molecules in the aqueous mucous

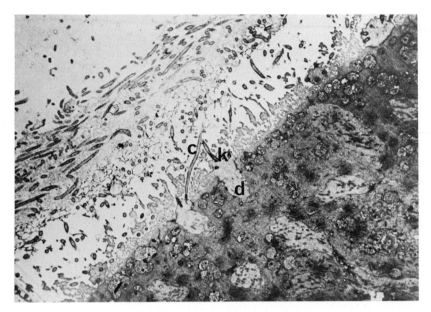

Fig. 3.1: Olfactory epithelium of the frog, showing dendrites (d) of receptor neurones, with cilia (c) projecting from the olfactory knob (k) into the aqueous mucous layer.

layer, and an unmyelinated axon which synapses with apical dendrites of secondary neurones (mitral cells) in the olfactory bulb. The distal end of the dendrite of the primary neurone has a knob-like shape from which extend motile cilia, the number of which varies according to the species (Ohno *et al.*, 1981). As yet is is unclear whether receptor sites are on the membrane of the cilia or the olfactory knob, or on both. Olfactory neurones are also characterized by the absence of lateral connections at the epithelial level and centrifugal projections from other olfactory centres.

In addition to the primary neurones, the olfactory epithelium contains supporting cells whose function is unclear, and basal cells which undergo mitosis to form primary neurons. This latter phenomenon occurs in a wide variety of species and appears to be a common feature of the olfactory epithelium. In the mouse, mitosis occurs at a rate such that the entire population of neurones is replaced every 30 days (Moulton *et al.*, 1970). A constant turnover of neurones means that their axons and synaptic terminals in the olfactory bulb are being continually renewed. Hence, the connectivity between the olfactory epithelium and the olfactory bulb provides an opportunity to study mechanisms of neural plasticity in the central nervous system of adult animals.

A significant feature of the anatomy of the peripheral olfactory system is that the axons of neurones from a single region of the epithelium project to a discrete region of the olfactory bulb (Constanzo and O'Connell, 1978; Le Gros Clark, 1951), thereby providing a topographic relationship between the epithelium and bulb, a feature crucial to the main topic of this chapter.

Data from a small number of studies on the physiology of primary neurones indicate that individual cells respond to a wide range of odours (Gesteland *et al.*, 1963; Getchell and Shepherd, 1978). Although this suggests the cells are "generalists", their response thresholds for different odours differ substantially, giving the impression that the cells are selective, but not specific, in response. This view is supported by data from cross-adaptation studies in the salamander (Baylin and Moulton, 1979) which indicated that a receptor cell can have several receptor site types so that the specificity of the cell is determined by the number of site types and the number of sites of each type.

Contrary to earlier thinking, primary neurones adapt slowly to odours (Ottoson, 1959). In part, this is possibly due to the absence of centrifugal input, and suggests that the rapid adaptation generally encountered when odours are sampled is due to bulbar or other central mechanisms. Modulation of the responses of olfactory receptor neurones, therefore, is effected only by their own intrinsic features, or by externally applied agents such as odours (for example, cross-adaptation effects), and protein or enzyme blockers (for example, sulphydryl reagents, war gases, or electrolytes added to the mucous).

B. Olfactory bulb

The bulb is a highly laminated structure in most vertebrates (Fig. 3.2). It has a glomerular layer where the axons of primary neurones synapse with dendrites of mitral, tufted, and periglomerular cells; an external plexiform layer containing tufted cells, whose axons either remain within the bulb, project to the opposite bulb, or to other olfactory centres (Macrides and Schneider, 1982); a layer of mitral cells which is often one cell thick; and an internal plexiform layer containing granule cells. The axons of mitral cells form the bulk of the lateral olfactory tract which is the main projection from the bulb to other olfactory centres. The main projections are to the primary olfactory cortex and the amygdala (Fig. 3.3). Other centres which receive ascending olfactory input from one or both of these central regions, are the thalamus, lateral and orbital prefrontal cortex, and the lateral hypothalamus. Major centrifugal fibres innervating the bulb originate in

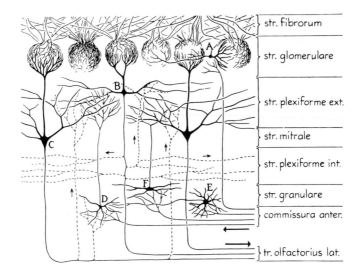

str. fibrorum

str. glomerulare

str. plexiforme ext.

str. mitrale

str. plexiforme int.

str. granulare

commissura anter.

tr. olfactorius lat.

Fig. 3.2: Diagram of bulbar pathways modified after Cajal. A = External granular or periglomerular cells. B = Tufted cells. C = Mitral cells. D = Internal granular cells. E = Golgi or Blanes cells. F = Cajal cells and horizontal fusiform cells. The collaterals of the mitral and tufted cell axons are shown by interrupted lines. From Lohman and Lammers (1967).

the primary olfactory cortex and anterior olfactory nucleus (Davis and Macrides, 1981; Macrides *et al.*, 1981).

The most relevant anatomical features of the bulb for this discussion concern the intrabulbar connections and activity of mitral cells. These cells are the principal neurone of the bulb and currently appear to be the cells which transfer most of the information from the periphery to other olfactory centres. The fact that each mitral cell receives input from hundreds of primary neurones (in the rabbit, 50 million receptor cells project to 50 000 mitral cells — Allison and Turner-Warwick, 1949) indicates it is a very important information processing (cell). However, intracellular connections appear to play a key role in modifying incoming information. Primary olfactory neurones, for example, are connected laterally in the glomerular layer by periglomerular cells, and mitral cells are connected through granule cells (Shepherd, 1972). Information from the periphery can therefore be modified at the glomerular level before passing to mitral cells, whilst mitral cell responses can be modulated by granule cells through reciprocal dendrodendritic synapses.

Like their primary counterparts these secondary neurones are selective rather than specific in their response. According to Mair (1982), the

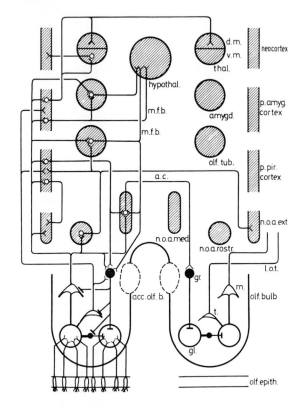

Fig. 3.3: Olfactory pathways. *acc. olf. b.* accessory olfactory bulb; *a.c.* anterior commissure; *amygd.* amygdaloid complex; *gl.* glomerulus; *gr.* granular cell; *l.o.t.* lateral olfactory tract; *m.f.b.* medial forebrain bundle; *m.* mitral cell; *n.o.a. ext.* anterior olfactory nucleus, pars externa;. *n.o.a. med.* anterior olfactory nucleus, pars medialis; *n.o.a. rostr.* anterior olfactory nucleus, pars rostralis; *olf. tub.* olfactory tubercle; *p. amygd. cortex* periamygdaloid cortex; *p. pir. cortex* prepiriform cortex; *thal., d. m.* thalamus, nucleus medio dorsalis; *thal., v.m.* thalamus, nucleus medio ventralis. From MacLeod (1971).

stimulating effectiveness of a particular odorant varies between different neurones. In addition, the number of evoked action potentials depends on the odorant used and the concentration at which it is delivered. The selectivity of mitral cells can be gauged from studies on the monkey by Tanabe *et al.* (1975), who found that the majority of responsive mitral cells responded to several of eight odours presented, whilst 12.5% responded to only one of the stimuli. In contrast, 50% of odour responsive cells in the lateroposterior region of the orbitofrontal cortex responded to only one of the eight odours used. These results prompted Tanabe *et al.* (1975) to conclude that a fine and specific discrimination of odours is performed in the neocortex, whilst gross discrimination occurs at the bulb.

As regards adaptation, some mitral cells adapt rapidly whilst others continue to respond even after one hour of continuous stimulation (Chaput and Panhuber, 1982). Although the exact role of the bulb during adaptation remains to be determined, these effects may account for the partial loss of sensitivity which occurs during psychophysical studies of adaptation in humans (Cain, 1974; Ekman *et al.*, 1967).

Overall, the very great similarity between the structures of the olfactory epithelia of humans and other vertebrates, and between their bulbs, despite some large phylogenetic differences (for example, humans and rats), provides confidence in assuming that the reception and perception of odours is characterized by a similar process in each.

C. Spatial coding of odour quality

The most popular theories of how odour quality is encoded are the chromatographic theory of Mozell (1964), and the spatio-temporal patterning approach of Adrian (1953) and Moulton (1976). The former maintains that, upon entering the nose, odorant molecules are absorbed by the receptor epithelium according to their polarity, with polar (water soluble) compounds being absorbed by cells nearest to the entrance of the nose, and non-polar (oil soluble) molecules in the rear or posterior section. The process is likened to the adsorption phenomenon in chromatography, and many of the data supporting the theory have been obtained by correlating retention times of odorants on gas chromatographic columns with neural activity in the anterior and posterior regions of the nose of the frog, and with the rate of migration of odour molecules across the olfactory mucosa (Mozell and Jagodowicz, 1973). On the other hand, in the spatio-temporal approach, it is proposed that odorants excite different parts of the olfactory epithelium by two methods. First, the theory suggests that olfactory receptor cells with similar response spectra are grouped in similar regions of the epithelium (inherent patterning). Second, odorants are dispersed differently after inspiration by physical factors imposed by the morphology of the nasal cavity, by the pattern of airflow during sniffing, and by differential absorption of the odorants as they pass over the nasal mucous (imposed patterning).

Recent studies by Kubie *et al.* (1980) and Mackay-Sim *et al.* (1982) with the salamander give strong support for both theories of odour quality encoding, suggesting that patterns of responsive cells arise from spatio-temporal factors, as well as from the polarity of the odour molecule. They showed, by delivering punctate odour stimuli directly onto the recording sites, that odorants can be classified into anterior, posterior, or general epithelial stimulators. The most responsive cells for polar odorants (for example, propanol) were sited anteriorly; for non-polar odorants (for example, pinene) highest responses occurred in the posterior region; whilst the most responsive cells for odorants that had polar and non-polar parts in their molecular structure (for example, amyl acetate) were located across the epithelium, at and between the anterior and posterior regions. Therefore it appears that receptor cells are arranged so that those responsive to non-polar odours are sited mainly in the posterior epithelium, whilst those which respond best to polar odours are sited in the anterior region. These studies in the salamander and frog have demonstrated that different odours will stimulate cells sited in discrete but different regions of the epithelium.

Now since anatomical and electrophysiological studies in rats, rabbits, hamsters, salamanders, and fish, have shown that axons of receptor cells in discrete regions of the epithelium project to discrete regions of the olfactory bulb (that is, a topographical relationship exists between the receptor epithelium and bulb), it follows that stimulation of the epithelium by an odour will result in discrete regions of activity in the epithelium and the bulb (Constanzo and O'Connell, 1980; Kauer and Moulton, 1974; Thommesen and Døving, 1977). Thus, for each odour there may be a specific set of regions stimulated at both centres. The resulting set or pattern of regions may be a spatial code used by the brain to recognize odours.

This notion has received further support from recent studies with the [^{14}C] 2-deoxyglucose technique for labelling of active nerve cells, which was first demonstrated by Kennedy et al. (1975). In this method, stimulation by an odour after injection of the radiotracer results in the production of small regions of intense radioactivity in the bulb (Sharp et al., 1975), some of which have been as small as a single glomerulus (Jourdan et al., 1980a). The overall patterns of these intensely labelled regions appear to be characteristic of specific odours. However, their topographical relationship with patterns of epithelial stimulation remains to be shown.

Nevertheless, spatial coding of odour quality at the level of the olfactory bulb is a well supported concept. It is this concept that is explored using another approach in the following section of this chapter.

III. EFFECTS OF PROLONGED EXPOSURE TO AN ODOUR

A. Selective degeneration of mitral cells

In 1973, Døving and Pinching reported that when two-week old rats are exposed to a constant stream of the odorant cyclo-octanone for periods of from two weeks to 11 months, there is degeneration of mitral cells in dorsomedial, ventral and mid-lateral regions of the olfactory bulb (Fig. 3.4 and Fig. 3.5). At the most anterior part of the mitral cell layer, degeneration extended around the whole circumference. Few cells showed signs of degeneration outside the three principal areas. All three zones of degeneration were evident throughout the anteroposterior extent of the bulb. In contrast, control rats exposed to room air for similar periods exhibited degeneration only in a small dorsomedial zone which extended throughout the bulb (Fig. 3.5).

Light microscopy showed that the main features of the degeneration were a darkening of nucleus and cytoplasm, and shrinkage of the cell. The darkening was shown by electron microscopy to be due to the nuclear and cytoplasmic contents, organelles and granular material becoming more closely packed. Free ribosomes and stacks of endoplasmic reticulum were evident and vacuolation just beneath plasma membranes was marked. However, nucleolar changes were rarely seen. In dendrites of the affected cells, neurotubules were closely packed, but in contrast, presynaptic and postsynaptic vesicles and thickenings were unaltered, as were the olfactory nerve terminals at the glomeruli, even where the glomeruli were opposite the most severely affected mitral cells. Regarding other types of cells in the bulb, similar morphological changes were seen in periglomerular, tufted and granule cells at slightly longer intervals after the commencement of exposure to an odorant.

Overall, the changes were likened to those observed with transneuronal degeneration of mitral cells following removal of the primary neurones by ablation of the olfactory receptor epithelium (Pinching and Powell, 1971). However, the authors stressed that there were important differences between the effects seen with both phenomena. Following exposure there was no degeneration of olfactory nerve terminals at the glomeruli, which suggested the phenomenon may be due to a "functional alteration" in the mitral cells rather than to anatomical degeneration, and, equally important, not all mitral cells were affected. This latter finding prompted the authors to use the term "selective degeneration" to indicate "an altered functional state, rather than cell death". Furthermore, they suggested that this change in functional state may have given rise to a change in the responses of cells to the fixation procedures used in the study. They therefore implied that before fixation it is possible the altered cells appear normal, but that subtle structural and/or biochemical changes have occurred in the cells during exposure. This is a particularly interesting point, since it has a direct bearing on the histological procedures that are used to identify affected cells. The consequences of using different fixation procedures will be discussed later (Section IV, B.).

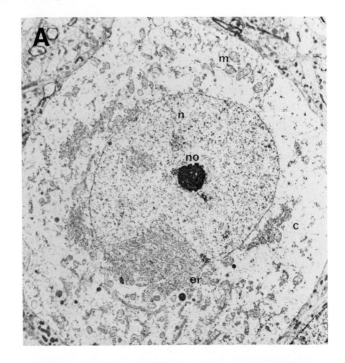

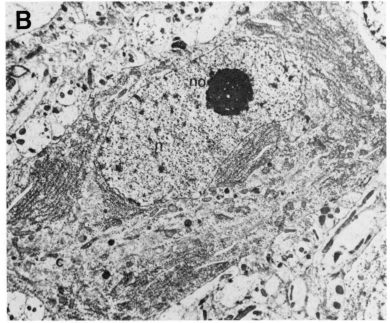

B. Possible mechanisms for selective degeneration

However, the initial study by Døving and Pinching (1973) did not provide a definite answer to how selective degeneration occurs. They suggested that although cells could degenerate from overstimulation, or understimulation, it was unlikely overstimulation could occur from long term excitation of mitral cells, since: (i) the stimulus is perceived phasically (that is, olfactory receptors are only stimulated during sniffs or inspiration); and (ii) Ottoson (1959) had shown that delivering repetitive stimuli to the rabbit olfactory mucosa for 10 seconds did not cause an appreciable decrease in the magnitude of responses in the bulb. In essence, they suggested that despite continuous exposure to an odour, adaptation of the receptor cells and mitral cells does not occur. Whether either reason is valid for the present prolonged exposure paradigm remains to be seen. So far the longest duration over which the responsivity of mitral cells has been continuously monitored is one hour (Chaput and Panhuber, 1982). This study showed that during one hour of continuous exposure to a moderately high concentration of odour, the magnitude of the responses of 50% of mitral cells was reduced, whilst that of others had disappeared. Why some ceased responding whilst others continued is not known, but this action may be related to the maintenance of a basic responsitivity. Whether the responses would have been reduced further with longer presentations of odour remains to be shown; however, these results do support the view that prolonged exposure to an odour does lead to a loss of responsivity. Therefore, overstimulation cannot be ruled out as the cause of cell changes on the evidence presented by Døving and Pinching (1973).

Exposure to an odour over many days or weeks could also involve other factors that may affect the responsivity of receptor and mitral cells. Continuous inhalation of an odorant, for example, can result in its build up in the body to a level which is dependent on its concentration and rate of metabolism. Some odorants have a half-life in the body of minutes (Longland et al., 1977), whilst for others it is several hours or days (Ahlborg and Thunberg, 1980). The slower metabolizing odorants could, therefore, reach quite high levels in the body and be exhaled into the nose following diffusion from the blood via the lungs, resulting in stimulation of the receptors. Thus, instead of odour delivery to the receptors occurring only

Fig. 3.4: A. Electron photomicrograph of a normal mitral cell from a control animal aged six weeks. Note the characteristically pale cytoplasm and nucleus and the wide separation of organelles. X6350: *n*, nucleus; *no*, nucleolus; *er*, endo-plasmic reticulum; *c*, cytoplasm; *m*, mitochondria. From Døving and Pinching (1973). B. Altered mitral cell from animal after two weeks exposure to cyclo-octanone. Note the marked shrinkage with darkening of cytoplasm and nucleus, close packing of organelles, but normal appearance of the membrane-bound organelles. X6350. From Døving and Pinching (1973).

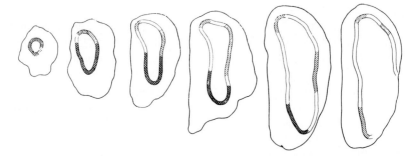

Fig. 3.5: Schematic representation of the mitral cell layer as seen in coronal sections of the olfactory bulb, showing regions of normal (open), sparse (single hatched) and severe (cross hatched) morphological changes in cells following exposure to cyclo-octanone for one month. Note there are three areas of degeneration. From Pinching and Døving (1974).

during inspiration, stimulation could also occur during expiration. This increased delivery of odour to the olfactory mucus, along with the possible build up of odour molecules through adsorption and desorption in the respiratory tissue in the nose, could result in the mucous layer in which the receptor cells bathe becoming saturated with the odour, in effect presenting the receptors with a truly continuous delivery of the stimulus. Receptor cells may not be able to cope with such stimulation and for intrinsic reasons could shut down. As yet, apart from the examination of olfactory nerve terminals in the glomeruli by Døving and Pinching (1973) which showed they were normal, no electrophysiological or anatomical study of the receptors during such prolonged exposure has been reported, nor have the levels of odorant in the blood or nasal tissue of exposed animals been determined. We therefore do not know the responsiveness of the receptors during prolonged exposure, and cannot rule out the possibility that degeneration of mitral cells has occurred through lack of olfactory input, as a result of overstimulation of the receptor cells.

Another mechanism for degeneration through overstimulation is the possible neurotoxic action of odour on receptor cells. At present we do not know what happens to odorants after they have stimulated a receptor cell. If the cells absorb odorants or secrete a factor upon stimulation which prevents re-stimulation of the cell by an odour molecule in a manner akin to that proposed by Vogt and Riddiford (1981) in insects, then excessive amounts of odorant in the vicinity of the cell, arising from constant odour delivery, could lead to a breakdown of this immobilizing pathway and result in constant stimulation of the cell, or of entry into the cell of large amounts of odorant. The altered responsivity of the cell resulting from these abuses could result in no input to their secondary neurones which, from deprivation, may degenerate. Overall then, there are at least two mechanisms by which overstimulation could cause degeneration, and both suggest the cells that are most responsive to the exposure odour are the ones which would appear altered.

Given our limited knowledge of how the olfactory systems operates, each of these mechanisms is possible; however, a more plausible reason given by Døving and Pinching (1973) is that cells degenerate because the primary neurones from which they normally receive input are not stimulated by the exposure odour. They likened the monotonous olfactory experience of the rats to the conditions employed by Wiesel and Hubel (1963) in studies of the visual system in the cat where animals were deprived of input to one eye during the critical period of development. During this treatment, cells in the lateral geniculate nucleus, which were dependent on input from the deprived eye, degenerated through lack of stimulation. This view implies that understimulation of some mitral cells may result in their degeneration, whilst those which are normally activated by the exposure odour receive sufficient input to retain their normal appearance and function. They also argued that the presence of normal receptor terminals at the glomeruli opposite the most degenerated mitral cells in animals exposed to cyclo-octanone indicates the receptor cells are unharmed and that this provides another parallel with the effects of monocular deprivation since no morphological changes were observed in the retinal cells of the deprived eye. If this proposal is correct, then it adds weight to the case that the degeneration of second order neurones is transneuronal, and is brought about by "functional deafferentation" (Døving and Pinching, 1973), or lack of olfactory input, with the end effect being similar to that produced by olfactory nerve section.

Thus, in summary, Døving and Pinching (1973) proposed that "cells responsive to the dominant stimulus (cyclo-octanone) are preserved" during prolonged exposure to an odour, "while other cells which do not respond to it, degenerate".

C. Functional implications

Whether or not the above interpretation is correct is overshadowed by the important functional implications of the exposure phenomenon. The fact that degeneration of all mitral cells did not occur and the pattern of normal and altered cells was reproducible across animals suggested to

Døving and Pinching (1973) that the phenomenon provides evidence for the functional localization of odour quality within the bulb that others had proposed from anatomical and physiological experiments. The method, therefore, appeared to have the potential for identifying mitral cells that are responsive to a specific odour (that is, the normal cells, if understimulation is the cause of degeneration). This proposal received firm support from a second study (Pinching and Døving, 1974) where specific degeneration patterns were obtained with 44 different odours (Fig. 3.6). As in the earlier study, the zones of change had the same relative position in coronal section through the antero-posterior extent of the bulb, and in the majority of animals degeneration was marked more anteriorly than posteriorly. As can be seen from Fig. 3.6, there is considerable overlap between patterns for some odours. This was taken to indicate the distribution of neurones affected by, but not specific to, a particular odour, or to represent properties shared by different odours. This seems reasonable in view of our current understanding of the specificity of receptor cells, which show a regional and differential sensitivity to different odours, and project to small regions of the bulb. The general conclusion of Døving and Pinching following their two studies indicated that each degeneration pattern reflected the spatial distribution of responsive receptor cells, and provided a unique method for identifying mitral cells which respond to a specific odour. However, these studies did not determine why selective degeneration occurs, or whether the normal cells remaining after exposure are the cells which respond to that specific odour. The significance of the patterns therefore had still to be established.

D. Evidence that understimulation causes degeneration

Recently Laing and Panhuber (1978) explored the significance of the patterns by examining the relationship between degeneration patterns and the olfactory acuity and preferences of rats raised in odorous and non-odorous environments. The rationale was that, if cells are altered through lack of stimulation, then the remaining normal cells would be those responding to the exposure odour, and no loss of acuity for this odour would occur. On the other hand, if overstimulation causes degeneration, then a loss of acuity for the exposure odour would be expected.

In these studies rats were exposed from postnatal day 14, for two or four months, to either rat colony air (normal environment), deodorized air,

Fig. 3.6: Patterns of mitral cell degeneration for 12 different odours. Dots in drawings for benzyl mercaptan (17) indicate marked tufted cell degeneration in that area. From Pinching and Døving (1974).

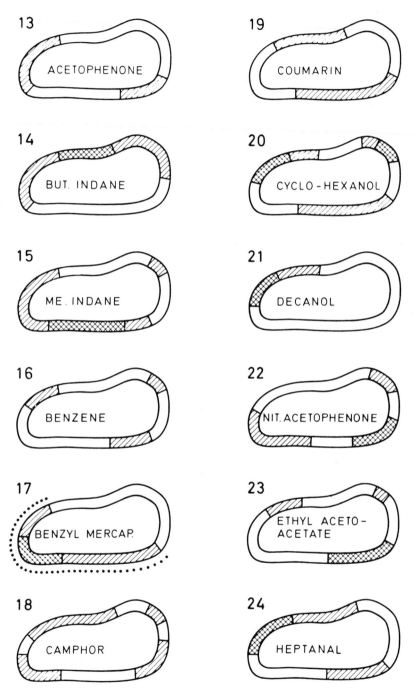

cyclohexanone, or acetophenone. The latter two odours had been used earlier by Pinching and Døving (1974), and clear patterns of altered and normal cells were reported. Results from behavioural measures with rats that had been exposed for four months indicated that continuous exposure to a single odour early in life can alter olfactory acuity and preferences. Animals exposed to acetophenone, for example, had a significantly poorer sensitivity for cyclohexanone than normal rats, or rats exposed to cyclohexanone, while the latter group were marginally worse than normal rats and rats reared with acetophenone in detecting acetophenone. Sensitivity to the exposure odour, therefore, was not altered, but animals exhibited a deficit in their ability to detect other odours. A deficit was also observed in the ability of rats reared in deodorized air to detect the two exposure odours. All these results were consistent with the proposal that the cells which appeared normal after exposure to an odour were the ones stimulated by the exposure odour. Further support for this view came from preference tests where animals were allowed to investigate four sampling stations from which deodorized air, rat odour, cyclohexanone, or acetophenone flowed. These showed that: rats exposed to cyclohexanone spent more time investigating cyclohexanone than the other three sources; rats exposed to acetophenone recorded their highest investigation times at the acetophenone and rat odour sources; rats reared in a laboratory colony (normal animals) spent equal times at the three odour sources, but showed little interest in the deodorized air; whilst rats reared in deodorized air did not differentiate between the sources, and spent similar times at each. The interest shown by animals for their exposure odour during preference tests, and the absence of any loss of acuity for this odour, suggested that no functional change in the neurones responsible for sensing the specific exposure odour had occurred. In contrast, the deficits in acuity exhibited by rats reared in deodorized air for both exposure odours, and the apparent inability of these rats to discriminate between the three odorous sampling stations and deodorized air in the preference tests, strongly suggested these animals had experienced changes in neuronal function. The behavioural data, therefore, supported the view that prolonged exposure to an odour preserves the cells that respond to that odour. On the other hand, the deficits in acuity and absence of interest in a novel odour during preference tests suggest that lack of exposure to other odours adversely affected the responsivity of cells needed to perceive these odours.

Histological examination of mitral cells from rats in each group was conducted in two phases. In the first phase, 50% of the animals were exposed for two months, then killed immediately, or within 50 days of removal from the exposure environment. A "blind" assessment of their bulbs showed that animals exposed to acetophenone or cyclohexanone could be distinguished by their degeneration patterns from normal (colony reared) rats, or those reared in deodorized air, but could not be distinguished from each other. This was not particularly surprising since the patterns published by Pinching and Døving (1974) for these two odours were similar (Fig. 3.6 and Fig. 3.9). Significantly, the patterns were similar to those reported earlier, with degeneration prominent throughout the dorsolateral and ventral regions of the bulb. Equally significant was the finding that rats reared in deodorized air showed a general degeneration of mitral cells. Not only was this group different from the odour exposed groups, but it was clearly distinguishable from normal rats because their cells were more heavily stained, whilst only the odd cell appeared to have degenerated in the latter. This was an unexpected finding since Døving and Pinching (1973) and Pinching and Døving (1974) had found only a small region of altered cells in their "control" (deodorized air) animals. As will be seen, this result has since proved to be a crucial one for assessing whether cells degenerate because of overstimulation or understimulation.

In the second phase of the histological study, the remaining animals were removed from the experimental cages after a total of four months exposure. Following the five months of behavioural testing described earlier, their brains were perfused and bulbs examined. As with animals exposed for two months, it was possible to distinguish the degeneration patterns of animals exposed to odours from the deodorized air and normal groups, but not between those of animals exposed to the two odours. However, contrary to the result obtained with rats that had been exposed for two months, it was not possible to differentiate between the bulbs of normal rats and animals reared in deodorized air, because the cells of both groups appeared normal. Since animals exposed for four months to deodorized air were expected to show the same or, perhaps, more severe degeneration of cells than those exposed for two months, it seemed that the cells had recovered their normal appearance during the five months of behavioural testing. This view was supported by the appearance of altered cells in the odour exposed rats which, although different from normal cells, were not as heavily stained as those of rats exposed to odours for two months. Histological evidence, therefore, indicated that the mitral cells of rats reared in a non-odorous environment degenerated from lack of olfactory input. Returning such animals to a normal environment, as occurred during behavioural tests, resulted in the restoration of normal appearance to the affected cells. Furthermore, since rats that had been exposed to odours received the same deodorized air as animals reared in deodorized air, but with a specific odorant added to it, the existence of normal cells in specific regions of the bulb was attributed to their stimulation by the added odorant.

Thus, both behavioural and neural data indicated that mitral cells which retained their normal morphology during continuous exposure to an odour were those receiving input from the peripheral receptor cells, whilst those showing morphological changes received little or no olfactory input. In addition, the existence of normal cells in specific regions of the bulb confirmed the earlier work of Pinching and Døving (1974), and provided further support for the view that a topographic relationship exists between the olfactory epithelium and the bulb.

The only significant difference between these early studies was the state of mitral cells in rats reared in deodorized air. In their first study Døving and Pinching (1973) reared "control" rats in unfiltered room air and consistently found a small number of altered cells in the dorsomedial region of the bulb. However, the same result was obtained when they reared animals in room air that had been filtered by charcoal and molecular sieves. This latter result is inconsistent with the interpretation given by Døving and Pinching (1973) and Pinching and Døving (1974) to their data, that lack of olfactory input or deprivation causes cells to degenerate. In contrast, Laing and Panhuber (1978) demonstrated that rats reared in a normal odorous environment have very few altered cells, whilst those reared in deodorized air have non-specific degeneration throughout the bulb. Two comments are relevant here. First, it would seem that the level of odour in the deodorized air used by Pinching and Døving (1974) was not low enough to deprive the mitral cells of general olfactory input arising from the many odorants that are usually in room air. On the other hand, the air used by Laing and Panhuber (1978) was deodorized by passage through a refrigerated trap, oil filters, and charcoal, and would appear to have produced sufficient deodorization to deprive the mitral cells of olfactory input. Second, it may not matter that the air is slightly odorous (Pinching and Døving, 1974) or non-odorous (Laing and Panhuber, 1978), since the actual odour exposure effect may be caused by the continuous predominance of the single odorant used. Laing and Willcox (1983), for example, have shown that a weak odorant is not perceived in the presence of a significantly stronger one, and this may be what is happening in the exposure environment. Low intensity contaminants may have no effect on degeneration patterns induced by a specific exposure odour so that degeneration only occurs in cells that are not stimulated by the exposure odour. However, to ensure that the degeneration pattern is only due to the specific odour used, two control groups are clearly necessary: one consisting of littermates reared in a "normal" colony environment to provide bulbs with normally developed cells; the other to provide a check on the air quality delivered to the exposure cages. This need was emphasized in a later study by Laing and Panhuber (1980a) who again found that rats reared in a deodorized air environment had a poorer acuity for cyclohexanone than normal rats, or rats exposed to this odour for two months.

Since 1978, little additional information on the selective degeneration phenomenon has been reported. Laing and Panhuber (1980a) have confirmed some of their earlier behavioural findings, whilst Dalland and Døving (1981) explored recovery of olfactory function in animals maintained in a normal environment for different periods after exposure. At the same time, however, others have failed to replicate the original anatomical or behavioural effects (Cunzeman and Slotnick, 1980; As et al., 1980; Greer, personal communication). Naturally, this has cast some doubt upon the reliability of the aforementioned results. Indeed the present conflict parallels the disagreements that existed between workers studying visual deprivation in the 1960s where some resorted to transporting their treated animals to other laboratories for an independent confirmation of the changes. In view of this doubt and the relevance of the exposure phenomenon to the effects of environmental odours on public health and the spatial coding of odours, the next section of this chapter is an analysis of the procedures and results of those workers who have explored the effects of odour exposure in the rat.

IV. EVIDENCE FOR AND AGAINST SELECTIVE DEGENERATION

A. Exposure conditions

1. Cage and air flows

The exposure conditions used by different workers are summarized in Table 3.1. In the original studies by Døving and Pinching (1973) and Pinching and Døving (1974), animals were exposed to an odour or air without their dam from postnatal day 14 for between seven and 330 days, or seven and 77 days, respectively. They were housed in cylindrical Lucite cages, 20 cm in diameter and 20 cm high. Air or odour was blown in through the top of the cage at 36 litres per minute (2 cm s^{-1}), whilst water was available from a spout that protruded into the cage and food from a container on the wall. From Table 3.1 it can be seen that all workers have used the same size of cage and air flows except for Cunzeman and Slotnick (1980) who used a very slow one litre per minute flow, through a very large cage, and As et al. (1980), who reported relatively slow flows of between two and four litres per minute. As yet, the effect of flow rate through the cage on degeneration patterns has not been established. The flow of 36 litres per minute was originally chosen so that air on contacting an animal would not eddy upwards and contaminate the rest of the air with rat odour, but would pass essentially unperturbed at a rate of 2 cm s^{-1} to the base of the cage. Theoretically, slower flows would be subject to greater turbulence as a consequence of contact with an animal and the effect of body heat. In reality, measurement of the air currents within cages at a flow of 36 litres per minute (Døving et al., 1979), shows that turbulence occurs to a very significant extent, but can be overcome by insertion of a perforated baffle plate in the upper section of the cage. Odour exposure studies with these inserts in position are underway in the writer's laboratory, as are studies of the effect of flow rate on degeneration patterns. Whether the very low flow rates employed by Cunzeman and Slotnick (1980) and As et al. (1980) allowed sufficient contamination of the cage air by rat odour to offset the predominance of the exposure odour used is not known, but it could be a factor contributing to the absence of cell degeneration in these studies.

However, flow rate not only affects turbulence; it also determines the turnover of air within a cage. In the cages used by Døving and Pinching (1973), and most others since, turnover occurred at a rate of six air changes per minute, compared with only one air change every 90 s in the cages used by As et al. (1980). A greater turnover in the present context would mean a greater dilution of contaminants arising from within the cage, and a smaller chance of these competing or interfering with the action of the exposure odour. However, assessment of the cage environment in Cunzeman and Slotnick's study is complicated by the fact that, every two minutes during exposure, a fan with a capacity of 45 cubic feet per minute [1215 litres per minute] evacuated the 130 L space for 20 s, removing a volume of air which was approximately four times that of the cage. Since the one litre per minute odour flow would have only added two litres of odorized air to the 130 L cage in the two minute interval, the remainder would have had to come from the vicinity of the cage and may have been contaminated by the odour of faeces and urine. Against this is the comment by Slotnick (personal communication) that the level of exposure odour in the cage was fairly strong during the 20 s "fan on" period. However, contamination, if it had occurred, would have been maximal in the cage of control animals who received deodorized air, since at all times the bulk of the air in the cage would not have been purified. The control animals, therefore, may have been exposed to the broad spectrum of odours which are emitted by urine and faeces and would tend to maintain cells. In brief, the low flow rates used by Cunzeman and Slotnick (1980) and by As et al. (1980) may have contributed to the absence of degeneration, since there was a greater possibility that odours other than the exposure odour were present at levels which were sufficient to offset the predominance of the exposure odour. With control animals where only deodorized air was used, the background level of odour may have been sufficient to maintain cell integrity.

2. Strain of rat

The absence of significant anatomical differences between normal rats of the strains used (Table 3.1) and the fact that similar degeneration patterns were observed in Wistar (Pinching and Døving, 1974) and Sprague Dawley rats (Laing and Panhuber, 1978) suggests that the strain of Norwegian rat used in exposure studies is unimportant.

3. Age

In contrast to rat strain, the age of a rat at the start of exposure may influence the occurrence of cell degeneration. In preliminary studies, Laing and Panhuber (1978) noted that 80-day old rats showed no signs of mitral cell degeneration after 80 days of exposure to acetophenone or cyclohexanone. Since degeneration has been observed in 14-day old rats exposed for similar periods, this indicates that these cells may be vulnerable to the olfactory environment early in life.

Clear evidence of a critical period of vulnerability has not been demonstrated, but there are a substantial number of observations to support this notion. For example, the bulb develops rapidly during the first three weeks of postnatal life. Although receptor and mitral cells are all present by birth, the latter are cytologically immature (Singh and Nathaniel, 1977) and rapidly mature during the first postnatal week. Evolution of the granule cells is more striking since only 10% are present at birth compared to 90% by the end of the third postnatal week (Roselli-Austin and Altman, 1979). The number of glomeruli also increase dramatically from about 400 at birth to 3000 by two months (Meisami, 1979) whilst the bulk of the development of growth in the external and internal plexiform layers, which are the sites of interaction of granule cells with mitral and tufted cells, is seen during the first three weeks of life. This latter period is also characterized by the evolution of electrical activity in the bulb. Iwahara et al. (1973) found activity commenced about postnatal day 5, but this increased markedly to near adult levels within three to four weeks.

Behavioural data also support the concept of a critical period. Both Marr and Lilliston (1970) and Cornwell-Jones (1979) demonstrated that

TABLE 3.1: Exposure Conditions and Results

Reference	Strain of rat	Age at exposure (days)	Exposure duration (days)	Cage dimensions (cm)	Air flow (L min⁻¹)	Degeneration
Døving and Pinching, 1973	Wistar	14	7–330	20 × 20	36	Yes
Pinching and Døving, 1974	Wistar	14	7–35	20 × 20	36	Yes
Oakley, Døving, and Pinching[a]	Wistar	14	39–64	20 × 20	36	Yes
Laing and Panhuber, 1978	Sprague Dawley	14	60–120	20 × 20	36	Yes
Laing and Panhuber, 1980	Sprague Dawley	1,14	60	20 × 20	36	[b]
Cunzeman and Slotnick, 1980	Long Evans	5	65	46 × 46 × 61[c]	1[d]	No
As, Smit, and Košter, 1980	—	14	28	19 × 19	2–4	No
Jourdan, Holley, Glasø-Olsen, Thommensen, and Døving, 1980	Wistar	21	7	20 × 20	36	Yes
Dalland and Døving, 1981	Wistar	14	33[e],50,230[f]	20 × 20	36	Yes
Greer, 1982	—	18	42	20 × 20	36	No
Panhuber, Laing, Pittman, and Willcox, 1983	Sprague Dawley	1	42	20 × 20	36	Yes

a Unpublished manuscript.
b Morphological analysis not complete.
c 61 cm high.
d A 45-cfm fan operated for 20 sec at 2 minute intervals to evacuate the cage.
e Sacrificed 73 days after exposure was terminated.
f Sacrificed 350 days after exposure was terminated.

preferences for novel odours can be induced in infant rats (3 to 18 days old), but not so readily in juveniles (22 to 32 days old), whilst Cornwell-Jones was not successful with 66-day old adults.

As shown in Table 3.1, only Jourdan *et al.* (1980b), and Greer (personal communication) commenced exposures at or close to the end of the third postnatal week, and possibly reduced the period of vulnerability.

4. *Duration of exposure*

The duration of exposure to an odour is an important factor in determining the extent of degeneration. Although Pinching and Døving (1974) observed considerable degeneration in rats exposed to benzyl mercaptan for only six days, they found that the patterns obtained from a range of odours were in general better defined and more marked at two months than at earlier periods. It appears that only Jourdan *et al.* (1980b – Table 3.1) employed an exposure time (seven days) which may have been too brief to induce significant cellular changes. However, in that study, degenerating cells were found in the dorsal and ventral regions throughout the bulbs of rats exposed to ethyl acetoacetate. Unfortunately, since the pattern of degeneration was not given, it is not possible to assess if the pattern was similar to that reported by Pinching and Døving (1974) who found changes mainly in the medioventral and dorsolateral regions (Fig. 3.6) for this odour.

5. *Type of odour*

From the very wide range of odour-specific patterns described by Pinching and Døving (1974), it appears that degeneration can be induced by many odorants. Indeed Pinching and Døving (1974) did not find any that did not produce a pattern. All other workers have used odorants which according to Pinching and Døving (1974) induced degeneration, and, importantly, have employed them at concentration levels which were clearly detectable to the experimenters. These levels were well above the threshold of rats for the particular odorants (Davis, 1973; Laing, 1975; Laing and Panhuber, 1978; Pierson, 1974), and sufficient to induce degeneration.

6. *Environment after exposure*

Another factor which has been shown to have a significant effect on degeneration patterns is the time spent in a normal environment after exposure to an odour or deodorized air. As mentioned earlier, Laing and Panhuber (1978) were the first to observe that altered cells recover their normal appearance and apparent function when animals are maintained for several months in a normal environment after exposure. They found that the mitral cells of animals reared in deodorized air could not be distinguished from those of normal rats after five months in an animal colony, whilst specific regions in the bulbs of odour exposed rats contained cells which were darker than those of normal rats but not as heavily stained as rats killed immediately, or soon after two months of exposure to an odour. Dalland and Døving (1981) also reported this effect in experiments where rats were exposed to an odour for, respectively, 33 or 230 days, then housed in an animal colony for 73 and 350 days. Selective degeneration was less precise with regard to changes in morphology of the cells, and the pattern of degeneration (Fig. 3.7) was not consistent with the patterns reported earlier by Pinching and Døving (1974). However, the environment after exposure does not appear to have contributed to the absence of altered cells in studies where no changes were observed, since an adequate number of animals were killed immediately after exposure for histological analysis.

B. Histology

In the procedure used by Døving and Pinching (1973) to visualize altered and normal cells, the animals were anaesthetized with a 5% solution of Nembutal, and perfused under hypothermia with buffered saline and formaldehyde-glutaraldehyde fixative. The rats' heads were immersed in fixative solution for at least three hours, and the brains removed. The brain was treated with osmium tetroxide (2%), dehydrated with alcohol, and embedded in Araldite-Epon. Sections (2 μm thick) were then stained by the method of Richardson et al. (1960) using methylene blue and Azure II. This procedure was followed in all other exposure studies, except for that of Cunzeman and Slotnick (1980) who used a perfusion and post fixation procedure that was similar to the original method, but the brains were embedded in gelatin-sucrose and stored in a solution of 10% formalin and 30% sucrose for four days, before being sectioned (10 μm) on a freezing microtome. Sections were mounted on gelatin coated slides and stained with cresyl violet. The method therefore involved rehydration of the fixed tissue and a relatively slow freezing procedure, a combination which can expand the tissue (Bell and Mellor, 1984) and confound comparison with cells prepared by dehydration in alcohol and embedded in Epon resin. For example, slow freezing can cause expansion or destruction of tissue by inducing the formation of ice crystals (Meryman, 1960), and denaturing by

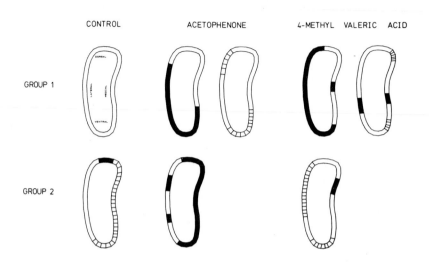

Fig. 3.7: Patterns of mitral cell degeneration (redrawn here) obtained by Pinching and Døving (1974) and Dalland and Døving (1981) following exposure of rats to acetophenone or 4-methyl valeric acid. Animals were sacrificed immediately after exposure ceased (Group 1), or after 73 days in a normal environment (Group 2). Patterns on the right side of each pair in the top row are from Pinching and Døving (1974), all other patterns are from Dalland and Døving (1981).

concentrating electrolytes (Meryman, 1960; Lovelock, 1953). Thus, the method used by Cunzeman and Slotnick could have extinguished any difference caused by the experimental treatment. Furthermore, if the morphological changes in degenerated cells are a result of an altered response to fixation procedures, and this is consequent upon their changed functional state (Døving and Pinching, 1973), then the histological procedure becomes a crucial step in demonstrating the effects of exposure. In this regard, Døving and Pinching (1973) reported that cellular structure was not so clearly visible in brains embedded in paraffin and stained with cresyl violet (Nissl method), although reduction in cell size was still apparent in the same zones as altered cells appeared in Araldite embedded material.

C. Identification of normal and altered cells

Døving and Pinching (1973) defined normal mitral cells as having a characteristically pale cytoplasm and nucleus, whilst the distinctive feature of altered cells was a darkening of nucleus and cytoplasm, along with a shrinkage of the cell. Their classification of cells into the two categories was primarily on the basis of experience. No objective measurement of cell darkening or size was used, nor were there statistical analyses to demonstrate the differences between control and exposed animals. In addition, in neither of their two studies did the authors indicate their classification of animals into control or odour exposed groups was achieved using a "blind" procedure. Although both authors have considerable experience with the anatomy of the bulb, appearance of normal mitral cells, and cells altered through transneuronal degeneration, the fact that others have failed to replicate the cell changes that occur with exposure stresses the need for development of objective methods for assessing cell changes. To be fair this need has been recognized by most workers in the area, and each has attempted to improve on the original procedure. Laing and. Panhuber (1978) used the same subjective procedure as Døving and Pinching (1973), but their successful assessment was done "blind". As et al. (1980) also used a "blind" subjective procedure, but arbitrarily divided the mitral cell layer in each histological section from the bulb into regions, and showed statistically that the populations of altered cells in these regions, in control and experimental animals, were not different. Dalland and Døving (1981) visually categorized cells into three types: those with a light cytoplasm and nucleus were considered normal; cells with a pale nucleus but dark cytoplasm were regarded as moderately degenerate; whilst in heavily degenerated cells, both cytoplasm and nucleus were dark. However, no statistical analysis was applied, and the patterns of normal and altered cells were inconsistent with those reported by Pinching and Døving (1974) (Fig. 3.7).

However, Cunzeman and Slotnick (1980) went a step further than this. In addition to looking for gross changes in mitral cell density and staining, cell counts were made at a magnification of 1000 in two sections (1.2 mm and 1.8 mm rostral to the accessory bulb) from the right bulb of each brain. In these two sections every identifiable mitral cell (whether this included cells with nucleolus only, cells with nucleus, or cells with only cytoplasm was not indicated) was counted, and every third cell measured along the short and along axes of the cell body. Cell counts were kept separate for the dorsomedial, ventromedial, ventrolateral, and dorsolateral quadrants of each section. For cell measurements, the quadrants were divided to yield eight separate areas in each section. Analyses of variance showed there was no difference in the number of mitral cells in rats sacrificed (i) immediately after exposure to ethyl acetoacetate or 4-methyl valeric acid, (ii) after several weeks in a normal environment, or (iii) reared from birth in the presence of the acid. Similarly, analyses performed on the lengths of the long and short axes of cells, indicated there were no differences between the rat groups.

Except for this limited attempt by Cunzeman and Slotnick to measure cell size and number, the other assessment methods used have been a refinement of the original "eyeballing" technique. One major reason for this apparent lack of initiative is that measurement of the differences of large numbers of individual mitral cells with the technology available in most laboratories is a daunting task. Another has been the assumption that the patterns of normal and altered cells described by Pinching and Døving (1974) are easily seen. Unfortunately, this does not appear to be so. Several years ago, whilst attempting to group tissue sections from the bulbs of animals exposed to cyclohexanone or deodorized air flowing at different rates through cages, it became obvious to Panhuber and myself that cells could be classified into more than just two or even three categories of degeneration, and they could also be classified according to cell size which varied markedly within a section. In addition, during histology, the task of maintaining an even uptake of stain over a section was difficult, and differences in stain density complicated classification of cells on the basis of the "degree of darkening". It was clear that, unless an objective method for measuring cell differences could be developed, it would be very difficult to proceed with studies of the exposure phenomenon. These thoughts appear to have been justified, since the patterns of altered cells shown by Dalland and Døving (1981) for rats exposed to acetophenone and 4-methyl valeric acid do not resemble those published originally by Pinching and Døving (1974) and were inconsistent within the experiment. The degeneration pattern produced by exposure to acetophenone (Fig. 3.7), for example, shows altered cells primarily in the lateral and ventral regions of the bulb in rats killed immediately following exposure, and in the dorsomedial, medial, and medioventral regions in rats killed 73 days after removal from the exposure environment. Although the authors suggest the variations most probably reflect the changing environment that rats have experienced after exposure, nevertheless, the patterns showed that altered cells existed in very different regions of the bulb in groups exposed to the same odour. Therefore, these differences did not arise simply because of the reduced uptake of stain by altered cells as observed by Laing and Panhuber (1978).

The absence of differences between control and experimental animals in the studies by Cunzeman and Slotnick (1980), As et al. (1980) and Greer (personal communication), and the inconsistent patterns of degeneration reported by Dalland and Døving (1981), suggest that another factor, "the dark cell" phenomenon, may be complicating some histological analyses. Dark or hyperchromic cells are well known to histologists and have similar features to the dark cells observed following odour exposure. The most common cause is believed to be *post mortem* traumatization (Cammermeyer, 1962) arising from removal of the brain from the skull too soon after death. A prime cause is understood to be mechanical damage even to tissue fixed by formalin perfusion. Thus, if variable numbers of artifactual dark cells are randomly distributed throughout the bulb, or damage gives rise to groups of dark cells in a particular region of the bulb, it would be difficult to identify the cells which were altered by odour exposure from those affected by trauma. For example, As *et al.* (1980) found degenerating cells in the bulbs of normal rats and in rats that had been reared with odours or deodorized air from 14 days of age for 28 days. Degeneration was significantly greater ($P < 0.01$) in the anterior regions of the bulb than in the posterior parts in animals from all groups, which suggests that post-traumatization damage was the cause. However, there is also a small chance that degeneration occurred in all groups for natural reasons, since there is a significant loss of mitral cells in rats aged between two and four weeks, and a small but gradual loss between four and 12 weeks (Roselli-Austin and Altman, 1979).

The darkening and shrinkage which characterize altered cells suggest two measurement methods: optical density measures of stain uptake in cells; and measurement of cell size. However, measurement of optical density is complicated by differential uptake of stain, not only in terms of uptake across a section of tissue, but also in that a device and method would have to differentiate and account for uptake in the cytoplasm and the nucleus — a difficult task. Measurement of cell size, though not without problems, is simpler, and a method was formulated recently (Laing and Panhuber, 1980b; Panhuber *et al.*, 1981) to determine if this parameter could differentiate between altered and normal cells. This method involved a projection microscope and a digitizer that is interfaced to a PDP15 computer for the measurement and calculation of cell cross-sectional areas. The latter measure was shown to correlate well with cell volume, and was chosen as the simplest indicator of cell size. With the procedure, ten coronal sections (5 μm thick) are cut from each of six regions of a bulb. The regions are equally spaced between the first complete mitral cell layer anteriorly and the start of the accessory bulb posteriorly. The best three sections (with little or no damage) from each batch of ten that are between 5 μm and 15 μm apart are selected for analysis. All mitral cells in each section are digitized after drawing their outlines at a magnification of 890, and are designated as cells having nucleoli, nucleus, or just cytoplasm, but only cells with nucleoli are used for calculation of cross-sectional area. Since section thickness is 5 μm and the diameter of the nucleolus is of the same order, by using sections that are at least 5 μm apart, there is little chance (approximately 5% according to our measurements) of measuring or counting the same cell twice. Angle changes incurred as digitizing of cells proceeds around the layer are obtained from the rotating stage of the microscope and typed into the computer. The data from all three "serial" sections are pooled to characterize the size of cells in a particular region of the bulb. The computer calculates cell cross-sectional area and is programmed to graph the location and size of each mitral cell in a serial section. For analysis, the data from the three sections from each of the six regions of the bulb are pooled, and each region divided into 40 subregions for comparison of cell size within a region, across a bulb, and across animals.

This method has so far been applied to studies of cell size distribution in the bulbs of normal rats and rats exposed for eight weeks to cyclohexanone or deodorized air. In the study with normal rats, approximately 15 000 cells were measured in ten bulbs from six rats compared with a total of about 300–400 cells in four bulbs by Cunzeman and Slotnick (1980). As mentioned above, it is not known if these authors counted only nucleolus-containing cells. If others were included, they are likely to have confounded any differences between the eight regions of each section that was examined, since cell sections without a nucleolus are generally smaller.*

Analysis of our data (Panhuber *et al.*, 1983) indicated that there was a significant variation in the size, but not the frequency, of mitral cells around the coronal extent of the bulb (Fig. 3.8), and that the variation in size did not exist along the rostrocaudal axis. The smallest cells were invariably found in the dorsal (282 μm^2) and ventral (276) quadrants, whilst lateral and medially located cells were substantially larger, being 326 μm^2 and 307 μm^2 respectively. However, the most critical finding was that the pattern of size variation in the coronal plane was consistent within and across animals.

Comparison of this normal pattern with those obtained from the bulbs of animals reared in an environment of cyclohexanone or deodorized air, showed that the patterns of all three groups were significantly different, and mitral cells in the experimental groups were substantially smaller than those in normal rats (Fig. 3.8 and Fig. 3.9). Statistical analyses also showed that cells in the medial and mediodorsal regions of bulbs from cyclohexanone exposed rats were not significantly different in size from cells in similar areas in normal rats, but were significantly larger than cells in these regions in rats reared in deodorized air (Fig. 3.8). The presence of normal cells in the medial region of the mitral cell layer had been reported by Pinching and Døving (1974) and Laing and Panhuber (1978). The "cell size" method also indicated that cells in the lateral region of the bulb are reduced in size in rats exposed to cyclohexanone. This change was not reported by Pinching and Døving (1974), or Laing and Panhuber (1978). However, these normally large cells may have been incorrectly classified because even with degeneration they were larger, or similar in size, to any normal cells that remained in the adjacent dorsal and ventral regions. A particularly

---

* This has been verified by research in this laboratory, the results of which are as yet unpublished.

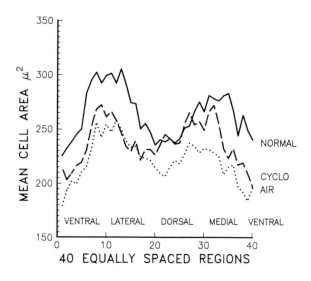

Fig. 3.8: Plots of the mean cross-sectional areas of mitral cells in 40 equally spaced sub-regions in bulbs of rats reared in a normal (*n* = 10 bulbs), cyclohexanone (five bulbs), or deodorized air (eight bulbs) environment. The approximate position of each sub-region in the coronal plane is indicated by ventral, lateral, dorsal and medial. Mean cross-sectional areas for the cells of each rat group are normals (263.8); cyclohexanone-exposed (238.0); deodorized air-exposed (221.1). Standard error for each group is 8.

important result was the demonstration that mitral cells in almost all regions of the bulbs of rats reared in deodorized air were smaller than those in normal rats (Fig. 3.9). This provides strong support for the report by Laing and Panhuber (1978) that all mitral cells appeared to have been altered in rats reared in deodorized air.

Measurement of cell size has therefore shown that a consistent pattern of size variation of mitral cells is present in normal rats, and that significant changes occur in this pattern in rats reared in cyclohexanone, or deodorized air. These results prove that mitral cells are vulnerable to the olfactory environment, and support the earlier report by Laing and Panhuber (1978) that the cells which remain normal after prolonged exposure are those which are deprived of olfactory input and are morphologically changed.

D. Selective degeneration and [^{14}C]-2-deoxyglucose activity patterns

Selective degeneration of mitral cells has also been investigated using the 2-deoxyglucose [2DG] cell labelling method of Kennedy *et al.* (1975).

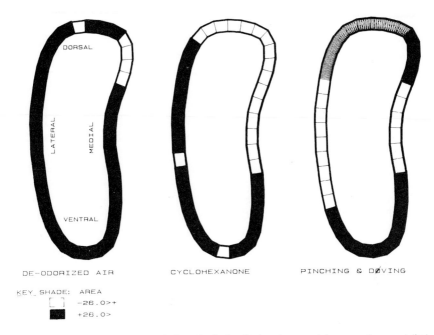

KEY SHADE: AREA

☐ −26.0>+

■ +26.0>

Fig. 3.9: Patterns of normal and altered mitral cells in rats reared in an environment that contained cyclohexanone or deodorized air. The pattern on the right is for cyclohexanone and was redrawn from Pinching and Döving (1974); patterns on the left are from Panhuber et al. (1983). Heavily shaded areas indicate regions that had significantly smaller ($P < 0.05$) cells than in normal rats (Panhuber et al., 1983), or had dense mitral cell degeneration (Pinching and Döving, 1974). Single hatching indicates a region containing both normal and degenerate cells. Unshaded areas contain normal cells (Pinching and Döving, 1974), or cells that are not different in size from those in normal rats (Panhuber et al., 1983). Each marked division in the two patterns on the left represents one of the 40 sub-regions that were used for comparing cell size. The l.s.d. for cells to be classified as smaller than normal is 26 μm^2 ($P < 0.05$).

This method reveals bulbar regions of high glucose uptake which correspond to increased neural activity (Greer et al., 1981). Jourdan et al. (1980b) treated rats with 2DG immediately after a one week exposure to ethyl acetoacetate, deodorized air, or normal air, and found that the pattern of 2DG related activity in the glomerular layer, in response to a stimulation of 45 minutes after exposure with ethyl acetoacetate was similar in all groups, although activity was less intense in the odour exposed group. This decrease in 2DG activity, and retention of the usual 2DG activity pattern, could have occurred for two reasons. First, rats were only exposed to ethyl acetoacetate for one week (hardly enough for significant degeneration to occur in receptor cells, mitral cells, or their related glomeruli). Second, treatment with 2DG immediately followed one week of exposure to the odour, so that receptor and mitral cells normally responsive to the odour are likely to have been partly adapted. Accordingly, this could have led to a reduced level of activity in glomeruli, where the two cell types synapse.

Greer (personal communication) also explored the relationship between selective degeneration and 2DG activity in the olfactory bulb. In this study no differences in the morphology of the mitral cells of normal rats and those reared with amyl acetate for six weeks were seen. Treatment with 2DG, followed by 45 minutes of stimulation with amyl acetate immediately after exposure, produced the same patterns of glomerular activity in both groups.

Neither study was successful in establishing a relationship between the two phenomena. Although both studies reproduced previously reported patterns of 2DG activity, neither obtained the specific pattern of normal and altered cells following prolonged exposure that was reported by Pinching and Døving (1974). Possible reasons for the differences were given earlier (Section IV).

In contrast to these two studies, Kauer and Greer (1983) found little evidence of 2DG uptake in the olfactory bulbs of mice reared in an environment of formaldehyde for four to six weeks when either amyl acetate or formaldehyde were the stimulants after exposure. As yet there has been no report about the condition of the mitral and receptor cells in the exposed animals. Therefore it remains to be seen whether there is a relationship between the location of normal mitral cells in an animal exposed to an odour for a long period, and the regions of high 2DG activity in the glomerular layer that are produced in response to postexposure stimulation with the same odour.

E. Physiological responses of mitral cells following odour exposure

So far Oakley, Døving and Pinching (personal communication, 1983) have conducted the only electrophysiological study of mitral cells following prolonged odour exposure. Regions of the bulb that contained predominantly normal cells, or altered cells (according to Pinching and Døving, 1974), were sampled, and several effects noted. Cells from regions which were presumed to contain altered cells, were less responsive to stimulation by the exposure odour and nine other odorants. Essentially lower responsivity was reflected by cells being less frequently excited, less frequently inhibited, and more frequently unresponsive to a given odour. Overall, cells which were presumed to be normal responded to a larger number of the odours tested. The activity of altered cells, therefore, appeared to have been changed but not necessary abolished by exposure. These results provided some support for the suggestion by Døving and Pinching (1973) that degeneration may arise from an imbalance of excitatory and inhibitory inputs to the affected cells. Since receptor axon terminals in the glomeruli appear normal after exposure (Døving and Pinching, 1973), Oakley, Døving and Pinching (personal communication, 1983) suggested such a change in synaptic activation of mitral cells could be due to changes in centrifugal input arising from altered cells in the horizontal limb of the diagonal band, which is a major source of centrifugal fibres to the bulb.

A possible shortcoming of this study was that responsivity of cells in normal and exposed rats was not compared. Reasons given for not comparing the two groups were that (i) there is a great variation in response between mitral cells within an animal, and (ii) the cells are very sensitive to anaesthesia. However, "within-animal" sampling does not overcome the variation in cell responsivity. The particular objection that is raised here concerns the state of olfactory adaptation of bulbar cells when responses were measured. The period after exposure before recording commenced appears to have been limited to the day rats were removed from the exposure cages. Cells may have been partially adapted and their responsivity altered accordingly. Therefore failure to compare responses with those of normal rats leaves some doubt as to the general responsivity of cells. A second shortcoming was the assumption that a cell in a particular region of the bulb was morphologically normal, or altered. Location of each cell type was based on the subjective "maps" of Pinching and Døving (1974), and the same procedure for identifying cells was used to confirm the location of sampling regions after recordings were completed. Difficulties with this subjective approach have been dealt with in Section IV, C, but, in addition, work in this writer's laboratory has shown that areas containing altered cells often have normal cells, which would add to the difficulty of obtaining significant effects in an electrophysiological study. Nevertheless, significant differences in responsivity were found between cells which were assumed to be normal or altered. The lower responsivity of "altered" cells to the wide range of odours presented, therefore, suggests a general or non-specific loss of sensitivity occurred, as might be expected from olfactory deprivation, or prolonged inhibition.

F. Behavioural studies of odour exposed rats

The results of the behavioural tests by Laing and Panhuber (1978) were described earlier in Section III, D. Later tests (Laing and Panhuber, 1980a) with rats reared from postnatal day 1 or 14 for two months, to concentrations of cyclohexanone ranging from approximately threshold level (rat) to 30 000 times this concentration confirmed that the acuity of rats for their exposure odour was not affected, and that rats reared in deodorized air had a deficit in their ability to detect cyclohexanone. An important feature of their initial study was that behavioural and anatomical data indicated recovery of function occurred during the five-month period of behavioural testing when rats were housed in an animal colony. However, significant behavioural differences were obtained between test groups within three months of removal from the "exposure" environment. Since other workers have conducted their behavioural tests within this three-month period, lack of differences between test groups cannot be attributed to this factor. As yet, no other workers have found behavioural differences that were consistent with anatomical changes following odour exposure. Cunzeman and Slotnick (1980), for example, found no differences in the acuity of rats reared in clean air (control animals), ethyl acetoacetate, or 4-methyl valeric acid for the latter odour, but control animals had a significantly lower threshold than either of the two experimental groups for ethyl acetoacetate. However, although the decreased sensitivity of animals reared in 4-methyl valeric acid or ethyl acetoacetate for ethyl acetoacetate suggests a non-specific loss of smell had occurred, this is not supported by the absence of a deficit in sensitivity for 4-methyl valeric acid. On the other hand, since the deficit in acuity was not accompanied by obvious changes in mitral cell morphology (at least not according to the method of anatomical analysis used) the result may be fortuitous, due either to the small number of animals in each group ($n = 4$), or to a change elsewhere in the olfactory system. Nevertheless, the fact that deficits were exhibited by both experimental groups is inconsistent with the specific effects described by Laing and Panhuber (1978), and are difficult to account for in terms of an "exposure–deprivation" model.

In contrast, Dalland and Døving (1981) found evidence of morphological changes in mitral cells of rats reared in the presence of ethyl acetoacetate, or 4-methyl valeric acid, but did not find differences between control and experimental groups in passive avoidance tests where these odours were used as the conditioning stimuli. Unfortunately, interpretation of these results is complicated because the patterns of altered and normal cells were not similar to those described by Pinching and Døving (1974), and were not consistent within the experiment (Fig. 3.7). The inconsistent degeneration patterns, therefore, cast some doubt on the specificity of the degeneration seen in this study, and may account for the absence of distinct behavioural changes.

V. CONCLUSIONS

The conflicting results obtained from exposing animals for prolonged periods of time to an odour indicate a specific need for co-operation between workers. There is no doubt that differences between the methods of exposure, histology, and identification of normal and altered cells have contributed to the lack of consistency between findings. Rigorous objective methods, one of which was described here, and standardization of techniques (Døving *et al.*, 1979) are needed if the occurrence of the effect is to be consistently demonstrated.

The evidence presented by Døving and Pinching (1973), Pinching and Døving (1974), Laing and Panhuber (1978), and Panhuber *et al.* (1983) indicates that prolonged exposure to an odour results in the selective degeneration of mitral cells in the rat. As yet, the degeneration has only been demonstrated in animals that have been exposed to an odour during the early months of life, when neural development is most rapid. Similar changes were not observed in a preliminary study with adult rats (Laing and Panhuber, 1978), and further work is needed to determine if the effects are confined to the developing nervous system.

Although the mechanisms of selective degeneration are not known, the evidence suggests that deprivation, or lack of olfactory input, is the cause. Deprivation could result in changes of receptor cell turnover, reduction in the number of mitral-granule cell synapses, and reduced levels of bulbar neurotransmitters. Each of these needs to be investigated if the mechanisms of degeneration are to be understood.

Responsivity of receptor and bulbar cells during exposure has yet to be determined. Different views have been presented here, but ultimately it will need electrophysiological studies to answer this question. Also, problems associated with testing after exposure are unsolved. How rapidly olfactory adaptation disappears must be determined, particularly for behavioural studies which often involve many weeks or months of tests. For example, should animals be returned to their exposure environment after each test session? How long should they be maintained in a normal environment before testing, and what effect does testing have on recovery of function? These are important questions that have to be answered if the differences induced by odour exposure are to be maintained during tests.

The specific patterns of normal and altered mitral cells produced by exposure to an odour suggest that may relate to the spatial coding of odour quality. Since there is substantial anatomical and electrophysiological evidence for this mode of coding, the selective degeneration method appears to have the potential for identifying large numbers of cells which respond to specific odours, and could make a substantial contribution to explaining how the sense of smell operates.

An important area for further research is the relationship between the selective degeneration of mitral cells and the patterns of bulbar activity obtained with radioactive 2DG. Since it is widely accepted that high 2DG uptake occurs with increased neural activity, comparison of the two sets of patterns should provide information on whether regions of high 2DG uptake in normal rats, in response to the odour used during prolonged exposure studies, corresponds to normal or altered cells in treated rats, and whether the same patterns of 2DG activity appear in exposed and normal rats in response to the exposure odour. Such information could be most useful for resolving whether deprivation is the cause of degeneration.

The effect of prolonged exposure to odours on human olfactory cells has not been investigated. In addition, occupational health surveys and family clinicians rarely measure olfactory capability thoroughly, despite the exposure of many workers to high concentrations of odours for extensive periods in a variety of industries. However, in this chapter the effects described with the rat from very low concentrations of odorants suggest that humans too may be vulnerable to odours in a manner not previously noticed by the clinicians.

For example, the maximum allowable eight-hour daily average concentration for exposure of humans to cyclohexanone is 2×10^{-6} mol L^{-1} (Occupational Safety and Health Administration, 1972), yet mitral cells were altered in rats exposed for two months to 4×10^{-8} mol L^{-1} of this odorant (Panhuber *et al.*, 1983). Whether exposure of a human to a variety of odours during the period away from the workplace is sufficient to maintain normality in cells likely to be deprived of input during worktime, is unknown, but as mentioned in Section III, B, the rate of removal of an odour from the body could govern the total time of exposure.

Another question to be resolved concerns the likelihood that humans could be exposed to an odour for prolonged periods in and around the home. In both environments, children as well as adults can be exposed to odours from factories, sewage treatment plants, etc. and the presence of children in any exposure group should cause authorities to closely monitor the health of recipients and the levels of odorants. A source of possible continuous exposure in the "home" environment that has arisen in recent years is the use of deodorants in central air conditioning systems in apartments and hotels. This practice clearly exposes young children to a potential cause of damage to developing brain cells.

Finally, the olfactory system is not an isolated entity in the body. It interacts with other parts of the brain associated with feeding, reproduction, and emotion (Section II, B). Changes in these behaviours are likely to be difficult to measure, or detect. However, since it is possible that the changes in the olfactory system during odour exposure are accompanied by changes in "non-olfactory" behaviour, workers in the field of occupational hygiene and community health need to look more critically upon the effects of odour exposure that has been done in the past.

Therefore, considerable work is needed before agreement can be reached on the effects of prolonged exposure to odours in animals and humans, the cause and mechanisms of degeneration, and the relationship between the patterns of selective degeneration and spatial coding of odour quality. This area of research is at about the same stage of development as studies on the effects of visual deprivation and exposure two decades ago, and it remains to be seen whether the same level of success and advances in our understanding of the sense of smell can be achieved from this avenue of research.

REFERENCES

Adrian, E.D. Sensory messages and sensation. *Acta Physiologica Scandinavica*, 1953, 29: 5–14.

Ahlborg, U.G. and Thunberg, T.M. Chlorinated phenols: Occurrence, toxicity, metabolism, and environmental impact. *Critical Reviews in Toxicology*, 1980, 7: 1–35.

Allison, A.C. and Turner-Warwick, R.T. Quantitative observations on the olfactory system of the rabbit. *Brain*, 1949, 72: 186–197.

As, W. van, Smit, K.G.J. and Köster, E.P. Effects of long-term odor exposure on mitral cells of the olfactory bulb in rats. In H. van der Starre (Ed.), *Olfaction and Taste* (Vol. VII). London: Information Retrieval, 1980: 296.

Baylin, F. and Moulton, D.G. Adaptation and cross-adaptation to odor stimulation of olfactory receptors in the tiger salamander. *Journal of General Physiology*, 1979, 74: 37–55.

Bell, G.A. and Mellor, J.D. Olfactory mitral cell integrity after freeze-fixation. *Neuroscience Letters*, 1984, in press.

Cain, W.S. Perception of odor intensity and the time-course of olfactory adaptation. *ASHRAE Transactions*, 1974, 80: 53–70.

Cammermeyer, J. An evaluation of the significance of the "dark" neuron. *Ergebnisse der Anatomie und Entwicklungsgeschichte*, 1962, 36: 1–61.

Chaput, M.A. and Panhuber, H. Effects of long duration odor exposure on the unit activity of olfactory bulb cells in awake rabbits. *Brain Research*, 1982, 250: 41–52.

Constanzo, R.M. and O'Connell, R.J. Spatially organized projections of hamster olfactory nerves. *Brain Research*, 1978, 139: 327–332.

Constanzo, R.M. and O'Connell, R.J. Receptive fields of second-order neurons in the olfactory bulb of the hamster. *Journal of General Physiology*, 1980, 76: 53–68.

Copley International Corporation. A Study of the Social and Economic Impact of Odors. Phase III. Development and Evaluation of a Model Odor Control Ordinance. *Report to the US Environmental Protection Agency*. Washington, D.C.: US Environmental Protection Agency, February 1973 (NTIS No. EPA-650/5-73-001).

Cornwell-Jones, C.A. Olfactory sensitive periods in albino rats and golden hamsters. *Journal of Comparative and Physiological Psychology*, 1979, 93: 668–676.

Cunzeman, P.J. and Slotnick, B.M. Olfaction after prolonged odor exposure. Paper presented at the Second Annual Meeting of the Association for Chemoreception Sciences, Sarasota, Florida, April 1980.

Dalland, T. and Døving, K.B. Reaction to olfactory stimuli in odor-exposed rats. *Behavioral and Neural Biology*, 1981, 32: 79–88.

Damstra, T. Environmental chemicals and nervous system dysfunction. *Yale Journal of Biology and Medicine*, 1978, 51: 457–468.

Davis, R.G. Olfactory psychophysical parameters in man, rat, dog and pigeon. *Journal of Comparative and Physiological Psychology*, 1973, 85: 221–232.

Davis, B.J. and Macrides, F. The organization of centrifugal projections from the anterior olfactory nucleus, ventral hippocampal rudiment, and piriform cortex to the main olfactory bulb in the hamster: An autoradiographic study. *Journal of Comparative Neurology*, 1981, 203: 475–493.

Døving, K.B., Holley, A., Köster, E.P. and Laing, D.G. Selective alteration of olfactory bulb cells following exposure to an odor. *European Chemoreception Research Organization Newsletter*, 1979, (no.) 17: 123–125.

Døving, K.B. and Pinching, A.J. Selective degeneration of neurones in the olfactory bulb following prolonged odor exposure. *Brain Research*, 1973, 52: 115–129.

Ekman, G., Berglund, B., Berglund, U. and Lindvall, T. Perceived intensity of an odor as a function of time of adaptation. *Scandinavian Journal of Psychology*, 1967, 8: 177–186.

Gesteland, R.C., Lettvin, J.Y., Pitts, W.H. and Rojas, A. Odor specificities of the frog's olfactory receptors. In Y. Zotterman (Ed.), *Olfaction and Taste* (Vol. I). Oxford: Pergamon Press, 1963: 19–34.

Getchell, T.V. and Shepherd, G.M. Responses of olfactory receptor cells to step pulses of odour at different concentrations in the salamander. *Journal of Physiology*, 1978, 282: 521–540.

Greer, C.A., Stewart, W.B., Kauer, J.S. and Shepherd, G.M. Topographical and laminar localisation of 2-deoxyglucose uptake in rat olfactory bulb induced by electrical stimulation of olfactory nerves. *Brain Research*, 1981, 217: 279–293.

Iwahara, S., Oishi, H., Sano, K., Yang, K.M. and Takahashi, T. Electrical activity of the olfactory bulb in the postnatal rat. *Japanese Journal of Physiology*, 1973, 23: 361–370.

Jourdan, F., Duveau, A., Astic, L. and Holley, A. Spatial distribution of [^{14}C]2-deoxyglucose uptake in the olfactory bulbs of rats stimulated with two different odours. *Brain Research*, 1980a, 188: 139–154.

Jourdan, F., Holley, A., Glasø-Olsen, G., Thommensen, G. and Døving, K.B. Comparison between the patterns of selective degeneration and marking with [^{14}C]2-deoxyglucose in the rat olfactory bulb. In H. van der Starre (Ed.), *Olfaction and Taste* (Vol. VII). London: Information Retrieval, 1980b: 295.

Kauer, J.S. and Greer, C.A. The effect of chronic formaldehyde exposure on 2-deoxyglucose uptake in the olfactory bulbs of mice. Paper presented at the Fifth Annual Meeting of the Association for Chemoreception Sciences, Sarasota, Florida, April 1983.

Kauer, J.S. and Moulton, D.G. Responses of olfactory bulb neurones to odour stimulations of small nasal areas in the salamander. *Journal of Physiology*, 1974: 243: 717–737.

Kennedy, C., DesRosiers, M.H., Jehle, J.W., Reivich, M., Sharp, F.R. and Sokoloff, L. Mapping of functional neural pathways by autoradiographic survey of local metabolic rate with ^{14}C deoxyglucose. *Science*, 1975, 187: 850–853.

Kubie, J., Mackay-Sim, A. and Moulton, D.G. Inherent spatial patterning of responses to odorants in the salamander olfactory epithelium. In H. van der Starre (Ed.), *Olfaction and Taste* (Vol. VII). London: Information Retrieval, 1980: 163–166.

Laing, D.G. A comparative study of the olfactory sensitivity of humans and rats. *Chemical Senses and Flavour*, 1975, 1: 257–269.

Laing, D.G. and Panhuber, H. Neural and behavioral changes in rats following continuous exposure to an odor. *Journal of Comparative Physiology*, 1978, 124: 259–265.

Laing, D.G. and Panhuber, H. Olfactory sensitivity of rats reared in an odorous or deodorised environment. *Physiology and Behavior*, 1980a, 25: 555–558.

Laing, D.G. and Panhuber, H. Quantification of mitral cell changes in rat olfactory bulb following prolonged odour exposure. In H. van der Starre (Ed.), *Olfaction and Taste* (Vol. VII). London: Information Retrieval, 1980b: 294.

Laing, D.G. and Willcox, M.E. Perception of components in binary odour mixtures. *Chemical Senses*, 1983, 7: 249-264.

Le Gros Clark, W.E. The projection of the olfactory epithelium on the olfactory bulb in the rabbit. *Journal of Neurology, Neurosurgery and Psychiatry*, 1951, 14: 1-10.

Lohman, A.H.M. and Lammers, H.J. On the structure and fibre connections of the olfactory centres in mammals. In Y. Zotterman (Ed.), *Progress in Brain Research* (Vol. 23). Amsterdam: Elsevier, 1967: 65-82.

Longland, R.C., Shilling, W.H. and Gangolli, S.D. The hydrolysis of flavoring esters by artificial gastric intestinal juices and rat tissue. *Toxicology*, 1977, 8: 197-204.

Lovelock, J.E. The haemolysis of red blood cells by freezing and thawing. *Biochimica et Biophysica Acta*, 1953, 19: 414.

Mackay-Sim, A., Shaman, P. and Moulton, D.G. Topographic coding of olfactory quality: Odorant specific patterns of epithelial responsivity in the salamander. *Journal of Neurophysiology*, 1982, 48: 584-596.

MacLeod, P. Secondary olfactory projections. In L.M. Beidler (Ed.), *Handbook of Sensory Physiology* (Vol. 4, part 1: Olfaction). Berlin: Springer-Verlag, 1971: 182-204.

Macrides, F., Davis, B.J., Youngs, W.M., Nadi, N.S. and Margolis, F.L. Cholinergic and catecholaminergic afferents to the olfactory bulb in the hamster: A neuroanatomical, biochemical, and histochemical investigation. *Journal of Comparative Neurology*, 1981, 203: 495-514.

Macrides, F. and Schneider, S.P. Laminar organization of mitral and tufted cells in the main olfactory bulb of the adult hamster. *Journal of Comparative Neurology*, 1982, 208: 419-430.

Mair, R.G. Response properties of rat olfactory bulb neurones. *Journal of Physiology*, 1982, 326: 341-359.

Marr, J.N. and Lilliston, L.G. Social attachment in rats by odor and age. *Behavior*, 1970, 33: 277-282.

Meisami, E. The developing rat olfactory bulb: Prospects of a new model system in developmental neurobiology. In E. Meisami and M.A.B. Brazier (Eds.), *Neural Growth and Differentiation*. New York: Raven Press, 1979: 183-206.

Meryman, H.T. General principles of freezing injury in cellular materials. *Annals of the New York Academy of Sciences*, 1960, 85: 503-509.

Moulton, D.G. Spatial patterning of response to odors in the peripheral olfactory system. *Physiological Reviews*, 1976, 56: 578-593.

Moulton, D.G., Celebi, G. and Fink, R.P. Olfaction in mammals — two aspects: Proliferation of cells in the olfactory epithelium and sensitivity to odors. In G.E.W. Wolstenholme and J. Knight (Eds.), *Taste and Smell in Vertebrates*. London: Churchill, 1970: 227-250.

Mozell, M.M. Evidence for sorption as a mechanism of the olfactory analysis of vapors. *Nature*, 1964, 203: 1181-1182.

Mozell, M.M. and Jagodowicz, M. Chromatographic separation of odorants by the nose: Retention times measured across *in vivo* olfactory mucosa. *Science*, 1973, 191: 1247-1249.

National Research Council. *Odors from Stationary and Mobile Sources*. Washington, D.C.: National Academy of Sciences, 1979.

Occupational Safety and Health Administration. *Federal Register*, October 18, 1972: 37 (22 140).

Ohno, I., Ohyama, M. Hanamure, Y. and Ogawa, K. Comparative anatomy of olfactory epithelium. *Biomedical Research*, 1981, 2 (Supplement): 455-458.

Ottoson, D. Studies on slow potentials in the rabbit's olfactory bulb and nasal mucosa. *Acta Physiologica Scandinavica*, 1959, 47: 136-148.

Panhuber, H., Laing, D.G. and Pittman, E.A. A method for measuring the size of mitral cells in the olfactory bulb of the rat. Paper presented at the 1st Australian Symposium on Stereology, Image Analysis and Mathematical Morphology, September 1981.

Panhuber, H., Laing, D.G., Pittman, E.A. and Willcox, M.E. The size and distribution characteristics of mitral cells in the olfactory bulbs of rats exposed to different olfactory environments. Paper presented at the Fifth Annual Meeting of the Association for Chemoreception Sciences, Sarasota, Florida, April 1983.

Pierson, S.C. Conditioned suppression to odorous stimuli in the rat. *Journal of Comparative and Physiological Psychology*, 1974, 86: 708–717.

Pinching, A.J. and Døving K.B. Selective degeneration in the rat olfactory bulb following exposure to different odours. *Brain Research*, 1974, 82: 195–204.

Pinching, A.J. and Powell, T.P.S. Ultrastructural features of transneuronal degeneration in the olfactory system. *Journal of Cell Science*, 1971, 8: 253–287.

Richardson, K.C., Jarrett, L. and Finke, E.H. Embedding in epoxy resins for ultrathin sectioning in electron microscopy. *Stain Technology*, 1960, 35: 313–323.

Roselli-Austin, L. and Altman, J. The postnatal development of the main olfactory bulb of the rat. *Journal of Developmental Physiology*, 1979, 1: 295–313.

Sharp, F.R., Kauer, J.S. and Shepherd, G.M. Local sites of activity-related glucose metabolism in rat olfactory bulb during olfactory stimulation. *Brain Research*, 1975, 98: 596–600.

Shepherd, G.M. Synaptic organization of the mammalian olfactory bulb. *Physiological Reviews*, 1972, 52: 864–917.

Singh, D.N.P. and Nathaniel, E.J.H. Postnatal development of mitral cell perikaryon in the olfactory bulb of the rat. A light and ultrastructural study. *The Anatomical Record*, 1977, 189: 413–432.

Tanabe, T., Iino, M. and Takagi, S.F. Discrimination of odors in olfactory bulb, pyriform-amygdaloid areas, and orbitofrontal cortex of the monkey. *Journal of Neurophysiology*, 1975, 38: 1284–1296.

Thommesen, G. and Døving, K.B. Spatial distribution of the EOG in the rat: A variation with odor quality. *Acta Physiologica Scandinavica*, 1977, 99: 270–280.

Vogt, R.G. and Riddiford, L.M. Pheromone binding and inactivation by moth antennae. *Nature*, 1981, 293: 161–163.

Wiesel, T.N. and Hubel, D.H. Effects of visual deprivation on morphology and physiology of cells in the cat's lateral geniculate body. *Journal of Neurophysiology*, 1963, 26: 978–993.

4
OLFACTORY BULBECTOMY AS A MODEL OF DEPRESSION

K. D. CAIRNCROSS

I. INTRODUCTION

The first dibenzazepine, or tricyclic antidepressant (TCA), drug introduced into clinical practice was imipramine. This happened almost 25 years ago, and the discovery of the beneficial therapeutic action of imipramine in depression was based on astute clinical observation rather than pharmacological design. Indeed, examination of the chemical structure of imipramine and other tricyclic antidepressant drugs shows the striking similarity of structure to the phenothiazines (Fig. 4.1) and, indeed, the series were originally synthesized as potential antipsychotic drugs. That Kuhn (1959) was able to recognize their antidepressant action in patients not being primarily treated for depression was quite remarkable, given that 30 per cent of depressive patients display a placebo effect, and that we now know that endogenous or unipolar depression can present in the clinic with homogeneous symptoms having heterogeneous aetiology (Cairncross *et al.*, 1981a; Cobbin *et al.*, 1981). Thus, not all cases of endogenous depression will respond with equal facility to the same antidepressant drug indicating that subtle differences in pharmacological properties are existent in different cyclic antidepressants. This observation will be discussed in greater detail below.

At this point it is pertinent to note that, following demonstration of the clinical efficacy of imipramine, it was a natural progression to examine the pharmacological properties of this drug in detail. Sigg (1959) was the first to point out that imipramine could potentiate the actions of peripherally

ANIMAL MODELS IN PSYCHOPATHOLOGY
ISBN   0 12 114180 2

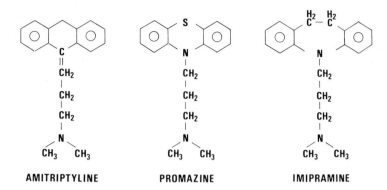

AMITRIPTYLINE   PROMAZINE   IMIPRAMINE

Fig. 4.1: The phenothiazines are characterized as a three-ringed molecule in which two benzene rings are linked by a sulphur and a nitrogen atom, as in promazine. The similarity in structure to amitriptyline (a dibenzocycloheptadiene) and imipramine (a dibenzazepine derivative) is clearly seen. All three drugs have a common side-chain. Imipramine and amitriptyline and their derivatives were commonly referred to as the tricyclic antidepressant drugs. The second generation of cyclic antidepressants (for example, mianserin) are characterized by modification of the common side-chain.

administered noradrenaline (NA). He suggested that, if imipramine had a similar action in the central nervous system, this could be the basis of the observed clinical antidepressant action. Thus, was born the "catecholamine theory of depression", and in 1983, almost a quarter of a century later, many would argue that, from a pharmacological stand-point, knowledge has changed but little! For example, "These studies support the view that the antidepressant efficacy of mianserin may be explained in terms of increasing the availability of noradrenaline to receptor sites in the brain by blockade of α_2-adrenoceptors rather than noradrenaline uptake blockade" (Rose *et al.*, 1982). The terminology may be different, but the inference is similar!

The important conclusion to be derived from these remarks relates to the fact that, after 25 years of intensive study, the precise mode of action of the cyclic antidepressants remains obscure, as does the aetiology of the disease they were not originally designed to treat! The questions that might reasonably be asked are: (i) what advances have been made in our understanding of depressive illness since 1959; (ii) does our knowledge of the pharmacology of the antidepressant drugs add materially to an understanding of the clinical condition; and (iii) does any fundamental discrepancy exist between the answers to questions (i) and (ii), and, if so, how can they be mediated?

To answer these questions, it is pertinent to review briefly several critical experimental observations made during this period, and to then relate these to experimental animal models of depression, including the bulbectomy model.

II. WHAT IS BULBECTOMY?

There are many references in the literature which relate to bulbectomy (that is, bilateral ablation or removal of the olfactory bulbs in the rat). The behavioural effects of bilateral bulbectomy have been reviewed by Leonard and Tuite (1981). Description of the behavioural changes induced by bulbectomy are varied, and inevitably lead to the conclusion that bulbectomy has wide ranging effects on emotional and reproductive behaviour (Murphy, 1976). However, in studies relating to the use of bulbectomy in examining the actions of the tricyclic antidepressant (TCA) drugs two behavioural parameters are generally monitored. These are a deficit in aquisition of a passive avoidance response (considered originally by Cairncross and King (1971) as a motivational deficit) and a hyperactivity syndrome, often referred to as an increase in irritability (Sieck, 1972; van Riezen et al., 1977). It was demonstrated in 1971 that both of these behavioural paradigms occurring after bulbectomy can be normalized by chronic (14 day) treatment of bulbectomized rats with the TCA drug amitriptyline at a dose of 1.5 mg kg^{-1} administered intraperitoneally. The rationale underlying such an approach is considered in detail by Cairncross et al. (1979). Briefly, the case was reasoned that if unilateral destruction of the olfactory bulbs produced a reduction in noradrenaline (NA) content of the pyriform cortex in the side of the brain ipsilateral to the lesion (Pohorecky et al., 1969), then bilateral bulb ablation should produce a bilateral reduction in the NA content of the pyriform cortex. If the changes in the behavioural paradigms previously mentioned following bilateral bulbectomy were related to a reduction in NA availability, then chronic treatment with a TCA drug which increased NA availability by inhibition of the neuronal re-uptake mechanism should normalize these behavioural parameters. Such proved to be the case (Cairncross et al., 1973). These results seemed to confirm the "noradrenaline hypothesis" of depression as suggested by Schildkraut (1965) and prefaced by Sigg (1959).

However, in 1972, there was proposed the "permissive amine hypothesis" of affective illness. This hypothesis was expanded by Prange et al. (1974) to suggest not only that NA was involved in the disease development, but also that there was a serotonergic (5-HT) involvement. Thus, it was suggested that limbic 5-HT concentration was low in depression and in mania (a situation producing endogenous or unipolar depression). In manic depressive states (bipolar depression), 5-HT content was low, but NA concentrations were high.

Geyer and his colleagues (1976) were among the first to lend some credence to this hypothesis in experiments derived from original data. Their experiments indicated that activation of a serotonergic inhibitory system, the mesolimbic pathway originating in the B8 raphe nucleus, reduced locomotor activity when used as an indicator of behavioural arousal. Lesions placed in the B8 region resulted in hyperactivity and hypermobility, and were correlated negatively with hippocampal tryptophan hydroxylase and positively with striatal tyrosine hydroxylase. As the behavioural changes following dorsal raphe lesions closely resemble those described following bilateral ablation of the olfactory bulb, it was necessary to suppose that, in addition to a NA component in bulbectomy, there also existed a serotonergic component in the basis of the bulbectomy model for depression. This might necessitate re-examination of the permissive amine hypothesis of affective illness.

Such a supposition would be pertinent to the three questions raised in Section I, and the results to be presented give an indication of the complexity of the problem. However, before the contribution made by bulbectomy to our understanding of depression is considered, the surgical and chemical methods which reliably reproduce the model are discussed in some detail as recent studies suggest that both the behavioural and endocrine parameters examined following bulbectomy are subject to circadian variation (Leigh and Cairncross, 1981). Experiments conducted with the model can give conflicting or misleading results if conducted outside the behavioural and environmental conditions described, due to circadian variation in endocrine activity which reflects also in behavioural measurements.

A. Methodology

1. Housing animals

Male rats (Sprague-Dawley, Macquarie strain) were removed from the central animal house when aged 70 to 75 days. They were placed in plastic boxes 41 cm × 27 cm × 16 cm deep, in racks which allowed access to both a drinking nipple and a drinking bottle (Section II, B, 1). Three rats were housed in each box, and were fed standard rat chow *ad libitum*. The rats were then housed in animal rooms adjacent to the main laboratory and were placed on a reverse night–day schedule (lights on at 8 p.m. [2000 h] to 8 a.m. [0800 h]). The temperature was $21° \pm 0.5°C$ at 45% humidity. There was no recirculation of air.

The animals were given 14 days to acclimatize to the housing conditions. The doors of the animal rooms were opened briefly whilst feeding chow was replenished between 0830 and 1000 h (Section II, B, 2). Animals destined for experimentation were removed from their home cage in a specific order and handled by the experimenter each day during the period prior to behavioural testing. This included the postoperative period (Section II, B, 3).

In a general laboratory routine, the animals were rehoused in clean boxes with fresh sawdust each Friday afternoon. Apart from these times, the animals were undisturbed in the animal rooms, but were exposed to routine noise from the main laboratory area. Thus, they were exposed to minimum stress. The importance of adherence to this regimen will be discussed (Section II, B, 4).

2. Surgical procedures

Following environmental adaptation, a rat was removed from its home cage (in the usual removal order) and anaesthetized with an intraperitoneal injection of Equithesin (3.3 mL kg^{-1}). Surgery was undertaken between 0830 and 1030 h (Section II, B, 5). When anaesthetized, the head of the animal was immobilized in a stereotaxic frame, and the head shaved. A longitudinal incision was made through the skin and periosteum, in the mid-line, extending at least 1 cm anterior and 1 cm posterior to bregma. The skin and periosteum were retracted, and superficial bleeding points in the skull were sealed with bone wax. Bregma was identified, and, using calipers, two points were marked on the skull surface 8 mm anterior to bregma and 2 mm lateral to the mid-line (Fig. 4.2B). Using a dental drill fitted with an ash round 4 burr, two holes, 2 mm in diameter, were drilled through the skull at the marked points, care being taken not to penetrate the dura. The area was then cleaned with sterile saline and dried with sterile gauze swabs. The dura was then perforated using the point of a sterile hypodermic needle.

At this point, two procedures could be followed:

(A) A rat destined to be a sham operated control (SO) had the skull holes packed with absorbable gelatin foam, and the wound closed; or

(B) In a rat undergoing bulbectomy, a small curved knife was introduced through the burr hole (Fig. 4.2B). Experience and care is necessary at this point to avoid damage to the frontal pole of the cortex (Section II, B, 6). The olfactory bulbs were then sectioned, and the excised bulbs aspirated with a sterile Pasteur pipette using a water suction pump. Following aspiration, bleeding often occurred; blood was removed by aspiration and sterile swab. The burr holes were then packed with absorbable gelatin foam as described for the SO procedure.

Closure of the wound was similar in the sham operated and bulbecto-mized animals. The retractor was removed, and penicillin dusting power placed in the wound which was then closed with silk sutures. With experience, the surgical technique can be completed in less than eight

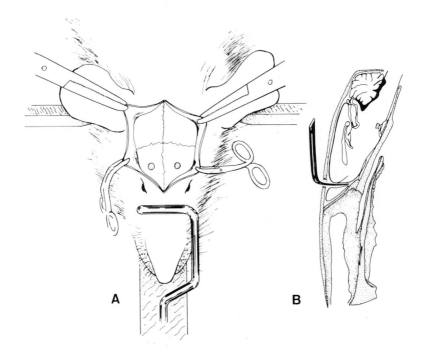

Fig. 4.2: A. A diagramatic illustration of the head of the rat immobilized in a stereotaxic frame, the ear and mouth bars in place. Bregma can be identified, and the two drill holes made in the skull 8 mm anterior to the reference point can be identified. B. The lower frame demonstrates section of the olfactory bulb, with severance of all afferent and efferent connections. The frontal pole of the cerebral cortex remains undamaged. Following severance of the bulb, the neuronal tissue is removed by aspiration.

minutes. Recovery from surgery and anaesthesia takes some 60 minutes with the animals wrapped in towelling and warmed under a lamp to minimize heat loss (Section II, B, 7).

On recovery, the rats were replaced in cages with their original cage mates. Shredded paper was used as bedding for a 48 h postoperative period. Thereafter, the animals were allowed a seven-day period for recovery. Handling was continued as described in Section I, A, 1. Generally, recovery was uneventful. It did not prove necessary to remove sutures, these being ruptured naturally as a result of mutual grooming behaviour.

3. Drug treatment and behavioural testing

Psychotropic drugs of various categorisation were injected intraperitoneally to sham operated and bulbectomized rats on a chronic basis over a 10–14 day period. Thereafter, two behavioural and one biochemical tests were performed. Reactivity and step-down passive avoidance tests were conducted between 0830 and 1030 h for each individual rat. On completion of behavioural testing, animals were sacrificed by cervical dislocation and exsanguinated.

Reactivity testing: A rat was removed from its home cage in the usual numerical order of handling, and placed on a clean, flat perspex surface 30 cm^2. Reactivity was assessed on the basis of the response of the animal to two novel stimuli: (i) a puff of air blown sharply on to the back of the rat's head whilst facing away from the observer; and (ii) a loud clap delivered close to and in front of the rat's nose (discharge of a toy cap pistol). A ranked scoring system was devised similar to that described by King (1958) (see Table 4.1). A rank was assigned to each rat in every group and the results subjected to a Mann-Whitney U test (Siegel, 1956).

Passive avoidance: Passive avoidance testing was carried out on the day subsequent to reactivity testing. The same time period was employed. The apparatus consisted of a perspex box with a 55 cm^2 stainless steel grid floor, the bars of which were 1.5 cm apart, connected to a random shock generator (Macquarie design) which delivered a constant current (0.5 mA) 50 Hz square wave scrambled footshock.

A 10.0 cm × 17.8 cm perspex platform was centrally placed 7.6 cm above the grid floor, and a 15 W red pilot light was centrally hung approximately 55 cm above the platform. The platform was connected via a fulcrum and rested on a micro-switch which was onset when a rat was placed on the platform and offset when the rat stepped down off the platform. The time taken for the rat to step off the platform was automatically recorded and printed out by a modified Sodeco timer. A universal scheduler (Macquarie design and manufactured) was used to control the equipment.

The rat's paws were dampened to improve electrical conductivity, and it was placed on the central platform. The latency time for the rat to step off the platform was recorded. The procedure was repeated with an inter-trial interval of one minute until the animal remained on the platform for at least one minute. The number of trials needed by each rat to reach this criterion was recorded.

Assay of plasma 11-hydroxycorticoids (11-OHCS): On the completion of behavioural testing, the rat was returned to its home cage. One hour later, using the established handling procedure previously described, the rat was taken to an adjoining laboratory, decapitated and exsanguinated. The whole process took less than two minutes, thus preventing the parameter of novelty from affecting circulating 11-OHCS levels. Blood was collected in heparinized tubes and centrifuged to obtain cell free plasma which was stored at $-20°C$.

TABLE 4.1: Scoring System for Reactivity Test

Score*	Response
0	No response
1	Slight jump and moves away
2	Slight jump and freezes for 0–2 sec
3	Rat jumps and freezes for 2–15 sec
4	Rat jumps and freezes for 15 sec

* Maximum score for the two novel stimuli was 8.

Before 1977, the corticosterone assay was performed using the fluoro-metric method of Mattingly (1962). This remains a well tried and accurate method for 11-OHCS determination. However, it is time-consuming, only 12 samples of plasma being assayed per day. In 1977, our laboratory reworked the competitive protein binding assay as described by Murphy (1967) and modified by Barnes *et al.* (1972). The method involved extraction with redistilled Analar grade dichloromethane, and used ³H corticosterone (TRK 133, Amersham) and reconstituted human sera (Hyland Control Service 1). The competitive protein binding assay was found to be cheaper and more robust than radioimmune assay methods.

Histology: Following decapitation, the head of the animal was skinned, and the occiput opened through the foramen magnum. This exposed the brain, and avoided damage to the frontal pole and adjacent structures. The head was then placed in 10% formol saline for at least seven days. This allowed time for brain fixation and facilitated removal. Brains were embedded in paraffin for sectioning and staining.

B. Comments on some methodological points

1. Following bulbectomy

Following surgical bulbectomy, a number of behavioural changes occur in the rat. Leonard and Tuite (1981) have considered one change in some detail, and note: "Sex and strain differences appear to play a role in the 'irritability responses'; for irritable reactions, female < male, and Hooded < Wistar < Sprague-Dawley". The experiments described use the Macquarie Sprague-Dawley strain of rat. These animals show rapid growth, the male animal usually weighing some 400 g at 90 days of age. They exhibit infraspecies aggression without surgery or drug treatment, and it is not uncommon for the dominant male in a group to exercise a territorial imperative regarding the water-nipple. Thus, additional access to a water-bottle prevents water deprivation and dehydration stress in other animals in a group. Following bulbectomy, aggressive behaviour on the part of particular males can become overt, necessitating their removal from the group.

2. Night–day schedule

The animals were acclimatized to a reverse night–day schedule. Thus, chow replenishment and activity within their home environment occurred with the onset of their activity cycle, the rat being a nocturnal animal. The timing of this phase of routine laboratory activity ensures that their circadian rhythm is "in phase" with exogeneous events.

3. Handling and stress

Bassett *et al.* (1973) drew attention to: "Parameters of novelty, shock predictability and response contingency in corticosterone release in the rat". The basis of their observations was that the degree of elevation of plasma corticosterone levels in response to stress was not an all or none phenomenon. These observations were subsequently extended to include bulbectomy when Cairncross *et al.* (1977) demonstrated that bulbectomy *per se* apparently elevated plasma corticosterone (11-OHCS) levels, and that the degree of elevation of 11-OHCS levels was related to infraspecies interaction in that individually housed rats (both sham operated and bulbectomised) had a lower 11-OHCS level than their group housed counterparts. Levine (1980, personal communication) drew attention to what he termed: "the match–mismatch theory" of 11-OHCS elevation. He proposed that exposure of an animal to a novel situation induces a potential threat (stress) response which results in elevated plasma 11-OHCS concentrations (a mismatch); however, if the animal is repeatedly exposed to what was a novel situation, it learns that this is "no threat" (a match). The hypothalamic-anterior pituitary-adreno-cortical (HPA) axis is not activated. Consequently, there is no elevation of 11-OHCS levels. The animal is in a match–match situation.

Experiments in my laboratory have indicated that animals handled on a regular daily basis exhibit a match–mismatch response if removed from their home cage in a random fashion. This results in elevation of plasma 11-OHCS levels. To prevent this eventuality, it is necessary to follow a strict and always reproducible regimen in the handling, removal, and replacement of animals in their home environment. The rats are tail-marked to allow their removal from the home cage in the same order.

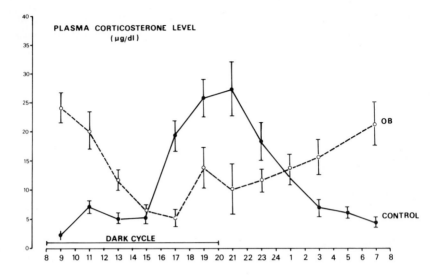

Fig. 4.3: This shows the effect of olfactory bulbectomy on the circadian rhythm for plasma corticosterone secretion. The continuous line shows the normal secretion pattern for control or sham-operated animals maintained in conditions described in the text. Following bulbectomy there is a marked shift in the circadian peak for corticosterone secretion. Each point represents the mean of 10 control (•) and 10 bulbectomized (o) animals. Horizontal bars designate ± s.e.

4. *Reducing stress*

As indicated, departure from established laboratory routine creates a stress "match–mismatch" situation. This produces activation of the HPA axis, and an elevation of plasma 11-OHCS levels. The positive and negative feedback loops of the glucocorticoids on central regulatory processes are well documented. The overall effect is one of behavioural unpredictability. This unpredictability is particularly important in dealing with the bulbectomized animal, which appears to lose a form of central tonic inhibition following this form of surgery, producing a form of compulsive behaviour. The central pathways underlying this behaviour are considered elsewhere.

5. *Time of surgery*

The time of day at which surgery is conducted is important in determining the rate of recovery and the mortality rate of the bulbectomy procedure. The procedure is certainly a serious traumatic experience for the animal. It was found that the best results were obtained if surgery was performed between 0830–1030 h (with the animals on a reverse night day schedule and lights out 0800 h, surgery is undertaken at the beginning of their activity cycle — a time when plasma 11-OHCS levels are minimal in terms of circadian rhythm: see Fig. 4.3). The reasons for the increased surgical risk in animals exposed to surgery outside this time-schedule is not immediately apparent, but could relate to the inhibitory effect of the glucocorticoids and ACTH on myocardial neuronal uptake mechanisms for noradrenaline (Bassett and Cairncross, 1976). Undertaking surgical procedures when the natural release of these hormones and prohormones is minimal apparently decreases surgical trauma by reducing cardiac stress.

6. Frontal pole damage

The effects of frontal pole damage are described by Cairncross *et al.* (1979) and considered in more detail by Hill (1982), and the implications of such damage are detailed by Iversen (1984).

7. Maintaining postoperative temperature

In addition to conforming to a rigorous time schedule in the surgical procedures, it proved necessary to maintain the animals at 35°C in the immediate postoperative period. Failure to adhere to this regimen increased mortality. As reported by Forster and Cox (1980), bulbectomy results in a loss of temperature regulatory mechanisms in the rat.

8. Other pertinent observations

Apart from the methodological comments described above, various other observations are important. Following surgery, bulbectomized rats apparently suffer a loss of gut motility, resulting in an accumulation of faecal material in the large gut. To overcome this, after the operation rats were given 5% magnesium sulphate in their drinking water. This treatment was found to enhance recovery as it reduced central nervous system oedema.

Adherence to the methodology, the time schedules and the handling procedures described resulted in a better than 98% recovery, and produced a behaviourally and biochemically robust, bulbectomized animal which some laboratories have been unable to achieve.

Rats subjected to the bulbectomy procedure described here show a differentiation in response to various classes of psychoactive drugs (Cairncross *et al.*, 1979). Such a difference is evident in both behavioural and glucocorticoid paradigms. Thus, Fig. 4.4 shows that three antidepressant drugs (amitriptyline, mianserin and viloxazine) which do not have a common spectrum of pharmacological activity show similar actions on acquisition of the passive avoidance response. This spectrum of activity is not evident with amphetamine (a central stimulant), chlorpromazine (a major tranquillizer) and chlordiazepoxide (an anxiolytic agent). Fig. 4.5 demonstrates that the antidepressant drugs previously mentioned normalize the glucocorticoid response. Amphetamine in high doses (3 mg kg^{-1}) exacerbates the 11-OHCS response in both the sham operated and bulbectomized animal.

Fig. 4.6 introduces two other antidepressant compounds to the bulbectomy model and compares these with mianserin and amitriptyline. Thus, nomifensine and iprindole show a positive predictive value in the model within the lower dose range. At high doses, nomifensine shows evidence of a central stimulant effect, an action in keeping with its described clinical effects. The monoamine-oxidase inhibitor tranylcypromine, which has been used as an antidepressant drug, did not show a positive predictive value in the bulbectomy model.

C. Olfactory bulbectomy: What are the pathways and systems affected?

Before this question can be considered in detail, it is necessary to review the afferent and efferent connections of the bulb. It is not the purpose of this article to reiterate the detailed studies of nineteenth century anatomists or to reconsider the observations of Le Gros Clark and Meyer (1947) and the detailed work of Scalia and Winans (1976). However it is pertinent to consider current thinking regarding olfactory bulb function, and to reconsider this in terms of broader concepts; that is, in terms of a limbic "rhinencephalon" axis.

At present, the olfactory bulb is viewed by most experimenters as a sensory organ, whose function is to project environmental information to the limbic brain, and in particular the pyriform cortex. It is accepted that olfactory information can also be projected to the encephalized brain. It is at this point that a paradoxical contradiction becomes evident. It is not clear which of the two systems is controlling or dominant in the evocation of behavioural, and, hence, biochemical, paradigms.

Modern anatomical descriptions take cognizance of, and perhaps lay too much emphasis on, telencephalic connections. But what of the role of

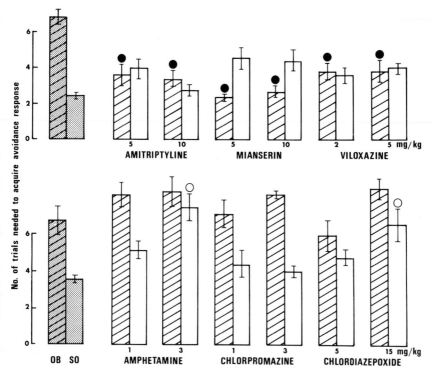

Fig. 4.4: The effect of chronic drug treatment (drugs administered intraperitoneally daily for 10 days) on the performance of bulbectomized (OB-hatched columns) and sham operated (SO- open columns) rats on passive avoidance. Each column represents the mean (± s.e.) of results from at least 10 animals. • represents significant difference from saline treated bulbectomized groups, and o represents significant difference from saline treated sham operated groups ($P < 0.05$). Drug doses per day are illustrated in the figure.

the primitive brain (the so-called limbic system, a system which the original anatomists in the field referred to as the rhinencephalon)? By the very use of this term they implied a non-sensory function for the bulb.

Modern technology has enabled us to study the rhinencephalon in a way unavailable to our experimental predecessors: neurotoxins, for example, specifically produce degeneration in particular neurotransmitter systems. It is possible to inject such neurotoxins directly into the olfactory bulb and to examine the behavioural and biochemical changes so induced. In a series of experiments, the following neurotoxins were injected into the bulb: 6-hydroxydopamine (6-OHDA); 5,7 dihydroxytryptamine (5,7-DHT) and 5,6 dihydroxytryptamine (5,6-DHT). These neurotoxins have been demonstrated to affect the following systems: 6-OHDA destroys noradrenergic nerve terminals; 5,6-DHT destroys serotonergic terminals; and

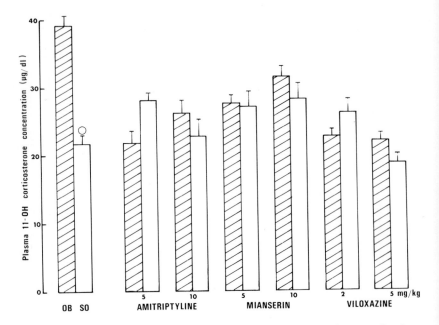

Fig. 4.5: The effect of chronic antidepressant treatment on mean plasma corticosterone levels (± s.e.) of bulbectomized (hatched column) and sham operated (non-hatched) rats. Dosage is indicated at the base of each column pair, and is given in mg kg⁻¹. o represents significant difference between saline injected bulbectomized and sham operated rats ($P <$ 0.01, $n = 6$).

5,7-DHT, though less specific, affects both noradrenergic and serotonergic terminals. However, noradrenergic terminals can be protected from the neurotoxic action of 5,7-DHT by pretreatment with desmethyl-imipramine (DMI) which inhibits the neuronal uptake mechanism for noradrenaline. In the latter case, 5,7-DHT acts primarily as a serotonergic neurotoxin. Observation of the effects of such neurotoxins on the behavioural and endocrine changes associated with bulbectomy enables examination of the role of the bulb in terms of extrasensory function and within the confines of the permissive amine hypothesis. Further, it offers the opportunity for investigation of the apparent contradictory situation that primary unipolar affective disorder, as diagnosed in the clinic, has a diffuse pathological basis not generally recognized.

There are two ways in which a study of neurotoxin action can be undertaken in relation to the olfactory bulb in particular and the rhinencephalon (or limbic system) in general. These relate to (i) neurotoxin injection into

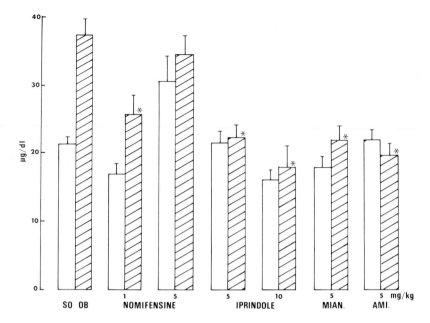

Fig. 4.6: The effects of two further "second generation" cyclic antidepressants on plasma corticosterone levels in the bulbectomy model. The results are discussed in the text. Drugs administered at the dosage indicated for 14 days. * represents significant difference between corticosterone elevation in bulbectomized rats and those exposed to different drug treatments ($P < 0.01$, $n = 6$).

the bulb (intrabulb injection); and (ii) injection of neurotoxin directly into the raphe nucleii.

1. Intrabulb injection

The animal was anaesthetized and secured in a Kopf stereotaxic frame as previously described. Burr holes were drilled as for bulbectomy. A blunt ended hypodermic needle (gauge 25 g) was fixed to a Kopf electrode carrier attached to a 10 μL microsyringe via polyethylene tubing, (internal diameter 0.2 mm). The blunt-ended needle was lowered through the burr holes to rest exactly on the brain surface. The probe was then lowered a further 4 mm from this reference. A total volume of 2 μL was administered by slow infusion over a period of one minute. The needle was removed and a similar injection made into the contralateral bulb.

Of the neurotoxins, two concentrations of each were used; 5,6-DHT (2 mg mL^{-1} and 4 mg mL^{-1}, injected dose 4 μg and 8 μg); 5,7-DHT (2 mg mL^{-1}, injected dose 4 μg and 8 μg) and 6-OHDA (2.5 mg mL^{-1} and 5 mg mL^{-1}, injected dose 5 μg and 10 μg). Control animals received vehicle injections of 0.2% ascorbic acid in isotonic saline.

2. Dorsal raphe injections

The animal was anaesthetized and prepared as described above. However, as the venterolateral dorsal raphe nuclei were the proposed injection target the burr holes were drilled 6 mm posterior to bregma, 2 mm lateral to the midline, and 10° from the vertical. This was necessary to protect the superior sagittal sinus from rupture. The injection needle was lowered to the brain surface at a lateral distance of 1.14 mm. The needle was lowered exactly 6.6 mm from the brain surface and neurotoxin infusions made as previously described.

As a measure of further control it was decided in both procedures to undertake protection experiments. This was to ensure that any behavioural or hormonal change produced by neurotoxin injection was due to destruction of serotonergic or noradrenergic neurones, and was therefore a lesion induced by lack of particular neurotransmitter or pathway. Protection of noradrenergic neurones was achieved by prior injection of desmethyl-imipramine as a single injection (25 mg kg^{-1} administered intraperitoneally) 30 minutes before the injection of 5,7-DHT. Org 6582 (d,1-8-chloro-11-anti-amino-benzo-(b)-bycyclo [3,3,1] nona 3,6a (10a) diene hydrochloride) has been described by Sugrue et al. (1976) as inhibiting the central neuronal uptake of serotonin. Thus pretreatment of an animal with desmeythl-imipramine will protect noradrenergic neurones in the brain from destruction with 6-OHDA or 5,7-DHT, and pretreatment with Org 6582 will prevent destruction of central serotonergic neurones by 5,6-DHT or 5,7-DHT. Thus, a precise experimental lesion can be produced in which noradrenergic and/or serotonergic neurones can be preferentially destroyed, whilst preserving the alternative neurotransmitter system. Thus, the use of neurotoxins produces an experimental format in which the chemical lesion can be characterized. Surgical bulbectomy produces a lesion affecting both noradrenergic and serotonergic pathways thereby producing a less precise experimental model. However, Org 6582 (10 μg in 2 μL was injected into the bulb or the dorsal raphe 15 minutes prior to the injection of 5,6-DHT. A second 5-HT uptake inhibitor, fluoxitine was injected in a similar manner.

The behavioural and glucocorticoid estimations were conducted as described previously. Treatments were compared using a one-way analysis of variance. Particular differences were determined by the Scheffé method of multiple comparisons. In the experiment using dorsal raphe lesions, there was a one-tailed application of Student's t-test. Monoamine determinations were undertaken 14 days after surgery t and noradrenaline, dopamine and 5-HT were assayed simultaneously by the fluorimetric method of Welch and Welch (1969). The results obtained following intrabulb neurotoxin administration are summarized in Table 4.2 and are discussed by Cairncross *et al.* (1979). However, the summarized results have not been hitherto published in detail, and are presented in the following figures.

Fig. 4.7 shows the effects of injection of 6-OHDA, 5,6-DHT and 5,7-DHT directly into the olfactory bulb, compared with the consequences of bulbectomy, on passive avoidance. The vehicle alone produced no significant change in the number of trials needed to acquire the passive avoidance response. Rats injected with 6-OHDA directly into the olfactory bulbs also showed no change in the passive avoidance response test, suggesting that a noradrenergic lesion was not involved in the passive avoidance deficit. Such a conclusion is supported by the observation that the neurotoxin 5,7-DHT was ineffective at the 8 μg dose level. Thus, 5,7-DHT which does not differentiate between noradrenergic and serotonergic systems was without significant effect on passive avoidance responding when injected directly into the olfactory bulb. However, rats pretreated with desmethyl-imipramine (25 mg kg^{-1} intraperitoneally) prior to the injection of 5,7-DHT into the bulbs did display a performance deficit in passive avoidance responding. In this group the number of trials required to avoid foot shock for one minute was not significantly different from that of bulbectomized rats. Thus protection of the noradrenergic system by desmethyl-imipramine prior to exposure of the bulb neurones to 5,7-DHT, a situation producing a preferential serotonergic lesion, produced a decrement in passive avoidance response. Similar results were obtained when the 8 μg dose of 5,6-DHT was injected into the olfactory bulbs, in this case without the need for prior treatment with desmethyl-imipramine, although the 4 μg dose of 5,6-DHT was without significant effect, a result which supports the arguments formulated.

The reactivity results of this test are shown in Fig. 4.8. Bulbectomized rats had a significantly higher total reactivity than the sham operated controls. The injection of vehicle, 6-OHDA or 5,7-DHT produced no significant change in reactivity. However, injection of 5,7-DHT after desmethyl-imipramine pretreatment and injection of 5,6-DHT at both dose levels increased reactivity to a level similar to that obtained in bulbectomy. This series of results again supports the hypothesis that the bulbectomy syndrome relates to a serotonergic deficit. Sham operated rats in their home environment had a plasma glucocorticoid (11-OHCS) level of 220 $\pm$ 21 μg L^{-1}.

TABLE 4.2: The effects of OB and intra-bulb injection of neurotoxins on plasma corticosterone levels (11-OHCS), passive avoidance (PA) deficit and reactivity

Procedure	11-OHCS	PA deficit	Reactivity
Bulbectomy	↑	↑	↑
6-OHDA	o	o	o
5,7-DHT	o	o	↑
5,7-DHT + DHI	↑	↑	?
5,6-DHT	↑	↑	↑
5,6-DHT + Org 6582	o	o	o

Arrows indicate direction of observed response.
Abbreviations as described in text.

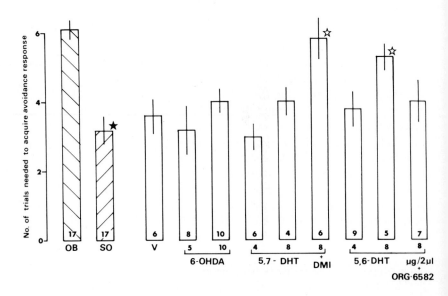

Fig. 4.7: The performance of bulbectomized (OB) and sham operated (SO) rats in the passive stepdown avoidance test compared to that of rats receiving intrabulb injections of vehicle alone (V), 6-OHDA, 5,6-DHT and 5,7-DHT in the doses shown. ★ indicates a significant difference between bulbectomized and sham operated rats following exposure to a one-way analysis of variance (F8, 73 = 7.74, $P < 0.001$). ☆ indicates results which are not significantly different ($P > 0.05$) to bulbectomized rats. Columns represent mean (± s.e.) number of trials needed by each group to acquire the appropriate avoidance response, that is, avoidance of footshock by remaining on the safety platform for at least one minute. Numbers at base of columns indicate group size.

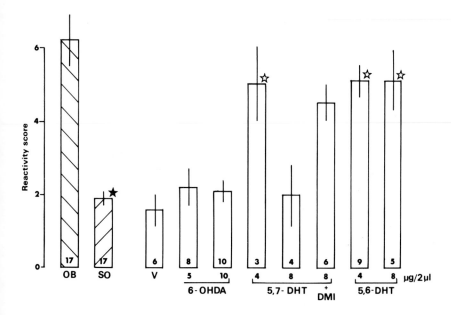

Fig. 4.8: The reactivity scores of bulbectomized (OB) and sham operated (SO) rats compared with animals receiving intrabulb injections of vehicle (V) alone, 6-OHDA, 5,6-DHT and 5,7-DHT in the doses shown. ★ indicates significant differences between bulbectomised and sham operated groups (F8, 73 = 13.86, $P < 0.01$). ☆ indicates results which are not significantly different ($P > 0.05$) between groups. Columns represent mean scores ($\pm$ s.e.). Numbers at the base of the columns indicate group size.

Bulbectomized rats in a similar situation and on a similar time schedule had a plasma 11-OHCS level of 391 $\pm$ 23 μg L^{-1}. The plasma 11-OHCS level in bulbectomized rats was significantly higher, (F[9,65] = 16.93, $P <$ 0.001) than that obtained in sham operated rats (Fig. 4.9). Intrabulbar injections of vehicle, 6-OHDA, or 5,7-DHT did not elevate plasma 11-OHCS levels in rats compared to the sham operated group. However, 5,7-DHT injection after DMI pretreatment, and intrabulbar injection of 5,6-DHT (8 μg) elevated plasma 11-OHCS concentrations to 382 $\pm$ 32 μg L^{-1} and 396 $\pm$ 22 μg L^{-1}, respectively. Thus, the biochemical (endocrine) results add further support to the hypothesis of a serotonergic deficit underlying the bulbectomy syndrome. Such a conclusion can be tested further by examining the actions of Org 6582 pretreatment on intra-bulb neurotoxin administration. This substance which has the property of inhibiting serotonin (5-HT) uptake must act predominantly through 5,6-DHT. The results of intrabulbar pretreatment with Org 6582 15 minutes

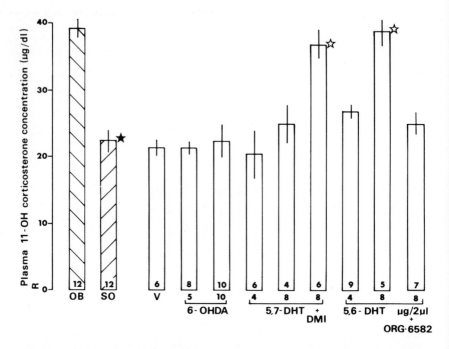

Fig. 4.9: Plasma 11-hydroxycorticosterone concentrations in bulbectomized (OB) and sham operated (SO) rats, compared with corticosterone levels in rats receiving intrabulb injections of vehicle (V) alone, 6-OHDA, 5,7-DHT and 5,7-DHT with DMI pretreatment and 5,6-DHT and 5,6-DHT with Org 6582 pretreatment. ★ indicates a significant difference (F9, 65 = 16.93, $P < 0.001$) between OB and SO rats. ☆ indicates results which are not significantly ($P > 0.05$) from OB rats. Columns represent mean (± s.e.) concentrations of corticosterone. Group size is shown at the base of each columns.

prior to intrabulbar injection of 5,6-DHT on passive avoidance responding, reactivity score and plasma 11-OHCS levels are shown in Fig. 4.10. Org 6582 itself produced no significant changes in these parameters in comparison with vehicle injected controls. However, intrabulbar 5,6-DHT produced changes in all three parameters. Pretreatment with Org 6582 significantly prevented the deficit in passive avoidance and the rise in plasma 11-OHCS produced by injection of 5,6-DHT. Again, these results are consistent with the hypothesis that the major behavioural and biochemical (endocrine) manifestations of the bulbectomy syndrome are not primarily induced by a noradrenergic lesion, and that a serotonergic malfunction is involved.

Such a premise can be further critically examined by neurotoxin treatment inducing a chemical lesion in the dorsal raphe. The effects of injecting 8 μg of 5,6-DHT into the ventrolateral area of the dorsal raphe are

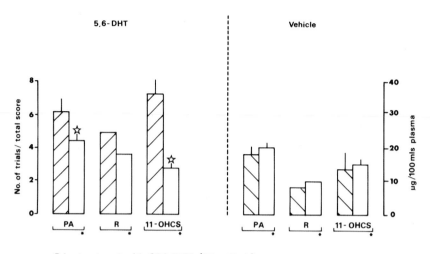

Fig. 4.10: The results of a 2 microlitre injection of Org 6582 (10 g 2 L⁻¹) injected 15 minutes prior to 5,6-DHT (8 g 2 L⁻¹) or ascorbic acid vehicle (2 μL) into each olfactory bulb. The left panel represents all groups receiving 5,6-DHT, and the right panel all groups receiving vehicle. The open column of each pair represent those groups pretreated with Org 6582. The columns show passive avoidance (PA), reactivity (R) and plasma corticosterone (11-OHCS). ☆ represents a significant difference ($P < 0.01$, Student's t test) between 5,6-DHT-saline treated and 5,6-DHT-Org 6582 treated animals.

shown in Fig. 4.11. Fifteen days after the injection of 5,6-DHT, rats showed a deficiency in acquisition of the passive avoidance response ($P < 0.01$) and an elevation of plasma 11-OHCS ($P < 0.01$) compared with vehicle controls. The reactivity response was not significantly affected.

In another series of experiments, 5,6-DHT (8 μg) was injected bilaterally into the dorsal raphe projection area of the rat brain (as previously described). Ten days later these animals had developed a deficit in passive avoidance behaviour similar to the 15 day preinjected animals, and had elevated plasma 11-OHCS levels. Pretreatment with the 5-HT uptake inhibitors Org 6582 or fluoxetine 30 minutes before raphe injection prevented these changes. Treatment of the raphe lesioned animals for 10 days following neurotoxin administration with mianserin 5 mg kg⁻¹ d⁻¹ normalized the aberrant parameters. Yohimbine treatment (0.08 mg kg⁻¹ d⁻¹ and 0.8 mg kg⁻¹ d⁻¹) in the same time period did not (Cairncross et al., 1981b). Perusal of Fig. 4.12 and Fig. 4.13 illustrates these results, and shows that the 0.8 mg dose of yohimbine exacerbates the glucocorticoid elevation.

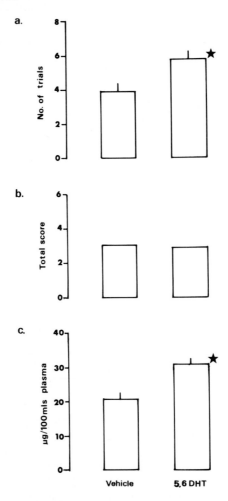

Fig. 4.11: The effect of a 2 microlitre injection of vehicle (0.2 % ascorbic acid) or a similar volume of 5,6-DHT (8 g L⁻¹) directly into the B8 area of the dorsal raphe 15 days prior to testing. Panel (a) shows number of trials required to achieve passive avoidance criteria, (b) shows reactivity scoring and (c) shows plasma corticosterone levels (in g 100 mL⁻¹ plasma). Each column represents the results of six experiments (± s.e., except in (b) where mean results are shown). ★ represents significant difference ($P < 0.01$) from vehicle injected control.

In all, this series of experiments supports the argument that a noradrenergic deficit is not the primary cause of the bulbectomy syndrome. The results support the premise that the primary lesion lies in a serotonergic system which relies on a noradrenergic pathway for its expression.

Thus, an overall examination of the evidence presented would confirm

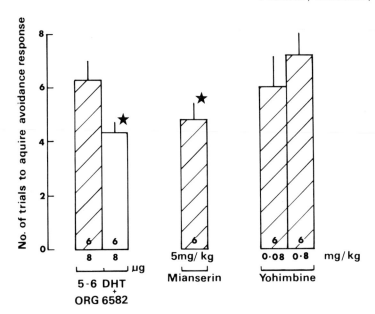

Fig. 4.12: The effect of injecting 2 microlitres of 5,6-DHT (8 g 2 L⁻¹) directly into the dorsal raphe B8 area on the passive avoidance response. The response is normalized by prior treatment with Org 6582 (10 g 2 L⁻¹), as is pretreatment (10 days) with the cyclic antidepressant drug mianserin (5 mg kg⁻¹ d⁻¹). Yohimbine at doses of 0.08 mg kg⁻¹ and 0.8 mg kg⁻¹ is without significant effect. ★ represents a significant difference ($P < 0.01$) from 5,6-DHT treated animal.

the behavioural and biochemical consequences of bulbectomy and suggests that a serotonin deficiency plays a crucial role in the development of the syndrome. The demonstration that a chemical lesion induced by intrabulbar injection of 5,6-DHT or 5,7-DHT (under appropriate conditions) or that injection of 5,6-DHT directly into the dorsal raphe could mimic the surgical lesion, whereas intrabulbar 6-OHDA could not, provides the firm evidence for such a connection (Schnieden *et al.*, 1978; Cairncross *et al.*, 1981b). This notion is supported by the observation that the serotonin uptake inhibitors Org 6582 and fluoxetine, when administered as pretreatment to the neuro-toxin and thus preventing the neurotoxins reaching their site of action, prevented manifestations of the syndrome (Cairncross *et al.*, 1981b).

Further, that the majority of serotonergic neurones in the central nervous system originate in the mid-brain raphe (Bobiller *et al.*, 1976) where direct injection of 5,6-DHT produces a similar, if not identical, syndrome, emphasizes the role of serotonin in the development of the bulbectomy syndrome.

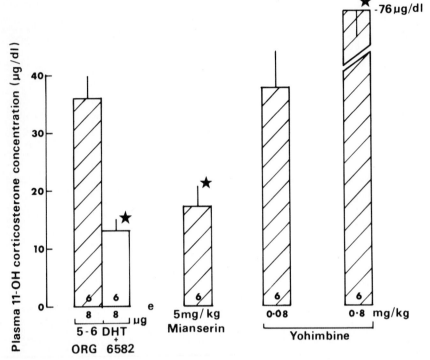

Fig. 4.13: The effect of injecting 2 microlitres of 5,6-DHT (8 g 2 L⁻¹) directly into the dorsal raphe on plasma corticosterone levels. Org 6582 (10 g 2 L⁻¹) pretreatment maintains plasma corticosterone levels within the normal range. Pretreatment with mianserin (5 mg kg⁻¹ d⁻¹ for 10 days) prevents corticosterone elevation. Yohimbine (0.08 mg kg⁻¹) is without effect, but at a dose of 0.8 mg/kg exacerbates corticosterone elevation. ★ represents a significant difference ($P < 0.01$) from 5,6-DHT treated animal.

However, cognizance must be taken of the fact that although both 5,6-DHT and 5,7-DHT after desmethyl-imipramine administration lowered serotonin concentration in the bulb and produced the syndrome, destruction of noradrenergic neurones with 6-OHDA did neither. The role of dopamine in the bulbectomized rat seems of little importance since no association was apparent between this amine and the appearance of the syndrome. The experiments described do suggest a role for noradrenaline in development of the syndrome, since depletion of serotonin and noradrenaline, as with 5,7-DHT alone, failed to produce the syndrome. This is further evidence that serotonin plays a primary role in the development of the syndrome, but an intact noradrenergic system is required for expression of the syndrome.

The complexity of the total situation is emphasized when examining the pharmacological and clinical profile of the quadracyclic antidepressant, mianserin. This drug, one of undisputed clinical efficacy, has been shown by Cerrito and Raiteri (1981) to be a central α_2-adrenoceptor antagonist. However, yohimbine, which is also a central α_2-adrenoceptor antagonist, failed to modify the behavioural and glucocorticoid response to the injection of 5,6-DHT into the B7 area of the raphe, reiterating the premise that the effect of mianserin on the noradrenergic system is not of fundamental importance. Mianserin also antagonizes the behavioural changes induced by quipazine, but not by 5-methoxy-N,N-dimethyltryptamine. Green (1981) suggests that these contrasting behavioural responses are due to interaction of the drugs mentioned with different serotonergic receptor populations. The effect of mianserin on 5,6-DHT treated animals may thus be due to its antagonism of certain central serotonergic and/or noradrenergic receptors. Leigh and Cairncross (1982) were able to differentiate the actions of mianserin and maprotiline on pineal hydroxy-O-methyl transferase (HIOMT) activity. Both these antidepressant agents antagonize the α_2-adrenoceptor, but mianserin was reported by Maunsey et al. (1982) to also antagonize the prejunctional 5-HT autoreceptor (5-HT$_2$ receptor). More recently, Liebman et al. (1983) have examined the pharmacological properties of CGS 7525A, a new centrally active α_2-adrenoceptor antagonist. They found the new compound to be marginally more effective than mianserin in displacing clonidine binding, but neither compound was effective in preventing or displacing prazosin binding. This work confirms, therefore, the α_2-adrenoceptor antagonist properties of mianserin, and demonstrates also (by examination of $_3$H-spiroperidol binding) that mianserin can displace this substance from 5-HT$_2$ sites in the frontal cortex. Yohimbine had little affinity for the 5-HT$_2$ receptor. Thus, current evidence would appear to establish the premise that the primary lesion in bulbectomy has a serotonergic basis, needing an intact α_2-adrenoceptor system for its expression.

Further evidence for such a contention is derived from the recent work of Raiteri et al. (1983) who presented functional evidence for two stereochemically distinct α_2-adrenoceptors regulating central noradrenaline and serotonin release. These workers demonstrated that in nerve terminals isolated from rat cerebral cortex, exogenous noradrenaline inhibited in a dose-dependent manner both the release of noradrenaline and serotonin. The inhibitory effect was antagonized by yohimbine and mianserin, but not by prazosin. This work confirms the conclusions of previously quoted studies concerning the involvement of α_2-adrenoceptors.

Raiteri and colleagues (1983) showed that mianserin exists as two enantiomorphs, each of which has contrasting pharmacological properties, giving greater weight to the "serotonin theory". Thus, the positive form was demonstrated to be an antagonist of the α_2-autoreceptor mediating regulation of noradrenaline release whereas the minus enantiomorph was inactive in this regard. By contrast, both enantiomorphs of mianserin antagonized the effect of exogenous noradrenaline on the α_2-andrenoceptors modulating serotonin release. Raiteri *et al.* (1983) concluded that the α_2-adrenoceptors which regulate noradrenaline and serotonin release are located presynaptically and represent two stereochemically different populations of α_2-adrenoceptors. Thus, it would appear the ratio of the positive to the negative enantiomorph in any mianserin preparation could regulate the pharmacological response to the drug. This in turn would modulate the clinical effectiveness of mianserin in particular groups of patients under treatment with the drug.

It will be remembered that Cobbin *et al.* (1981) demonstrated that patients diagnosed as unipolar depressives and having homogeneous symptomatology in fact could be shown to fall into two distinct biochemical subgroups. One of the criteria examined was the response of the patient to the dexamethasone suppression test (DST). This test uses a synthetic glucocorticoid, dexamethasone, which in normal physiological circumstances acts through an inhibitory feedback mechanism, to suppress adrenocorticotrophic hormone (ACTH) release from the anterior pituitary gland. This prevents further release of cortisol from the cortex of the adrenal gland (HPA axis). Certain patients diagnosed as suffering from endogenous (unipolar) depression do not suppress cortisol secretion in the presence of dexamethasone, such patients are said to "escape" from DST. Other patients exhibit the normal, or predictable, response; in these patients glucocorticoid secretion is suppressed by dexamethasone (Cobbin *et al.*, 1981). The pharmacological basis of escape or suppression of dexamethasone remains to be elucidated. Nonetheless, the premise that patients can present in the clinic with homogeneous symptoms having heterogeneous aetiology remains pertinent.

Those patients who showed suppression to dexamethasone challenge showed a positive response to mianserin; those patients who escaped dexamethasone suppression failed to respond to mianserin (indeed, their symptoms were often exacerbated). In a separate, but relatively concurrent, study Brown and Qualls (1982) demonstrated that escape from dexamethasone equated with a positive clinical response to desmethyl-imipramine (DMI) a cyclic antidepressant acting primarily on the noradrenergic α_2-adrenoceptor. Thus, it would be anticipated that the (positive) enantiomorph of mianserin, which is the α_2-autoreceptor antagonist modulating NA release, would be effective in those patients responding to DMI, and who did not respond to dexamethasone with reduction in cortisol secretion. Conversely, the (negative) enantiomer of mianserin should be effective in those patients who respond positively to dexamethasone suppression, and in whom the bulbectomy model postulates a serotonergic lesion requiring an effective α_2-adrenoceptor mechanism for its expression. An investigation in the clinic to examine such a hypothesis has not been undertaken, but is a matter of some import.

III. CONCLUSIONS

At this point, it is pertinent to refer back to the three questions asked in Section I, and to view current discussion in the light of these questions. Obviously great advances have been made, but these advances can only be fully appreciated and understood when viewed as part of a whole organism, irrespective of whether the organism is subhuman or human. *In vitro* studies can supply vital information which can only be realistically evaluated by study of the whole animal. Thus, the answers to the first two questions in Section I are affirmative.

The answer to the third question broaches many areas which remain unclarified. Perhaps the most urgent of the problems remaining to be answered relates to the physiological/pathological basis of the dexamethasone suppression test (DST). Is it a test useful in psychiatry purely as a diagnostic tool, or does it serve as a basis for investigative progress? Studies of the bulbectomy model, and in the clinic, suggest that activation of the HPA axis requires a noradrenergic–serotonergic interaction, the basis of which is not fully understood. Experimental studies and projected clinical studies suggest two possibilities: (*a*) there can exist a malfunction in pathways controlling the HPA axis which is fundamentally noradrenergic controlled by a β_1-adrenoceptor mechanism (Corderoy-Buck and Cairncross, 1983); and (*b*) a serotonergic malfunction could exist, which prevents efficient functioning of the NA pathway.

Malfunction in either of these two pathways produces a common behavioural/biochemical/endrocrine profile which can be interpreted as a clinical manifestation of depression *or* as an animal model commonly referred to as the bulbectomy syndrome. Further, the total profile can be reversed in the clinic and experimentally by the judicious use of cyclic antidepressant drugs, taking cognizance of the subtle differences in the pharmacological profiles of the cyclic antidepressant drugs discussed.

It is tempting to speculate further on the outcome of these observations; however, at this junction such speculation would serve no useful purpose. Suffice it to say that the basis exists for meaningful research questions to be examined both in the clinic and in the animal model.

Carefully couched questions, planned with specific endpoints, must materially add to our understanding of the animal model; that is, bulbectomy. Experience has shown that further elucidation of the model could be extrapolated cautiously into experiments in clinical pharmacology with a deliberately conceived, limited endpoint. After 25 years of effort in which basic research has remained singularly divorced from clinical progress, there exists a common ground which, if utilized carefully by both experimental scientist and clinician, could open the door to a new horizon of understanding of affective disease.

ACKNOWLEDGEMENT

The author wishes to acknowledge the contributions of many colleagues in the development of this work. In particular, the contributions of Dr Barry Cox, Dr Christine Forster and Emeritus Professor H. Schnieden must be mentioned. Dr Henk van Riezen of the Organon Company, Oss, Holland, and many of his colleagues have given enthusiastic support and advice. In my own laboratory, Mrs Kerry Pearce and Ms Ann Parks deserve thanks for their support and help.

REFERENCES

Barnes, N.D., Joseph, J.H., Atherden, S.H. and Clayton, B.E. Function tests of adrenal axis in children with measurement of plasma cortisol by competitive protein binding. *Archives of the Diseases of Children*, 1972, 47: 66–73.

Bassett, J.R., King, M.G. and Cairncross, K.D. Parameters of novelty, shock predictability and response contingency in corticosterone release in the rat. *Physiology and Behaviour*, 1973, 10: 901–907.

Bassett, J.R. and Cairncross, K.D. Myocardial sensitivity to catecholamines following exposure of rats to irregular, signalled footshock. *Pharmacology Biochemistry and Behaviour*, 1976, 4: 27–33.

Bobiller, P., Seguin, S., Petitjean, F.,Solvert, D., Tauret, M. and Jarret, M. The raphe nuclei of the rat brain stem: A topographical atlas of their efferent projections as revealed by autoradiation. *Brain Research*, 1976, 113: 449–486.

Brown, W.A. and Qualls, C.B. Pituitary–adrenal regulation over multiple depressive episodes. *Psychiatry Research*, 1982, 1: 263–269.

Cairncross, K.D. and King, M.G. Facilitation of avoidance learning in anosmic rats by amitriptyline. *Proceedings of the Australian Physiological and Pharmacological Society*, 1971, 2: 1–2.

Cairncross, K.D., Schofield, S.P.M. and King, M.G. The implication of noradrenaline in avoidance learning. *Progress in Brain Research*, 1973, 39: 481–485.

Cairncross, K.D., Wren, A.F., Cox, B. and Schnieden, H. Effects of olfactory bulbectomy and housing on stress induced corticosterone release in the rat. *Physiology and Behaviour*, 1977, 19: 485–487.

Cairncross, K.D., Cox, B., Forster, C. and Wren, A.F. Olfactory Projection Systems, drugs and behaviour: A review. *Journal of Psychoneuroendrocrinology*, 1979, 4: 253–272.

Cairncross, K.D., Cobbin, D.M. and Pohlen, G.H. The new psychiatry. *British Medical Journal*, 1981a, 283: 991.

Cairncross, K.D., Cox, B., Forster, C. and Schnieden, H. The ability of 5,6-DHT injected into dorsal raphe projections to mimic surgical bulbectomy. *Proceedings of the Australian Society of Clinical and Experimental Pharmacology*, 1981b, 15: 147.

Cerrito, P. and Raiteri, M. Supersensitivity of central noradrenergic presynaptic autoreceptors following chronic treatment with the antidepressant mianserin. *European Journal of Pharmacology*, 1981, 70: 425–426.

Cobbin, D., Cairncross, K.D., Jurd, S., Veltman, D.G. and Pohlen, G.H. Urinary MHPG levels and the dexamethasone test predict clinical response to the antidepressant, mianserin. *Neuroendocrinology Letters*, 1981, 3:253–272.

Corderoy-Buck, S. and Cairncross, K.D. The effect of β receptor antagonists on hydroxy indole-O-methyltransferase activity in the pineal gland of the rat. *Proceedings of the Australian Society for Medical Research*, 1983, 14: 55.

Forster, C. and Cox, B. Effects of olfactory bulbectomy and peripherally induced anosmia on thermoregulation: Susceptibility to antidepressant type drugs. *Journal of Pharmacy and Pharmacology*, 1980, 32: 630–634.

Geyer, H.A., Puerto, A., Menkes, D.B. and Mandell, A.J. Behavioural studies following lesions of the mesolimbic and mesostriatal pathways. *Brain Research*, 1976, 106: 257–270.

Green, A.R. Pharmacological studies on serotonin mediated behaviour. *Journal of Physiology*, 1981, 77: 437–447.

Hill, D. *A critical evaluation of the effects of bulbectomy in the rat.* M.Sc. Thesis, Macquarie University, Sydney, Australia (1982).

Iversen, S.D. Recent advances in the anatomy and chemistry of the limbic system. *Experiments in Brain Research*, 1984, in press.

King, F.A. Effects of septal and amygdaloid lesions on emotional behaviour and conditioned avoidance responses in the rat. *Journal of Nervous Disease*, 1958, 126: 221–236.

Kuhn, R. The treatment of depressive states with G-22355 (imipramine hydrochloride). *American Journal of Psychiatry*, 1959, 115: 449–464.

Leibman, J.H., Lovall, R.A., Braunwalder, A., Stone, G., Bernard, P., Barbaz, B., Welch, J., Kim, H.S., Walsey, J.W. and Robson, R.D. CGS 7525A, a new centrally active alpha adrenoceptor antagonist. *Life Sciences*, 1983, 24: 355–363.

Leigh, D.H. and Cairncross, K.D. The effect of olfactory bulbectomy and antidepressant drugs on pineal function in the rat. *Neuroendocrinology Letters*, 1982, 4: 195.

Leonard, B.E. and Tuite, M. Anatomical, physiological and behavioural aspects of olfactory bulbectomy in the rat. *International Reviews in Neurobiology*, 1981, 22: 251–286.

Le Gros Clark, W.E. and Meyer, M. The terminal connections of the olfactory tract in the rabbit. *Brain*, 1947, 70: 304–328.

Mattingly, D. A simple fluorimetric method for the estimation of free 11-hydroxy corticoids in plasma. *Journal of Clinical Pathology*, 1962, 15: 374–379.

Maunsey, I., Brady, K.A., Carroll, J., Fisher, R. and Middlemiss, D.N. K$^+$ evoked [^{3}H]-5-HT release from rat frontal cortex slices: the effect of 5-HT agonists and antagonists. *Biochemistry and Pharmacology*, 1982, 31: 49–53.

Murphy, B.E.P. Some studies of the protein binding of steroids and their application to the routine micro and ultra-micro measurement of various steroids in body fluids by competitive protein binding assay. *Journal of Clinical Endocrinology*, 1967, 27: 973–990.

Murphy, M.R. Olfactory impairment, olfactory bulb removal and mammalian reproduction. In R.L. Doty (Ed.), *Mammalian Olfaction, Reproductive Processes and Behaviour.* New York: Academic Press, 1976: 96–112.

Pohorecky, L.A., Zigmond, H.J., Heimer, L. and Wurtman, R.J. Olfactory bulb removal: Effects on brain norepinephrine. *Proceedings of the National Academy of Sciences*, 1969, 62: 1052–1055.

Prange, A., Wilson, I. and Lynn, C.W. L-tryptophan in mania: Contribution to a permissive amine hypothesis of affective disorders. *Archives of General Psychiatry*, 1974, 30: 50–62.

Raiteri, M., Maura, G. and Versace, P. Functional evidence for two stereochemically different alpha-2 andrenoceptors regulating central norepinephrine and serotonin release. *Journal of Pharmacology and Experimental Therapeutics*, 1983, 224: 679–684.

Rose, A., McCulloch, M.W. and Sarantos-Laska, C. Effects of mianserin or noradrenergic mechanisms. *Proceedings of the Australian Society of Clinical and Experimental Pharmacologists*, 1982, 16: 16.

Scalia, F. and Winans, S.S. Olfactory and vomeronasal pathways in mammals. In R.L. Doty (Ed.), *Mammalian Olfaction, Reproductive Processes and Behaviour*. New York: Academic Press, 1976: 8–26.

Schildkraut, J.J. The catecholamine hypothesis of affective disorder: A review of supporting evidence. *American Journal of Psychiatry*, 1965, 122: 509–522.

Schnieden, H., Wren, A.F., Forster, C. and Cairncross, K.D. Olfactory bulbectomy and anti depressant drugs. *Abstracts from the 7th International Congress in Pharmacology*, Paris, 1978: 187.

Sieck, M.H. The role of the olfactory system in avoidance learning and activity. *Physiology and Behaviour*, 1972, 8: 705–710.

Siegel, S. *Non parametric statistics for behavioral scientists*. New York: McGraw-Hill, 1956.

Sigg, E.G. Studies on the action of "Tofranil". *Canadian Psychiatric Association Journal*, 1959, 4 (Suppl.): 75–83.

Sugrue, M., Goodlet, I. and Mireylees, S.E. On the selective inhibition of serotonin uptake *in vivo* by Org 6582. *European Journal of Pharmacology*, 1976, 40: 121–130.

Van Riezen, H., Schnieden, H. and Wren, A.F. Olfactory bulb ablation in the rat: Behavioural changes and their reversal by anti-depressive drugs. *British Journal of Pharmacology*, 1977, 60: 521–528.

Wren, A.F., van Riezen, H. and Rigter, H. A new model for the prediction of antidepressant activity. *Pharmakopsychology*, 1977, 10: 96–100.

Welch, A.S. and Welch, B.L. Solvent extraction method for simultaneous determination of norepinephrine, dopamine, serotonin and 5-hydroxy indole acetic acid in a single mouse brain. *Annals of Biochemistry*, 1969, 30: 161–179.

5

THE AETIOLOGY OF STRESS INDUCED ISCHAEMIC HEART DISEASE: THE USE OF ANIMAL MODELS

J. R. BASSETT

I. INTRODUCTION

Prolonged exposure to psychological stressors such as anxiety, apprehension or fear is now known to induce many degenerative disease states (Bassett and Cairncross, 1975). The cardiovascular system appears to be most susceptible to damage in the face of prolonged exposure to such stressors. Hypertension, arteriosclerosis and atherosclerosis, thrombosis, myocardial ischaemia, necrosis and fibrosis have all been linked with the exposure to stressful situations in which the psychological parameters of anxiety or fear play a major role. For example, Myers and Dewar (1975), in a study of 100 sudden deaths from coronary artery disease, found that acute psychological stress showed the most significant relationship when compared with other risk factors.

The study of psychosomatic disease in humans has profited enormously from the availability of experimental models of these diseases in animals. This is particularly so in the case of ischaemic heart disease. Whereas studies using human subjects are limited in both the range and intensity of investigation, the use of animal models has allowed detailed investigation of the aetiology of the stress related disease. Without the use of animal models our understanding of the mechanisms of stress induced heart disease would have progressed little further than a suggested correlation.

ANIMAL MODELS IN PSYCHOPATHOLOGY
ISBN 0 12 114180 2

II. LIMITATION OF HUMAN STUDIES

Medical authorities throughout the ages have ascribed cardiac diseases almost exclusively to emotional disorders (Russek, 1967). However, the failure to provide solid scientific evidence has led to the concept of the causal relationship between psychological stress and disease of the heart being repeatedly challenged in modern times. Originally it was thought that only epidemiological assessment of the way coronary artery disease arose, evolved and terminated fatally in the general population could provide an undistorted picture of ischaemic heart disease (Kannel, 1973). Psychological assessment of patients presenting with cardiac disease demonstrated the prevalence of certain personality traits and behavioural patterns in subjects prone to ischaemic heart disease. The typical coronary patient was described as an aggressive, ambitious individual with intense physical and emotional drives, who concentrates all his* energy within the narrow scope of his career; a person with an intense sense of urgency and preoccupation with deadlines (Minc, 1967; Sobel, 1962; Jenkins, 1971). Psychological stress of occupational origin appeared to be far more significant in the aetiological picture of coronary disease than did heredity, high fat diet, obesity, cigarette smoking, or exercise (Russek, 1967). Such reports allowed possible candidates with an increased susceptibility to clinical coronary disease to be defined, but made little contribution to our understanding of the disease process. These observations suffered from the common weakness that they arose from retrospective analysis of values which could only be qualitatively estimated. They were based on clinical impression which has been recognized as the most inaccurate of all research modalities (Russek, 1967). A more scientific approach to the mechanisms by which behaviour may be associated with a higher prevalence of coronary heart disease was required, and this could only be obtained by the development of successful animal models. Without such models there could be no clear understanding of the manner in which emotional stress could hasten the advent of clinical coronary artery disease.

Studies on human subjects had shown that emotional stress could produce marked haemodynamic effects. However, such studies were confined to measurement of blood pressure, electrocardiography (ECG), cardiac output, or changes in blood flow to individual vascular beds. Anxiety or anticipatory tension can evoke marked to moderate acceleration in heart rate (Bogdonoff *et al.*, 1960; Bord *et al.*, 1959) and an augmented cardiac output (Hickam *et al.*, 1948). Electrocardiographic abnormalities in patients exhibiting anxiety are also observed. These changes take the form

---

* The masculine pronoun has been used as the "typical coronary patient" is more likely to be male.

of S-T segment displacements and inversion of T waves (Fig. 5.1); changes indicative of myocardial hypoxia (Magendantz and Shortsleeve, 1951; Schiffer et al., 1976). Increased blood pressure in stressful situations is also common. Blood pressure changes may result from either the increase in cardiac output or changes in total peripheral resistance; the change in total peripheral resistance depends upon the balance between simultaneous muscular vasodilation and visceral vasoconstriction (Brod et al., 1959).

Since the stress induced changes in cardiovascular function are almost identical to those that can be induced by stimulation of the sympathetic-adrenal medullary system, the activation of this system has long been linked with stress induced ischaemic heart disease. Cannon's classic studies concerning the activation of the peripheral sympathetic nervous system under the influence of emotional stress laid the foundations for today's concepts of psychosomatic inter-relationships in cardiovascular pathology (Cannon, 1920). It is now well established that an augmented liberation of the adrenosympathetic catecholamines (adrenaline and noradrenaline) is a typical sequelae of emotional stress (Fig. 5.2). Adrenaline discharge is characteristic of situations involving passive anxiety or apprehension, whereas noradrenaline is mobilized during attitudes of aggression, anger or violent action (Feuerstein and Gutman, 1971).

III. THE SYMPATHETIC–ADRENAL MEDULLARY SYSTEM

Exposure to emotional stress involves activation of the limbic system, the emotional centre of the central nervous system. From a component of the limbic system, the hypothalamus, there are two basic outflows, both travelling initially via the spinal chord. The first of these outflows represents the sympathetic branch of the autonomic nervous system. This neuronal system innervates the viscera; heart, gut, blood vessels, etc. The neurotransmitter released on stimulation of the sympathetic nervous system is the catecholamine noradrenaline. The second outflow leaves the spinal cord as the splanchnic nerve and innervates the chromaffin cells of the adrenal medulla. When stimulated these cells release mainly the hormone adrenaline but also noradrenaline in varying amounts. The catecholamines, adrenaline and noradrenaline prepare the animal for an immediate response to the stressor, a response which may be "flight" or "fight" (Fig. 5.3).

Increased adrenosympathogenic catecholamine discharge has been shown to occur following exposure to emotional stress. Much of the evidence for this comes from studies of the levels of both catecholamines and their metabolites found in the blood and urine under a wide variety of

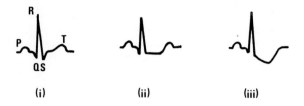

Fig. 5.1: Stress induced changes in ECG pattern. (i) control electrocardiogram; (ii) and (iii) electrocardiograms from stressed animals showing; (ii) depressed *ST* segment and (iii) inverted *T* peak both characteristic of myocardial hypoxia.

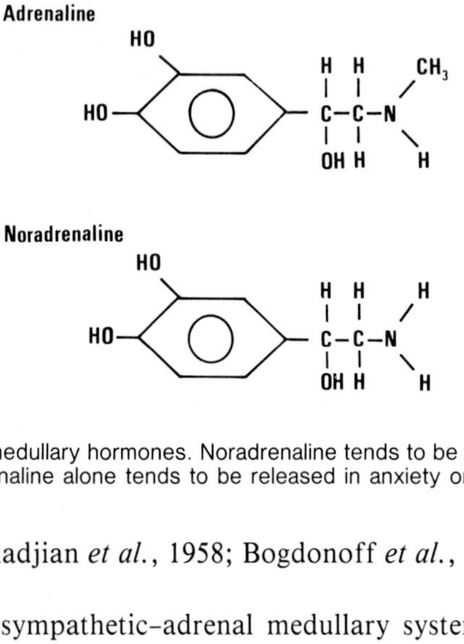

Fig. 5.2: The adrenal medullary hormones. Noradrenaline tends to be released in aggression and anger, where adrenaline alone tends to be released in anxiety or fear.

such stressors (Elmadjian *et al.*, 1958; Bogdonoff *et al.*, 1960; Raab, 1968; Mason, 1968b).

However, the sympathetic–adrenal medullary system is not the only system known to be activated in response to exposure to emotional stress. Most stressors that activate the sympathetic–adrenal medullary system also activate a second system, the pituitary–adrenocortical system, resulting in the release of the steroid hormones, cortisol and corticosterone. This system also appears to play an important role in stress induced heart disease. Troxler *et al.* (1977) found a significant correlation between plasma cortisol levels and the other major risk factors normally associated with coronary artery disease.

IV. THE PITUITARY–ADRENOCORTICAL SYSTEM

Emotional stress activates the supraoptic and paraventricular nuclei of the hypothalamus resulting in the release, from neurosecretory cells in the

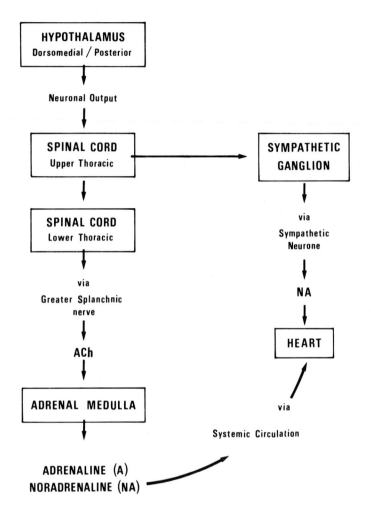

Fig. 5.3: The sympathetic–adrenal medullary system.

median eminence, of corticotropin releasing factor (CRF) which travels via the hypothalamic-hypophyseal portal system to the anterior lobe of the pituitary gland (Fig. 5.4). Here the releasing factor causes the release of the adrenocorticotrophic hormone (ACTH) which then travels via the systemic blood stream to the zona fasciculata of the adrenal cortex. ACTH stimulates the release from the fasciculata cells of the glucocorticoid hormones, cortisol and/or corticosterone. The ratio of cortisol to corticosterone varies according to species. In humans, the only glucocorticoid

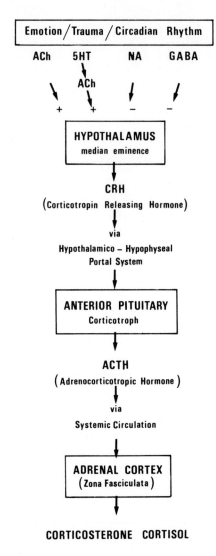

Fig. 5.4: The pituitary–adrenocortical system. Ach = acetylcholine. 5-HT = 5 hydroxy-tryptamine. NA = noradrenaline. GABA = gamma aminobutyric acid. + = stimulation. − = inhibition.

secreted in an appreciable amount is cortisol; in the rat it is corticosterone (Ganong, 1971; Peron, 1960).

Situations involving psychological stress are associated not only with an elevated level of catecholamines but also with an elevation in glucocorticoid levels, the levels of both rising simultaneously (Mason, 1968a,b). While the pituitary–adrenocortical system is activated by a wide range of psychological stressors, situations of uncertainty or unpredictability produce a far greater elevation of circulating glucocorticoids (Mason, 1968a; Bassett *et al.*, 1973).

V. ANIMAL MODELS

A point at issue with animal models is the extent to which the experimental disease is similar to its human analogue. Each human disease has its own characteristic gross and histological morphology, pathogenesis, natural history, time of onset, and factors predisposing to its occurrence. The experimental model of the disease may have some features in common with the human situation and yet lack others. In most cases the degree of homology cannot be predicted, and it may be only after extensive investigation with the model that the degree of similarity becomes apparent. What can be made of these human and animal model similarities? Normally one cannot say emphatically that the data obtained from the animal model are pathogenetically the same as the disease state in humans. One can only notice the similarities and hope that by perhaps elucidating the pathogenesis of the animal model we can better understand the process in the human situation. The animal model is successful if it gives rise to potential research questions leading to further insight into the problem.* A single animal model may not provide all the answers. It may help us to understand certain aspects of the disease state, while casting no light on other aspects, or the disease state as a whole. This is particularly so for animal models concerned with the pathogenesis of emotionally induced ischaemic heart disease. In general, animal models in this area can be broadly divided into two different approaches. The first approach is associated with the involvement of mechanisms associated with the action of the catecholamines and glucocorticoids. These models have utilized exogenously administered catecholamines and glucocorticoids or catecholamines liberated by nerve stimulation. While these models have mainly involved the administration of the exogenous hormones *in vivo*, there are numerous *in vitro* studies which should be put into this class. The second approach is where an attempt has been made to produce a model which emulates exposure to an emotional stressor; that is, to duplicate the human condition. Both of these approaches have had their successes and failures, but both have made major contributions to our knowledge of how a psychosomatic situation can lead to a genuine pathological disease.

---

* This point is considered in detail by Bond in Chapter 1.

A. Models involving the use of exogenous hormones

Hypoxic changes in electrocardiography and necrotic foci similar to those seen in ischaemic heart disease can be produced by continuous elevation of the circulating catecholamine level, whether this is achieved by exogenous administration or following prolonged electrical stimulation of the sympathetic innervation to the heart (Raab and Gigee, 1955; Johansson and Vendsalu, 1957; Barger *et al.*, 1961; Greenhoot and Reichenbach, 1969; Moss and Schenk, 1970). The foci of such necroses appear to be regularly located in the subendocardium. The fact that there is a lowered creatine phosphate level in the inner portions of the myocardium suggests that there is a catecholamine-induced reduction in coronary blood flow to the endocardial surface (Boerth *et al.*, 1969). Such a reduction in blood flow could lead to myocardial hypoxia and cell death, thus explaining the necrotic foci. The implication of catecholamines in the aetiology of ischaemic heart disease is supported by clinical findings. Lown *et al.* (1979) reported that in humans, as well as in experimental animals, the administration of catecholamines would induce ventricular arrhythmia similar to that provoked by various psychological states. Plasma levels (Bertel *et al.*, 1978) and urinary excretion of noradrenaline and adrenaline are also found to be greatly elevated in cases of myocardial infarction (Jewitt *et al.*, 1969), and there is a striking correlation between the secretion of medullary adrenaline and cardiac arrhythmias after an infarction (Ceremuzynski *et al.*, 1969). Animal models using exogenous catecholamines have, therefore, provided considerable evidence linking an emotionally induced neurohormonal mechanism, involving catecholamine discharge, and myocardial hypoxia and necrosis.

What then is the role of the glucocorticoids (Fig. 5.5)? There is now considerable evidence from studies involving exogenously administered corticosteroids which shows a marked intensification of the cardiotoxic overproduction of catecholamines by a glucocorticoid–catecholamine interaction. There is a marked increase in the extent of myocardial destruction induced by psychological stressors or exogenously administered catecholamines when these factors are combined with exogenously administered glucocorticoids (Raab, 1966; Nahas *et al.*, 1958; Raab and Bajusz, 1965). Daily injections of glucocorticoids to mice or rats have been shown to produce myocardial necrosis with leucocyte invasion in the absence of other controlled stress factors (Clark *et al.*, 1968; Ashburn *et al.*, 1962; Górny, 1968). As with the catecholamines, the involvement of the glucocorticoids in cardiopathogenesis is supported by numerous clinical findings. There is a frequent occurrence of sudden cardiac attack during early morning when the glucocorticoid level is rising due to diurnal rhythm and rapid eye

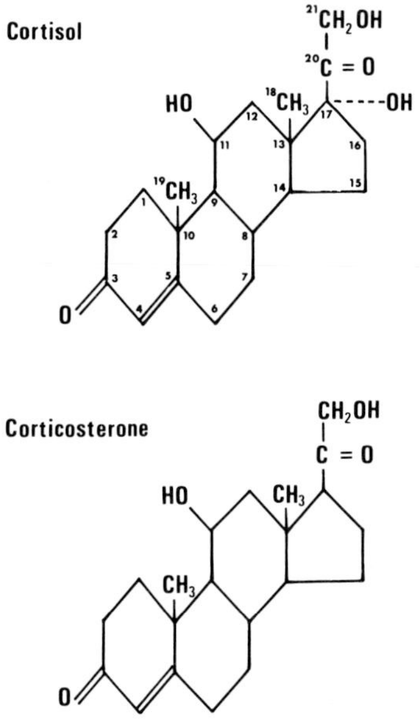

Cortisol

$^{21}CH_2OH$

$^{20}C = 0$

HO $^{18}CH_3$ $_{17}$ -----OH

$^{19}CH_3$

Corticosterone

CH_2OH

$C = 0$

HO CH_3

CH_3

Fig. 5.5: The glucocorticoids. The cortisol molecule shows the standard numbering of the carbon atoms. Both cortisol and corticosterone are C21 steroids. Cortisol is a 11,17-hydroxy-steroid where corticosterone is an 11-hydroxysteroid.

movement (REM) associated dreams are accompanied by adrenergic cardiac manifestations. Concomitant with high endogenous steroid levels due to the diurnal rhythm, the half-life of the steroids is longer as there appears to be a relationship between the activity of the pituitary–adrenal axis and the activity of metabolizing enzymes in the liver (Marc and Morselli, 1969). Plasma corticosteroid levels are found to be elevated in acute myocardial infarction, the degree of elevation correlating well with the gravity of the prognosis (Nitter Nauge et al., 1972; Wiener, 1977).

The use of animal models has also given some insight into the nature of the catecholamine–glucocorticoid interaction. While the glucocorticoids themselves do not appear to exert a positive inotropic or chronotropic effect on the myocardium, they do potentiate many of the effects of the sympathomimetic amines on the cardiovascular system (Ramey and Goldstein, 1957). The potentiating effects are variable, however; the glucocorticoids potentiate the action of adrenaline in some vascular beds, but do not potentiate noradrenaline or sympathetic nerve stimulation (Kadowitz and Yard, 1970, 1971; Yard and Kadowitz, 1972). Conversely, in vitro studies using isolated aortic strips show that cortisol will potentiate the response to both adrenaline and noradrenaline (Kalsner, 1969).

Animal models involving the use of exogenously administered hormones have provided strong evidence implicating the involvement of the catecholamines, and, more particularly, a catecholamine–glucocorticoid interaction, as an essential factor in stress related cardiovascular disease. However, despite considerable investigation, no clear picture has emerged from these models regarding the exact nature of the catecholamine–glucocorticoid interaction on the cardiovascular system.

The fact that the foci of experimentally induced necroses were isolated in the subendocardium and this region showed a lowered creatine phosphate level led to the hypothesis that the catecholamine–glucocorticoid interaction resulted in a reduction in coronary blood flow to the endocardial surface. Raab (1966) proposed that the hypoxic changes seen in situations of psychological stress are due to the inadequate compensatory dilatability of the coronary arteries supplying the myocardium, particularly the left ventricle. Discharge of catecholamines during stress, which may be potentiated by a concomitant release of glucocorticoids, would produce an increased workload on the heart and thus an increased oxygen consumption by the myocardium. If the dilatation of the coronary arteries by the catecholamines is insufficient to provide the oxygen requirements of the excited heart, ventricular anoxia will be produced and areas of myocardial ischaemia will develop.

B. Animal models of psychological stress

Animal models which have attempted to duplicate the human psychological stress situation, and thus allow investigation of its link with degenerative disease states, have been faced with two basic problems. First, it has proved difficult to quantify the stressor. In many cases assessment of the aversiveness of a situation on the grounds of behavioural parameters does not agree with an assessment based on physiological variables. For example, behavioural studies of signalled and unsignalled shock typically find that signalled shock is consistently preferred. A common feature of the behavioural explanations for signal-shock preference is that signalling reduces the aversiveness of the subsequent shock (Berlyne, 1960; Seligman, 1968; Perkins et al., 1966). By contrast physiological studies of signalled and unsignalled shock have typically found that variables which are generally regarded as indices of aversiveness, namely, adrenal hypertrophy, weight loss and plasma corticosterone elevation, are greater with signalled shock (Bassett et al., 1973). However, while it has been difficult to reconcile the differences between the behavioural and physiological findings, it must be realized that many physiological variables are not only indices of aversiveness but are also associated with the organism's physiological preparedness to respond to the stressor. In the case of the signal-shock situation, the animal may not choose the signalled shock on the basis of reduced aversiveness, as postulated in the behavioural explanations. An effective signal may initiate physiological responses, such as elevation of the plasma levels of catecholamines and glucocorticoids, which best prepare the organism to cope with the threatened physical stressor. The signal-shock "choice" can thus be explained on the basis that the animal in that situation is optimally prepared physiologically to respond to the physical stressor. In their study of the psychological factors involved in corticosterone response, Bassett *et al.* (1973) found that variation in the intensity and duration of the physical stressor was not accompanied by corresponding variation in plasma corticosterone elevation. However, by varying factors such as novelty and unpredictability of the stressor the plasma level of corticosterone could be elevated reliably to predictable levels. It was postulated that it was the psychological component of the stressor which was mainly concerned with the elevation in plasma glucocorticoids, and that increments in the level of the psychological stressor would be mirrored in corticosterone output.

The second problem facing animal models of psychological stress is that not all models result in the initiation of the same disease process, even though they all result in an activation of the sympathetic–adrenal medullary and pituitary–adrenal cortical axes. For example Weiss (1971a,b,c) could induce gross gastric ulceration using a model consisting of electrical shock and restraint in rats. However, even though plasma levels of catecholamines and glucocorticoids were elevated, Weiss never found any indication of changes associated with ischaemic heart disease. On the other hand Bassett and Cairncross (1975, 1977), subjecting rats to unpredictable, signalled footshock from which the animal could escape, observed gross morphological changes in the coronary vascular system. These changes included congestion and dilatation of components of the venous system, lipid deposition in the arteriole walls, platelet adhesion to the endothelial wall and aggregation, and the opening up of junctional gaps in the endothelial lining. Even under microscopic examination Bassett and Cairncross (1975, 1977) could not find any evidence of gastric ulceration in their stressed animals. Corley *et al.* (1973), investigating the influence of environmental stress on the myocardium of squirrel monkeys, used two forms of stressor. In one group animals were subjected to restraint stress alone. In the other group the animals were restrained and trained in Sidman avoidance of electrical tail shock. In this second group the stress procedure was very similar to that used by Weiss (1975a,b,c) to induce gastric ulceration in his rats. Corley *et al.* (1973) could observe no gastric lesions in any of their monkeys. However, the stressed monkey showed myocardial lesions ranging from necrosis, cellular infiltration and fibroblastic proliferation to acellular collagen formation. In the animals subjected to the avoidance procedure the lesions were more extensive than those seen in the animals subjected to restraint stress alone. It would appear that the physiological response to a stressor is not limited to the activation of just the two systems we have already discussed, it also involves other endocrine systems. Exposure to a stress procedure may elicit a multiplicity of hormonal response which, through their metabolic effects, are interdependent and may lead to disturbed physiological function. Mason (1974) presented evidence which suggests that specific endocrine profiles can be obtained for particular stressors. In most cases the hormones liberated in response to the various stressors are the same, but the magnitude of their response is different. Bassett *et al.* (1973) found that not only could the degree of glucocorticoid elevation in response to stress be quantified, but that the magnitude of the plasma steroid elevation is related to the types of stressor to which the animal is exposed. It appears, then, that this complex inter-relationship between the same hormones may determine the type of pathology seen in a particular animal model.

In the case of models involved in the study of stress induced ischaemic heart disease, a further problem has been that ischaemic heart disease appears to have two quite different aetiologies. It has been a widespread belief among clinicians and pathologists that lesions of the coronary vascular system (particularly the coronary arteries) were a necessary prerequisite for degenerative disease states of the myocardium. This idea still persists. However, there are now numerous clinical and experimental studies to suggest that myocardial ischaemia, necrosis and infarction can occur with or without a major contribution from coronary occlusion. Psychological stress can be involved as a major contributing factor in both situations. Henry (1975) proposed that sustained arousal of neuroendocrine response patterns may produce both an acute and a chronic disturbance in cardiovascular function. The acute disturbance may result in sudden death, normally associated with primary arrhythmia, whereas the chronic disturbance is associated with arteriosclerotic lesions in coronary arteries. Elliot *et al.* (1977), in a study of aerospace workers at Cape Kennedy (a work situation associated with excessive occupational stress), showed that the population exhibited a higher than normal incidence of sudden cardiac death and acute myocardial infarction. In this study, myocardial necrosis was much more frequently demonstrated than was acute coronary obstruction of any type. Regan *et al.* (1975) reported a high incidence of toxic cardiomyopathy in acute myocardial infarction where there was no significant coronary artery obstruction. Again, the study of Topolianski *et al.* (1978) also found normal coronary arteries in a high proportion of patients with ischaemic heart disease. While the major proportion of patients suffering acute myocardial infarction would be expected to show obstructive disease (Roberts, 1972), the exclusive role of such obstructive disease must be questioned.

Most of the animal models which have attempted to simulate the effect of psychological stress on the myocardium have seen the formation of lesions of the myocardium without any apparent effect on the coronary vessels. Corley *et al.* (1973), who subjected their monkeys to restraint stress and restraint stress plus tail shock, observed that the coronary arteries in both cases were patent with no obstructive lesions. Necroses and scars in the heart muscle in the absence of vascular lesions have been observed in baboons as the result of mixed sensory and emotional stresses (Raab *et al.*, 1964).

In the animal models, the failure to observe any discernible lesions in the coronary vascular system may relate to the period of exposure. Myocardial damage without any vascular change has been reported for most psychological stressors, and in most animal species examined after less than seven days exposure. Bassett and Cairncross (1976) found that exposing rats to a stressor associated with a large psychological component and extreme corticosterone response resulted in an enhanced sensitivity of the myocardium to the catecholamines. Enhanced sensitivity to noradrenaline and adrenaline was observed immediately following an initial exposure to the stressor and persisted unchanged in animals stressed daily over a 28-day period. The enhanced sensitivity was dependent upon the plasma levels of glucocorticoids, only being observed when there was an extreme elevation of the steroid. No enhanced sensitivity was observed in animals where exposure to the stressor induced only a moderate steroid elevation. However, while the level of circulating glucocorticoids tended to return to normal values within 3 h of completion of the stress period, the enhanced sensitivity persisted for at least 24 h. Such a persistent change in sensitivity suggests that only one glucocorticoid surge in a 24 h period is sufficient to maintain the heart in a state of constant enhanced sensitivity. If these findings are looked at in the light of the hypothesis of Raab (1966) then an explanation can be offered for a possible first phase to the stress induced pathology of ischaemic heart disease. Raab postulated that, in psychological stress, there is an inadequate compensatory dilation of the coronary arteries to match the increased workload on the heart, thus leading to myocardial ischaemia. Where high circulating levels of glucocorticoids were involved, this would be exacerbated. The enhanced myocardial sensitivity to the catecholamines induced by high circulating levels of the glucocorticoids would result in an even greater workload on the heart and compound the already inadequate coronary blood flow. This first phase of the stress induced myocardial ischaemia, then, would depend upon high circulating levels of the glucocorticoids, and not be associated with any coronary occlusion.

Bassett and Cairncross (1976) found that, if they continued to expose their animals to the same stressor that was associated with the enhanced myocardial sensitivity, for periods in excess of 20 days, then changes to the coronary vasculature occurred. There was an opening up of endothelial junctions and an accumulation of lipid material in the arterial wall. There was a distension of the venules and constriction of the veins, as well as adhesion of platelets to the endothelial lining and platelet aggregation (Bassett and Cairncross, 1976, 1977). Such inflammatory responses would result in a reduction in coronary blood flow due to coronary obstruction. However, the high circulatory levels of the glucocorticoids induced by the stressor should have inhibited these inflammatory reactions, and they should not be manifest until adaptation to the steroid response has occurred. Bassett and Cairncross (1977) were able to show a close correlation between the adaptation of the steroid response to stress and the onset of a progressive degeneration of the coronary vascular system. It would appear that there is a second phase in the stress induced aetiology of ischaemic heart disease. This second phase involves an inflammatory response resulting in coronary occlusion and occurs only after the steroid response to stress has adapted.

VI. DANGERS IN THE USE OF ANIMAL MODELS

As already mentioned, a point justifiably at issue with the use of animal models is the extent to which the model is similar to its human analogue. While it is not essential that the experimental model disease should have all features in common with its human counterpart, it is important that at least the features being studied should be similar in both cases. As we have seen, the investigation of psychosomatic diseases in humans has profited enormously from the availability of experimental models of these diseases in animals. However, in the search for animal models suitable for the study of the human disease, the similarities must be closely examined. It is often easy to induce a particular state in an animal that, on the surface, is very similar to the human state under investigation, but the two situations may not be the same. Studies involving vascular permeability are examples of this. The rabbit has an exceedingly permeable vascular system resulting from the presence of endothelial gaps. While at first sight the choice of the rabbit in studies involving vascular permeability may be a good one, in actual fact the choice is a poor one. In the human situation the passage of materials across the endothelial lining occurs via vesicular transport and not by passage through endothelial gaps. The basic systems are different in the two species. Studies of the effect of emotional stress on reproductive function have often used the rat as an animal model; however, the oestrous cycle of the rat is quite different from the menstrual cycle of humans. The hormone profiles and triggers are completely different. Again, studies of the function of the pineal gland in seasonal breeding animals may have little relevance to humans, which are not seasonal breeders. When choosing an animal model, one must ensure that the basic morphology and physiology of the model is similar (if not the same) to what we are modelling it against. Choosing a model on the basis that it can produce similar symptoms to that seen in the disease state under investigation, or that it is easy to work with, can lead to conflicting results. Such studies only hamper the search for an understanding of the aetiology of emotionally induced degenerative disease states.

VII. CONCLUSION

The animal model of Bassett and Cairncross (1976, 1977) bears a close similarity to the human clinical situation and allows a better understanding of the stress induced disease state. With the use of such models it is possible now to see that the aetiology of the disease state consists of two phases, one leading to the other. Data which were difficult to explain or apparently conflicting previously can now be understood. For example, animal models have allowed an understanding of how psychological stress can induce a myocardial ischaemia, in some cases with obvious coronary occlusion and in some cases without any apparent vascular lesions. It is now possible to explain why most animal models induced myocardial lesions without any coronary obstructions. Animal models have allowed our understanding of the human clinical state to progress further and more rapidly than would have been the case if our studies had been confined to the human situation alone.

REFERENCES

Ashburn, A.D., Lane Williams, W. and Arlander, T.R. Comparative actions of cortisone, adrenogens and vitamin B12 on body weight and incidence of disease in mice. *Anatomical Records*, 1962, 144: 1-17.

Barger, A.C., Herd, J.A. and Leibowitz, M.R. Chronic catheterization of coronary arteries: Induction of ECG pattern of myocardial ischemia by intracoronary epinephrine.

Proceedings of the Society for Experimental Biology and Medicine, 1961, 107: 474–477.

Bassett, J.R. and Cairncross, K.D. Morphological changes induced in rats following prolonged exposure to stress. *Pharmacology, Biochemistry and Behaviour*, 1975, 3: 411–420.

Bassett, J.R. and Cairncross, K.D. Myocardial sensitivity to catecholamines following exposure of rats to irregular, signalled footshock. *Pharmacology, Biochemistry and Behaviour*, 1976, 4: 27–33.

Bassett, J.R. and Cairncross, K.D. Changes in the coronary vascular system following prolonged exposure to stress. *Pharmacology, Biochemistry and Behaviour*, 1977, 6: 311–318.

Bassett, J.R., Cairncross, K.D. and King, M.G. Parameters of novelty, shock predictability and response contingency in corticosterone release in the rat. *Physiology and Behaviour*, 1973, 10: 901–907.

Bertel, O., Bluhler, F.R., Steiner, A., Baitsch, G., Ritz, R. and Burkart, F. Severely increased plasma catecholamine values in myocardial infarct with ventricular fibrillation: Doubling during intensive care monitoring. *Schweizerische Medizinische Wochenschrift*, 1978, 108: 1729–1731.

Berlyne, D.E. *Conflict, Arousal and Curiosity.* New York: McGraw-Hill, 1960.

Boerth, R.C., Covell, J.W., Seagren, S.G. and Pool, P.E. High energy phosphate concentrations in dog myocardium during stress. *American Journal of Physiology*, 1969, 216: 1103–1106.

Bogdonoff, M.D., Estes, E.H., Harlan, W.R., Trout, D.L. and Kirshner, N. Metabolic and cardiovascular changes during a state of acute central nervous system arousal. *Journal of Clinical Endocrinology*, 1960, 20: 1333–1340.

Brod, J., Fencl, V., Hejl, Z. and Zirka, J. Circulatory changes underlying blood pressure elevation during acute emotional stress (mental arithmetic) in normotensive and hypertensive subjects. *Clinical Science*, 1959, 18: 270–281.

Cannon, W.B. *Bodily Changes in Pain, Hunger, Fear and Rage.* New York: Appleton-Century, 1920.

Ceremuzynski, L., Staszewska, Barczak, J. and Cedro, K. 1969, [Cardiac rhythm disturbances and the release of catecholamines following acute coronary occlusion in dogs. *Cardiovascular Research*] (in Russian) cited in J.R. Vane, 1969. The release and fate of vasocative hormones in the circulation. *British Journal of Pharmacology*, 35: 209–242.

Clarke, T.B., Ashburn, A.D. and Lane Williams, W. Cortisone induced hypertension and cardiovascular lesions in mice. *American Journal of Anatomy*, 1968, 123:429–440.

Corley, K.C., Shiel, F.O'M., Mauck, H.P. and Greenhoot, J. Electrocardiographic and cardiac morphological changes associated with environmental stress in squirrel monkeys. *Psychosomatic Medicine*, 1973, 35: 361–364.

Eliot, R.S., Clayton, F.C., Pieper, G.M. and Todd, G.L. Influence of environmental stress on pathogenesis of sudden cardiac death. *Federation Proceedings*, 1977, 36: 1719–1724.

Elmadjian, F., Hope, J.M. and Lamson, E.T. Excretion of epinephrine and norepinephrine under stress. *Recent Progress in Hormone Research*, 1958, 14: 513–553.

Feuerstein, G. and Gutman, Y. Preferential secretion of adrenaline and noradrenaline by the cat adrenal *in vivo* in response to different stimuli. *British Journal of Pharmacology*, 1971, 43: 764–775.

Ganong, W.F. *Review of Medical Physiology.* Los Altos: Lange, 1971.

Górny, D. Changes in the content of adrenaline and noradrenaline in the brain, heart and suprarenal gland of rats with necrotic inflammatory lesions of the myocardium and other diseases induced by the administration of sodium phosphate, hydrocortisone and desoxycorticosterone. *Acta Physiologica Polonica*, 1968, 19: 835–842.

Greenhoot, J.H. and Reichenbach, D.D. Cardiac injury and subarchnoid hemmorrhage: A clinical, pathological and physiological correlation. *Journal of Neurosurgery*, 1969, 30: 521–528.

Henry, J.P. The induction of acute and chronic cardiovascular disease in animals by psychosocial stimulation. *International Journal of Psychiatry in Medicine*, 1975, 6: 147–158.

Hickam, J.B., Cargill, W.H. and Golden, A. Cardiovascular reactions to emotional stimuli: Effect on the cardiac output, arteriovenous oxygen difference, arterial pressure and peripheral resistance. *Journal of Clinical Investigation*, 1948, 27: 290-298.

Jenkins, C.D. Psychologic and social precursors of coronary disease. *New England Journal of Medicine*, 1971, 284: 307-317.

Jewitt, D.E., Mercer, C.J., Reid, D., Valori, C., Thomas, M. and Shillingford, J.P. Free noradrenaline and adrenaline excretion in relation to the development of cardiac arrhythmias and heart-failures in patients with acute myocardial infarction. *Lancet*, 1969, 3: 635-641.

Johansson, B. and Vendsalu, A. The influence of adrenaline, noradrenaline and acetylcholine on the electrocardiogram of the isolated perfused guinea-pig heart. *Acta Physiologica Scandinavica*, 1957, 39: 356-369.

Kadowitz, P.J. and Yard, A.C. Circulatory effects of hydrocortisone and protection against endotoxic shock in cats. *European Journal of Pharmacology*, 1970, 9: 311-318.

Kadowitz, P.J. and Yard, A.C. Influence of hydrocortisone on cardiovascular responses to epinephrine. European Journal of Pharmacology, 1971, 13: 281-286.

Kalsner, S. Mechanism of hydrocortisone potentiation of responses to epinephrine and norepinephrine in rabbit aorta. *Circulation Research*, 1969, 24: 383-396.

Kannel, W.B. *The natural history of myocardial infarction: The Framingham study.* Leiden: Leiden University Press, 1973.

Lown, B., Verrier, R.L. and Rabinowitz, S.H. Neural and psychologic mechanisms and the problem of sudden cardiac death. *American Journal of Cardiology*, 1977, 39: 890-902.

Magendantz, H. and Shortsleeve, J. Electro-cardiographic abnormalities in patients exhibiting anxiety. *American Heart Journal*, 1951, 42: 849-857.

Marc, V. and Morselli, P.L. Metabolism of exogenous cortisol in the rat in various experimental conditions. *Journal of Pharmacy and Pharmacology*, 1969, 21: 864-866.

Mason, J.W. A review of psychoendocrine research on the pituitary adrenal cortical system. *Psychosomatic Medicine*, 1968a, 30: 576-607.

Mason, J.W. A review of psychoendrocine research on the sympathetic adrenal medullary system. *Psychosomatic Medicine*, 1968b, 30: 631-653.

Mason, J.W. Specificity in the organization of neuroendrocrine response profiles. In P. Seeman and G.M. Brown (Eds.), *Frontiers in Neurology and Neuroscience Research*, Toronto: University of Toronto Press, 1974: 68-80.

Minc, S. Emotions and ischemic heart disease. *American Heart Journal*, 1967, 73: 713-716.

Moss, A.J. and Schenk, E.A. Cardiovascular effects of sustained norepinephrine infusion in dogs. Previous treatment with adrenergic blocking agents. *Circulation Research*, 1970, 27: 1013-1022.

Myers, A. and Dewar, H.A. Circumstances attending 100 sudden deaths from coronary artery disease with coroner's necropsies. *British Heart Journal*, 1975, 37: 1133-1143.

Nahas, G.G., Brunson, J.G., King, W.M. and Cavert, H.M. Functional and morphologic changes in heart-lung preparations following administration of adrenal hormones. *American Journal of Pathology*, 1958, 34: 717-725.

Nitter Hauge, S., Kirkeby, K., Alvsaker, J.O. and Aakvaag, A. Plasma 11-hydro-corticosteroids in acute myocardial infarction. *Acta Medica Scandinavica*, 1972, 192: 533-538.

Perkins, C.C., Seymann, R.G., Levis, D.J. and Spencer, H.R. Factors affecting preference for signal-shock over shock-signal. *Journal of Experimental Psychology*, 1966, 72: 190-196.

Peron, F.G. The isolation and identification of some adrenocorticosteroids released by rat adrenal tissue incubated *in vitro. Endocrinology*, 1960, 66: 458-469.

Raab, W. Emotional and sensory stress factors in myocardial pathology: Neurogenic and hormonal mechanisms in pathogenesis, therapy and prevention. *American Heart Journal*, 1966, 72: 538-564.

Raab, W. Correlated cardiovascular adrenergic and adrenocortical responses to sensory and mental annoyances in man: A potential accessory cardiac risk factor. *Psychosomatic Medicine*, 1968, 30: 809-818.

Raab, W. and Bajusz, E. Epinephrine induced early, prenecrotic derangements of myocardial potassium, glycogen and phosphorylase. *Circulation*, 1965, 32: 174–178.

Raab, W., Chaplin, J.P. and Bajusz, E. Myocardial necroses produced in domesticated rats and in wild rats by sensory and emotional stresses. *Proceedings of the Society for Experimental Biology and Medicine*, 1964, 116: 665–669.

Raab, W. and Gigee, W. Specific avidity of the heart muscle to absorb and store epinephrine and norepinephrine. *Circulation*, 1955, 3: 553–558.

Ramey, E.R. and Goldstein, M.S. Adrenal cortex and sympathetic nervous system. *Physiological Review*, 1957, 37: 155–195.

Regan, T.J., Wu, C.F., Weisse, A.B., Moschos, C.B., Ahmed, S.S., Lyons, M.M. and Haider, B. Acute myocardial infarction in toxic cardiomyopathy without coronary obstruction. *Circulation*, 1975, 51: 453–461.

Roberts, W.C. Coronary arteries in fatal acute myocardial infarction. *Circulation*, 1972, 45: 215–230.

Russek, H.I. Emotional stress in the etiology of coronary heart disease. *Geriatrics*, 1967, 22: 84–89.

Schiffer, R., Hartley, L.H., Schulman, C.L. and Abelmann, W.H. The quiz electrocardiogram: A new diagnostic and research technique for evaluating the relation between emotional stress and ischaemic heart disease. *American Journal of Cardiology*, 1976, 37: 41–47.

Seligman, M.E.P. Chronic fear produced by unpredictable electric shock. *Journal of Comparative and Physiological Psychology*, 1968, 66: 402–411.

Sobel, H. Stress and emotions in problems bearing on experimental atherosclerosis. *Progress in Cardiovascular Disease*, 1962, 4: 500–525.

Topolianski, V.D., Alperovich, B.R. and Strukovskaia, M.V. Ischaemic heart disease in normal coronary vessels. *Kardiologiia*, 1978, 18: 140–149.

Troxler, R.G., Sprague, E.A., Albanese, R.A. Fuchs, R. and Thompson, A.J. The association of elevated plasma cortisol and early atherosclerosis as demonstrated by coronary angiography. *Atherosclerosis*, 1977, 26: 151–162.

Weiss, J.M. Effects of coping behaviour in different warning signal conditions on stress pathology in rats. *Journal of Comparative and Physiological Psychology*, 1971a, 77: 1–13.

Weiss, J.M. Effects of punishing the coping response (conflict) on stress pathology in rats. *Journal of Comparative and Physiological Psychology*, 1971b, 77: 14–21.

Weiss, J.M. Effects of coping behaviour with and without a feedback signal on stress pathology in rats. *Journal of Comparative and Physiological Psychology*, 1971c, 77: 23–30.

Weiner, K. Plasma cortisol, corticosterone and urea in acute myocardial infarction: Clinical and biochemical correlations. *Clinica Chemica Acta*, 1977, 76: 243–250.

Yard, A.C. and Kadowitz, P.J. Studies on the mechanism of hydrocortisone potentiation of vasoconstrictor responses to epinephrine in the anesthetized animal. *European Journal of Pharmacology*, 1972, 20: 1–9.

6
ANIMAL MODELS OF OBESITY

LEONARD H. STORLIEN

I. INTRODUCTION

The study of weight regulation in laboratory animals is multifaceted, embracing a range of disciplines from psychology and nutrition to physiology and endocrinology. Each has contributed significantly and, while integration of the various approaches has often been tortuous, a rational overall picture is now emerging. This contrasts markedly with the human work where even the most tenuous results are pounced upon by the popular press to bolster or refute the current *zeitgeist*. It is intended that this chapter be an overview of the laboratory animal literature, updating some of the critical issues and relating these to the emerging body of human work where, happily, the same issues are now receiving profitable attention.

In a number of respects the current study of obesity via animal models is a satisfying one. As will become clear over the course of this chapter, there are a number of excellent animal models whose aetiologies focus on either energy intake or expenditure. The genetic preparations provide excellent models for obesity predicated largely on reduced energy expenditure. On the other hand, increased intake has provided the focus of dietary models where the induction of obesity is by exposure to a varied, high-fat, sugar-rich series of foods. The initial exploring of the parameters of this model has laid to rest the myth that humans are gluttons and thus incapable of resisting the obesity-inducing blandishments of our modern society with its plethora of refined and palatable foods, and that sub-human animals are

ANIMAL MODELS IN PSYCHOPATHOLOGY
ISBN 0 12 114180 2

cool discriminators of nutrient offerings, not only maintaining a lean, healthy bodyline but a balanced macronutrient intake in the face of myriad challenges. Such is obviously not the case. A basic literature, long ignored, and the millions of pet owners throughout the world could have informed researchers that given access to the types of diets to which we humans are exposed animals sink (or rise) to impressive levels of gluttony and obesity. The appealing aspects of obesity research and the available models are: the research attacks a major health problem; the crucial findings of the animal literature are proving applicable to the human situation; and discoveries at the human level are proving amenable to animal research into their aetiology.

This chapter is an update on genetic, diet-induced, lesion-induced and natural rhythm animal models of obesity. The weight regulation equation to be borne in mind is energy intake = energy expenditure + energy stored. Both input and output will be examined but expenditure claims the limelight. Thus the following section will provide an overview of the nature of energy expenditure.

II. THERMOGENESIS

Energy expenditure can be compartmentalized as follows. First, basal metabolic rate refers to that energy consumed as a minimal requirement for the basic processes of life to proceed: for example, breathing, muscular contractions of the heart, endogenous production of glucose, etc. It is classically determined at thermoneutrality for the animal (that is, that temperature at which the heat loss to the environment exactly balances the heat generated by these basic processes). Second is exercise metabolic rate: that energy consumed as a result of physical activity. A subset of exercise metabolic rate is shivering thermogenesis, the rapid reflexive muscular contractions which generate heat in the face of a low temperature environment. In the normal homeotherm the generation of heat to maintain core temperature also involves non-shivering thermogenesis which is the generation of heat by methods other than muscular activity. Finally, and what is perhaps an extension of non-shivering thermogenesis, is the wastage of energy following a meal. Termed the "heat increment to a meal", it is the energy loss above basal level in the period following a meal and undoubtedly more than that necessary just for the actual ingestion, digestion and disposal of the incoming nutrients (Boyle *et al.*, 1981).

Increased basal metabolic rate and increased heat increment to a meal are the two components of the controversial concept of "luxuskonsumption" (the burning off of excess calories) which is so important in our present attempts to understand the aetiology of obesity. As stated, an animal can generate heat metabolically by two mechanisms; those of shivering and non-shivering thermogenesis. In the former, with which we are all familiar, the rapid muscular contractions of shivering require energy and the energy transformation is work into heat. In the latter phenomenon of non-shivering thermogenesis heat is generated, and hence energy used, by substrate cycles of metabolism (Jansky, 1973; Sellers *et al.*, 1954). A simplified substrate cycle can be schematized as follows:

Metabolite "A" can be made into metabolite "b" by the action of enzyme "a" and "B" can be made back into "A" by courtesy of enzyme "b". One or both of these reactions will require energy to proceed. The usage of that energy is reflected in the generation of heat. However, the net result of creating "A" from "B" and then recreating "A" again is, of course, nil.

A clever demonstration of the cellular basis of non-shivering thermo-genesis was made as a result of investigations into the flight muscles of the bumble bee (Newsholme *et al.*, 1972). The extremely high oscillation rate of bumble bee wings is achieved by the unique arrangement of the fibrillar muscles. Bumble bees in the cold are unable to fly unless the temperature of these critical flight muscles is high. In a typically academic abstracting of some truly exciting findings, we have the description of these substrate cycles in resting bumble bees in a cold environment from Newsholme *et al.* (1972): "It is proposed that both fructose diphosphatase and phospho-fructokinase are simultaneously active and catalyse a cycle between fructose 6-phosphate and fructose diphosphate in resting bumble-bee flight muscle. Such a cycle would produce continuous hydrolysis of adenosine triphos-phate (ATP), with the release of energy as heat, which would help to maintain the thoracic temperature during rest periods at a level adequate for 'flight'."

The particular enzymes and metabolites are not important; what is elegantly uncovered is the cellular basis of energy-consuming substrate cycles in the body whose sole purpose under particular circumstances would appear to be the generation of heat. It is easy to accept that the generation of heat is adaptive in situations where keeping certain tissues "on the back burner" is conducive to the survival of the organism. What is less clear is why substrate cycles might occur in situations where the heat generated is of no apparent advantage to the animal. Such a situation is the heat increment to a meal where energy in excess of need is wasted following ingestion of a meal. As we shall see later, this energy wastage may be of central importance in the aetiology of obesity.

While it is beyond the scope of this Chapter (and this author) to go into all the various reasons why non-shivering thermogenesis might exist unrelated to thermoregulation, one explanation that I favour is by Newsholme and coworkers (see Newsholme and Start, 1972). This argument, as I understand it, distills to the following. Let us go back to our basic substrate cycle of

$$A \underset{b}{\overset{a}{\rightleftarrows}} B.$$

Also let us suppose that the activities of enzymes "a" and "b" might range from 0 to 100 on some artibrary scale. In a system totally at rest, and thus not "wasting" energy, the activities of "a" and "b" would be zero. In a system just idling, as it were, the activities of "a" and "b" might be, for example, 10 each on our artibrary scale. Now a sudden stimulus for change to, for example, the production of metabolite "B" from "A" might be capable of a 10% alteration in enzymatic activity. In a system totally at rest this would result in the level of activity of enzyme "a" going from 0 to 10 with a resultant shift in flux through the system from zero to 10% capacity. However, with the system ticking over at an enzyme level of 10 for both enzymes "a" and "b" then a stimulus capable of changing enzymes by one-tenth of their range will be able not only to increase "a" from 10 to 20 but also to reduce "b" from 10 to 0. The flux through this system will thus change from zero to 20%, not zero to 10%, as in the zero activity system. This doubling of response capability in a given time has obvious survival value for the organism and makes the explanation of Newsholme and Start (1972) particularly attractive.

What is of concern here, and what is particularly controversial, is whether non-shivering thermogenesis plays a role, via the energy expenditure side of the equation, in body weight regulation. Inherent in this question is whether differences in heat wastage might account for carcass fat accumulation in obesity. It is a surprisingly complex question and clear answers have not appeared. What has been shown is the existence of a thermogenic defect in some genetically obese animals. It is the extrapolation to obesity of non-genetic origins that is less clear. The reader is referred to recent articles by Hervey and Robin (1983) and Rothwell and Stock (1983) for expositions of the divergent positions. The concept of non-shivering thermogenesis will reappear at intervals throughout this Chapter, as will its major site of generation, brown adipose tissue (see Nicholls, 1983, for a recent review).

If this Chapter stimulates your interest at all in the nature of metabolism then I highly recommend two books. Max Kleiber's *Fire of Life* is a classic and the second edition in 1975 makes it relatively modern. It is written with enviable grace and style. Newsholme and Start's *Regulation in Metabolism* (1973) is also a fine book and well worth the time.

III. GENETIC MODELS OF OBESITY

Of the animal models, the genetic and hypothalamic-lesion induced obesities are undoubtedly the most studied. The ob/ob obese mouse and the Zucker fa/fa "fatty" rat are the classic genetic models.

A. ob/ob Obese mouse

The ob/ob obese mouse, a mutation on the sixth chromosome, was described over 30 years ago (Ingalls *et al.*, 1950) and the "obese" gene has been transferred to, and maintained on, a number of mouse strains (Herberg and Coleman, 1977). The mutation is an autosomal recessive. The obese mice (homozygous "ob/ob") are generally infertile and procreation is confined to the mating of the (ob/+) heterozygote lean mice. This means, rather tediously, that the production of obese mice involves the identification of the heterozygote leans (which are, upon gross physical examination, undistinguishable from homozygous lean mice—designated +/+) by breeding. Even then heterozygous pairs will only produce, on average, one-quarter obese mice, one-quarter homozygous leans and one-half heterozygous leans.

This obese mutation is characterized by a series of metabolic abnormalities which synergize in the ultimate obesity. Hyperphagia and hyperinsulinaemia are central characteristics, being detectable by four weeks and persisting into late adulthood. The hyperinsulinaemia is associated with an increase in both the number and size of the insulin-secreting beta cells of the pancreas (Wrenshall *et al.*, 1955). There is a marked insulin resistance and loss of insulin receptors, a condition which can be mostly reversed by eliminating the hyperinsulinaemia (see Herberg and Coleman, 1977, for numerous references). Hyperglycaemia is also present in the "dynamic" phase of the animal's weight gain. The rate of lipogenesis is increased, both in liver and fat (Assimacopoulos-Jeannet *et al.*, 1974; Renold *et al.*, 1960), and precedes the hyperinsulinaemia (Joosten and van der Kroon, 1974). The accumulation of fat involves both increases in size and number of adipocytes (Johnson and Hirsch, 1972) and continues at the expense of lean tissue even when insulin levels and food intake are normalized (Alonso and Maren, 1955; Hollifield and Parson, 1958).

A major component of the ob/ob obese mouse syndrome is

undoubtedly a thermogenic defect. It is now 30 years since Davis and Mayer (1954) first reported that obese mice were unable to maintain their core temperature in a 3°C environment and died of hypothermia within a few hours. This is in contrast to their lean littermates who apparently had no difficulty in adjusting to such conditions by appropriately increasing heat production. Since then numerous studies have explored the nature of the deficit in the obese mouse. First of all the ob/ob mice can be separated from their lean littermates as early as day 18 following birth with over 90% success rate on the basis of their lower oxygen consumption at 25°C (Kaplan and Leveille, 1974). Indeed, as early as day 12, the ob/ob mice are retaining significantly more energy in their carcasses (Thurlby and Trayhurn, 1978) despite the fact that hyperphagia (Jeanrenaud, 1978) and hyperinsulinaemia (Dubuc, 1977) cannot be detected at that time. The presumption is that an initial thermogenic defect is primary to the hyper-adipositic condition of the obese mouse, and not secondary to either hyperphagia or hyperinsulinaemia.

Since then, numerous studies have explored the nature of the defect at a cellular level. Himms-Hagen and Desautels (1978) demonstrated a mitochondrial defect in brown adipose tissue of reduced binding of purine nucleotide and a failure in the ob/ob mice to respond to cold stress with an increase in purine binding. Knelans and Romsos (1982) also showed reduced noradrenaline turnover in brown adipose tissue. In skeletal muscle, the levels of sodium, potassium and ATPase are decreased in the obese mice (Lin *et al.*, 1978). These findings combine to provide a cellular basis for the gross behavioural observation of reduced thermogenic capacity in the ob/ob mouse.

Finally, Kaplan and Leveille (1974) made an interesting observation which, to my knowledge, has not been pursued. As previously discussed, these investigators were able to distinguish with high reliability prior to weaning ob/ob mice from +/? mice on the basis of the low oxygen consumption of the former, being generally less than 2 mL h^{-1} g^{-1} as against greater than 3 mL h^{-1} g^{-1} for the +/? mice. The observation which, if substantiated, would prove of immense interest is that the heterozygous +/ob lean (determined on the basis of breeding) mice had, in general, preweaning oxygen consumptions intermediate to ob/ob and +/+ mice. There is other evidence hat +/+ and ob/+ mice can be distinguished metabolically. Joosten and van der Kroon (1974) presented data suggestive of a difference between ob/+ and +/+ in fat cell diameter, in 13 day old mice. The most convincing demonstraton, however, probably comes from Yen *et al.* (1968). These workers took adipose tissue from three and five month old +/? mice and performed an *in vitro* glucose oxidation test. This involves incubating fat cells with C^{14}-labelled glucose and assaying for labelled carbon dioxide after, in their case, 90 minutes. The radioactivity in the carbon dioxide comes from the labelled glucose and gives a measure of the rate of metabolism of that glucose. Very clear, highly significant differences appeared between all three groups, the ob/ob, ob/+ and +/+ with, in fact, the ob/+ being closer to the ob/ob animals in glucose oxidation than to the +/+.

These are all very important findings. They suggest that we have a group of mice genetically predisposed to obesity, but without the grossly different characteristics of hyperinsulinaemia and insulin resistence that distinguishes the ob/ob from +/?. I am not aware of any studies which have attempted to exploit the +/+ as against the +/? difference by, for example, exposing the heterozygous and homozygous lean mice to high fat or "cafeteria" style diets (see the following section on dietary-induced obesity).

B. Zucker fa/fa "fatty" rat

The Zucker fa/fa "fatty" rat was first reported as a spontaneous genetic abnormality by Zucker and Zucker (1961) in their colony of Wistar rats. The obesity occurred along predictable Mendelian genetic lines associated with a single recessive gene. Unfortunately, as with the ob/ob mouse, the homozygous (fa/fa) "fatties" are generally infertile and breeding is usually by mating of fertile lean (fa/Fa) heterozygotes. However, it is possible to induce fertility in young "fatty" males by a combination of testosterone injections and food restriction. The basic elements of the Zucker "fatty" syndrome have been well characterized and the reader is referred to comprehensive reviews by Bray (1977) and Coleman (1978). Briefly, the "fatty" rat is similar in most respects to the ob/ob mouse with hyperphagia (Stern and Johnson, 1977), hyperinsulinaemia (Lemmonier, 1971), hypertriglyceridaemia (Barry and Bray, 1969) and insulin resistance (Zucker and Antoniades, 1972). Again, the beta cells are increased both in size and number (York et al., 1972) as are adipocytes (Johnson et al., 1971). A dipocyte proliferation continues into adulthood. Unlike the ob/ob mouse, the Zucker "fatties" do not appear to be hyperglycaemic at any time in their lives.

Interestingly, accumulation of fat can be demonstrated well before hyperinsulinaemia appears (Zucker and Antoniades, 1972) and the adult "fatty" is characterized by gross accumulation of fat with reduced lean tissue and some stunting. These characteristics, along with the hyper-insulinaemia and hypogonadism, should be kept in mind and compared to the effects of lesions in the area of the ventromedial hypothalamus (Section

V). Even when insulin levels are controlled (Chan *et al.*, 1982), or food intake restricted to lean control levels (Cleary *et al.*, 1980), the "fatty" rat lays down fat at the expense of lean tissue, suggesting a basic metabolic alteration, independent of insulin, in the partitioning of nutrient supply.

In common with the ob/ob mouse, Zucker "fatties" have been reported to show thermogenic deficits. However, where that defect is clear in the ob/ob mouse, much controversy surrounds the issue in the Zucker. The extremes are represented by two studies. Trayhurn *et al.* (1976) reported a profound thermogenic defect in their Zucker "fatties" leading to death within 10 hours in a 4°C environment. In contrast, Armitage *et al.* (1980) were able to demonstrate no defect whatsoever and their "fatties" coped perfectly well over a number of days at 4°C, increasing their metabolic rate appropriately (presumably first by shivering and then by increasing non-shivering thermogenesis).

We have invesitgated the Zucker "fatty" in the cold room with the thought of supporting one of these disparate positions. Unfortunately (and possibly why a definite article has not yet appeared on the issue), our results fall between the two extremes. Most Zucker rats, both fat and lean, cope perfectly with a 4°C environment, maintaining a normal core temperature over long periods of time. A few "fatties" and a lesser proportion of leans are incapable of such homeostasis in their core temperatures drop precipitously within a few hours of cold exposure. Interestingly, all animals cope well with a second exposure to cold a few days later. Thus if there is any thermogenic deficit, as certainly suggested by investigations at the cellular level (see Levin *et al.*, 1982), it would appear to be in the ability to rapidly induce brown adipose tissue thermogenesis. Certainly the capability is there. It would just seem to need turning on. Doi and Kuroshima (1979) demonstrated a longlasting effect of early cold exposure on thermogenic capability and one would expect that colony conditions in early life (that is, ambient temperature and the tightness of its control) could markedly affect the results of any test of thermogenic capability.

This suggestion and our results are very much in line with the recent report of Bertin *et al.* (1983) who found that Zucker "fatties" acclimatized to a 10°C coped perfectly with exposure to 0°C over a 10-hour period. Both leans and fatties increased their metabolic rates, and to a similar extent, and both maintained core temperatures. There is also a further interesting facet of their data. As previously noted, both ob/ob mice and fa/fa rates characteristically display lower core temperatures than their lean littermates at normal ambient colony temperatures (approximately 22°C). Bertin *et al.* (1983) found that this difference disappears when both lean and fat Zucker rats are maintained at 10°C. Also, their basic metabolic rates (expressed as $J\ m^{-2}\ h^{-1}$) were identical at this temperature.

IV. DIETARY-INDUCED OBESITY

What has been surprising in many respects is the huge amount of work done on the obviously flawed models of obesity, such as the genetic and ventromedial hypothalamic lesion preparations (see next section), in comparison with the only recently revived interest in dietary-induced obesity, which was first described over 30 years ago. In the early studies, the manipulation was primarily an increase in the proportion of fat. The modern revival of dietary-induced obesity has implicitly, in the usage of "cafeteria" or "supermarket" style diets, manipulated energy density, macronutrient proportions and palatability (see Faust *et al.*, 1978; Orcai, 1982; Rolls *et al.*, 1980; Sclafani and Springer, 1976). In these experiments the animals (usually rats) are offered varied and presumably palatable foods and allowed to choose freely among the offerings. The individual foods range from things like chocolate-chip cookies to corn chips to salami. However, the central characteristics of the foods are that they are high in fat and simple sugars. These would appear to be the prime culprits in the obesity-generating effects of these foods in accordance with the following analysis of the original studies which manipulated a single macronutrient.

Many of the basic parameters of obesity generated by exposure to varied diets were elucidated in the 1940s and early 1950s. Essentially the studies most relevant to the present discussion increased the fat content in the diets of a number of strains of rats and mice (see Fenton and Dowling, 1953; Forbes *et al.*, 1946a,b; Mickelsen *et al.*, 1955; Schemmel *et al.*, 1970). In the large proportion of these studies, fat made up some 60% by weight of the diet at the expense of carbohydrate, protein being maintained at between 20% and 25%. Fat, of course, also has a higher energy concentration than either carbohydrate or protein. Metabolizable energy is usually assessed as 38 kJ g^{-1} of fat and 17 kJ g^{-1} of both carbohydrate and protein. This means that in these high fat diets over 80% of energy was being derived from fat, a very high proportion indeed.

However, the results of these studies are still interesting. First, excess weight gain was consistently observed over a number of strains of mice and rats and in both sexes. A very complete later study by Schemmel *et al.* (1970) illustrates this point nicely. Seven strains of rats of both sexes were fed with either a "grain" (23.4% protein, 3% fat, 53.5% carbohydrate) or "high fat" (24.5% protein, 60% fat, 7.5% carbohydrate; 81% of the energy as fat) diet for 20 weeks after weaning. Compared to the "grain" fed groups, all of the male and six of the seven female groups gained significantly more weight on the "high fat" diet. However, the diversity of gains is striking, ranging from an excess of only four and 12% in female and male S5B/f1 rats to 50 and 56% respectively for Osborne-Mendel rats. Interestingly, the S5B/fl rats were the result of a cross between Sprague-Dawley and NIH Black rats, both of which are susceptible to high fat diets.

Further, the variability in weight gain induced in some strains by exposure to the high fat diet is also striking. Take, for example, the male Wistar-Lewis and Hoppert groups. At weaning the standard error of the mean was 3.4 g and 1.8 g respectively and 12.9 g and 12.1 g after 20 weeks on the "grain" ration. Twenty weeks exposure of the Wistar-Lewis males to a high fat diet resulted in a 42% excess weight gain but actually a slight reduction in variability (from 12.1 go to 8.0 g). However, the same diet in Hoppert males resulted in a lesser excess weight gain (25%) but a massive increase in variability (from 12.9 g to 68.3 g). Thus there is the genetic basis for wide variability, both between and within strains, in the susceptibility of rats to the obesity-inducing blandishments of high fat diets and the Hoppert rat might be a particularly interesting one for further study. It should also be pointed out that a large proportion of the excess weight gain of the rats on high fat diets appeared as carcass fat. Thus they are obese, not just larger; an important distinction.

The effects of simple sugars in a diet are less easy to demonstrate than those of fat. This is not surprising as the rat's normal diet is very high in carbohydrate. To further increase the proportion of carbohydrate at the expense of fat and protein one runs the risk of creating a diet deficient in essential amino or fatty acids. However, increased weight gain has been demonstrated in situations where carbohydrate is provided separately as an extra fluid source, usually as a sucrose or glucose solution of up to 32% (weight/volume). In these experiments (Castonquay et al., 1981; Kanarek and Hirsch, 1977), the experimental animals consume large amounts of the sugar solutions while reducing the intake of their normal chow diet, but not sufficiently to fully compensate for the extra carbohydrate energy. The extra intake is slowly translated into extra body weight gain.

A subset of the above experiments has compared access to a simple sugar, such as sucrose, with access to complex carbohydrate as some form of starch. This has been done essentially in two ways. Hallfrisch et al. (1981) fed a high fat diet containing either 30% sucrose or 30% starch as the carbohydrate while Hill et al. (1980) provided chow and separate access to either 32% sucrose or destrinized starch. In both of these studies the rats with access to sucrose gained significantly more weight than those with access to starch, despite the fact that they consumed the same number of total kilojoules and the same proportions of macronutrients (Hill et al., 1980). Additionally, Hallfrisch et al. (1981) demonstrated increased fat deposition, increased insulin levels and insulin resistance in their sucrose-fed group. These latter are all warning signals for the adult-onset type of diabetes mellitus. In fact the diabetogenic action of simple sugars has recently been directly demonstrated in the spontaneously diabetic (db/db) mouse (Leiter *et al.*, 1983).

An interesting and potentially important aspect of carbohydrate intake is the demonstration of an apparent synergism of sucrose (as the commonly explored simple sugar) and saccharin. It has been known for many years that giving rats access to a fluid source containing small amounts of sucrose and saccharin induces polydipsia. For example, Valenstein *et al.* (1967) reported that a solution containing 0.125% saccharin and 3.0% sucrose increased fluid intake tenfold, the total daily fluid intake being at times equal to the animal's body weight. In experiments where up to 32% sucrose has been applied as a nutrient source in addition to lab chow, the increase in energy intake has reflected the failure to entirely compensate for the sugar solution intake. In these experiments, carbohydrate finally makes up some 65% of the energy ingested (Castonquay *et al.*, 1981).

Interestingly, we have recently applied the synergism apparent at low levels of sucrose and saccharin to much higher proportions of sucrose. Animals exposed to "lab chow", 24% sucrose and 0.6% saccharin overeat by 32%, gain weight and consume close to 90% of their energy as carbohydrate, reducing fat and protein intake to what must be barely minimal levels. These results focus on palatability as a major determinant of intake.

The effect of high fat and simple sugar diets on young animals is not completely clear. With high fat diets, a significant increase in body weight and accumulation of fat is seen in rats as early as five weeks after weaning (see Schemmel *et al.*, 1972). However, over the same period access to a sucrose solution has only a minimal effect. It is only after seven to eight weeks on the sugar solution and approximately 70 days of life that a divergence in body weight emerges (Muto and Miyahara, 1972). This may indicate a difference in the obesity-generating properties of sugars and fats. Palatability may account for this difference. However, the young rat is likely to be eating just about as much as is comfortably possible in terms of sheer stomach capacity. The difference between sugars and fats may then just represent the fact that fat is more dense in terms of kilojoules. Thus the young rat can ingest more kilojoules for the same bulk on high fat, but not high sugar, diets.

Orcai (1982) observed the normal obesity-generating effects of high fat diets in young rats given access to that diet from post-weaning to adulthood. He further demonstrated that rats, which he refers to as "programmed high intake" (by restricting litter size to 4) in the pre-weaning period, amass more fat than rats "programed for low intake" (litters of 22) when allowed free access to food (either laboratory chow or high fat diets) in the post-weaning period. Thus Orcai suggests that adult obesity is not only dependent upon the high fat diet but also on the animal's nutritional status in early life.

However, this conclusion must be contrasted with the results of a study by Rothwell and Stock (1982). The two groups from this study most relevant to the present discussion received either a cafeteria diet or laboratory chow over the first 30 days after weaning. Both groups then received laboratory chow for the next 30 days (days 31–60 after weaning). Interestingly, the group *re-exposed* to the cafeteria diet for 22 days (days 61–82 after weaning) ate more, but gained less weight, than the group fed only laboratory chow throughout. Thus the energetic efficiency (grams of body weight gained/kilojoule energy intake) was significantly lower in the group with prior experience of high energy diets. Further, while the resting metabolic rates of these two groups were similar, the response of the post-weaning cafeteria-fed group to an injection of noradrenaline (a method of assessing non-shivering thermogenesis) was significantly greater than that of the non-exposed group. These data can also be related to the results of Doi and Kuroshima (1979) who found that cold exposed neonatal rats showed improved cold tolerance as adults. Both these publications suggest a prolonged effect of early experience on the thermogenic capability of the animal. In fact the cross-link has been nicely provided by Rothwell *et al.* (1982) who showed that early cold experience enhanced diet-induced thermogenesis in the adult. These results are interesting from the point of view of notions about adult obesity predicating upon hypernutrition of the young.

The point central to this issue has undoubtedly been fat cells. The notion that fat cell number and an optimum size for each cell thus determine the "set point" (discussed at the end of this Section) of body weight regulation for a given animal at a given point in its life is an attractive one. However, the opening sentence of an article by Peckham *et al.* summarizes the field: "Of the several aspects of tissue physiology yet to be elucidated is the extent of change, if any, in the number of fat cells in adipose tissue with its acquisition or loss of fat". Unfortunately, this article was published in 1962 and giant strides have not been made with respect to the issues to which these authors alluded. Certainly advances have been made and interesting data accumulated but the difficulty is in establishing any causative relationships in the face of conflicting images. Faust *et al.* (1978) looked specifically at dietary-induced obesity (with a cafeteria style diet) and fat cell proliferation. In brief they provided adult rats with the cafeteria diet for five months and essentially found significant fat cell proliferation, fat and weight accumulation. This then countered suggestions (see Greenwood and Hirsch, 1974) that fat cell number was fixed by late adolescence.

How do we reconcile these results and those of Orcai (1982) with those just discussed in which early exposure to obesity-inducing diets or cold (Rothwell and Stock, 1982; Rothwell *et al.*, 1982) results in an increased thermogenic capability, and thus the tendency to waste, and not sequester, energy? Two possibilities come to mind. First is the time of exposure and the second is the length of exposure. Orcai's (1982) "programed high intake" group were exposed to a surplus in the time period from birth to weaning while the Rothwell and Stock rats were exposed only in the post-weaning period. Doi and Kuroshima's (1979) study is interesting in respect to this in that their rats were exposed to cold in the same growth period considered by Orcai and, with cold exposure, brown adipose tissue, but not white adipose tissue, may proliferate. Thus storage capacity may not be increased but thermogenic capability may. The integration of Faust *et al.*'s (1978) results may reflect the much longer exposure to enriched diets. Thus the thermogenic benefit of short exposure may eventually be overwhelmed by fat cell proliferation which is reflected in a drive for higher body weight maintenance. I'm afraid none of this really resolves the questions surrounding fat cell number and obesity. Maybe the concluding sentence of the abstract of a paper by Gurr *et al.* (1982) will suffice for now: "We conclude that the whole concept of adipocyte hypercellularity as a causal factor in obesity has been overemphasized".

From studies of the genetic and dietary-induced models of obesity it is clear that both energy intake and expenditure play significant roles. This accords well with the human data (as we shall see in Section VII). In the past most attention has been paid to gluttony as pre-eminent in the aetiology of human obesity and undoubtedly that is the case in numerous individuals. However, it is clear from recent human studies that there is a significant subgroup of the obese population whose obesity owes itself more to reduced energy expenditure than to increased intake. For this group, the genetic models, or some subset (such as the heterozygotes), may be most relevant. In fact, a genetic component may somehow have predisposed a segment of a given population towards obesity. Thus, cultures generally in close balance with their food supply may have favoured the metabolically efficient in the periodic times of reduced food supply. Such societies would be particularly susceptible to the blandishments of readily available supplies of high fat/simple sugar diets attendant upon their exposure to the "Western" diet. Thus is undoubtedly the case with numerous native peoples, ranging from the Pima Indians of North America to the Aborigines of Australia and Melanesians of the Pacific Basin who develop marked obesity (and attendant health problems such as diabetes) upon exposure to the Western diet. What is obviously needed is an animal model for these effects. The attempts to create a subgroup within a strain of animals which exhibit a tendency to obesity have been largely concentrated within animal husbandry, with the primary aim being the production of much larger, rather than necessarily fatter, animals.

It is clearly important to exploit the diversity available in different strains of laboratory animals suitable for the study of obesity to identify the leanest and fattest animals among siblings, matched for length, of each generation. Breeding, with appropriate further selection, within these subgroups over successive generations will result in groups of animals with differing propensities to adiposity. If, concurrently, studies were carried out to identify further subgroups with low and high metabolic rates, and with low and high responsivity to palatable and energy dense diets, then we would be in a position to properly model the various obesity syndromes seen among the human population. That such genetic diversity exists among rats and mice is clear from studies like the one already discussed by Schemmel *et al.* (1970). Indeed the following is taken from an article by Lyon *et al.* (1953): "Mice of the C_{57} and C_3H strains voluntarily consumed more calories [kilojoules] when fed a 50% fat ration than when fed a 5% fat diet. This is in agreement with the findings of Deuel, Meserve, Straub, Hendrick and Scheer (1947) and others. From the work of Forbes *et al.* (1934) it might be expected that this increased caloric [energy] intake would result in increased oxygen consumption. This in fact proved to be true for mice of the C_{57} strain. In contrast, however, were the findings with animals of the C_3H strain; these consumed no more oxygen when fed with the high fat ration, although their caloric [energy] intake was significantly greater than that for the C_3H strain mice on the low fat diet. Thus it appears that mice of the C_{57} strain possess a mechanism for the oxidation of the extra calories [kilojoules] consumed on a high fat diet. This mechanism seems to be lacking, or at least poorly developed, in mice of the C_3H strain. The latter thus seem to be forced to deposit the extra calories [kilojoules] consumed as carcass fat". In some ways it is sad that this critical observation over 30 years ago made so little impact on our thinking about human obesity which is only now coming to reconsider energy expenditure as a significant variable in the energy balance equation. It may be that the heterozygous/homozygous leans of the genetically obese strains will provide us with a shortcut to reinvestigating these phenomena.

Finally, another possible casualty of the resurgence of interest in dietary-induced obesity is the notion of "set point". In respect of weight regulation "set point" means, in its strictest sense, that an animal's growth weight curve is genetically determined. Any deviations from this curve will be resisted behaviourally and metabolically with the endpoint being to re-establish the individual on its curve at the level appropriate for its age (Keesey *et al.*, 1976; Mrosovsky and Powley, 1977). Using temperature regulation as a model of "set point", there should be a set of neurons whose firing rate is optimized (either high or low) at a particular temperature (in the case of humans, approximately 37°C). It is against the firing rate of these stable neurons that the body may compare its present state *vis à vis* the desired 37°C. Neurons with the necessary characteristics indeed have been demonstrated (Mason *et al.*, 1978). Fever is given as an example of a condition where the temperature "set point" may be adjusted to cope with special circumstance. The concept of temporary adjustability was necessary, in the case of a body weight "set point", to cope with consistent observations that, for example, body weight fluctuated rhythmically over the oestrous cycle of the female.

However, in the case of dietary obesity we have a condition where, by dietary means alone, body weight is markedly increased (by increases mainly in fat, but also in lean tissue) and remains elevated in some cases even when the original feeding conditions are reintroduced. It is difficult for a "set point" notion to cope with such observations. Keesey and Corbett (1983) have addressed these difficulties and agreed that a less inflexible "set point" is necessary. However, notions of a "settling point" (see Booth, 1978), based on modelling of energy flow patterns, still perhaps cope best with the data. Thus the organism's body weight will "settle" at a particular level depending on the integration of the entire range of external (ambient temperature and humidity, palatability, energy density, availability of nutrient supply, etc.) and internal (cephalic reflexes, gastric emptying time, current energy needs, storage capacity, endocrine status, etc.) factors. Presumably the genesis of the "weight" given to each of the range of factors will be found in the extent to which leanness and fatness dispose any particular species to survival.

V. HYPOTHALAMIC LESION MODELS OF OBESITY

A. Surgical

By far the most studied non-genetic animal model of obesity over the past quarter of a century is the obesity resultant upon surgical perturbations of the ventromedial hypothalamus (VMH). Lesions, either electrolytic, radio-frequency or chemical, and knife cuts round the VMH all result in varying degrees of hyperphagia and weight gain of which the great proportion is as fat.

The following summarizes the VMH lesion preparation as it has been characterized over the 30 years since the initial demonstration of the obesity generating effects of the VMH electrolytic lesion (Hetherington and Ranson, 1940). Hyperphagia and rapid weight gain were the dramatic, overt characteristics. The pattern of food intake was interesting. The rat is normally a nocturnal feeder, taking frequent, small meals in the dark and eating little during the light period. Following VMH lesions, the day–night difference disappears and feeding is characterized by regular taking of large meals (Thomas and Mayer, 1968). There is also an exaggerated effect of palatability with sweet/greasy diets being consumed in even greater excess and unpalatable diets markedly reducing intake (see Powley, 1977, for an extensive listing). The exaggerated affect is also seen in a characteristic viciousness. The weight gain is made up almost entirely of an accumulation of fat (Kemnitz et al., 1977). As in the genetic models, hyperphagia does not fully account for the obesity. Excess lipogenesis occurs even when lesioned animals are pair-fed with controls (Han, 1968). Again like the genetic models, physical stunting and hypogonadism are both usually evident (Bernardis and Skelton, 1965; Brobeck, 1946). Activity is reduced.

Of the hormonal changes, hyperinsulinaemia, in the face of normoglycemia, is prominent and will be discussed at length later. Growth hormone levels are reduced with a suppression of the normally occurring spikes (Martin et al., 1974). This is consistent with the stunting of growth. Glucagon levels are also reduced (Inoue et al., 1977) reflecting a reduced sympathetic nervous system activity in general (Vander Tuig et al., 1982). Direct effects on the liver (Shimazu, 1981), white adipose tissue (Nishizawa and Bray, 1978) and brown adipose tissue (Seydoux et al., 1981) can be demonstrated and all are consistent with an anabolic state when the VMH is suppressed and catabolism is linked with VMH activity.

Curiously, prior to the 1970s, investigations into VMH function essentially diverged. One body of literature focused on the overt behavioural characteristics. This work concentrated on the affective changes, particularly related to taste, the motivational defects, the characteristics of the "dynamic" and "static" phases of weight regulation and, through this, the emerging concept of a change in "set point" (see Grossman, 1966 for a synthesizing review of that period).

Enormous amounts were written from this perspective, viewing the VMH as a "satiety center" which acted upon the lateral hypothalamic (LHA) "feeding center". The assumption was that certain unspecified circulating metabolites might signal, via specialized receptors in the VMH, the animal's state of current and long-term energy repletion or depletion. The VMH would then, presumably behaviourally by modification of intake through the LHA "feeding center", respond appropriately and ensure an adequate energy supply and, hence, the long-term survival of the organism. The metabolic signal received considerable attention. Mayer's (1953) glucostatic signal, Kennedy's (1953) lipostatic signal, Hamilton's (1963) non-circulating metabolite dependent thermostatic signal and, recently, Pitt's (1978) concentration on the stability of protein reserves have offered a multitude of putative short-term and long-term satiety signals.

This work, prior to the 1970s, appeared to pay little attention to the second body of literature dealing with hypothalamic function; that of the relationships of the hypothalamus to the visceral organs via the autonomic nervous system. These latter studies were spawned by the elegant and extensive work of, predominantly, Japanese workers in the 1950s and 1960s led by Ban and Shimazu. They (see Ban, 1966; Shimazu et al., 1966; Shimazu and Ogasawara, 1975; Shimazu, 1981) established the close homology of the VMH with the sympathetic nervous system and the LHA with the parasympathetic division of the autonomic nervous system. Since then an extensive literature has developed which focuses on a nervous control, either directly or indirectly via the adrenals, or via the visceral organs critical to energy balance, both in the disposition of incoming nutrients and the use of endogenous energy stores. There have been demonstrations of nervous control over pancreatic secretion of the sole anabolic hormone, insulin, and of glucagon, the slow-acting adrenalin-like hormone. Control has also been demonstrated over gluconeogenesis in the liver (the supply of glucose being critical for brain functioning); and over triglyceride breakdown in adipose tissue and subsequent free fatty acid and glycerol efflux as, respectively, glucose energy substitute and gluconeogenic substrate.

The critical synthesis of these disparate literatures was undoubtedly forged by Powley in 1977 with his "cephalic phase hypothesis". Powley ambitiously proposed a synthesis of the vast "psychological" literature concentrating on the effective, sensory, and motivational aspects of the syndrome and the growing awareness that the demonstrations by the Japanese of visceral perturbations resultant upon hypothalamic manipulation must mean something to the energy balance equation.

In simple overview, Powley (1977) suggested: "... that VMH lesions produced their major effects on feeding behavior by directly heightening the phasic autonomic and endocrine responses triggered by oropharyngeal contact with food stimuli — the cephalic reflexes of digestion". However, since Powley's initial foray the expected rush of definitive articles on an obviously testable hypothesis have not appeared. Powley himself (Weingarten and Powley, 1981) has demonstrated an increased cephalic axis gastric acid secretion in VMH lesioned animals, but no other evidence either way has surfaced to bear on his hypothesis. In my own work I could elicit no cephalic insulin release at all in VMH-lesioned rats using a conditioning procedure with light, odour and sound but a good, if highly variable, release in intact rats.

However, there is other evidence to suggest the post-ingestional (and perhaps oropharyngeal, if Weingarten and Powley's (1981) work generalizes to other metabolic responses) consequences are exaggerated in the VMH-lesioned animals, even within minutes of the lesion being produced (Rohner et al., 1977). It should be noted from this study that destruction of the VMH does not result in a change in basal levels of insulin, but only in an exaggerated response to nutrients. My own analysis has the VMH initiating (rather than suppressing) the anticipatory insulin release (co-ordinated, of course, with the tuning of other metabolic pathways to anabolism); suppressing prandial insulin; and reinstituting the post-prandial catabolism to provide a rising flow of endogenous nutrients to counter the falling influx from digestion. The overall *raison* of this system is to stabilize ambient blood glucose to the brain in the face of the discontinuous supply attendant upon meal feeding.

B. Chemical

It is also possible to induce destruction of the medial, basal area of the hypothalamus by chemical means using systemic injections of goldthioglucose (GTG) or monosodium glutamate (MSG, Olney, 1969). Goldthioglucose induced obesity caused great excitement when first noted as it was seen as direct support for Mayer's glucostatic theory (Mayer, 1953). Gold is toxic to cells and when complexed to glucose it was considered that it would destroy cells which rapidly uptake glucose. The demonstrations that systemic injections of GTG preferentially destroyed cells in the area of the ventromedial hypothalamus (Mayer and Marshall, 1956), but not in the absence of insulin (Debons et al., 1968) was very exciting indeed. However, Caffyn (1972) pointed out that it was blood vessels rather than neurons which primarily suffered damage from GTG and that a range of anti-inflammatory drugs could also protect the VMH. Further non-specific damage throughout the brain could also be observed.

The issue of specificity has not been resolved satisfactorily. Kataoka et al. (1978) found binding of GTG to both vascular endothelium *and* to cell membrane. Powley and Laughton (1981) suggest that, with sufficient care in choosing the dosage and strain of mouse, non-specific damage may be largely avoided. They have further explored GTG lesions and found that, as well as VMH damage, cell groups of the dorsal motor nerve of the vagus are destroyed. It is interesting that the cell groups primarily destroyed are at the level of the largest number of vagal cells projecting to the pancreas (Van Houten and Posner, 1981). Cells in that region were identified (by these latter authors) as having insulin receptors suggesting the possibility of a direct feedback loop involving brain-vagus-pancreas in the neural control of insulin secretion.

Overall, then, the GTG lesion may provide a model closely akin to the electrolytic VMH lesion but which is characterized by selective damage to subgroup of hypothalamic neurons which have special glucoreceptor properties. With additional damage to the relevant (perhaps reflex) midbrain components of the insulin control group, the GTG lesion syndrome may provide an enlightening variation on other models of central control of energy balance. Finally, there is an unfortunate drawback to the use of GTG. It is lethally toxic to rats at dose levels sufficient to damage the VMH (Mayer and Marshall, 1956). However, attempts to induce local VMH damage with intrahypothalamic GTG implants have had some success (Smith and Britt, 1971).

Obesity following medial, basal hypothalamic lesions caused by injections of monosodium glutamate (MSG) was first reported by Olney (1969). Once again, this is different from other hypothalamic lesion syndromes in some important respects. The damage appears to be more in the arcuate, rather than the ventromedial, nuclei. Lesions are only possible in neonatally-treated animals. Hyperphagia is not seen and fat accumulation proceeds even in the face of reduced food intake, with reduced energy expenditure having been directly demonstrated (Djazyery et al., 1979; Poon and Cameron, 1978). However, there are certain similarities with electrolytic and GTG hypothalamic lesions in that stunting and hypogonadism (Arango and Mayer, 1973; Olney, 1969) are features of all three syndromes.

It should not escape the reader that, in the genetic, electrolytic VMH lesion, GTG, and MSG models of obesity, there is a critical common feature: lean tissue and growth are sacrificed in the cause of accumulation of fat. When intake is restricted to control levels (voluntarily in the case of MSG-treated animals) this tendency becomes pronounced and severe stunting, with gross accumulation of fat, can be seen in any of these preparations. This is one of the critical issues which must be addressed. Certainly hyperinsulinism is a central feature of all these preparations, but insulin has proteinogenic as well as lipogenic properties and, in any case, in the genetic models the accumulation of fat precedes hyperinsulinaemia. Discovery of the common component of all these preparations, which distributes incoming nutrient supply (or indeed redirects endogenous energy stores) disproportionately into adipose tissue, will be a major breakthrough in understanding the neural basis of obesity.

VI. "OTHER" MODELS—NATURAL RHYTHMS

There are numerous other obesity-producing procedures, including chronic insulin injection (Panksepp *et al.*, 1975) which likely provokes hyperphagia in response to hypoglycemia, and injections of bipiperdyl mustard, another hypothalamus-damaging inflammatory agent (Rutman *et al.*, 1966). Due to the limitations of space, a comprehensive examination of these and other models is not possible, despite their undoubted value. However, one set of intake–body weight fluctuations really must be mentioned, for potentially the set will be of immense benefit. The set is the natural rhythms of positive and negative energy balance encompassing everything from the massive circannual changes seen in hibernating animals to the modest but reliable fluctuations of the circadian and menstrual cycles.

Mrosovsky and Melnyk (1982) have recently organized their own investigations, and those of others, into various natural rhythms of extreme hyperphagia and anorexia associated not only with the circannual rhythm in hibernators but also with special requirements of certain breeding, incubating and nurturing styles. There are two demonstrations by Mrosovsky and coworkers that I find particularly interesting. The first is that the phases of weight loss and anorexia which are seen naturally are regulated. Thus the incubating jungle fowl keeps to a well programmed, reducing level of intake and body weight and, if challenged, will actively regulate at the level which is appropriate for the particular point in time (Sherry *et al.*, 1980). Second, superimposing VMH lesions on the normal circannual rhythm of the golden-mantle ground squirrel appears only to exaggerate the hyperphagia and body weight gain of the "spring", but fails entirely to interfere with the anorexia, weight loss and weight nadir attained during the "winter" (Mrosovsky, 1975). Undoubtedly, these animals, and the very conveniently rhythmic fluctuations at normal colony temperatures in the dormouse (*Glis glis*), offer marked changes in energy balance without external interference which should be amenable to comprehensive analysis of neural, hormonal and metabolic status. Finally, even the normal diurnal cycle offers a short-term situation where an animal such as a rat eats over 30% in excess of requirement during the dark period of a 12–12 light/dark cycle, but 24% *less* than requirement during the light (Le Magnen and Devos, 1982); another example of a periodic hyperphagia and hypophagia.

VII. ON THE APPLICATION OF ANIMAL MODELS TO THE HUMAN CONDITION

There are many examples of where animal models have not been used wisely or profitably in exploring human medical problems involving obesity. One example which we have been investigating recently is that of excessive weight gain as a negative side effect of mood stabilizing drugs (Storlien *et al.*, 1984). Both weight gain and specific carbohydrate cravings were widely reported in the clinical literature as side effects of a range of psychotropic drugs. However, when we explored the literature very few animal studies had been performed appropriately and not a single one had offered the animal anything other than laboratory chow as a food source (the human equivalent might be seen as a clinical trial where the experimental subjects were offered a diet solely consisting of bran cereal, water and vitamin pills). As a model for the human effects, such experiments are clearly inappropriate.

In our first experiments two startling findings have come to light. Chronic injection of male rats with lithium indeed has little effect on intake or body weight in those animals offered only laboratory chow. However, with the added availability of sucrose (24% weight/volume) and saccharin (0.6% weight/volume) as additional fluid sources the lithium-treated rats show increased total/energy intake and, in some, spectacular weight gains (ranging up to four times that in normal rats). A second finding was that chronic mianserin treatment similarly had no effect on intake or weight gain on the laboratory chow diet. However, with access to sucrose and saccharin, again as additional fluid sources, the mianserin treated rats showed a marked loss of metabolic efficiency. They ate approximately 40% more than the saline control animals, but gained exactly the same amount of weight.

We are in the process of following up these findings but the point is that great care has to be taken to create conditions for the animals which are appropriate to the human situation. Thus a laboratory chow diet is quite clearly inappropriate for testing the induction of a carbohydrate craving as a result of drug treatment. Similarly, what has been reported as a carbohydrate craving in the human literature may, in fact, be a general energy craving, excess carbohydrate often being the most available macronutrient (especially in the case of lithium which induces thirst). In the present example, lithium is well known to depress the urine concentrating capacity of the kidney and thus weight gain may well result from an interaction of attractive, carbohydrate-rich fluid sources in our present range of soft drinks with this basically physiological property of the drug. Determining the critical variable is clearly possible with appropriately designed experiments. The separation of macronutrients as a proportion of intake is feasible in the experimental situation, but not in the human setting. Overall the message is that there must be a clear assessment of the issues involved and of the experimental situation most likely to be relevant to its elucidation.

VIII. RELATION OF ANIMAL TO HUMAN LITERATURE

We now find ourselves at the really critical issue. Is there sufficient information in the human literature on obesity to encourage the further exploration of animal models and, if so, in what direction does the literature point us? First of all, there is now ample evidence that human obesity may be due to inappropriate energy intake and/or expenditure. Gone, hopefully, are the days when the obese patient who was diagnosed as not having abnormal "glands" was automatically labelled a glutton. Indeed in the human literature documenting the food intake of obese and lean people there is now almost an embarrassment of findings showing *reduced* intake in the obese, even when uncorrected for the obviously increased tissue mass which these people must sustain.

For example, in a very recent study of 871 middle-aged men by Kromhout (1983) in Zutphen, The Netherlands (The Zutphen Study), the following results were abstracted: "Men in the highest quartile of the sum of two skinfolds or the Quetelet index (weight/height squared) distribution consumed on average 300 to 400 kcal [1255 to 1674 kJ] *less* than men in the lowest quartile". This same paper makes as the point in the opening sentence of the introduction: "Obese individuals in affluent cultures have generally a lower energy intake than their lean counterparts. . ." and quotes no less than seven studies of adults and children to support this contention, with none to gainsay it. In favour of this thesis there has accumulated over the last few years an impressive literature implicating a thermogenic defect in human obesity.

Following is a quick summary of some of this literature and hopefully it will not escape the reader that there are clear parallels with the defects already elucidated for the animal models of obesity. We have reports of the noradrenaline-induced increase in metabolic rate being less in the obese (Jung *et al.*, 1979) and as well, a reduced sodium and potassium pumping capacity of red blood cells (De Luise *et al.*, 1980; Klimes *et al.*, 1982). Pittet *et al.* (1976) found a reduced thermic effect of food in the obese. Moore *et al.* (1980) reported a negative correlation between weight loss on a diet and circulating level of the thyroid hormone triiodothyronine (T3), an accepted index of metabolic rate.

Morgan *et al.* (1982) neatly side-stepped the problem of studying populations differing significantly in weight and adiposity. They investigated two groups of "lean" men. One group was that disgusting lot who ate promiscuously and regulated perfectly. The second group, with which the most diligent of us can identify, were equally lean but professed to great difficulty in retaining this lean state. Testing these two groups on their metabolic response to both meals and ephedrine (an analogue of naturally occurring adrenaline and an index of non-shivering thermogenesis) revealed that the "naturally" lean indeed expended (wasted) significantly more energy for a given stimulus than the "will-power" leans. This is a particularly important finding and accords well with Robson *et al.*'s (1977) report of a negative correlation between the heat increment to a meal and proportion of ideal body weight. Zahorska-Markiewicz (1980) has added further to the issue with her study of a combination of heat increment to a meal and exercise. The increased metabolic rate to a meal has already been discussed. It is also well known that exercise in the postprandial hypermetabolic period results in an oxygen consumption which is in excess of the simply additive effects of the meal and exercise. What Zahorska-Markiewcz has shown is that this supersynergism is of some 17.8% in the lean subjects, but is entirely absent in obese subjects (0.8%). This finding has recently been confirmed by Segal and Gutin (1983).

Of the various physiological stimuli for energy expenditure caffeine is particularly interesting, being a drug taken regularly in high doses by a good proportion of our Western population. Acheson *et al.* (1980) have shown that while the thermic effect of caffeine is similar in obese and lean patients, caffeine results in a greater oxidation of fat in the lean compared to the obese subjects. The implication is that there is a "metabolic reluctance" in the obese to mobilize fat that must be compared to a similar pattern in the genetic and lesion animal models just discussed.

This brings us to the study which engenders, for me at least, a good deal of excitement. Griffiths and Payne reported in 1976 the results of a study in five to six year old children which closely parallels the study by Morgan *et al.* (1982) in regulated and non-regulated lean adult men. What Griffiths and Payne did was establish a group of normal weight children who were the offspring of "lean" parents. A second group of children were indistinguishable from the first group in terms of any physical characteristic. However, this second group had at least one parent who might be described as truly obese. The offspring of the lean parents consumed significantly more food than the offspring of the obese parents and the fact that both groups were in identical energy balance indicates the offspring of the obese parents were, as well as ingesting less, expending less. This important study demands replication and, if possible, a follow up from the original authors on what happened to these groups of "genetically" obese and lean children.

From the above accounting it could, but should not, be taken as a fact that the observation of obesity automatically supposes a metabolic predisposition. There are a number of studies which have failed to reveal any reduced metabolic rate in the obese (see for examples, the studies of Dore *et al.*, 1982; and Blaza and Garrow, 1983) and a recent one which showed some of the thermogenic defects of the obese to be partially reversible by weight loss (Davis *et al.*, 1983). However, I believe we have had the synthesis for as long as eight years in the results of an important study by Miller and Parsonage (1975). In their study 29 overweight women who claimed to be metabolically efficient were incarcerated for three weeks in a tightly controlled environment on an 7500 kJ d^{-1} diet. The synthesis was that nine women failed to lose weight and displayed lower basal metabolic rates. The others were widely spaced in terms of weight loss and metabolic rate. This study is important in that it clearly establishes categories for both the metabolically efficient and the obese whose excess weight gain would appear, for whatever reason, to be caused by overeating. Any further studies of obesity must characterize their subject population on those bases if spurious controversies are to be avoided.

IX. CONCLUSION

As I see it, there are two intertwined issues which the work of the last few years has revealed as central to our understanding of the regulation of body weight. These issues are, first, non-shivering thermogenesis and the possible existence of "luxuskonsumption" as a mechanism of limiting energy stores through wastage of excess energy as heat. The failure of "luxuskonsumption" or some part of it will undoubtedly come to be recognized as important in the aetiology of a significant proportion of human obesity. Second, is the multifaceted integration of information about the organisms's energy supply (both internal and external) with both the behavioural acts of food search and ingestion and the metabolic patterns which control the distribution and utilization of the incoming nutrients. Such control is undoubtedly effected via the autonomic nervous system with the hypothalamus still the focus as the prime integrating and control region. It is likely that non-shivering thermogenesis, and "luxuskonsumption" as a component of non-shivering thermogenesis, will eventually be seen as one segment of the centrally-regulated, integrated metabolic process of tissue depletion and repletion.

ACKNOWLEDGEMENTS

This work was supported by an N.H. & M.R.C. Program Grant to the Garvan Institute of Medical Research (E.W. Kraegen, Chief Investigator), St Vincent's Hospital, Sydney, Australia. Special thanks to the long suffering secretarial staff.

REFERENCES

Acheson, K.J., Zahorska-Markiewicz, B., Pittet, Ph., Anantharaman, K. and Jequier, E. Caffeine and coffee: Their influence on metabolic rate and substrate utilization in normal weight and obese individuals. *American Journal of Clinical Nutrition*, 1980, 33: 989–997.

Alonso, L.G. and Maren, T.H. Effect of food restriction on body composition of hereditary obese mice. *American Journal of Physiology*, 155, 1983: 284–290.

Aranjo, P.E. and Mayer, J. Activity increase associated with obesity induced by monosodium glutamate in mice. *American Journal of Physiology*, 1973, 225: 764–765.

Armitage, G., Harris, R.B.S., Hervey, G.R. and Tobin, G. Energy expenditure of Zucker rats in relation to environmental temperature. *Journal of Physiology*, 1980, 297: 33–34P.

Assimacopoulus-Jeannet, F., Singh, A., Le Marchand, Y., Loten, E.G. and Jeanrenaud, B. Abnormalities in lipogenesis and triglyceride secretion by perfused livers of obese-hyperglycaemic (ob/ob) mice: Relationship with hyperinsulinaemia. *Diabetologia*, 1974, 10: 155–162.

Ban, T. The septo-preoptico-hypothalamic system and its autonomic function. *Progress in Brain Research*, 1966, 21A: 1–43.

Barry, W.S. and Bray, G.A. Plasma triglycerides in genetically obese rats. *Metabolism*, 1969, 18: 833–839.

Bernardis, L.L. and Skelton, F.R. Growth and obesity following ventromedial hypothalamic lesions placed in female rats at four different ages. *Neuroendocrinology*, 1965/66, 1: 265–275.

Bertin, R., Razanamaniraka, I., De Marco, F. and Portet, R. Effects of cold acclimation on the feeding pattern and energetic metabolism of genetically obese Zucker rats. *Comparative Biochemistry and Physiology*, 1983, 74A: 855–860.

Blaza, S. and Garrow, J.S. Thermogenic response to temperature, exercise and food stimuli in lean and obese women, studied by 24 hour direct calorimetry. *British Journal of Nutrition*, 1983, 49: 171–180.

Booth, D.A. Prediction of feeding behaviour from energy flows in the rat. In D.A. Booth (Ed.), *Hunger Models — Computable Theory of Feeding Control*. London: Academic Press, 1978: 227–278.

Boyle, P.C., Storlien, L.H., Harper, A.E. and Keesey, R.E. Oxygen consumption and locomotor activity during restricted feeding and realimentation. *American Journal of Physiology*, 1981, 241: R392–R397.

Bray, G.A. The Zucker-fatty rat: A review. *Federation Proceedings*, 1977, 36: 148–153.

Brobeck, J.R. Mechanism of the development of obesity in animals with hypothalamic lesions. *Physiological Reviews*, 1946, 26: 541–559.

Caffyn, Z.E.Y. Early vascular changes in the brain of the mouse after injections of goldthioglucose and bipiperidyl mustard. *Journal of Pathology*, 1972, 106: 49–56.

Castonquay, T.W., Hirsch, E. and Collier, G. Palatability of sugar solutions and dietary selection *Physiology and Behavior*, 1981, 27: 7-12.

Chan, C.P., Koong, L.J. and Stern, J.S. Effect of insulin on fat and protein deposition in diabetic lean and obese rats. *American Journal of Physiology*, 1982, 242: E19-E24.

Cleary, M.P., Vaselli, J.R. and Greenwood, M.R.C. Development of obesity in the Zucker obese (fa/fa) rat in the absence of hyperphagia. *American Journal of Physiology*, 1980, 238: E284-E292.

Coleman, D.L. Genetics of obesity in rodents. In G.A. Bray (Ed.), *Recent Advances in Obesity Research*, Vol. 2. London: Newman, 1978: 142-152.

Davis, J.R., Tagliaferro, A.R., Kertaer, R., Gerado, T., Nichols, J. and Wheeler, J. Variations in dietary-induced thermogenesis and body fatness with aerobic capacity. *European Journal of Applied Physiology*, 1983, 50: 319-329.

Davis, T.R.A. and Mayer, J. Imperfect homeothermia in the hereditary obese-hyperglycemic syndrome of mice. *American Journal of Physiology*, 1954, 177: 222-226.

Debons, A.F., Krimsky, I., Likuski, J., From, A. and Cloutier, R.J. Gold thioglucose damage to the satiety center: Inhibition in diabetes. *American Journal of Physiology*, 1968, 214: 652-658.

De Luise, M., Blackburn, G.L. and Flier, J.S. Reduced activity of the red-cell sodium-potassium pump in human obesity. *New England Journal of Medicine*, 1980, 303: 1017-1022.

Deuel, H.J., Jr, Meserve, E.R., Straub, E., Hendrick, C. and Scheer, B.T. The effect of fat level of the diet on general nutrition. I. Growth, reproduction and physical capacity of rats receiving diets containing various levels of cottonseed oil or margarine fat *ad libitum*. *Journal of Nutrition*, 1974, 33: 569.

Djazyery, A., Miller, D.S. and Stock, M.J. Energy balance in obese mice. *Nutrition and Metabolism*, 1979, 23: 357-367.

Doi, K. and Kuroshima, A. Lasting effect of infantile cold experience on cold tolerance in adult rats. *Japanese Journal of Physiology*, 1979, 29: 139-150.

Dore, C., Hesp, R., Wilkins, D. and Garrow, J.S. Prediction of energy requirements of obese patients after massive weight loss. *Human Nutrition: Clinical Nutrition*, 1982, 36C: 41-48.

Dubuc, P.D. Development of obesity, hyperinsulinaemia and Hyperglycaemia in ob/ob mice. *Metabolism*, 1977, 26: 1567-1574.

Faust, I.M., Johnson, P.R., Stern, J.S. and Hirsch, J. Diet-induced adipocyte number increase in adult rats: A new model of obesity. *American Journal of Physiology*, 1978, 235: E279-E286.

Fenton, P.F. and Dowling, M.T. Studies on obesity. I. Nutritional obesity in mice. *Journal of Nutrition*, 1953, 49: 319-331.

Forbes, E.B., Kriss, M. and Miller, R.C. The energy metabolism of the albino rat in relation to the plane of nutrition. *Journal of Nutrition*, 1934, 8: 535-546.

Forbes, E.B., Swift, R.W., Elliott, R.F. and James, W.H. Relation of fat to economy of food utilization. I. By the growing albino rat. *Journal of Nutrition*, 1946a, 31: 203-212.

Forbes, E.B., Swift, R.W., Elliott, R.F. and James, W.H. Relation of fat to economy of food utilization. II. By the mature albino rat. *Journal of Nutrition*, 1946b, 31: 213-221.

Greenwood, M.R.C. and Hirsch, J. Postnatal development of adipocyte cellularity in the normal rat. *Journal of Lipid Research*, 1974, 15: 474-480.

Griffiths, M. and Payne, P.R. Energy expenditure in small children of obese and non-obese parents. *Nature*, 1976, 260: 698-700.

Grossman, S.P. The V.M.H.: A center for affective reactions, satiety or both? *Physiology and Behavior*, 1966, 1: 1-10.

Gurr, M.I., Jung, R.T., Robinson, M.P. and James, W.P.T. Adipose tissue cellularity in man: The relationship between fat cell size and number, the mass and distribution of body fat and history of weight gain and loss. *International Journal of Obesity*, 1982, 6: 419-436.

Hallfrisch, J., Cohen, L. and Reiser, S. Effects of feeding rats sucrose in a high fat diet. *Journal of Nutrition*, 1981, III: 531-536.

Hamilton, C.L. Interaction of food intake and temperature regulation in the rat. *Journal of Comparative and Physiological Psychology*, 1963, 56: 476–488.

Han, P.W. Energy metabolism of tube-fed hypophysectomized rats bearing hypothalamic lesions. *American Journal of Physiology*, 1968, 215: 1343–1350.

Herberg, L. and Coleman, D.L. Laboratory animals exhibiting obesity and diabetes syndromes. *Metabolism*, 1977, 26: 59–99.

Hervey, G.R. and Tobin, G. Luxuskonsumption, diet-induced thermogenesis and brown fat: A critical review. *Clinical Science*, 1983, 64: 7–18.

Hetherington, A.W. and Ranson, S.W. Hypothalamic lesions and adiposity in rat. *Anatomical Record*, 1940, 78: 149–172.

Hill, W., Castonquay, T.W. and Collier, G.H. Taste or diet balancing? *Physiology and Behavior*, 1980, 24: 765–767.

Himms-Hagen, J. and Desautels, M. A mitochondrial defect in brown adipose tissue of the obese (ob/ob) mouse: Reduced binding of purine nucleotides and a failure to respond to cold by an increase in binding. *Biochemical and Biophysical Research Communications*, 1978, 83: 628–634.

Hollifield, G. and Parson, W. Body composition of mice and goldthioglucose and hereditary obesity after weight reduction. *Metabolism*, 1958, 7: 179–183.

Ingalls, A.M., Dickie, M.M. and Snell, G.D. Obese, a new mutation in the house mouse. *Journal of Heredity*, 1950, 41: 317–318.

Inoue, S., Campfield, L.A. and Bray, C.A. Comparison of metabolic alterations in hypothalamic and high fat diet-induced obesity. *American Journal of Physiology*, 1977, 233: R162–R168.

Jansky, L. Non-shivering thermogenesis and its thermoregulatory significance. *Biological Review*, 1973, 48: 85–132.

Jeanrenaud, B. An overview of experimental models of obesity. In G.A. Bray (Ed.), *Recent Advances in Obesity Research*, Vol. 2. London: Newman, 1978: 111–122.

Johnson, P.R. and Hirsch, J. Cellularity of adipose depots in six strains of genetically obese mice. *Journal of Lipid Research*, 1972, 13: 2–11.

Johnson, P.R., Zucker, L.M., Cruce, J.A.F. and Hirsch, J. Cellularity of adipose depots in the genetically obese Zucker rat. *Journal of Lipid Research*, 1971, 12: 706–714.

Joosten, H.F.P. and van der Kroon, P.H.W. Enlargement of eipdidymal adipocytes in relation to hyperinsulinemia in obese hyperglycemic mice (ob/ob). *Metabolism*, 1974, 23: 59–66.

Jung, R.T., Shetty, P.S., James, W.P.T., Barrand, M.A. and Callingham, B.A. Reduced thermogenesis in obesity. *Nature*, 1979, 279: 322–323.

Kanarek, R.B. and Hirsch, E. Dietary-induced overeating in experimental animals. *Federation Proceedings*, 1977, 36: 154–158.

Kaplan, M.L. and Leville, G.A. Core temporation O_2 consumption and early detection of ob/ob genotype in mice. *American Journal of Physiology*, 1974, 227: 912–915.

Kataoka, K., Danbara, H., Sunayashiki, K., Okuno, S., Sorimachi, M., Tanaka, M. and Chikamori, K. Regional and subcellular distribution of gold in brain of goldthioglucose obese mouse. *Brain Research Bulletin*, 1978, 3: 257–263.

Keesey, R.E., Boyle, P.C., Kemnitz, J.W. and Mitchel, J.S. The role of the lateral hypothalamus in determining body weight set point. In D. Novin, W. Wyrwicka and G. Bray (Eds.), *Hunger: Basic Mechanisms and Clinical Implications*. New York: Raven, 1976: 243–255.

Keesey, R.E. and Corbett, S.W. Metabolic defense of the body weight set-point. In A.J. Stunkard and E. Stellar (Eds.), *Eating and its Disorders*. New York, Raven, 1983: 87–96.

Kemnitz, J.W., Goy, R.W. and Keesey, R.E. Effects of gonadectomy on hypothalamic obesity in male and female rats. *International Journal of Obesity*, 1977, 1: 259–270.

Kennedy, G.C. The role of depot fat in the hypothalamic control of food intake in the rat. *Proceedings of the Royal Society*, Series B, 1953, 140: 578–592.

Kleiber, M. *The Fire of Life*. New York: Wiley, 1975.

Klimes, I., Nagulesparan, M., Unger, R.H., Aronoff, S.L. and Mott, D.M. Reduced

Na⁺K⁺ATPase activity in intact red cells and isolated membranes from obese man. *Journal of Clinical Endocrinology and Metabolism*, 1982, 54: 721–724.

Knehans, A.W. and Romsos, D.R. Reduced norepinephrine turnover in brown adipose tissue of ob/ob mice. *American Journal of Physiology*, 1982, 242: E253–E261.

Kromhout, D. Energy and macronutrient intake in lean and obese middle-aged men (the Zutphen Study). *American Journal of Clinical Nutrition*, 1983, 37: 295–299.

Leiter, E.H., Coleman, D.L., Ingram, D.K. and Reynolds, M.A. Influence of dietary carbohydrate on the induction of diabetes in C57BL/KsJ-db/db diabetes mice. *Journal of Nutrition*, 1983, 113: 184–195.

Le Magnen, J. and Devos, M. Daily body energy balance in rats. *Physiology and Behavior*, 1982, 29: 807–811.

Lemonnier, D. Hyperinsulinism in genetically obese rats. *Hormone and Metabolic Research*, 1971, 3: 287–288.

Levin, B.E., Comai, K., O'Brien, R. and Sullivan, A.C. Abnormal brown adipose composition and beta-adrenoreceptor binding in obese Zucker rats. *American Journal of Physiology*, 1982, 243: E217–E224.

Lin, M.H., Romsos, D.R., Akera, T. and Leveille, G.A. Na⁺,K⁺-ATPase enzyme units in skeletal muscle from lean and obese mice. *Biochemical and Biophysical Research Communications*, 1978, 80: 398–404.

Lyon, J.B., Jr, Dowling, M.T. and Fenton, P.F. Studies on obesity. II. Food intake and oxygen consumption. *Journal of Nutrition*, 1953, 51: 65–70.

Martin, J.B., Renaud, L.P. and Brazeau, P., Jr. Pulsatile growth hormone secretion: Suppression by hypothalamic ventromedial lesions and by long-acting somatostatin. *Science*, 1974, 186: 538–540.

Mason, P., Hasan, H. and Valis, M. Spontaneous firing of hypothalamic neurones over a narrow temperature interval. *Nature*, 1978, 273: 242–243.

Mayer, J. Glucostatic mechanisms of regulation of food intake. *New England Journal of Medicine*, 1953, 249: 13–16.

Mayer, J. and Marshall, N.B. Specificity of gold thioglucose for ventromedial hypothalamic lesions and hyperphagia. *Nature*, 1956, 178: 1399–1400.

Mickelson, O., Takahashi, S. and Craig, C. Experimental obesity. I. Production of obesity in rats by feeding high-fat diets. *Journal of Nutrition*, 1955, 57: 541–554.

Miller, D.S. and Parsonage, S. Resistance to slimming, adaption or illusion? *Lancet*, 1975, 2: 773–775.

Moore, R., Howard, A.N., Grant, A.M. and Mills, I.H. Treatment of obesity with triiodothyronine and very low calorie liquid formula diet. *Lancet*, 1980, 1: 223–224.

Morgan, J.B., York, D.A., Wasilewska, A. and Portman, J. A study of the thermic responses to a meal and to a sympathomimetic drug (ephedrine) in relation to energy balance in man. *British Journal of Nutrition*, 1982, 47: 21–32.

Mrosovsky, N. The amplitude and period of circannual cycles of body weight in golden mantled ground squirrels with no medial hypothalamic lesions. *Brain Research*, 1975, 99: 97–116.

Mrosovsky, N. and Melnyk, R.B. Towards new animal models in obesity research. *International Journal of Obesity*, 1982, 6: 121–126.

Mrosovsky, N. and Powley, T.L. Set points for body weight and fat. *Behavioral Biology*, 1977, 29: 205–223.

Muto, S. and Miyahara, C. Eating behaviour of young rats: Experiment on selective feeding on diet and sugar solution. *British Journal of Nutrition*, 1972, 28: 327–337.

Newsholme, E.A., Crabtree, B., Higgins, S.J., Thornton, S.D. and Start, C. The activities of fructose diphosphatase in flight muscles from the bumble-bee and the role of this enzyme in heat generation. *Biochemical Journal*, 1972, 128: 89–97.

Newsholme, E.A. and Start, C. In D.F. Steiner and N. Freinkel (Eds.), *Handbook of Physiology: Section 7: Endocrinology I.* Washington, D.C.: American Physiological Society, 1972: 369–383.

Newsholme, E.A. and Start, C. *Regulation in Metabolism.* London: Wiley, 1973.

Nicholls, D.G. The thermogenic effect of brown adipose tissue. *Bioscience Reports*, 1983, 3: 431–441.

Nishizawa, Y. and Bray, G.A. Ventromedial hypothalamic lesions and the mobilisation of fatty acids. *Journal of Clinical Investigation*, 1978, 61: 714–721.

Olney, J.W. Brain lesions, obesity and other disturbances in mice treated with monosodium glutamate. *Science*, 1969, 164: 719–721.

Orcai, L.B. Dietary-induced severe obesity: A rat model. *American Journal of Physiology*, 1982, 242: R212–R215.

Panksepp, J., Pollack, A., Krost, K., Meeker, R. and Ritter, R. Feeding in response to repeated protamine zinc insulin injections. *Physiology and Behavior*, 1975, 14: 489–493.

Peckham, S.C., Entenman, C. and Carroll, H.W. The influence of a hypercaloric diet on gross body and adipose tissue composition in the rat. *Journal of Nutrition*, 1962, 77: 197–198.

Pittet, Ph., Chappuis, Ph., Acheson, K., de Techtermann, F. and Jequier, E. Thermic effect of glucose in obese subjects studied by direct and indirect calorimetry. *British Journal of Nutrition*, 1976, 35: 281–292.

Pitts, G.C. Physiologic regulation of body energy storage. *Metabolism*, 1978, 27: 469–478.

Poon, T.K.-Y. and Cameron, D.P. Measurement of oxygen consumption and locomotor activity in monosodium glutamate-induced obesity. *American Journal of Physiology*, 1978, 234: E532–E534.

Powley, T.L. The ventromedial hypothalamic syndrome, satiety and a cephalic phase hypothesis. *Psychological Review*, 1977, 84: 89–126.

Powley, T.L. and Laughton, W. Neural pathways involved in the hypothalamic integration of autonomic responses. *Diabetologia*, 1981, 20: 378–387.

Renold, A.E., Christophe, J. and Jeanrenaud, B. The obese hyperglycemic syndrome in mice: Metabolism of isolated adipose tissue *in vitro*. *American Journal of Clinical Nutrition*, 1960, 8: 719–726.

Robson, J.R.K., Olman, M.J., Coale, M.S. and Bradham, G.B. Metabolic response to food. *Lancet*, 1977, 2: 1367.

Rohner, R., Dufour, A.-C., Karakash, C., Le Marchand, Y., Ruf, K.B. and Jeanrenaud, B. Immediate effect of lesion of the ventromedial hypothalamic area upon glucose-induced insulin secretion in anaesthetized rats. *Diabetologia*, 1977, 13: 239–242.

Rolls, B.J., Rowe, E.A. and Turner, R.C. Persistent obesity in rats following a period of consumption of a mixed, high energy diet. *Journal of Physiology*, 1980, 298: 415–427.

Rothwell, N.J., Saville, M.E. and Stock, M.J. Factors influencing the acute effect of food on oxygen consumption in the rat. *International Journal of Obesity*, 1982, 6: 53–59.

Rothwell, N.J. and Stock, M.J. Effects of early overnutrition and undernutrition in rats on the metabolic responses to overnutrition in later life. *Journal of Nutrition*, 1982, 112: 426–435.

Rothwell, N.J. and Stock, M.J. Luxuskonsumption, diet-induced thermogenesis and brown fat: The case in favour. *Clinical Science*, 1983, 64: 19–23.

Rutman, R.J., Lewis, F.S. and Bloom, W.D. Bipiperidyl mustard, a new obesifying agent in the mouse. *Science*, 1966, 153: 1000.

Schemmel, R., Mickelsen, O. and Gill, J.L. Dietary obesity in rats: Body weight and body fat accretion in seven strains of rats. *Journal of Nutrition*, 1970, 100: 1041–1048.

Schemmel, R., Mickelsen, O. and Motawi, K. Conversion of dietary to body energy in rats as affected by strain, sex and ration. *Journal of Nutrition*, 1972, 102: 1187–1198.

Sclafani, A. Dietary obesity. In G.A. Bray (Ed.), *Recent Advances in Obesity Research*, Vol. 2. London: Newman, 1978: 123–132.

Sclafani, A. and Springer, D. Dietary obesity in adult rats: Similarities to hypothalamic and human obesity syndromes. *Physiology and Behavior*, 1976, 17: 461–471.

Segal, K.R. and Gutin, B. Thermic effects of food and exercise in lean and obese women. *Metabolism*, 1983, 32: 581–588.

Sellers, E.A., Scott, J.W. and Thomas, N. Electrical activity of skeletal muscle of normal and acclimatized rats on exposure to cold. *American Journal of Physiology*, 1954, 177: 372–376.

Seydoux, J., Rohner-Jeanrenaud, F., Assimacopoulos-Jeannet, F., Jeanrenaud, B. and Girardier, L. Functional disconnection of brown adipose tissue in hypothalamic obesity in rats. *Pflugers Archives*, 1981, 390: 1-4.

Sherry, D.F., Mrosovsky, N. and Hogan, J.A. Weight loss and anorexia during incubation in birds. *Journal of Comparative and Physiological Psychology*, 1980, 94: 89-98.

Shimazu, T. Central nervous system regulation of liver and adipose tissue metabolism. *Diabetologia*, 1981, 20 (suppl.): 343-356.

Shimazu, T., Fukuda, A. and Ban, T. Reciprocal influences of the ventromedial and lateral hypothalamic nuclei on blood glucose level and liver glycogen content. *Nature*, 1966, 210: 1178-1179.

Shimazu, T. and Ogasawara, S. Effects of hypothalamic stimulation on gluconeogenesis and glycolysis in rat liver. *American Journal of Physiology*, 1975, 228: 1787-1793.

Smith, C.J.V. and Britt, D.L. Obesity in the rat induced by hypothalamic implants of gold thioglucose. *Physiology and Behavior*, 1971, 7: 7-10.

Stern, J.S. and Johnson, P. Spontaneous activity and adipose cellularity in genetically obese Zucker rat (fa/fa). *Metabolism*, 1977, 26: 371-380.

Storlien, L.H., Higson, F.M., Gleeson, R.M., Smythe, G.A. and Atrens, D.M. Effects of chronic lithium, amitriptyline and mianserin on glucoregulation, corticosterone and energy balance in the rat. *Pharmacology, Biochemistry and Behavior*, in press.

Thomas, D.W. and Mayer, J. Meal taking and regulation of food intake by normal and hypothalamic hyperphagic rats. *Journal of Comparative and Physiological Psychology*, 1968, 66: 642-653.

Thurlby, P.L. and Trayhurn, P. The development of obesity in pre-weaning (ob/ob) mice. *British Journal of Nutrition*, 1978, 39: 397-402.

Trayhurn, P., Thurlby, P.L. and James, W.P.T. A defective response to cold in the obese (obob) mouse and the obese Zucker (fafa) rat. *Proceedings of the Nutrition Society*, 1976, 35: 133A.

Valenstein, E.S., Cox, V.C. and Kakolewski, J.W. Polydipsia elicited by the synergistic action of a saccharin and glucose solution. *Science*, 1967, 157: 552-554.

Vander-Tuig, J.G., Knehans, A.W and Romsos, D.R. Reduced sympathetic nervous system activity in rats with ventromedial hypothalamic lesions. *Life Sciences*, 1982, 30: 913-920.

Van Houten, M. and Posner, B.I. Cellular basis of direct insulin action in the central nervous system. *Diabetologia*, 1981, 20 (suppl.): 255-267.

Weingarten, W.P. and Powley, T.L. Pavlovian conditioning of the cephalic phase of gastric acid secretion in the rat. *Physiology and Behavior*, 1981, 27: 217-221.

Wrenshall, G.A., Andrus, S.B. and Mayer, J. High levels of pancreatic insulin coexistent with hyperplasia and degranulation of beta cells in mice with the hereditary obese-hyperglycemic syndrome. *Endocrinology*, 1955, 56: 335-340.

Yen, T.T., Lowry, L. and Steinmetz, J. Obese locus in *Mus musculus*: A gene dosage effect. *Biochemical and Biophysical Research Communications*, 1968, 33: 883-887.

York, D.A., Steinke, J. and Bray, G.A. Hyperinsulinemia and insulin resistance in genetically obese rats. *Metabolism*, 1972, 21: 277-284.

Zahorska-Markiewicz, B. Thermic effect of food and exercise in obesity. *European Journal of Applied Physiology*, 1980, 44: 231-235.

Zucker, L.M. and Zucker, T.F. Fatty, a new mutation in the rat. *Journal of Heredity*, 1961, 52: 275-278.

Zucker, L.M. and Antoniades, H.N. Insulin and obesity in the Zucker genetically obese rat "fatty". *Endocrinology*, 1972, 90: 1320-1330.

7
A CLINICIAN LOOKS AT ANIMAL MODELS OF ANOREXIA NERVOSA

P. J. V. BEUMONT

I. INTRODUCTION

Anorexia nervosa is an illness, characterized by the excessive use of behaviours directed at inducing weight loss, which usually occurs in adolescent girls and young women. Its incidence has increased in recent years, its treatment is difficult and controversial, and its prognosis remains unsatisfactory. The condition has been the subject of an extraordinary amount of research interest, and reasons for this are not difficult to find. It is one of the few psychiatric syndromes for which simple diagnostic criteria are generally accepted, the weight loss which it entails provides a parameter of change which can easily be measured, and the clinical picture has many features which are of interest not only to psychiatrists but also to endocrinologists, gynaecologists and psychologists.

Attempts to define diagnostic criteria for anorexia nervosa have concentrated on three major themes: (i) a thought content dominated by a desire to become thinner; (ii) the prominence of behaviours which bring about weight loss; and (iii) somatic symptoms arising from these behaviours such as emaciation and interruption of the menstrual cycle. Because two of these three sets of criteria are either behavioural or physical, anorexia nervosa is a suitable condition for study by the use of animal models. Comparisons of patterns of behaviour and of their physical consequences may obviously be helpful, and their validity does not depend on underlying assumptions as to similarity of motivation or other internal psychological

ANIMAL MODELS IN PSYCHOPATHOLOGY
ISBN 0 12 114180 2

variables between the animal subject and the human patient. Thus many of the difficulties discussed by Bond in the introductory chapter of this volume are not relevant in this context.

Before surveying some of the animal models that have been proposed, it is necessary to examine the concept of anorexia nervosa in some detail, if only to ensure that controversial or inconsistent aspects of the syndrome do not obscure those essential, central features that may be elucidated by study of the animal models. An historical approach is appropriate.

II. THE CLINICAL PICTURE OF ANOREXIA NERVOSA

A. Early descriptions

There are many reports of patients with anorexia nervosa in the early medical literature. For instance, Francis de Valangin (1768) of the Royal College of Physicians of London described the case of a "young lady who was inclined to be fat, was advised to make use of vinegar, to reduce her fat; she lived accordingly on pickled mangoes and other pickles which within a short time brought on a train of hysteric disorders; these she increased by too sparse a diet". Eventually her physician persuaded her to resume a normal diet and she recovered.

Clinicians such as de Valangin did not formulate a coherent view of the phenonemon with which they were dealing. It was not until the latter part of the nineteenth century that a proper concept of the illness was generated. Two excellent and independent descriptions appeared almost simultaneously. William Gull (1873, 1888) of Guy's Hospital in London, wrote of "a peculiar form of disease" characterized by extreme emaciation for which no physical cause could be found. Physical signs included amenorrhoea, slow pulse, slow respiration, oedema of the lower extremities and hypothermia. He remarked that the patients displayed an unexpected degree of activity despite their emaciation. Gull believed that the illness was due to a "morbid mental state", and that all the physical symptoms were caused by starvation.

Jean Lasegue (1873), of the Pitie in Paris, gave a detailed description of the progression of the illness, from dieting through increasing preoccupation with weight, to complete and obstinate food refusal and eventual physical exhaustion. He remarked that only then would the patient accept treatment and refeeding, albeit reluctantly. Lasegue concluded that his patients so much resembled each other that he had little difficulty in deciding the diagnosis, and that many of them persisted in their illness for years.

B. Doubts and queries

Both Gull and Lasegue clearly recognized the unique and neurotic nature of the condition they had described. Subsequent authors, however, were less clear in this regard. Anorexia nervosa has been termed a *forme fruste* of schizophrenia, a variant of depression or of manic-depressive psychosis, a type of obsessional neurosis and even a symptom complex within the setting of psychoneurosis, rather than a diagnosis itself (see review by Beumont, 1968).

Psychoanalytical studies sought to discover symbolic meaning in the behavioural manifestations of the illness, at the cost of obfuscating the clarity and simplicity inherent in Gull's and Lasegue's original descriptions. Anorexia nervosa patients were considered to have particular problems in relation to sexuality — to be psychosexually immature. Freud (1902) wrote that "the well known anorexia nervosa of girls seems to me a melancholia occurring when sexuality is undeveloped. The patient asserts she has not eaten simply because she has no appetite. Loss of appetite [is] in sexual terms, loss of libido". Waller *et al.* (1940) suggested that anorexia nervosa patients have fantasies of oral impregnation and that the food refusal is a direct consequence of these fantasies. Others considered the basic problem to be the patient's inability to assume an adult sexual role (Thoma, 1967; Selvini, 1974).

The third deviation from the original concept of the illness resulted from developments in endocrinology. In 1914 and 1918, Morris Simmonds, a German physician, elucidated the clinical picture arising from destruction of the anterior pituitary gland. Fortuitously, some of the patients he described were cachetic. Their emaciation was due to the diseases that had caused their hypopituitarism (malignancy, tuberculosis) and was not the result of the endocrine disturbance. Nevertheless, a misconception arose which was to recur in the literature for years, namely that pituitary dysfunction brought about severe weight loss. It followed that anorexia nervosa was a kind of "functional hypopituitarism", a view which has led to the unnecessary investigation of many anorexia nervosa patients, in futile attempts to find evidence of underlying endocrine disease.

C. Current views

Current acceptance of anorexia nervosa as a distinct clinical entity owes much to the influential writings of Hilda Bruch (1974) who emphasized that the behaviours of these patients is characterized by a relentless pursuit of thinness. This key symptom is accorded proper recognition by the term *pubertatsmagersucht* which is used as a synonym for the illness in the German literature. It distinguishes anorexia nervosa from other psychiatric illnesses which are associated with weight loss. Nosology is no longer considered a problem. In place thereof, attention has shifted to another question, namely, are there distinct subgroups of anorexia nervosa?

Beumont *et al.* (1976a) proposed a division between patients who lose weight entirely by abstinence behaviours such as dieting, and those who employ more bizarre methods such as induced vomiting and purgation. Subsequent investigation indicated that the latter group almost invariably had episodes of gorging or "binge-eating" against a background of long-standing food restriction (Russell, 1979). Bulimia nervosa is now recognized as a different albeit related condition to anorexia nervosa. In a more recent development, Yates *et al.* (1982) pointed to the many similarities between anorexia nervosa (the pursuit of thinness) and exercise "addiction" (the relentless pursuit of fitness). Obligatory exercising seems to be yet another variant of the illness.

Garfinkel and Garner (1983) stress that anorexia nervosa is a multi-dimensional condition with multifactorial causation. The recent increase in its frequency is undoubtedly related to the social pressures that lead many normal people to go on diets or to become health conscious exercisers (Hsu, 1983). The distinction between anorexia nervosa, bulimia and exercise addiction on the one hand, and "normal" dieting and exercise commitment on the other, is difficult and confused. A way in which these various phenomena may be related is shown in Fig. 7.1.

The alleged predominance of sexual conflicts in the genesis of anorexia nervosa has not been confirmed by attempts to study the issue objectively. Beumont *et al.* (1981) reported that anorexia nervosa patients show a wide spectrum of sexual knowledge, attitudes and behaviour, and that their sexual experience is generally equivalent to that of age-matched control subjects up until the time they become emaciated. Severe weight loss is the most likely cause of decreased libido during the illness. The view that anorexia nervosa is a symbolic response to deep-seated psychological problems of a sexual nature is difficult to disprove. There is, however, little evidence to support it.

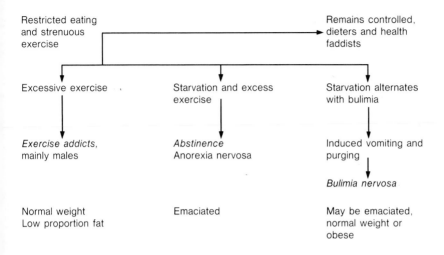

Fig. 7.1: Relations of the Magersucht disorders.

The confusion between anorexia nervosa and pituitary disease has been resolved. Sheehan and Summers (1948), in a painstaking analysis of patient's records, showed that the two conditions could easily be distinguished on clinical grounds. The ceaseless activity of most anorexia nervosa patients contrasts with the lethargy characteristic of panhypopituitarism, while the endocrine profile of anorexia nervosa patients is quite different from that of any known endocrine disease (Beumont, 1979).

Various hypothalamic disturbances have been reported in anorexia nervosa patients such as abnormalities of water metabolism and of thermoregulation. All these disturbances of endocrine and hypothalamic function appear to be secondary manifestations of the illness, and a variety of factors are involved in their pathogenesis. Important amongst these are the emaciation itself, with an alternation in body composition and decreased adipose content; the nutritional deficiency, with a low energy, low fat and low carbohydrate diet; strenuous exercise, which is known to affect endocrine parameters; self-induced vomiting and purgation and the consequent disturbances of blood chemistry, particularly potassium depletion; and the effects of dysfunctions in one endocrine system contributing to abnormalities in another (Beumont and Russell, 1982).

III. THE PLACE OF ANIMAL MODELS

The prior discussion indicates that anorexia nervosa is characterized by a variety of weight losing behaviours, motivated by a desire for thinness, and is related to other behavioural sequences with similar goals. There is no evidence of a basic disturbance of the physiological mechanisms controlling eating. Rather these mechanisms are deliberately over-ridden by the patient. Frequently, restricted eating leads on to a pattern of alternating starvation and gorging, the associated condition of bulimia nervosa. Loss of sexual interest and endocrine and hypothalamic dysfunctions are common in anorexia nervosa, but they appear to be the results of the illness rather than its cause.

Animal models may be postulated at various stages in this development. In some instances, the models are of interest in that they contrast with the human illness, illustrating the basic differences that exist between behaviours that only appear to be similar. In others, the animal models accurately reflect the mechanisms by which the physical symptoms are produced.

The remainder of this chapter will be concerned with a discussion of examples of both types of model. First, spontaneously occurring hypophagias, the so called animal anorexias, will be described and their features compared and contrasted with the human illness. Next, the long term effects of alteration of dietary intake on weight maintenance will be explored. Third, the effects of hypothalamic lesions on feeding behaviour will be presented, and comments will be made on the role of central neurotransmitter systems. Finally the effects of energy deprivation on one important aspect of endocrine activity, namely the control of reproductive function, will be compared in animals and humans.

IV. SPONTANEOUS HYPOPHAGIAS

A. Hibernation and incubation

Fasting in response to religious dictates, dieting for cosmetic or health reasons and anorexia nervosa are examples of restrained eating in humans. These behaviours derive from a deliberate decision to abstain and, initially at least, they are not associated with a loss of appetite. Other animals also have phases during which they eat little and lose weight. An inference that is sometimes drawn from a detailed analysis of these latter phenomena is that they do result from a true loss of appetite; hence, the term animal anorexias appears appropriate. They may be distinguished from food refusal due to illness in that they occur regularly, at specific stages during the life cycle. Examples include the interrupted and decreased feeding associated with hibernation in certain small mammals, and the marked restraint or even fasting seen in many avian species during incubation.

Hibernation is a process whereby an animal spends the inhospitable winter season in a state of torpor. It is usually considered to have an adaptive function, enabling the animal to survive a period of relative food shortage. The relationship between hibernation and feeding in the ground squirrel, *Citellus lateralis*, a small mammalian obligate hibernator, was studied by Mrosovsky and Sherry (1980). In an experimental setting, they found that these animals become torpid and markedly decrease their feeding at the appropriate season even in the presence of plentiful supplies of food. If the animals are repeatedly aroused and forced to rewarm themselves, so that they expend more energy, their feeding increases correspondingly. But irrespective of whether their energy output is high or low, ground squirrels continue to lose weight at a constant rate throughout the winter. On the other hand, if they are totally deprived of food their weight loss accelerates. When food is again made available, they regain weight to a level appropriate to the stage of hibernation they have by now attained, not to their predeprivation levels.

Remarkably similar changes are found during *incubation*. The hen of the red junglefowl, *Gallus gallus*, loses between 10% and 20% of her weight during a 20 day incubation period in which feeding is markedly decreased. The bird leaves the eggs in order to feed for less than 20 minutes per day. This change in feeding behaviour is more important as a cause of weight loss than either the energy expenditure of incubation itself or the resorption of ovary and oviduct that occurs at this time. Yet the hen does not significantly increase her intake when food is placed directly next to the nest so that she can feed without leaving her eggs. However, if incubating birds are totally deprived of food, their weight falls even more rapidly. Once access to food is again allowed, weight is regained — but only to levels appropriate to the stage of incubation the birds have reached, not to preincubation or predeprivation levels (Mrosovsky and Sherry, 1980).

Penguins have very long periods of total fasting associated with their reproductive activity. The male Adelie penguin, *Pygoscelis adeliae*, abstains for a continuous period of about 40 days during which it travels across the ice to its breeding site, selects its territory and mate, awaits the laying of the two-egg clutch and then undertakes the first stint of incubation while the female returns to the sea to feed. When the female relieves him of incubation duty, the male bird has lost about 30% of its body weight (Johnson and West, 1973).

The incubation fast of the Emperor penguin, *Aptenodyte forsteri*, is even more dramatic. By the time the male is relieved of incubation duty by the return of the female, he has undergone a fast of approximately 120 days undertaken in a season of severely inclement weather with high winds and average minimal ambient temperatures as low as minus 48°C. During this fast he loses about 40% of his body weight. Despite this remarkable display of parenting, the male bird will abandon his eggs and return to the seas to feed if his partner's return is delayed so that his body weight falls below a critical value of about 20 kg (Le Mayo, 1977).

B. Programmed lowering of set point

To explain findings such as these, Mrosovsky and Powley (1977) adduce the concept of a programmed decline in the set-point for body weight, or more precisely for body fat. They use the term set-point in an entirely descriptive way to indicate the value at which a stable weight, or a programmed alteration of weight, is apparently defended in the face of external threats, without implying that a physiological feedback system is necessarily involved. In fact, they specifically state that phenomena of this type, which superficially appear similar, are probably controlled by entirely different effector mechanisms in differing species.

Mrosovsky and Sherry (1980) suggest that these animal anorexias have a survival value for the animals concerned, or at least for the species. They occur at times when there is a potential conflict between the drive to feed and other important biological activities. Anorexia is clearly of value in making incubating birds less likely to neglect their eggs in order to seek food. Similarly the apparent loss of hunger of the female octopus during brooding ensures the survival of her eggs. The animal is less likely to eat the eggs herself, although this does occasionally occur, nor does she expose them to other predators while she forages for food, but she remains available to assist in their hatching (Wodinsky, 1977). Another example is that of the hypophagia which is associated with moulting in penguins (Williams et al., 1977). Feeding and moulting are mutually incompatible in the Antarctic as the poorly insulated bird would not be able to survive the excessive heat loss consequent on swimming in extremely cold water.

The advantage occasioned by hypophagia in relation to hibernation is a little more difficult to postulate. Perhaps the anorexia renders the animal less likely to experience thermogenically-expensive arousals induced by hunger. Besides, decreased food intake lessens the need to clear metabolic end products and hence allows renal function to be markedly reduced (Deavers and Musacchia, 1980).

It is interesting to speculate why set-point should be lowered gradually and progressively (Mrosovsky and Sherry, 1980). If the process were rapid, a marked dissonance would occur between the animal's current weight and the newly acquired target value. Mechanisms other than a reduced rate of feeding might then be activated in order to resolve this dissonance, such as an accelerated breakdown of body's energy reserves and the dissipation of excess kilojoules in the form of heat. This would obviously be extremely wasteful, as the reserves have accumulated at considerable cost to the animal. Besides, it would significantly shorten the period of decreased feeding because the animal would soon exhaust its stores and face starvation.

The set-point theory may be criticized as being essentially a teleological explanation deriving from the assumption that the observed hypophagia is the result of a true loss of appetite. Can that really be inferred from the observation that the animal will not eat more if given the opportunity? Can the restoration of a normal response to food by further and artificial reduction of weight be used as evidence that hunger has been only temporarily repressed, but is again elicited to defend a lower weight? It is on these specific observations and inferences that the theory depends (Mrosovsky, 1983).

C. Contrasts with anorexia nervosa

Viewed in the light of the set-point theory, spontaneous hypophagias in animals appeal to clinicians not so much because of their similarities to anorexia nervosa, but rather because of the ways they differ from that condition (Mrosovsky, 1983).

First, they are thought to convey a biological advantage, while anorexia nervosa does not. In fact the illness is associated with a significant mortality, with infertility and with persistent morbidity.

Second, the reduced feeding in animals is assumed to be associated with a true loss of appetite. Even when large amounts of food are available, the animal consumes only small quantities. In contrast, patients with anorexia nervosa often admit they are ravenously hungry, but will not allow themselves to eat. Moreover, they fear that if they start to eat they will be unable to stop and occasionally, when their resolve to abstain does break down, they gorge themselves. Most patients with anorexia nervosa admit to having experienced at least a few episodes of gorging (Beumont et al., 1983a), while in some bulimia assumes over-riding importance (Russell, 1979; Beumont et al., 1983b).

Third, the weight loss in animals is seen as being regulated, and similar in nature to the changes in body temperature during fever or in hormone levels at puberty. The alteration occurs gradually and the new value of weight is subsequently defended (Mrosovsky and Powley, 1977). Characteristic of anorexia nervosa is the precipitous nature of the weight loss and the insatiable desire of the patients to be ever thinner, to weigh less today than yesterday, which is perhaps a reflection of the distortion of their body image that makes them see themselves as obese even when they are really emaciated (Bruch, 1974).

Fourth, activity during hibernation and incubation is markedly decreased. Anorexia nervosa, on the other hand, is usually associated with increased activity up until the stage of physical exhaustion.

Fifth, spontaneous hypophagias stop short once energy reserves have been exhausted. The weight loss involves little catabolism of protein tissue, hence health is not impaired and normal activity can readily be resumed. In anorexia nervosa patients the weight loss is massive and protein tissue as well as fat is broken down. Disturbances in blood chemistry and serious debilitation ensue. The patient is physically ill and presents a picture of severe malnutrition or even starvation.

In view of these contrasting features Mrosovsky (1983) concludes that animal anorexias are of limited value in advancing our understanding of anorexia nervosa. But are the contrasts as vivid as they appear on first appraisal? Do they really arise from an objective observation of the phenomena, or are they dependent on the theoretical stances adopted by the observers? In the sections that follow, some of the apparent contrasts between anorexia nervosa and animal hypophagias will be explored more critically. Anorexia nervosa is defined as an illness with a clearly defined and bizarre symptomology, but it may also be considered an extreme manifestation of voluntary weight control behaviours (Abraham *et al.*, 1983). The spectrum of such behaviours shows greater similarity to the spontaneous hypophagias than does the illness itself. Furthermore, incubation in birds and hibernation in small mammals are but two examples of naturally occurring hypophagia. Other related but dissimilar phenomena may be better models for the human condition.

D. Fatal hypophagia

Anorexia nervosa is not unique in its propensity to lead to a fatal outcome. Perhaps the spontaneous hypophagias of animals do convey an advantage to the species, but their effect on the individual concerned is often disastrous. The abstinence of the female *Octopus hummelincki* during the brood is a case in point (Wodinsky, 1977). The animal spawns only once in its lifetime. Its feeding is markedly decreased while it cares for its eggs, and it invariably dies shortly after the eggs are hatched. These events are controlled by the secretory activity of the optic glands, and, if these organs are removed, the animal resumes eating and survives.

The effects of the incubation fast of the Emperor penguin (*Aptenodytes fosteri*) are more directly comparable to the human situation. The parent birds faithfully incubate their eggs until fat reserves are almost exhausted. They must then return to the sea to replenish their energy stores — often a distance of more than 50 km — and protein catabolism may be needed to provide the necessary energy. It is hardly surpising that many die in the attempt. Their orphaned offspring contribute to the high mortality rate among chicks. At Point Geologie during the winter of 1972, when an unusually long stretch of unbroken sea ice separated the rookery from the open sea making the journeys of the adult birds more hazardous, more than 90% of the chicks did not survive (Le Mayo, 1977). Obviously the complicated interplay of hypophagia and parenting activity was singularly ineffective in preventing a major calamity for the colony.

E. Nutritional aspects

1. Spontaneous hypophagias

The metabolic changes that occur during spontaneous hypophagias in animals are varied, but they are clearly different from those that result from simple starvation. In many instances there is almost an exclusive utilization of lipid stores to provide the required energy. This is well illustrated during the incubation fast of the Emperor penguin. Lipid catabolism accounts for 55%, water loss for 35% and protein breakdown for only 9% of the decrease in weight. Once the bird's weight falls below 20 kg, the value at which it is likely to abandon its eggs, fat reserves are completely exhausted, protein catabolism increases dramatically and the rate of weight loss accelerates (R. Groscolas and C. Clement, quoted by Mrosovsky and Sherry, 1980).

During the incubation fast of the Adelie penguin, only 5% of the weight loss is due to protein breakdown, 95% being the result of fat catabolism. There is a marked decrease in blubber thickness and a corresponding dimunition in other extractable fat. On arrival at the breeding site, the proportion of fat in the bird's dry weight is about 45%. Twenty-seven days later this proportion has fallen to 20%, while carcass water content has increased from 48% to 60% during the same period. Each bird has utilized fat at a rate of approximately 55 g d^{-1} and protein at a rate of less than 5 g d^{-1} to yield some 2050 kJ d^{-1} (Johnson and West, 1973).

Levels of energy expenditure as high as this may seem excessive for such a small animal during a period of relative inactivity. But it must be remembered that the demands on energy reserves are extraordinary. Basic existence, parenting and incubation behaviours, locomotion, territory defence and heat replacement are all occurring in the face of an extreme Antarctic environment, with sub-zero temperatures and high winds.

Of particular interest in relation to the incubation fast of the Adelie penguin is the finding that the fatty acid composition of the lipids that remain does not change appreciably despite the great decrease in the total mass of adipose tissue. This indicates that the metabolic process concerned is very different to that associated with simple starvation (Johnson and West, 1973).

Metabolic changes during mammalian hypophagias have been the subject of a recent symposium (Folk, 1980). Such hypophagias are not uniform but vary greatly from species to species. There are at least four major patterns. First, there are non-dormancy fasts such as the hypophagias found in deer during the rut, or the long fasts of whales during migration and the breeding season. Second, there is the hibernation of small mammals, such as the woodchuck, which remain dormant at low body temperatures for about a week at a time. They arouse periodically to a normothermic condition, but do not feed on these occasions, hence they have no need of a food cache. They have fairly substantial reserves of adipose tissue. Third, there are other small mammalian hibernators, such as the chipmunk, which are dormant and hypothermic for a few days, then arouse to feed avidly on stored supplies of food before again relapsing into dormancy. They have little depot fat, but do hoard food. Finally, there are the large mammalian hibernators, such as bears, which have an uninterrupted period of dormancy of several months with a reduced heart rate, but no hypothermia. They live off their massive reserves of adipose tissue.

Some hibernating mammals satisfy their energy needs by occasional recourse to caches of food. Others live off lipid reserves. And some species also make use of protein catabolism to provide energy (Riedesel and Steffen, 1980). This last strategy is found in small animals such as rodents, whose fat reserves are necessarily small in relation to their body surface, rather than in large animals like bears that can acquire a massive adipose tissue.

2. *Anorexia nervosa*

Metabolic changes during starvation in humans have been reviewed by Davidson *et al.* (1975). The picture in patients with anorexia nervosa is quite atypical. These subjects choose a diet which is very low in energy dense foods, but relatively high in proteins (Beumont *et al.*, 1982). Weight loss at first is almost entirely due to loss of adipose tissue, and only when fat reserves are exhausted is protein broken down. Twenty to thirty per cent of the total body mass in the average woman consists of fat (Davidson *et al.*, 1974); hence it follows that lipid catabolism predominates until the subject has reduced to a weight of about 80% of the original value. Increased exercise, so characteristic of anorexia nervosa, not only enhances the weight loss but further ensures that it is fat rather than protein that is broken down.

Two comments may be made about this initial phase of deliberate weight reduction. First, it is hardly pathological in itself. Although it may lead to anorexia nervosa, this is by no means invariable. Most subjects stop at some point before their fat reserves are exhausted. They may suffer minor physiological disturbances as a consequence of their behaviour, a menstrual disorder euphemistically called hypothalamic amenorrhoea being perhaps the most common, but they are not ill and are usually considered as "healthy dieters". Perhaps they would best be categorized as having subclinical anorexia nervosa.

Second, the point at which fat reserves are exhausted and protein catabolism begins corresponds closely to the weight criterion necessary for the diagnosis of the illness. Thus Russell (1970) mentions a loss of body weight to below 80% of standard while Feighner *et al.* (1972) and the American Psychiatric Association (1980) insist on a loss of at least 25% of original body weight. At levels such as these the patient has very little adipose tissue.

The initial stage of a progressive depletion of fat stores with preservation of protein tissue closely resembles the changes that occur in many forms of animal hypophagia, in which lipid catabolism is the major source of energy. It would be interesting to know whether the adipose tissue that remains in anorexia nervosa patients has an unaltered fatty acid composition, as is the case in the incubating Adelie penguin (Johnson and West, 1973).

As the illness declares itself and weight loss accelerates, protein catabolism is activated to provide energy. Physiological functions are disrupted and the patient becomes physically ill. Starvation has now intervened. An analysis of the way in which animals cope with a prolongation of hypophagia beyond the point of exhaustion of lipid reserves would be relevant to an understanding of this progression. Reference to small mammalian species might be appropriate, as they often need to utilize protein catabolism during hibernation. However it must be remembered that while most animal hypophagias occur at times of reduced activity, anorexia nervosa is usually associated with strenuous exercise until the patient becomes physically exhausted.

F. Variations in the size of energy reserves

Social factors are undoubtedly involved in the aetiology of anorexia nervosa (Hsu, 1983). They are thought to account for the increased occurrence of the illness in recent years, and for its virtual confinement to affluent communities. The illness is seen as a response to the sorts of social pressures that have made dieting endemic in the United States and other Western countries, particularly amongst women. These pressures include the equation of slenderness with sexual attractiveness, and the widely publicized and often exaggerated propaganda that points to the dangers of obesity. The intensity of such pressures led Apfelbaum (1976) to comment that one of the major aims in the treatment of obesity should be to persuade moderately fat subjects to accept their condition! The context wherein these concerns have arisen is a society in which large amounts of energy dense foods are constantly available and obesity is becoming more prevalent. Can there be an animal analogy for so complex a causal relationship?

Variations in habitual body size and composition dependent on the availability of food have been recorded in several animal species, although it is not clear whether the variation is acquired or the result of selection. For instance, Brodie (1975) commented on the discrepancy in body size within rorqual whales. Antarctic blue and fin whales (balaenoptera) have a larger body size than specimens from the Northern Hemisphere. The large size of the Antarctic whale serves an adaptive function. It ensures a body proportion optimal for the reduction of specific metabolic rate and the establishment of an appropriate surface area for the deposition of lipids. Hence, the Antarctic variant is able to make short forays into very cold water where food is densely concentrated and then spend the majority of the year in a warmer environment where food is scarce. In contrast, Northern Hemisphere whales spend a far larger proportion of the year in waters which are always moderately rich in food and consequently do not need to adopt the larger size and body proportions of their southern cousins. In a similar vein, Brodie (1975) remarks that the relatively "poor" condition — from a commercial point of view — of rorqual whales on the Nova Scotia coast implies that these animals live in an area of reliable food resources and have little need to store energy in the form of blubber. In other words, where animals live in an environment in which food is fairly constantly available, the need for stored energy reserves is diminished.

Perhaps, as Brodie (1975) suggests, one should consider the energy reserve of hoarding species of mammals such as rodents as the sum of their fat reserves and their food caches. If the cache is large, the need for fat stores is lessened. Relevant to this concept is the frequent occurrence of hoarding of foodstuffs by patients suffering from anorexia nervosa. As their fat reserves are depleted, patients accumulate large larders of foods whose very existence is a closely guarded secret.

A plump figure, with ample fat reserves, and a larder stacked full with high energy dense foods may be seen as desirable when food supplies are scarce or precarious. In contrast, large segments of our present day communities have constant access to food with minimal effort. The combination of plentiful supplies and ease of access is probably unique in human history. Energy reserves are no longer necessary, although more easily accumulated than ever before. This dissonance must surely be relevant to the disproportionate presentation of obesity and of anorexia nervosa in modern affluent Western type societies.

V. LONG TERM EFFECTS OF DIETARY CHANGE

A. Defence of energy stores

Animal anorexias may be seen as biological strategies directed at minimizing the dissonance between actual and physiologically defended stores of fat. How large is that dissonance in anorexia nervosa patients, and does the illness involve a shift in set-point in one or other direction?

If an animal's fat stores exceed the defended level, energy will be dissipated. If the dissonance is in the opposite direction, the animal not only feeds avidly when given the opportunity, but also utilizes food more efficiently (Boyle *et al.*, 1978). Although patients with anorexia nervosa protest that they *feel* they are at the right weight, there can be little doubt that fat stores are below physiologically defended levels, at least early in the course of the illness. It is true that the patients eat little but their behaviour is contrary, dictated by their psychopathology and difficult to interpret. A better indication of their true condition is probably given by their expressed fear that if they were to allow themselves to eat, they would not be able to stop.

Less subjective is the finding that the more emaciated a patient is, the less energy cost of each kilogram of weight regained (Walker *et al.*, 1979). This suggests that at very low weights the efficiency of food utilization is increased, as it is in animals below a defended weight level. Incidentally, this finding contradicts the view that the homeostatic system regulating body weight is disrupted in anorexia nervosa (Russell *et al.*, 1975).

Another approach to the issue of dissonance is provided by the alliesthesia phenomenon described by Cabanac (1971). Under usual circumstances, a person preloaded with glucose rates a standard sugar solution as less pleasant than if no preloading were given. After dieting and significant weight loss, the effect of preloading is no longer apparant. Similar findings have been reported in relation to anorexia nervosa (Garfinkel *et al.*, 1978), and may be interpreted as indicating that the patients are below their defended levels.

Does the set point for body fat shift during the course of the illness? There are other situations in humans in which such an alteration is suspected. For instance, weight changes during the puerperium suggest a programmed decline (Dennis and Blytheway, 1965). In this context it is appropriate to consider animal experiments that have demonstrated changes in set-point consequent on alterations in diet.

B. Dietary manipulation of set point

Rolls *et al.* (1980) exposed rats over a long period to a palatable high energy "cafeteria" diet. Not only did the animals gain weight, but they subsequently defended a higher set-point.

A corresponding, but opposite, down regulation of set-point might be induced by the continued low energy intake of anorexia nervosa patients. If so, it would account for the common clinical observation that many chronic anorexia nervosa patients appear to need an excessive amount of food to maintain a normal body weight. However the little information that is available in the animal literature does not support the concept that chronic deprivation leads to a down regulation of set-point. Animals can not be maintained at subnormal body weights without substantial reductions in daily energy intake (Quimby, 1948; Kaunitz *et al.*, 1975).

In contrast, the chronic undernutrition of patients with anorexia nervosa may lead to upwards regulation of the body fat set-point, in a manner analogous to a model described by Coscina and Dixon (1983). These authors reported a study in which female rats were deprived of food during adolescent growth. The experimental rats lost 18% of their initial weight after four days of deprivation, but rapidly regained it in the post-deprivational phase together with an extra amount equivalent to the gain registered by control subjects over the same period. The experimental rats achieved this gain without taking more food than the control subjects, suggesting an increased efficiency of utilization.

At a later stage in the experiment, both the experimental and the control rats were exposed to palatable, high energy diet supplements. Both responded with a major rise in weight due to increased feeding and to better utilization. However the experimental animals, which had previously been deprived, ate significantly more than the controls and gained more weight. When returned to the basic low diets, both groups ate less and lost weight, but the difference between the experimental and control groups persisted. That is, the rats that had previously been deprived were now heavier than the control subjects, and maintained this differential. Further, some of the experimental rats later began to gain weight without any change in the diet. Coscina and Dixon (1983) suggest that their findings relate to an alteration in the cephalic phase insulin response, which can be amplified by prior deprivation and which correlates with the severity of dietary induced obesity in rats.

Thus the animal literature suggests that both downwards and upwards alterations in body fat set-point are conceivable in relation to anorexia nervosa patients. It may be that downwards regulation occurs in those who remain chronically emaciated while upwards regulation is found in patients whose anorexia nervosa is subsequently superseded by bulimia and the ultimate development of obesity.

C. Food deprivation resulting in overactivity

The decreased food intake of anorexia nervosa patients is often coupled with extreme overactivity and excessive exercise, which further depletes energy stores. This picture is strongly reminiscent of the self-starvation observed in rats on a restricted diet with ready access to activity wheels (Routtenberg and Kuznesof, 1967).

Routtenberg had observed that rats given a choice between food essential for survival and rewarding self-stimulation chose the latter option and died. He speculated that a similar phenomenon might be involved in the excessive weight loss found in rats living in activity wheels (Spear and Hill, 1962). This concept was explored in a series of elegant experiments.

Rats were maintained on 23 hour deprivation cycles. Some were kept housed in laboratory cages (controls) while others were allowed periodic access to an activity wheel (experimental subjects). The control subjects were soon able to adapt and maintain a stable weight despite the dietary deprivation, but the experimental subjects lost weight and eventually died. In conjunction with the fall in weight, activity levels steadily increased. Furthermore, the experimental subjects ate significantly less than the controls, despite their increased output of energy, a finding that must be considered paradoxical (Routtenberg and Kuznesof, 1967).

Routtenberg and Kuznesof (1967) and Routtenberg (1968) investigated the effects of administering certain drugs and of various alterations in the experimental procedure on the phenomenon. It would seem that the major factor contributing to the self starvation is a "stress" arising from food deprivation itself. But why the rat runs in response to food deprivation, and why this activity causes a further reduction in food intake, remains unclear.

Routtenberg's original suggestion that the phenomenon is related to stimulation at a hypothalamic level sounds reasonable, but the effect of a negative energy balance on hypothalamic self-stimulation is itself a matter of considerable disagreement. Food deprivation has variously been reported as enhancing, not affecting and inhibiting rates of self-stimulation. The exact siting of the stimulating electrode is an important determinant of which of these effects is seen, negative energy balance appearing to selectively increase excitability of reward-related neurones in the lateral hypothalamus. Furthermore, not only does energy balance effect self-stimulation, but self-stimulation effects energy balance (Atrens et al., 1982).

The inverse relationship between activity and energy intake is seen in less dramatic situations than that described by Routtenberg. Levitsky (1974) demonstrated that rats on a free food schedule show a significant decrease in food intake for the first four to six days following the introduction of an activity wheel into their cages. Similar findings have been reported in other species, including humans. Thus Edholm et al. (1955) found that cadets eat less on days of military training than they do on days of less activity, while Katch et al. (1969) showed that participation in sport activities moderately decreases energy intake in young women who are usually inactive. Given time, however, both animals and humans adapt to the activity and take adequate amounts of food to maintain their weights *provided their diets are not restricted* (Epling et al., 1983). The key factor in anorexia nervosa and in the animals studied by Routtenberg is that the increased activity occurs in a setting in which food is restricted, compensation cannot occur and the phenomenon became non-adaptive. The animal model is clearly apposite to the human illness, and warrants further investigation (Epling et al., 1983).

One may speculate as to the teleological significance of the inverse relationship between activity and eating. In the direction of a lessened food intake leading to an increase in exercise levels it would seem reasonable to suggest a potential benefit to the animal concerned. As food resources became scarce, the animal is prompted to become more active in order to seek fresh supplies. Viewed in this way, the overactivity of anorexia nervosa patients, and their characteristically disturbed sleep pattern which is reversed on refeeding, may be seen as direct effects of the starvation to which they have subjected themselves. On the other hand, excessive exercise is often the initial behavioural disturbance, prompted by a desire to become "fit" and "not flabby", rather than a secondary effect resulting from the dietary restriction. As always, the interaction of voluntary and involuntary factors in the determination of human behaviour is more complex than that modelled in animal experiments.

VI. LESIONS OF THE HYPOTHALAMUS

A. Obesity and emaciation resulting from hypothalamic lesions

To maintain constancy of the *milieu interieur*, energy balance is regulated through the adjustment of four important variables, namely, food intake, stored energy, work and heat production. Research interest has usually focused on the first of these factors, although lately the importance of the others has received increasing recognition (see Chapter 6). In the regulation of food intake, as in that of other visceral activities, the hypothalamus plays a crucial role. The effects of lesions in this area of the brain on eating behaviour have been the subject of numerous studies.

Frohlich's syndrome, of obesity and genital underdevelopment, has long been known to arise from pathology in the region of the sella turcica. Originally ascribed to pituitary hyposecretion, it is now realized that the syndrome is due to hypothalamic damage as it can be induced in experimental animals by bilateral lesions in the hypothalamus without concomitant pituitary damage. The region whose bilateral destruction induces obesity is the medial hypothalamic area, which contains the ventromedial nuclei. The obesity appears to arise from hyperphagia — voracious overeating — and not from any associated metabolic disturbance (Anand, 1961).

Anand and Brobeck (1951) produced a different kind of feeding disturbance by lesioning another area of the hypothalamus in rats. They reported that bilateral destruction of the extreme lateral part of the lateral hypothalamus, in the same rostrocaudal plane as the ventromedial nucleus, produces complete aphagia and death due to inanition. Anand (1961), from his own and other work, proposed two "centres" concerned with feeding: a facilitatory centre in the lateral hypothalamus; and a satiety or inhibitory centre sited medially. He believed the lateral centre to be dominant, as its bilateral destruction leads to death by starvation irrespective of whether the medial centre is intact or not. Lesions of the medial centre produce the effect of hyperphagia only in the presence of an intact lateral system.

Anand (1961) was concerned not only with the results of selective lesioning, but also with work in which the relevant hypothalamic areas were directly stimulated by implanted electrodes. During these latter experiments he observed that various behaviours were associated with the "urge to eat" and with satiation. Hyperactivity (restlessness, searching) anticipates feeding and increases the likelihood that food will be encountered, while satiation is usually accompanied by inactivity and lethargy.

The interruption of feeding by lateral hypothalamic lesions is prolonged, but not permanent. With adequate maintenance after lesioning a characteristic course can be discerned, culminating in the restoration of normal feeding (Teitelbaum and Epstein, 1962).

B. Altered body weight regulation

Powley and Keesey (1970) criticized previous hypotheses concerning the effects of hypothalamic lesions on feeding behaviour. They noted that the theories propounded had been of two kinds, namely, (i) motor theories that suggest the lesions disrupt feeding by damage to specific motor systems involved in its co-ordination; (ii) motivational theories that explain the behaviour as being due to a loss of appetite or anorexia. In both instances, the gradual return of feeding that eventually occurs, was seen to reflect a gradual recovery of normal functioning.

In contrast, Powley and Keesey (1970) proposed a theory involving an alteration of the set-point for weight regulation. Rather than abolish appetite or disrupt the motor control of feeding, lateral hypothalamic lesions lower the set-point. Animals stop feeding and lose weight until they reach the level of the lowered set-point and it is this lag, rather than the gradual recovery of normal function, that accounts for the animals' subsequent progress. In support of their theory, Powley and Keesey reported the results of two experiments. First, they showed that rats that had recovered normal feeding behaviour after a phase of aphagia induced by lateral hypothalamic lesions persisted in maintaining weight levels substantially below those of control subjects despite a relatively normal food intake. Second, they demonstrated that reduction of the animals' weight by partial starvation prior to lesioning greatly reduces the periods of aphagia and anorexia that follow such operations. Nevertheless, these animals stabilize their weights at a level similar to those that have not been subjected to prior deprivation.

Keesey *et al.* (1978) went on to monitor food intake and utilization in animals with lateral hypothalamic lesions. While control animals cannot be maintained at a reduced body weight without a substantial reduction in energy intake, those that have been lesioned continue to do so. When lesioned rats and controls are subjected to progressive restrictions in food intake, both show equivalent falls in body weight. When given access to the same amounts of food they had access to before restriction, indexed to their reduced metabolic mass, both sets of animals regain weight rapidly and at an equivalent rate. Thus the lesioned animals, like the control subjects, appear to utilize food in a normal manner and to adapt to weight loss by increasing the efficiency of food utilization. However, the lesioned animals stabilize again at a weight considerably below that of the control subjects, indicating that the adjustments, in their case, occur around a set-point for body weight that has been reduced as a result of the operation.

Recent work suggests that concept of hypothalamic feeding "centres" may be unwarranted, at least in as far as that term implies a nucleus of neurons concerned with a specific function.

Stricker and Andersen (1980) have pointed out that the extreme lateral lesions of the lateral hypothalamus most effective in producing aphagia interrupt dopaminergic fibres coursing through the hypothalamus, and lower dopamine concentrations in the forebrain. Injecting the toxin 6-hydroxydopamine destroys the distant cell bodies of these fibres without causing local damage, and produces the same behavioural effects. Thus it seems that damage to ascending dopaminergic tracts passing through the region is more important in the causation of the so-called lateral hypothalamic syndrome than is the destruction of local neurons.

C. Involvement of neurotransmitters

Liebowitz (1983) studied the role of brain monoamine systems in feeding behaviour using a cannula to deliver drugs to discrete areas of brain in freely-moving rats. She proposed the existence of four distinct mono-aminergic systems within the hypothalamus that modulate feeding and weight. First, an α-noradrenergic system within the medial hypothalamus stimulates feeding and is involved in the appetite-stimulating effects of drugs such as clonidine and the tricyclic antidepressants. Second, a serotonergic system, also within the medial hypothalamus, inhibits feeding and is associated with the appetite suppressant effect of fenfluramine which releases serotonin. Third, a beta-adrenergic system in the lateral hypothalamus inhibits feeding and participates in the appetite suppressant effects of amphetamines. Fourth, and finally, a dopaminergic system in the lateral hympthalamus also inhibits feeding. The appetite stimulating action of phenothiazine antipsychotic drugs is due to the blockade of dopamine receptors in this last system.

It is clear that several different neurotransmitter systems are involved in the control of feeding. To some extent, at least, these various systems appear directed at controlling the intake of specific nutrient substances, and the relationship is reciprocal, that is, changes in plasma composition which follow the ingestion of certain nutrients have modulating effects on the production and release of specific neurotransmitters (Wurtman and Wurtman, in press). For instance, plasma amino acid concentrators after a meal rich in carbohydrate and poor in protein are such as to cause a rise in brain tryptophan levels which in turn accelerates the production and release of tryptophan's neurotransmitter product, serotonin. Such a change predisposes the individual to choose a protein rich meal on the next occasion and it may also lead to increased sleepiness and impaired mental efficiency. On the other hand, a protein rich, low carbohydrate meal has exactly opposite effects.

D. Implications for anorexia nervosa

Anand's original concepts provided two potential models for anorexia nervosa. The illness may result either from bilateral destruction of the lateral hypothalamus, or from chronic overstimulation of the medial hypothalamus. Because he believed lateral lesions invariably lead to death by starvation, Anand favoured the second hypothesis and sought evidence to support it. Later, when it was understood that recovery could take place from lateral lesions, it was the lateral hypothalamic syndrome that was usually proposed as the model of anorexia nervosa (Russell, 1970).

Stricker and Andersen (1980) discussed the comparison of anorexia nervosa with the lateral hypothalamic syndrome. They noted that the behavioural effects of the hypothalamic lesion are rather more diffuse than the original reports suggested. Although aphagia is a prominent feature, other alterations of behaviour are also present, such as loss of thirst, disinclination to seek warmth and inability to learn simple tasks. There appears to be a broad impairment of all voluntary activity, so that the animal is lethargic unless specifically provoked. In addition, neurological deficits such as akinesia, catalepsy and sensory neglect are prominent. Rather than resemble anorexia nervosa with its hyperactivity, the behaviour of lesioned animals is reminiscent of patients with advanced Parkinson's disease, a known dopamine-deficiency condition.

The performance of lesioned animals can be improved by administering a number of pharmacological substances, all of which have a net dopaminergic effect. DOPA (dihydroxyphenylalaline), the precursor of dopamine, apomorphine and amphetamine, which are dopamine agonists, and drugs that augment the post-synaptic effects of dopamine such as theophylline and caffeine, have all been shown to be effective (Stricker and Andersen, 1980). It warrants noting that Johansen and Knorr (1977) claimed that low doses of L-dopa exert a beneficial effect in anorexia nervosa, but their study was uncontrolled and the findings have not been replicated.

Although the effect of lateral hypothalamic lesions is neither as specific a syndrome as was originally proposed, nor as appropriate a model as was hoped, it has nevertheless been useful in drawing attention to the role of neurotransmitters in the regulation of feeding behaviour. The involvement of dopaminergic mechanisms in feeding, together with the observation that dopamine is important in controlling the secretion of LHRH and hence menstrual function, led Barry and Klawans (1976) to suggest that anorexia nervosa is a state not of dopaminergic deficiency, but rather of dopaminergic excess! On the other hand, evidence of an adrenergic system concerned with satiety prompted Redmond et al. (1977) to propose that increased activity of the satiety mechanism was important in the pathogenesis of the illness.

Leibowitz believes that the four hypothalamic monoaminergic systems she described also exist in humans, and that their disturbance is a factor in the pathogenesis of anorexia nervosa and bulimia. Her own research has focused on the noradrenergic system in the medial hypothalamus. She proposes that anorexia nervosa is produced in part by a decrease in hypothalamic noradrenergic activity, a theory supported by the finding of a decreased level of the metabolite MHPG in the urine of anorexia nervosa patients (Halmi et al., 1978; Abraham et al., 1981). Food deprivation in turn has dramatic effects on noradrenergic activity within the medial hypothalamus which may account for the oscillating eating patterns associated with the reactive hyperphagia of bulimia patients.

All such theories are almost certainly too simplistic, but they open up areas of study that should be pursued. In view of the specificity of the relationships between neurotransmitters and the intake of nutrients that Wurtman and Wurtman (in press) have described, future investigators could profitably explore the precise relation of changes in nutrient intake and neurotransmitter concentrations with specific behavioural manifestations. The two prime candidates for such investigation are the avoidance of energy dense foods, a characteristic of the behaviour of most patients with anorexia nervosa, and the episodic hyperphagia on sweet, highly palatable "cafeteria" type foods that is the usual disturbance in bulimia.

VII. UNDERNUTRITION AND REPRODUCTIVE ENDOCRINE FUNCTION

A. The hypothalamic pituitary gonadal axis

Undernutrition has profound effects on reproductive function in animals. Ball *et al.* (1947) reported a decreased pregnancy rate in mice on a kilojoule restricted diet, while Marrian and Parkes (1929) found that inanition leads to anoestrous and atrophy of the ovaries and uterus in rats. The most prominent defect is an endocrine disturbance, that is, gonadal hypofunction. It is not due to a refractory condition of the gonads themselves, but to decreased circulating levels of the gonadotrophic hormones secreted by the anterior pituitary. Evidence to support this statement is provided by the finding that the atrophy of the genital system can readily be arrested by injecting gonadotrophins (Marrian and Parkes, 1929) or by pituitary implants (Werner, 1939).

Lowered levels of circulating gonadotrophins may result from impaired synthesis or from defective release of hormone by the pituitary. Impaired synthesis does not appear to be the mechanism involved, as the pituitary content of gonadotrophins in undernourished rats has been found to be unchanged or even increased, on a potency per milligram basis (Marian and Parkes, 1929; Meites and Reid, 1949). Consequently, Ershoff (1952) suggested that the basic defect during inanition is a failure of the gonadotrophin mechanism.

The recent advent of radioimmunoassay techniques, which provide sensitive, reliable and convenient methods for measuring circulating hormone values, has led to a spurt in endocrine research. The findings of the earlier studies mentioned above have now been confirmed and extended. The secretory ability of the gonads is not impaired by starvation (Pirke and Spyra, 1981). But the restriction of food to 50% of *ad libitum* intake for 10 to 20 days does result in a significant decrease in serum levels of the gonadotrophin, luteinizing hormone (LH), in both female and male rats (Howland, 1972; 1975). The other pituitary gonadotrophin, follicle-stimulating hormone (FSH), appears to be less effected. Campbell *et al.* (1977) reported that seven days of complete starvation in male rats results in only a 32% reduction of circulating FSH levels as opposed to a 75% reduction of LH. It would indeed appear that the secretion of LH is more sensitive to undernutrition than is that of FSH, and that LH levels are effected earlier and more severely in conditions of complete starvation.

Ershoff (1952) assumed that the reduced secretion of gonadotrophins was a direct consequence of the effects of inanition on the pituitary. This view is difficult to reconcile with the finding that female rats that have developed anoestrus due to underfeeding show evidence of renewed release of pituitary gonadotrophins (namely, resumption of pro-oestrous and oestrous vaginal smear patterns) when exposed to constant illumination for 10 days, but without alteration to their nutritional status (Piacsek and Meites, 1967). A central nervous system (CNS) mechanism must be postulated to account for the phenomenon. Recent understanding of neuro-endocrine relationships provides an answer. It is now realized that the CNS controls pituitary function through releasing hormones secreted by the hypothalamus into a portal system which leads down the pituitary stalk. Luteinizing hormone releasing hormone (LHRH) is the releasing hormone responsible for the control of LH secretion, and to a lesser extent of FSH secretion as well (Pasteels and Franchimont, 1976).

The disturbance of reproductive function during inanition could be due to a decreased sensitivity of the pituitary to LHRH (Root *et al.*, 1975). This appears to be unlikely as Campbell *et al.* (1977) reported a normal LH response to exogenous releasing hormone in starved rats. It would seem more likely that there is a decrease in either the hypothalamic production of LHRH or of its release.

Piacsek and Meites (1967) reported that the hypothalamic content of LHRH in female rats subjected to 50% food restriction was reduced to 75% after 21 days, while Negro-Vilar *et al.* (1971) reported a reduction of "FSH" releasing hormone in male rats that had been starved for seven days. However, Pirke and Spyra (1981), using modern techniques, found that the LHRH content of the preoptic area and the basal medial hypothalamus in rats is not altered by starvation, while that of the median eminence is significantly increased! Although Pirke and Spyra's data do not necessarily reflect production rates, they do indicate that there is more than sufficient LHRH present in the area from which it is normally secreted. Moreover, under *in vitro* conditions, the release of LHRH from the median eminences of starved rats is greater than that from control tissue of normal animals (Warnhoff *et al.*, 1983). However, the relevant point is that the *in vitro* release of LHRH is markedly decreased in the starved animals (Pirke and Spyra, 1981).

It thus appears that LHRH secretion is diminished in instances of undernutrition, and this diminution underlies the reduced pituitary secretion of gonadotrophins and consequent gonadal hypofunction that is associated with inanition.

Ibrahim and Howland (1972) suggested that the activity of the LHRH secreting cells is affected by a decrease in insulin levels that occurs in undernutrition as a compensatory mechanism to prevent fatal hypoglycemia. Their hypothesis has not yet been confirmed by experimental study.

The activity of the LHRH neuron is modulated by a number of factors, including the feedback system by which gonadal hormones influence activity at the pituitary and the hypothalamic level. Pirke and Spyra (1981) demonstrated that the testosterone-LH feedback system is preserved in the starved rat, although its sensitivity is greatly increased, while Pirke *et al.* (in press) found that no clear relationship could be established between the decreased secretion of LHRH and the changes in noradrenergic neurotransmission, the endophinergic system on the mediator prostaglandin E2. Other neurotransmitter and neuromodulator systems have still to be investigated, but as yet the mechanisms responsible for the effects of starvation on LHRH secretion remains unknown.

B. The type of deprivation, its latency and the effects of nutritional rehabilitation

Perhaps the deficiency of energy intake itself is the prime factor causing the reproductive endocrine disturbance in undernutrition. An alternative explanation is that an inadequate intake of kilojoules necessitates the use of available protein to meet energy requirements, and hence leads to a relative protein deficiency. Platt (1966) has commented on the interdependence of protein and energy requirements, noting that the dietary value of protein is reduced under conditions of inadequate energy intake. Protein restriction *per se* is known to cause anoestrous and its effects are said to be more rapid and severe than simple kilojoule deficiency (Srebnik and Nelson, 1963). Deficiencies of various vitamins and minerals are also known to affect gonadal functioning. Unfortunately, widely differing dietary regimes have been used in studying the effects of undernutrition on laboratory animals and it is not always possible to discern which are the relevant deficiencies causing the disturbance.

The latency of the endocrine changes during undernutrition has received relatively little attention, as most investigators have drawn blood samples, or have sacrificed their animals, only at fixed intervals, for example, seven, 10 or 20 days after starting the reduction in dietary intake. Howland and Skinner (1973) were exceptional in reporting that LH levels fell within 24 hours of the initiation of starvation, and FSH levels within 48 hours.

Vaginal smear patterns in female rats provide indirect evidence of hormonal status, but as anoestrous occurs only after a significant fall in circulating gonadotrophin levels, vaginal smears are at best an imprecise measure of reduced secretion. Nevertheless studies based on their use are of interest in view of the general paucity of literature concerning the timing of the endocrine changes. Srebnik and Nelson (1963) reported that female rats became anoestrous after five days on a protein free diet, while pair-fed animals did not become anoestrous until 21 days. Lamming and Krause (1963) found that anoestrous occurred in rats after three weeks on a severely restricted diet that caused a weight loss of 2–3 g d⁻¹. Similarly, Piacsek and Meites (1967) found that female rats on a 50% normal food intake stopped oestrous cycling after 14 to 21 days.

Reproductive endocrine function recovers rapidly following the restoration of normal nutrition. Widdowson *et al.* (1964) refed nutritionally deprived immature rats. They found that vaginal opening occurred after five days of feeding being restarted, and that the ovaries were as large as those of control subjects of the same age, with many corpora lutea, after only seven days of nutritional rehabilitation. Campbell *et al.* (1977) fed male rats again after a period of chronic undernutrition. After seven days of feeding, circulating LH levels were elevated to values well above those of normal control subjects. They found no evidence of an increased pituitary responsiveness to LHRH and concluded that the LH rebound effect was due to an increased release of LHRH by the hypothalamus.

De Wet (1981) has recently performed a comprehensive investigation of the effect of undernutrition and subsequent refeeding on sexually mature female rats. Using a modification of the casein diet described by Harper (1959), he systematically reduced energy value by withdrawing dextrin and fats. He found that oestrous functioning was relatively resistant to modification by energy deprivation. Serum LH levels and ovarian and uterine weights were significantly decreased only after more than seven days on a severely depleted dextrin and fat free diet. Anoestrus was initiated between the 7th and 13th day, and appeared to relate to the animal having undergone a weight loss of approximately 20%. Anoestrous rats had a significantly diminished response of LH to infused LHRH, but this abnormality was corrected by prior priming of the animal with LHRH.

Animals were rehabilitated by allowing them access to *ad libitum* feeding on the full casein diet with dextrin and fats. Serum LH levels rose promptly, reaching near normal values by the 15th day. There was no evidence of persisting damage to the reproductive system, and the resumption of oestrous cycles appeared to relate to the animal regaining its original weight.

De Wet (1981) reported a significant reduction of pituitary LH content in his undernourished animals, a finding at variance with most recent reports in the literature. Nevertheless the finding that a normal LH response to LHRH could be induced in these animals by prior priming with LHRH supports the generally accepted hypothesis that the main effect of undernutrition is a diminution of hypothalamic releasing hormone secretion rather than a decrease in pituitary LH synthesis.

C. Relevance to human undernutrition

Research in animals over many decades and using different methodologies has shown that serum gonadoptrophin levels are reduced during states of undernutrition. Associated with this reduction is atrophy of gonads and the secondary sex organs. The reduction of circulating hormone levels is due to an impairment of the pituitary secretory mechanism, itself caused by a defective release of hypothalamic LHRH.

Most of the work reported was undertaken using rats as the laboratory species. The physiological mechanisms controlling the rat oestrous cycle are similar in many important respects to the mechanisms involved in the human menstrual cycle (Tepperman, 1973), but there are some major differences. Specifically, the positive feedback regulating the cycle is different in rodents and primates. In the former there is a very powerful central signal, while in the latter the clock triggering the mechanism appears to be in the gonad rather than in the brain (Knobil et al., 1980).

The effects of undernutrition on reproductive endocrine functioning, as studied by animal experiment, bears a striking resemblance to findings in patients with anorexia nervosa (see reviews by Beumont, 1979 and Beumont and Russell, 1982). In both situations: (i) the disorder is characterised by low levels of circulating gonadotrophins, LH being affected more than FSH; (ii) the basic problem appears to be defective stimulation of the pituitary by LHRH which in turn leads to a temporary disturbance of the pituitary's ability to respond to exogenous LHRH, which can be overcome by prior priming with releasing hormone; (iii) refeeding leads to a rapid restoration of hormone levels; and (iv) during refeeding, a rebound effect may be noted.

Certain important and unexplained differences remain. First, anoestrous occurs in animals only after a significant fall in body weight. In humans, amenorrhoea is often the first symptom of an anorexia nervosa illness. Perhaps this difference reflects the stronger central signal that regulates the cycle in rats as opposed to primates (Knobil et al., 1980). Second, the rebound effect in animals, leading to supranormal levels of gonadotropin during refeeding, seems to be due to an increased secretion of LHRH by the hypothalamus. In humans, on the other hand, there is good evidence that it is pituitary sensitivity which is increased (Beumont et al., 1976b). Third, restoration of normal hormone levels by refeeding leads to a prompt resumption of oestrous cycle in the rat. In the human, return of the menses may be long delayed. This delay suggests the presence of an additional factor in the anorexia nervosa subject that contributes to the persistence of disordered functioning. Once again, it may be that this factor is also a matter of sensitivity to response — in this instance, of the hypothalamus rather than of the pituitary. Wakeling *et al.* (1977) have shown altered feedback to exogenous ethinyloestradiol in anorexia nervosa patients, persisting long after weight restoration and the return of normal tonic values of hormones.

The findings of the animal studies strongly support the conclusion that the nutritional deprivation is the prime cause of the reproductive endocrine dysfunction underlying the menstrual disorder of anorexia nervosa. However, other factors in addition to nutritional deprivation may be involved in the human situation which could account for the differences mentioned above. It has been suggested that emotional stress can bring about menstrual disturbances (Rakoff, 1968) and psychological factors may contribute to the endocrine disturbance in anorexia nervosa patients (Russell *et al.*, 1975). De Wet (1981) found evidence that a combination of nutritional deprivation and repeated stress was more effective than either in isolation in the production of anoestrous in rats. Another possibility is that activity plays a key role, as overexercising is known to affect reproductive endocrine function (Abraham *et al.*, 1982) and overexercising is often an important element in anorexia nervosa. As yet there have been no studies of endocrine function in animals subjected to a combination of increased physical activity and energy deprivation.

VIII. CONCLUSION

Anorexia nervosa is a complex disturbance that has been termed a paradigm of psychosomatic illness. It is a very human ailment, largely restricted to certain types of society, and to certain groups within those societies. It would indeed be expecting too much to imagine that any animal model would accurately reflect all aspects of the illness. However, animal models have provided a series of observations through which our understanding of the pathogenesis of many symptoms of the condition has been significantly advanced.

The deficiencies of existing models point to new areas which should be explored and new models that need to be sought. Anorexia nervosa is an unfortunate term for an illness that is characterized by a variety of behaviours, all aimed at inducing weight loss, but in which loss of appetite *per se* is not invariable and perhaps not even usual. Yet attempts to define an animal model almost always start from the premise that hypophagia is the essential criterion for the condition, and assume an underlying anorexia.

Clinicians now realize that anorexia nervosa patients may ingest relatively large amounts of food, but rid themselves of the kilojoules by regurgitating, vomiting or inducing diarrhoea. Are there animal anologies in these forms of behaviour? Equally important is the question of exercise. The anorexia nervosa patient is usually hyperactive until the stage of physical exhaustion is reached. Animal anorexias, whether they occur naturally or are induced, often involve lethargy or at least relative inactivity.

Models in which animals lose weight through a combination of restricted eating and increased physical exertion such as that proposed by Routtenburg and Kuznesof (1967) seem more appropriate. They might also help unravel some of the problems that still obscure our understanding of the physical disturbance in anorexia nervosa. For example, the early onset of amenorrhoea that often occurs before significant weight loss may well be related directly to the exercise in which these patients so frequently indulge.

Many problems remain to be solved, and animal models will undoubtedly help in their resolution.

REFERENCES

Abraham, S.F., Beumont, P.J.V. and Cobbin, D.M. Catecholamine metabolism and body weight in anorexia nervosa. *British Journal of Psychiatry*, 1981, 138: 244–247.

Abraham, S.F., Beumont, P.J.V., Fraser, I.S. and Llewellyn-Jones, D. Body weight, exercise and menstrual status among ballet dancers in training. *British Journal of Obstetrics and Gynaecology*, 1982, 89: 507–510.

Abraham, S.F., Mira, M., Beumont, P.J.V., Sowerbutts, T. and Llewellyn-Jones, D. Eating behaviours among young women. *Medical Journal of Australia*, 1983, 2: 225–228.

American Psychiatric Association. *Diagnostic and Statistical Manual of Mental Disorders*, 3rd Ed., 1980, Washington, DC.

Anand, B.K. and Brobeck, J.R. Nervous regulation of food intake. *Physiology Reviews*, 1961, 41: 677–708.

Anand, B.K. and Brobeck, J.R. Hypothalamic control of food intake. *Yale Journal of Biology and Medicine*, 1951, 24: 123–140.

Apfelbaum, M. The effects of very restrictive high protein diets. *Clinical Endocrinology and Metabolism*, 1976, 5: 417–430.

Atrens, D.M. Williams, M.P., Brady, C.J. and Hunt, G.E. Energy balance and hypothalamic self-stimulation. *Behavioural Brain Research*, 1982, 5: 131–142.

Ball, Z.B., Barnes, R.H. and Visscher, M.B. The effects of caloric restriction on maturity and senescence, with particular reference to fertility and longevity. *American Journal of Physiology,* 1947, 150:511–519.

Barry, V.C. and Klawans, H.L. On the role of dopamine in the pathophysiology of anorexia nervosa. Journal of Neural Transmission, 1976, 38:107–122.

Beumont, P.J.V. Anorexia nervosa: A review. *South African Medical Journal,* 1968, 44:911–915.

Beumont, P.J.V. The endocrinology of anorexia nervosa. *Medical Journal of Australia,* 1979, 1:611–613.

Beumont, P.J.V., George, C. and Smart, D.E. 'Dieters' and 'vomiters and purgers' in anorexia nervosa. *Psychological Medicine,* 1976a, 6:617–622.

Beumont, P.J.V., George G.C.W., Pimstone, B.L. and Vinik, A.I. The pituitary response to hypothalamic releasing hormones in patients with anorexia nervosa. *Journal of Clinical Endocrinology and Metabolism*, 1976b, 43:487–496.

Beumont, P.J.V., Abraham, S.F. and Simson, K.G. Sexual experiences and attitudes in girls and women with anorexia nervosa. *Psychological Medicine,* 1981, 11:131-140.
Beumont, P.J.V. and Russell, J. Anorexia nervosa. In P.J.V. Beumont and G. Burrows (Eds), *Handbook of Psychiatry and Endocrinology,* Amsterdam: Elsevier, 1982.
Beumont, P.J.V. and Abraham, S.F., Episodes of ravenous overeating or bulimia: Their occurrence in patients with anorexia nervosa and with other forms of disordered eating. In P.L. Darby, P.E. Garfinkel, D.M. Garner and D.V. Ciscina (Eds), *Recent Developments in Research,* New York: Alan R. Liss, 1983a: 149-157.
Beumont, P.J.V., Booth, A.L., Abraham, S.F., Griffiths, D.A. and Turner, T.R. A Temporal Sequence of Symptoms in Patients With Anorexia Nervosa: A preliminary report. In P.L. Darby, P.E. Garfinkel, D.M. Garner and D.V. Coscina (Eds), *Anorexia Nervosa: Recent Developments in Research,* New York: Alan R. Liss, 1983b:129-136.
Boyle, P.C., Storlien, L.H. and Keesey, R.C. Increased efficiency of food utilization following weight loss. *Physiology and Behaviour,* 1978, 21:261-264.
Brodie, P.F. Catacean energetics, an overview of intra-specific size variation. *Ecology,* 1975, 56:152-161.
Bruch, H. *Eating Disorders, Obesity, Anorexia Nervosa and the Person Within.* London: Routledge and Kegan Paul, 1974.
Cabanac, M. Physiological role of pleasure. *Science,* 1971, 173:1103-1107.
Campbell, G.A., Kurcz, M., Marshall, S. and Meites, J. Effects of starvation in rats in serum levels of follicle stimulating hormone, luteinizing hormone, growth hormone and prolactin response to LHRH and TRH. *Endocrinology,* 1977, 100:580-587.
Coscina, D.V. and Dixon, L.M. Body weight regulation in anorexia nervosa: Insights from an animal model. In P.L. Darby, P.E. Garfinkel, D.M. Garner and D.V. Coscina (Eds), *Anorexia Nervosa: Recent Developments in Research.* New York: Alan R. Liss, 1983: 207-219.
Davidson, S., Passmore, R., Brock, J.F. and Truswell, A.S. *Human Nutrition and Dietetics.* Edinburgh: Churchill Livingstone, 1975: 13: 281-287.
Deavers, D.R. and Musaacchia, X.J. Water metabolism and renal function during hibernation and hypothermia. *Federation Proceedings,* 1980, 39: 2969-2973.
Dennis, K.J. and Blytheway, W.R. Changes in body fat after delivery. *Journal of Obstetrics and Gynaecology,* 1965, 72: 94-102.
De Valangin, F. *A treatise on diet.* London: J. & W. Oliver, 1968.
De Wet, J.M. *Psychological and nutritional factors influencing the dynamics of gonado-trophin secretion in the female rat.* Ph.D Thesis, University of Cape Town, 1981.
Edholm, O.G., Fletcher, J.G., Widdowson, E.M. and McCance, R.A. The energy expenditure and food intake of individual men. *British Journal of Nutrition,* 1955, 9: 286-300.
Epling, W.F., Pierce, W.D. and Stefan, L. A thoery of activity based anorexia. *International Journal of Eating Disorders,* 1983, 3: 7-46.
Ershoff, B.H. Nutrition and the anterior pituitary with special reference to the general adaptation syndrome. *Vitamins and Hormones,* 1952, 10: 79-140.
Feighner, J.P., Robins, E., Guze, S.B., Woodruf, R.A., Winokur, G. and Munoz, R. Diagnostic criteria for use in psychiatric research. *Archives of General Psychiatry,* 1972, 26: 57-63.
Folk, G.E. Protein and fat metabolism during mammalian hypophagia and hibernation. *Federation Proceedings,* 1980, 39: 2953-2954.
Freud, S. *The Origins of Psychoanalysis. Letters to Wilhelm Fliess. Drafts and Notes.* London: Hogarth Press, 1902.
Garfinkel, P. and Garner, D.M. *Anorexia Nervosa, a Multidimensional Perspective.* Montreal: Brunner/Mazel, 1983.
Garfinkel, P.E., Moldofsky, H., Garner, D.M., Stancer, H.C. and Coscina, D.V. Body awareness in anorexia nervosa: Disturbances in body image and satiety. *Psychosomatic Medicine,* 1978, 40: 487-498.
Gull, W. Anorexia hysterica (apepsia hysterica). *British Medical Journal,* 1873, 2: 527.
Gull, W.W. Anorexia nervosa. *Lancet,* 1888, 1: 516.
Halmi, K.A., Dekirmenjian, H., Davis, J.M., Casper, R. and Goldberg, S. Catecholamine

metabolism in anorexia nervosa. *Archives of General Psychiatry*, 1978, 35: 458-460.

Harper, A.E. Amino acid balance and imbalance. 1. Dietary level of protein and amino acid imbalance. *Journal of Nutrition*, 1959, 68: 405-418.

Howland, B.E. Effect of restricted feed intake on LH levels in female rats. *Journal of Animal Science*, 1972, 34: 445-447.

Howland, B.E. The influence of feed restriction and subsequent re-feeding on gonadotrophin secretion and serum testosterone levels in male rats. *Journal of Reproduction and Fertility*, 1975, 44: 429-436.

Howland, B.E. and Skinner, K.R. Effect of starvation on gonadotrophin secretion in intact and castrated male rats. *Canadian Journal of Physiology and Pharmacology*, 1973, 51: 759-762.

Hsu, L.K.G. Editorial: The aetiology of anorexia nervosa. *Psychological Medicine*, 1983, 13: 231-238.

Ibrahim, E.A. and Howland, B.E. Effect of starvation on pituitary and serum follicle stimulating hormone and luteinizing hormone following ovariectomy in the rat. *Canadian Journal of Physiology and Pharmacology*, 1972, 50: 768-773.

Johanson, A.J. and Knorr, N.J. The treatment of anorexia nervosa by levodopa. *Lancet*, 1974, 2: 591.

Johnson, S.R. and West, G.C. Fat content, fatty acid composition and estimates of energy metabolism of Adelie penguins (*Pygoscelis adeliae*) during the early breeding season fast. *Comparative Biochemistry and Physiology*, 1976, 45B: 709-719.

Katch, F.I., Michael, E.D. and Jones, E.M. Effects of physical training on the body composition and diet of females. *Research Quarterly*, 1969, 40: 99-104.

Kaunitz, H., Spanetz, C.A. and Johnson, R.E. Utilization of food for weight maintenance and growth. *Journal of Nutrition*, 1975, 62: 551-559.

Keesey, R.E., Boyle, P.C. and Storlien, L.H. Food intake and utilization in lateral hypothalamic lesioned rats. *Physiology and Behaviour*, 1978, 21: 265-268.

Knobil, E., Plant, T.M., Wildt, L., Belchetz, P.E. and Marshall, G. Control of the rhesus monkey menstrual cycle: Permissive role of hypothalamic gonadotrophin releasing hormone. *Science*, 1980, 207: 1371-1373.

Lamming, G.E. and Krause, J.B. The effect of a low plane of nutrition on the endocrine glands of the female rat. *Proceedings of the Sixth International Congress on Nutrition, Edinburgh*. Edinburgh: Livingstone, 1963.

Lasegue, C. De l'anorexie hysterique. Translated in M.R. Kaufman and M. Heiman (Eds), *Evolution of a Psychosomatic Concept: Anorexia Nervosa a paradigm*. New York: International Universities Press, 1929.

Leibowitz, S.F. Hypothalamic catecholamine systems controlling eating behaviour: A potential model for anorexia nervosa. In P.C. Darby, P.E. Garfinkel, D.M. Garner and D.V. Coscina (Eds), *Anorexia Nervosa: Recent Developments in Research*. New York: Alan R. Liss, 1983: 221-229.

Le Mayo, Y. The emperor penguin: A strategy to live and breed in the cold. *American Scientist*, 1977, 65: 680-693.

Levitsky, D. Feeding conditions and intermeal relationships. *Physiology and Behaviour*, 1974, 12: 779-787.

Marrian, G.F. and Parkes, A.S. Effects of anterior pituitary preparations administered during dietary anestrus. *Proceedings of the Royal Society London*, 1929, 105: 248-258.

Meites, J. and Reed, J.O. Effects of restricted feed intake in intact and ovariectomized rats on pituitary lactogen and gonadotrophin. *Proceedings of the Society for Experimental Biology and Medicine*, 1949, 70: 513-516.

Mrosovsky, N. Animal anorexias, starvation and anorexia nervosa: Are animal models of anorexia nervosa possible? In P.L. Darby, P.E. Garfinkel, D.M. Garner and D.V. Coscina (Eds), *Anorexia Nervosa: Recent Developments in Research*. New York: Alan R. Liss, 1983, 199-205.

Mrosovsky, N. and Powley, T.L. Set points for body weight and fat. *Behavioural Biology*, 1977, 20: 205-223.

Mrosovsky, N. and Sherry, D.F. Animal anorexias. *Science*, 1980, 207: 837–842.

Negro-Vilar, A., Dickerman, E. and Meites, J. Effects of starvation on hypothalamic FSH-RF and pituitary FSH in male rats. *Endocrinology*, 1971, 88: 1246–1249.

Pasteels, J.L. and Franchimont, P. The production of FSH by cell cultures of fetal pituitary. In P. Hubinat (Ed.), *Progress in Reproductive Endocrinology*. Basel: Karger, 1976.

Piacsek, B.E. and Meites, J. Reinitiation of gonadotrophin release in underfed rats by constant light of epinephrine. *Endocrinology*, 1967, 81: 535–541.

Pirke, K.M. and Spyra, B. Influence of starvation on testosterone-luteinizing hormone feedback in the rat. *Acta Endocrinologica*, 1981, 96: 413–421.

Pirke, K.M., Spyra, B., Warnhoff, M., Kuderling, I., Dorsch, G. and Gramsch, C. The effect of starvation on central neurotransmitter systems and on endocrine regulations. In D. Ploog and K.M. Pirke (Eds), *Anorexia nervosa*. Berlin: Springer Verlag, in press.

Platt, B.S. Protein-calorie deficiency. *Lancet*, 1966, 2: 283.

Powley, T.L. and Keesey, R.E. Relationship of body weight to the lateral hypothalamic feeding syndrome. *Journal of Comparative and Physiological Psychology*, 1970, 70: 25–36.

Quimby, F.H. Food and water economy of the young rat during chronic starvation and recovery. *Journal of Nutrition*, 1948, 36: 177–186.

Rakoff, A.E. Endocrine mechanisms in psychogenic amenorrhoea. In R.P. Michael (Ed.), *Endocrinology and human behaviour*. London: Oxford University Press, 1968.

Redmond, D.E., Huang, Y.H., Snyder, D.R. and Maas, J.W. Norepinephrine and satiety in monkeys. In R.A. Vigersky (Ed.), *Anorexia nervosa*. New York: Raven Press, 1977: 81–96.

Riedesel, M.L. and Steffen, J.M. Protein metabolism and urea recycling in rodent hibernations. *Federation Proceedings*, 1980, 39: 2959–2963.

Rolls, B.J., Rowe, E.A. and Turner, R.C. Persistent obesity in rats following a period of consumption of a mixed, high energy diet. *Journal of Physiology*, 1980, 298: 415–427.

Root, S.W., Reiter, E.O., Duckett, G.E. and Sweetland, M.L. Effect of term castration and starvation upon hypothalamic content of luteinizing hormone releasing hormone in adult male rats. *Proceedings of the Society for Experimental Biology and Medicine*, 1975, 150: 602–605.

Routtenberg, A. Self-starvation of rats living in activity wheels: adaptation effects. *Journal of Comparative and Physiological Psychology*, 1968, 66: 234–238.

Routtenberg, A. and Kuznesof, A.W. Self-starvation of rats living in activity wheels while on a restricted feeding schedule. *Journal of Comparative and Physiological Psychology*, 1967, 64: 414–421.

Russell, G.F.M. Anorexia nervosa: Its identity as an illness and its treatment. In J.H. Price (Ed.), *Modern Trends in Psychological Medicine*. London: Butterworths, 1970: 131–164.

Russell, G.F.M. Bulimia nervosa, an ominous variant of anorexia nervosa. *Psychological Medicine*, 1979, 9: 429–448.

Russell, G.F.M., Campbell, P.G. and Slade, P.D. Experimental studies on the nature of the psychological disorder in anorexia nervosa. *Psychoneuroendocrinology*, 1975, 1: 45–56.

Selvini, M.P. *Self-starvation: From the intrapsychic to the transpersonal approach to anorexia nervosa* (translated by A. Pomerans). London: Human Context Books, Chaucer Publishing Co., 1974.

Sheehan, H.L. and Summers, V.K.The syndrome of hypopituitarism. *Quarterly Journal of Medicine*, 1948, 18: 319–398.

Simmonds, M. Über hypophysisschwund mit todlichem ausgang. *Deutsche Medizinische Wochenschrift*, 1914, 40: 322–323.

Simmonds, M. Atrophie des kypophysisvordelappe und hypophysare kachexie. *Deutsche Medizinische Wochenschrift*, 1918, 44: 852–854.

Spear, N.E. and Hill, W.T. Methodological note: Excessive weight loss in rats living in activity wheels. *Psychological Reports*, 1962, 11: 437–438.

Srebnink, H.H. and Nelson, M.M. The influence of diet on the gonadotrophins of the anterior pituitary gland. *Proceedings of the 6th International Congress of Nutrition, Edinburgh.*

Edinburgh: Livingstone, 1963: 375–386.

Stricker, E.M. and Andersen, A.E. The lateral hypothalamic syndrome: Comparison with the syndrome of anorexia nervosa. *Life Sciences*, 1980, 26: 1927–1934.

Teitelbaum, P. and Epstein, A.N. The lateral hypothalamic syndrome. *Psychological Review*, 1962, 69: 74–90.

Tepperman, J. *Metabolic and endocrine physiology*, 3rd ed., Chicago: Year Book Medical Publications, 1973.

Thoma, H. *Anorexia nervosa* (translated by G. Brydone). New York: International Universities Press, 1967.

Wakeling, A., De Souza, V.A. and Beardwood, C.J. Assessment of the negative and positive feedback effects of administered oestrogen on gonadotrophin release in patients with anorexia nervosa. *Psychological Medicine*, 1977, 7: 397–405.

Walker, J.,Roberts, S.L., Halmi, K.A. and Goldberg, S.C. Caloric requirements for weight gain in anorexia nervosa. *American Journal of Clinical Nutrition*, 1979, 32: 1396–1400.

Waller, J.V., Kaufman, M.R. and Duetsche, F. Anorexia nervosa: A psychosomatic entity. *Psychosomatic Medicine*, 1940, 2: 3–16.

Warnhoff, M., Dorsch, G. and Pirke, K.M. Effect of starvation on gonadotrophin secretion and on in vitro release of LRH from the isolated median eminence of the male rat. *Acta Endocrinologica*, 1983, 103: 293–301.

Werner, S. Failure of gonadotrophic function of the rat hypophysis during chronic inanition. *Proceedings of the Society for Experimental Biology and Medicine*, 1939, 41: 101–105.

Widdowson, E.M., Mavor, W.O. and McCance, R.A. The effect of undernutrition and rehabilitation on the development of the reproductive organs: Rats. *Journal of Endocrinology*, 1964, 29: 119–126.

Williams, A.J., Siegfried, W.R., Burger, A.E. and Berruti, A. Body composition and energy metabolism of moulting eudyptid penguins. *Comparative Biochemistry and Physiology*, 1977, 56A: 27–30.

Wodinsky, J. Hormonal inhibition of feeding and death in octopus: control by optic gland secretion. *Science*, 1977, 198: 948–951.

Wurtman, R.J. and Wurtman, J.J. Nutritional control of central neutotransmitters. In D. Ploog and K.M. Pirke (Eds), *Anorexia nervosa*. Berlin: Springer Verlag, in press.

Yates, A., Leehey, K. and Shisslak, C.M. Running — an analog of anorexia? *New England Journal of Medicine*, 1983, 308: 251–255.

8
SCHEDULE-INDUCED SELF-INJECTION OF DRUGS: AN ANIMAL MODEL OF ADDICTION

G. SINGER AND M. WALLACE

I. INTRODUCTION

There are two reasons why animal models are necessary for the understanding of drug intake behaviour in humans. The first is that, although considerable knowledge can be gained from the *in vitro* study of the effect of drugs on tissues, the interaction of biochemical and anatomical variables with behaviour can only be studied in a living organism. In our studies, for example, we are concerned with a model for addiction and, since addiction implies self-administration of a drug, voluntary intake is a necessary attribute of such a model.

The second reason is that ethical considerations preclude the experimental use of drugs with humans. This does not prevent the study in humans of phenomena associated with the termination of drug intake such as withdrawal. However, one consequence of drug intake is the development of tolerance and dependence and a proper study of these requires continued drug taking by the subject, which is not acceptable in our society. At this stage, most methods of studying the interaction of biochemical and anatomical factors of drug intake involve invasive techniques, and this again prohibits the use of human subjects. These restrictions limit the scope of study in humans to a point where little understanding can be expected of the behavioural aspects of drug taking. While the assumption of a link between physical dependence and withdrawal symptoms provides a logically tenable but indirect method of

ANIMAL MODELS IN PSYCHOPATHOLOGY
ISBN   0 12 114180 2

approach acceptable in humans, empirical evidence does not support the existence of this equation. For example, both clinical and animal studies show that relief of withdrawal symptoms is unrelated to blood alcohol level. Despite this, in most studies physical dependence is assumed to exist when withdrawal symptoms are observed, without any behavioural test.

II. SCHEDULE-INDUCED SELF-INJECTION

We will now outline a method we have developed to obtain voluntary self-administration of drugs in animals and give examples of how this model can be used to understand drug intake behaviour. Since the terms "dependence" and "addiction" have conflicting descriptive and operational definitions, we refer to the behaviour we are studying as the initiation and maintenance of drug intake behaviour. The findings described here have provided the basis for a classification of the drugs studied in terms of behaviour. In addition we will show how the model can be used with traditional pharmacological, anatomical and biochemical methods. Finally, data on a reconciliation of the model with clinically and sociologically derived factors will be presented.

In our laboratory we have combined a self-injection technique with a food delivery schedule and developed the method of schedule-induced self-injection (SISI).

The rationale for this method is based on a non-regulatory behaviour first described by Falk (1961) as adjunctive behaviour. He found naïve rats, reduced to 80% of their free feeding weight, would drink excessive amounts of water in the presence of a contingent, or non-contingent, variable, or fixed, interval food schedule. Since then a variety of other behaviours (for example, wheelrunning, licking and gnawing in the rat [Cook *et al.*, 1983; Wallace and Singer, 1976a], motor responses, and smoking in humans [Wallace *et al.*, 1975; Wallace and Singer, 1976b; Clarke *et al.*, 1977; Wallace *et al.*, 1978]) has been found to increase in frequency under similar schedule conditions. The behavioural increases are usually referred to as schedule-induced. Falk himself has used this method to induce rats to drink larger quantities of alcohol than they will normally ingest by substituting alcohol solutions for drinking water in the schedule paradigm (Falk *et al.*, 1977).

A. Methods

The schedule-induced self-injection (SISI) paradigm seems to overcome the reluctance of animals to self-inject some drugs and allows us to observe the acquisition and maintenance patterns of dependence for most psycho-active substances. In this procedure, rats reduced below free feeding weight and implanted with venous catheters are placed in operant chambers with the drug available intravenously contingent upon bar pressing. A non-contingent fixed-time 60 s (FT 60) food delivery schedule operates through-out the test session.

The general experimental design for these studies compares drug intake (self-injection) with saline intake under conditions of 100% or 80% free feeding weight, with and without the FT 60 schedule, using eight independent groups. This design allows the comparison of drug with placebo, and the observation of nutritional and schedule effects on drug intake as well as their interactions. Before reviewing the results of experiments testing a number of drugs with this paradigm, we present a brief account of the general methodology. Detailed procedures can be found in the individual papers. For these experiments, only male rats were used. Early experiments employed experimentally naïve albino Wistar rats. Later experiments used experimentally naïve, male hooded Long-Evans rats with initial ages between 90 and 120 days and body weights between 370 g and 400 g. Rats were housed individually with water available at all times. A 12 h light/12 h dark cycle operated (lights on at 0600 hours) and the laboratories were maintained at 22°C ± 1. After four days acclimatization to the laboratory, rats were reduced over a 14 day period of restricted food intake to 80 per cent of their initial body weights. This reduced body weight was maintained throughout the experiments. They were normally tested for one hour per day during the light cycle at almost the same time each day with the exception of the Lang et al. (1977) experiment where they were tested for two hours per day. A priming dose of drug or saline solution was administered prior to each testing session. No liquid was available in the test chamber, but water was freely available in the home cages. Before each test session, animals were weighed and their catheters were flushed with a heparinized saline solution to prevent blood clotting.

Anaesthetized animals had a polythene catheter (CSP 28 Dural plastic) implanted in the left jugular vein, terminating above the left auricle of the heart and anchored to the midline neck muscles. Each animal wore a leather jacket to maintain the catheter in position. The catheter was connected to a flexible swivel system which allowed the animal unrestricted movement. Animals were given three days to recover from surgery before being assigned to experimental groups.

A modified operant chamber was used which contained a bar and a food pellet dispensing unit attached to one wall. The bar operated a syringe infusion pump which delivered 0.07 mL solution when triggered. A five seconds delay was incorporated into the drug delivery system so that any further bar presses during the five seconds infusion were not rewarded with drug or saline injections. When a FT 60 schedule was operating, Noyes food pellets (45 mg) were delivered noncontingently, one each minute.

Each drug was freshly prepared for intravenous administration prior to a test session by dissolving it in a 0.9% sterile saline solution, except that for Δ^9-tetrahydrocannabinol (Δ^9-THC) a solution of Tween 80 in physiological saline was used.

B. Experimental findings

The first results with this technique were reported by Lang *et al.* (1977) with regard to nicotine (see Fig. 8.1). It appears that the acquisition of nicotine intake is dependent on the interaction of three factors: (i) reduced body weight; (ii) the presence of the nicotine molecule in the injection solution; and (iii) the presence of a food delivery schedule. All of these are necessary, but none is a sufficient condition.

The acquisition patterns for nicotine and other drugs tested are shown in Table 8.1. It can be seen that there are four distinct patterns and that the necessary conditions vary from drug to drug. In another series of experiments, we have shown that the removal of some of the factors which are important in acquisition does not always disturb the drug intake behaviour, once established.

This work is incomplete, but we show some examples in Table 8.2. Saline is not normallly self-administered by rats, but in these experiments animals will continue to bar press for saline (which is the vehicle used with heroin) when it is substituted for the heroin. This supports our conclusions, derived from the acquisition studies, that dependency involves the interaction of several contributory factors. It suggests that the distinction between physical and psychological dependency must be rejected and that the notion of dependence must be re-examined. Data on faecal boli indicate that there was a considerable reduction in the usual physiological disturbances following heroin removal in the animals which were switched to saline self-injection. The implication is that withdrawal symptoms are also dependent on a number of factors.

This thesis is not unlike Wikler's (1974) suggestion that variables which can provide reinforcement for renewed self-administration of opioids include a protracted opioid-abstinence syndrome which may last at least six months, and a combination of classically conditioned facilitation of the acute abstinence syndrome and operantly conditioned opioid seeking behaviour. Siegel *et al.*'s (1982) findings of the role of drug associated cues in drug tolerance is even closer to our view. Siegel *et al.* would predict a negative correlation between severity of withdrawal and the similarity of the

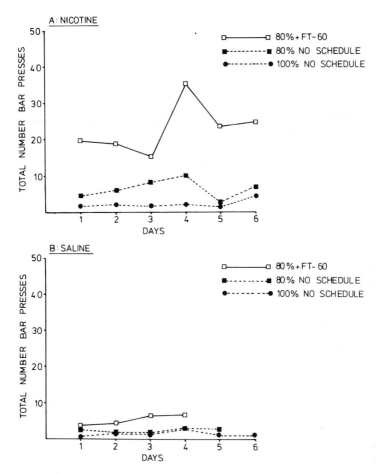

Fig. 8.1: A: Self-injection of nicotine under conditions of schedule and reduced body weight; no schedule and reduced body weight; no schedule and normal body weight. B: Self-injection of saline under the same conditions as in A.

total stimulus complex after withdrawal to the opiate intake stimulus complex. It appears that the attachment to classical and operant conditioning may need some modification in relation to ''driven'' behaviours such as drug intake. Garcia *et al.*'s (1976) work makes it clear that there are physiological limits to the occurrence of stimulus response connections in an operant framework. Changes in the biochemical *milieu interieur* related to the initiation and discontinuation of drug intake may fall into the same category. Siegel implies that a novel environment will elicit a more vehement withdrawal response, which is in accordance with Madden's

TABLE 8.1: A Classification of Drugs according to Acquisition Patterns

Group 1	Group 2	Group 3	Group 4
Alcohol Some opiates, e.g. heroin	Amphetamine Cocaine Phentermine	Δ⁹-THC Nicotine Methadone Acetaldehyde Benzodiazepam Barbiturates	Haloperidol Saline
Self-injections occur without schedule but are enhanced by the schedule and by reduced body weight	Self-injections occur only with reduced body weight	Self-injections occur only in the presence of the schedule plus reduced body weight	Unsuccessful in inducing self-injections so far

TABLE 8.2: Maintenance Patterns of Drug Self-Injection

Drug	Intake and response
Schedule Removal	
Heroin	Intake drops (Madden, Oei and Singer, 1980)
Nicotine	After 5 days of schedule, intake drops (Lang *et al.*, 1977). After 14 days, intake maintained (Lang, 1980). Will initiate intake without schedule, if body weight is 80% but acquisition is very slow (> 22 days) (Lang, 1980).
Cocaine	Intake high if body weight low (Papasava, Oei and Singer, 1981).
Alcohol	Intake drops (Oei and Singer, 1979).
Body Weight Restitution	
Nicotine	Intake maintained, if recovery period co-occurs with nicotine intake under SISI. Intake maintained if only saline available during recovery (Singer, Simpson and Lang, 1978).
Cocaine	Intake drops immediately (Papasava *et al.*, 1981).
Δ⁹-THC	Intake drops (Takahashi and Singer, 1980).
Substitution of Saline (Vehicle) for Drug	
Heroin	Responding maintained (Madden, Singer and Oei, 1979).
Antagonism of Drug Effect	
Heroin and Naloxone Pretreatment	Responding for drug drops to saline levels (Oei, 1979).

observation of attenuated withdrawal symptoms when the environment is maintained (Madden *et al.*, 1979).

Madden has suggested that the outcome of the substitution experiment has important implications for drug treatment. In methadone replacement therapies, for instance, substitution of the vehicle alone could facilitate the transition from the use of methadone to being completely drug free.

III. TRADITIONAL PHARMACOLOGICAL STUDIES

The schedule-induced self-injection (SISI) method can also be used in pharmacological experiments where the aim is to identify the biochemical substrates involved in the intake of a particular drug. The method allows inferences about the receptors with which a drug molecule will interact and is useful in the confirmation of *in vitro* findings. When drug administration is involuntary, indirect indices of the effect of the drug and blocker (such as changes in food or water intake, or activity) have to be used, whereas the use of SISI allows the direct observation of changes in the target behaviour; that is, the initiation and maintenance of drug self-injection.

A typical example of this is a comparison of the effect on the self-injection rate of Δ^9-THC of pretreatment with intraperitoneal injections of saline or agonists and antagonists of serotonin, dopamine and noradrenaline (Takahashi, 1980). In this case there was a significant decrease in Δ^9-THC self-injections when animals were pretreated with the dopamine blockers, haloperidol or pimozide, compared with saline pretreated rats, whereas there was no difference between the self-injection rates of rats pretreated with saline and those given noradrenergic receptor agonists and antagonists. This leads to the conclusion that dopaminergic, but not noradrenergic neurons, are involved in self-administration of Δ^9-THC.

Another finding obtained from this approach is that pretreatment with buprenorphine or naloxone reduced the rate of self-injection of ethanol and acetaldehyde, suggesting the involvement of opiate receptors in ethanol intake and acetaldehyde intake behaviour (see Table 8.3). In a recent extension of this work (Myers *et al.*, 1984) we have been able to show that extended treatment with alcohol or acetaldehyde will lead to the formation of salsolinol in the hypothalamus. Salsolinol is an opiate-like condensation product of acetaldehyde and dopamine which has been shown to increase alcohol intake when applied, exogenously, to the brain ventricles. Other experiments are shown in Table 8.3.

Related to this type of experiment is the technique of using cross self-administration. An example is a study of Takahashi and Singer (1981). The pharmacological classification of cannabis is controversial and, depending on dose, it has been shown to have stimulant, sedative, analgesic and psychedelic effects. In this experiment rats were switched from Δ^9-THC to amphetamine self-injection and returned to Δ^9-THC self-injection. Although the rats injected more amphetamine than Δ^9-THC when returned to Δ^9-THC there was no increase in the self-injection rate for this drug solution. It was concluded that the self-injection responses are related to the pharmacological properties of the drugs and that theories of progression or escalation were not supported by this experiment. Also, the argument that

TABLE 8.3: Pharmacological Studies

Self-injected drug	Substance used in pretreatment	Dose	Result	Experiment
A				
Heroin	Naloxone	3 mg kg⁻¹	B	Oei, 1980
		10 mg kg⁻¹	B	
Benzodiazepam	Haloperidol	0.15 mg kg⁻¹	B	Pilotto *et al.*, 1984
	Naloxone	3 mg kg⁻¹	O	Pilotto *et al.*, 1984
	Bicuculline	3 mg kg⁻¹	B	Pilotto *et al.*, 1984
	RO 15-1788	10 mg kg⁻¹	B	Pilotto *et al.*, 1984
Pentobarbital	Bicuculline	3 mg kg⁻¹	O	Martin, 1982
	RO 15-1788	10 mg kg⁻¹	O	Martin, 1982
	Haloperidol	0.15 mg kg⁻¹	B	Martin, 1982
Phentermine	Haloperidol	0.15 mg kg⁻¹	B	Papasava & Singer (pers. comm.)
	Pimozide	0.15 mg kg⁻¹	B	Papasava & Singer (pers. comm.)
		0.2 mg kg⁻¹	B	Papasava & Singer (pers. comm.)
	FLA-57	25 mg kg⁻¹	O	Papasava & Singer (pers. comm.)
	FLA- 57	50 mg kg⁻¹	O	Papasava & Singer (pers. comm.)
B				
Ethanol	Buprenorphine	0.3 mg kg⁻¹	B	Martin *et al.*, 1983
	Naloxone	3 mg kg⁻¹	B	Graham, 1981
Acetaldehyde	Buprenorphrine	0.03 mg kg⁻¹	O	Myers *et al.*, 1983a
		0.3 mg kg⁻¹	B	Myers *et al.*, 1983a
		3 mg kg⁻¹	B	Myers *et al.*, 1983a
	Naloxone	1 mg kg⁻¹	O	Myers *et al.*, 1983a
		10 mg kg⁻¹	O	Myers *et al.*, 1983a
		30 mg kg⁻¹	B	Myers *et al.*, 1983a
C				
Δ⁹-THC	Pimozide	0.125 mg kg⁻¹	O	Takahashi, 1980
		0.5 mg kg⁻¹	B	Takahashi, 1980
	Haloperidol	0.125 mg kg⁻¹	B*	Takahashi, 1980
		0.5 mg kg⁻¹	B†	Takahashi, 1980
	Apomorphine	0.5 mg kg⁻¹	B	Takahashi, 1980
		1.0 mg kg⁻¹	B	Takahashi, 1980
	Phentolamine	2.5 mg kg⁻¹	O	Takahashi, 1980
		5.0 mg kg⁻¹	O	Takahashi, 1980
	Phenoxybenza-amine	2.5 mg kg⁻¹	O	Takahashi, 1980
		10.0 mg kg⁻¹	B†	Takahashi, 1980
	Propranolol	2.5 mg kg⁻¹	O	Takahashi, 1980
		10.0 mg kg⁻¹	O	Takahashi, 1980
	Clonidine	0.025 mg kg⁻¹	O†	Takahashi, 1980
		0.05 mg kg⁻¹	O†	Takahashi, 1980
	Cyproheptadine	3.0 mg kg⁻¹	O	Takahashi, 1980
		10.0 mg kg⁻¹	O	Takahashi, 1980
	Clomipramine	5.0 mg kg⁻¹	O†	Takahashi, 1980

* Partial.
† Also reduces other operant behaviours.
B: Drug self administration blocked by prior administration of the substance listed. O: No effect on drug self administration.

drug self-administration behaviour is entirely the result of the increased activity generated by the schedule or a learning mechanism is untenable. The most interesting form of drug substitution has been shown recently by Myers *et al.* (1983b) where rats, after a 20-day period of schedule-induced self-injection of acetaldehyde, demonstrated a large and significant shift in preference for alcohol by an oral route.

Data from behavioural blocking studies are always difficult to interpret since some drugs may give rise to a non-specific reduction of general activity. In some experiments listed in Table 8.3 operant responses for food have been used in order to assess drug effects on operant response levels (Takahashi and Singer, 1980; Papasava *et al.*, 1981). However, it is possible that a drug may have a food specific effect without affecting the drug substrate involved in self-injection. Other experimenters have used measures of general activity to assess drug effect on activity (Graham, 1982). Where the same dose level of a drug blocks self-injection of one drug, but not another, it establishes a strong case for stereo-specific receptor blockade in the first case. As an example, it was found that naloxone blocks self-injection of ethanol and heroin, but not self-injection of benzodiazepam and barbiturate. Data on haloperidol may be difficult to interpret since there are no cases in the table where haloperidol did not lead to blockade. Since this also applies to pimozide, for which Papasava *et al.*, have shown no effect of the same dose of pimozide on phentermine self-injection and also no effect on food contingent operant responses (personal communication), it is possible that dopamine receptors are involved in all drug intake behaviour. This is also supported by the data on nucleus accumbens septum (NAS) lesions reported in the next section.

IV. BIOCHEMICAL AND ANATOMICAL LESIONS

The schedule-induced self-injection (SISI) paradigm also permits the investigation of biochemical and anatomical factors involved in the drug intake condition. A powerful determinant of the rate of drug intake in these studies is the schedule. In three of the four drug categories shown in Table 8.1 the rate of acquisition of self-injection behaviour is accelerated in the presence of this factor.

We have studied some of the endocrinological concomitants of schedule-induced behaviour and found increased levels of plasma corticosterone in rats which have been exposed to the classical schedule-inducing paradigm. After two or more days experience of one hour of schedule food delivery, male rats were found to have increased corticosterone levels before the testing session, compared with non-scheduled rats. After the one hour session the corticosterone levels were reduced, but not to the baseline levels of rats given the same amount of food in a single presentation (Table 8.4a). Brett and Levine (1979, 1981) showed the decrease was apparently related to schedule-induced drinking, and that rats with no opportunity to drink maintained the increased corticosterone levels. Our results are only in partial agreement since the presence or absence of the water tube did not change the corticosterone levels (see Table 8.4b).

The increases in corticosteroid levels demonstrate that an increase in arousal is associated with schedule-induced behaviour and that the schedule may constitute a mild stress. A tentative conclusion which might be drawn from these data is that an increased level of arousal may be responsible for enhancing the intake of all drugs tested except for haloperidol and the stimulants. Unlike Group 1 drugs, the increased arousal is a necessary condition for the intake of Group 3 compounds which suggest they have lower reinforcing efficacy. This is in accordance with human clinical reports in which the drugs are usually regarded as less addictive. However, there is no relationship with their legal classification.

Anatomical site of the control of schedule-induced behaviour is of particular interest. Robbins and Koob (1980) have shown a dissociation between schedule-induced drinking and deprivation-induced drinking brought about by dopaminergic lesions of the nucleus accumbens septum (NAS). We confirmed the greater generality of the involvement of the NAS in schedule-induced behaviour by demonstrating that schedule-induced wheel-running is abolished when a lesion is made in the NAS although there is no reduction in spontaneous wheel-running. Not only do these lesions abolish or reduce schedule-induced behaviour, they also reduce the level of corticosterone in the presence of scheduled food (Table 8.5; Wallace et al., 1983).

TABLE 8.4: Mean plasma corticosterone (μg L^{-1} ± SEM) for 16 groups (n = 8 per group).

Number of days	Scheduled food			Massed food presentation		
	2	10	20	2	10	20
A.						
Presession	284	450	463	113	191	292
	(35)	(51)	(64)	(14)	(16)	(41)
Postsession	274	265	264	134	111	125
	(14)	(40)	(15)	(21)	(21)	(17)
B.	253	270		131	112	
	(16)	(37)		(10)	(18)	

A. Water available to all groups.
B. Water available in home cage but not during test session.

TABLE 8.5: Effect of 6-OHDA lesions of the NAS on postsession plasma corticosterone levels (μg L^{-1}) for rats with or without scheduled food delivery.

	Scheduled Food	Massed Food Presentation
Lesion	124	192
Sham	265	136

Finally, if the schedule is a necessary factor in the accelerated acquisition of nicotine intake behaviour, then the creation of a lesion in the NAS should abolish the acquisition of nicotine intake behaviour. Results of this experiment are shown in Fig. 8.2.

Schedule-induced heroin self-injection is also reduced by 6-hydroxy-dopamine (6-OHDA) lesions of the NAS to the self-injection level of non-scheduled rats (Fig. 8.3).

The results from these experiments show that catecholaminergic neurons in the NAS are necessary for schedule-induced behaviours to occur and that components of the behaviour which are not schedule-induced can continue without disruption when lesions are present.

The link between anatomical and biochemical factors which affect drug intake behaviour differentially opens the way to the discovery of more specific connections between receptors which are not only related to the stereo chemical properties of drugs but to their reinforcement value.

V. STUDIES OF SPECIFIC DRUG PROPERTIES

The schedule-induced self-injection (SISI) method has been used to explore the chronopharmacological properties and associated biochemistry of ethanol and acetaldehyde. Smith *et al.* (1980) showed that ethanol self-injection in the dark phase of a 12:12 light/dark cycle could be achieved without body weight reduction and that daily administration of melatonin significantly increased self-injection in the dark but not in the light. Similarly, Myers *et al.* (1983b) showed that rats self-injected more acetaldehyde during the dark period of a 12:12 light/dark cycle. It has been shown that the potency of drugs varies with circadian rhythm patterns and it has been suggested that dose levels of therapeutic drugs may be adjusted according to the times of drug intake in the future. It seems that rats adjust their intake according to some cyclic patterns.

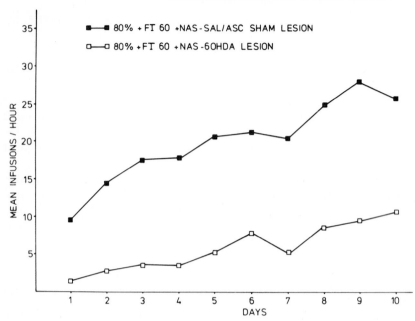

Fig. 8.2: Self-injection of nicotine following 6-hydroxydopamine (6-OHDA) lesions of the nucleus accumbens septum (NAS) or following sham lesioning.

VI. CONCLUSIONS

The data presented here show the importance of an interaction model in the understanding of the acquisition and maintenance of drug intake behaviour. It is clear that the molecule alone is rarely sufficient for the acquisition of drug intake behaviour, that the total stimulus complex needs to be considered and that salient aspects of the stimulus complex differ for different drugs. It seems counterproductive to make a distinction between physical and psychological dependence. We argue here that dependence can only be defined in behavioural terms. "Physical" dependence has been identified in terms of withdrawal symptoms, but there is no evidence that withdrawal symptoms lead to drug seeking behaviour or are a necessary step in the development of drug seeking behaviour. This is not to deny that there are physical changes in the central nervous system as a result of drug intake but these are not sufficient to lead to dependence. These changes are part of the total stimulus complex and may be necessary in the case of some

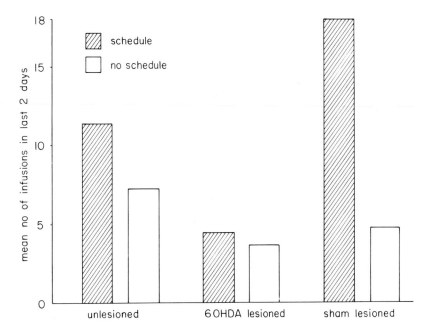

Fig. 8.3: Self-injection of heroin following 6-hydroxydopamine (6-OHDA) lesions of the nucleus accumbens septum (NAS), or following sham lesions.

drugs for the maintenance of drug seeking. It is also important to recognize the possible role of stress in this model and the specific role of the dopamine system in the nucleus accumbens septum and its effect on the corticosterone response. There are considerable theoretical implications for the model presented here as well as implications for legislation and therapeutic programmes.

REFERENCES

Brett, L.P. and Levine, S. Schedule-induced polydipsia suppresses pituitary-adrenal activity in rats. *Journal of Comparative and Physiological Psychology*, 1979, 93: 946–956.
Brett, L.P. and Levine, S. The pituitary-adrenal response to "minimized" schedule-induced drinking. *Physiology and Behavior*, 1981, 26: 153–158.
Clarke, J., Gannon, M., Hughes, I., Keogh, C., Singer, G. and Wallace, M. Adjunctive behaviour in humans in a group gambling situation. *Physiology and Behavior*, 1977, 18: 159–161.
Cook, P., Wallace, M. and Singer, G. A reinterpretation of schedule-induced behaviors based on a systematic analysis of behavior. *Neuroscience and Biobehavioral Reviews*, 1983, 7: 97–104.

Falk, J.L. The behavioral regulation of water-electrolyte balance. In M.R. Jones (Ed.), *Nebraska Symposium on Motivation*. Lincoln: University of Nebraska Press, 1961: 1–33.

Falk, J.L., Samson, H.H. and Winger, G. Behavioral maintenance of high concentrations of blood ethanol and physical dependence in the rat. *Science*, 1972, 177: 811–813.

Garcia, J., Hankins, W.G and Rusiniak, K.W. Flavor aversion studies. *Science*, 1976, 192: 265.

Graham, H.J. Acquisition and maintenance of ethanol self-injection behaviour: Effect of naloxone administration. Honours Thesis, La Trobe University, 1981.

Lang, W.J. Factors influencing the self-administration of nicotine and other drugs by rats. *Proceedings of The Australian Physiological and Pharmacological Society*, 1980, 11: 33–36.

Lang, W.J., Latiff, A.A., McQueen, A. and Singer, G. Self administration of nicotine with and without a food delivery schedule. *Pharmacology Biochemistry and Behavior*, 1977, 7: 65–70.

Madden, C., Oei, T.P.S. and Singer, G. The effect of schedule removal on the maintenance of heroin self-injection. *Pharmacology Biochemistry and Behavior*, 1980, 12: 983–986.

Madden, C., Singer, G. and Oei, T.P.S. The involvement of interoceptive factors in the maintenance of heroin seeking behavior. *Pharmacology Biochemistry and Behavior*, 1979, 11: 445–448.

Martin, A. Acquisition and maintenance of pentobarbital self-injection behaviour in rats: Effects of Bicuculline, RO 15/1788, Naloxone and Haloperidol. Honours Thesis, La Trobe University, 1982.

Martin, A., Pilotto, R., Singer, G. and Oei, T.P.S. The suppression of schedule-induced self-injection of ethanol in rats by buprenorphine. *Pharmacology Biochemistry and Behavior*, 1984, 19: 985–986.

Myers, W.D., Ng, K.T. and Singer, G. Effects of naxolone and buprenorphine on acetaldehyde self-injection. *Physiology and Behavior*, 1983a, in press.

Myers, W.D., Ng, K.T. and Singer, G. Ethanol preference in rats with a prior history of acetaldehyde self-administration. *Experientia*, 1983b, in press.

Myers, W.D., Mackenzie, L., Ng, K.T., Singer, G., Smythe, G. and Duncan, N. Increased salsolinol and dopamine levels in rat medial basal hypothalamus but not striatum following chronic ethanol consumption. *Pharmacology, Biochemistry and Behavior*, 1984, in press.

Oei, T.P.S. Reversal of schedule-induced self-injection of heroin by naloxone. *Pharmacology Biochemistry and Behavior*, 1980, 13: 457–459.

Oei, T.P.S. and Singer, G. Effects of a fixed time schedule and body weight on ethanol self-administration. *Pharmacology Biochemistry and Behavior*, 1979, 10: 767–770.

Papasava, M., Oei, T.P.S. and Singer, G. Low dose cocaine self administration by naive rats: Effects of body weight and a fixed time one minute food delivery schedule. *Pharmacology Biochemistry and Behavior*, 1981, 15: 485–488.

Pilotto, R., Singer, G. and Overstreet, D. Self-injection of diazepam in naive rats: Effects of dose, schedule and blockade of different receptors. *Psychopharmacology*, 1984, in press.

Robbins, T.W. and Koob, G.F. Selective disruption of displacement behaviour by lesions of the mesolimbic dopamine system. *Nature*, 1980, 285: 409–412.

Siegel, S., Hinson, R.E., Krank, M.D. and McCully, J. Heroin "overdose" death: Contribution of drug-associated environmental cue. *Science*, 1982, 216: 436–437.

Singer, G. and Wallace, M. Effects of 6-OHDA nucleus accumbens lesions in the acquisition of self-injection of heroin under schedule and non schedule conditions in rats. *Pharmacology Biochemistry and Behavior*, 1984, in press.

Smith, D., Oei, T.P.S., Ng, K.T. and Armstrong, S. Rat self-administration of ethanol: Enhancement by darkness and exogenous melatonin. *Physiology and Behavior*, 1980, 25: 449–455.

Takahashi, R.N. Behavioural and pharmacological effects of Δ^9-tetrahydrocannabinol self-administration in animals. Ph.D. Thesis, La Trobe University, Melbourne (December, 1980).

Takahashi, R.N. and Singer, G. Cross self-administration of Δ^9-tetrahydrocannabinol and D-amphetamine in rats. *Brazilian Journal of Medicine and Biological Research*, 1981, 14: 395-400.

Takahashi, R.N. and Singer, G. Effects of body weight levels on cannabis self-injection. *Pharmacology Biochemistry and Behavior*, 1980, 13: 877-881.

Wallace, M., Sanson, A. and Singer, G. Adjunctive behavior in humans on a food delivery schedule. *Physiology and Behavior*, 1978, 20: 203-204.

Wallace, M. and Singer, G. Adjunctive behavior and smoking induced by a maze solving schedule in humans. *Physiology and Behavior*, 1976a, 17: 849-852.

Wallace, M. and Singer, G. Schedule induced behavior: A review of its generality, determinants and pharmacological data. *Pharmacology Biochemistry and Behavior*, 1976b, 5: 483-490.

Wallace, M., Singer, G., Finlay, J. and Gibson, S. The effect of 6-OHDA lesions of the nucleus accumbens septum on schedule-induced drinking, wheelrunning and corticosterone levels in the rat. *Pharmacology Biochemistry and Behavior*, 1983, 18: 129-136.

Wallace, M., Singer, G., Wayner, M.J. and Cook, P. Adjunctive behavior in humans during game playing. *Physiology and Behavior*, 1975, 14: 651-654.

Wikler, A. Requirements for extinction of relapse-facilitating variables and for rehabilitation in a narcotic antagonist treatment program. In M.C. Braude, L.S. Harris, E.L. May, J.P. Smith and J.E. Villarreal (Eds.), *Advances in Biochemical Psychopharmacology: Narcotic antagonists*, (Vol. 8). New York: Raven, 1974: 399-414.

9
SELF-STIMULATION AND PSYCHOTROPIC DRUGS: A METHODOLOGICAL AND CONCEPTUAL CRITIQUE *

DALE M. ATRENS

I. INTRODUCTION

The 1954 discovery by Olds and Milner that rats will learn an arbitrary response to obtain electrical stimulation of the brain is a landmark in the history of the behavioural and neurosciences. The phenomenon of self-stimulation suggested that the behavioural process of positive reinforcement could be defined in neural terms. Direct intervention into the neural substrate of positive reinforcement offered enormous possibilities of behavioural control.

Whereas the self-administration of electrical stimulation of the brain was a reasonable operational definition of positive reinforcement, intervening variables were soon invoked to account for the behaviour. Self-stimulation was said to represent a rewarding effect of the brain stimulation. In turn the reward was said to be due to the fact that the brain stimulation elicited a feeling of pleasure. Self-stimulation has been used to explore the pleasure centres of the brain and to develop a psychobiology of hedonia (Olds, 1962; Olds and Fobes, 1981; Liebman, 1983; Wise, 1982).

Most researchers in this area maintain that whether self-stimulation reflects positive reinforcement, reward or pleasure is largely a matter of

* The author's research reported in this chapter was supported by grants from the Australian Research Grants Committee, the Australian Research Grants Scheme and the University of Sydney. The ideas expressed in this chapter are the outcome of collaboration with Jeff Bitterman, Glenn Hunt, and John Sinden.

semantics, with little real import for the conduct and interpretation of self-stimulation experiments. The position developed in this chapter is that the resolution as to which, if any, of these processes determines self-stimulation has far reaching consequences for both the conduct and interpretation of self-stimulation experimentation. It is argued that the failure to adequately resolve this issue forms the centre of a series of problems which renders most self-stimulation research to date largely irrelevant to most of the problems to which it has been addressed.

Soon after the discovery of self-stimulation, it was reported that rats would terminate longer trains of the same stimulation that they initiated (Bower and Miller, 1958). The obvious explanation for this apparently paradoxical termination of positive reinforcement was that longer durations of stimulation became negatively reinforcing. The hedonic interpretation of the termination was that longer durations of stimulation became aversive.

That the initiation of brain stimulation indicates reward has remained virtually unchallenged. However, there are a number of alternate explanations of stimulation termination which are not based upon stimulation-induced aversion. One alternate explanation of stimulation termination is that it is the incidental result of motor responses elicited and potentiated by the stimulation (Fibiger, 1978; Hu, 1971). If the termination is not a purposive response there is little justification for inferring an aversive component to it.

A more widely held explanation for stimulation termination is based upon the well-documented phenomenon on neural adaptation. Just as the neural responses to light diminishes or adapts during prolonged light stimulation (Kuffler and Nicholls, 1976), it was speculated that the response of "reward" neurons adapted during prolonged electrical stimulation (Duetsch and Hawkins, 1972). Adaptation would result in initially rewarding stimulation gradually becoming less rewarding. According to this view, the termination of rewarding brain stimulation is positively reinforced by the opportunity to reinitiate stimulation and to keep positive reinforcement at a maximal, relatively unadapted, level. Like the elicitation explanation described above, the adaptation of positive reinforcement hypothesis does not require an aversive process to account for stimulation termination.

The general lack of agreement as to whether the termination of positively reinforcing stimulation is reinforced and, if so, what reinforces it, has limited its use as a laboratory model. Stimulation termination is primarily used to control for the non-specific effects of drugs on stimulation initiation (Liebman, 1983). In marked contrast, the general agreement that stimulation initiation reflects positive reinforcement has resulted in its being widely used to model reward and pleasure (Liebman, 1983; Olds and Fobes, 1981; Wise, 1982).

Thus stimulation initiation appeared to be a reasonable operational definition of positive reinforcement. Stimulation termination perhaps suggested some sort of reinforcement process, but whether it was negative or positive reinforcement remained disputed. These tenuous neuro-behavioural associations were soon obscured by making gratuitous hedonic–affective inferences about reward and aversion. That brain stimulation is rewarding as opposed to being positively reinforcing is supported by only very indirect evidence (Rolls, 1976). In humans, who can give the most direct evidence of pleasure, Sem-Jacobsen (1976) is careful to point out that pleasure is probably only a minor determinant of self-stimulation.

We will see below that stimulation initiation may not even indicate positive reinforcement, let alone reward. That positively reinforcing brain stimulation becomes aversive is supported by even less evidence. The status of the initiation and termination of brain stimulation as models of neuro-affective processes such as reward and aversion is highly questionable — yet rarely questioned.

Since schizophrenia and the manic–depressive psychoses are character-ized by gross neuroaffective disturbances, it was perhaps inevitable that self-stimulation would be used to model various aspects of these major psychiatric problems. This logic was lent further credibility by numerous reports that drugs which attenuated psychoses also attenuated self-stimula-tion (for reviews see Liebman, 1983; Wise, 1982). Thus self-stimulation had evolved into an animal model of psychopathology.

The present chapter is a critical examination of some methodological and conceptual aspects of this model with particular reference to the psychopharmacology of positive and negative reinforcement processes. This examination will avoid making hedonic–affective inferences since, until the basic questions of reinforcement that form the foundations of these inferences are adequately resolved, such speculations remain premature. Nor will this chapter attempt to review the psychopharmacology of reinforcement processes. Such a review will be avoided not because of space limitations. On the contrary, such a review need only include a handful of studies in order to be comprehensive. Although there is a vast literature on the psychopharmacology of self-stimulation, the present analysis suggests that this literature is of little relevance to reinforcement processes. Commonly used self-stimulation and stimulation escape procedures are relevant to a variety of ill-specified performance processes, but they are, at best, only peripherally relevant to the reinforcement processes which they are claimed to measure. A psychopharmacology of reinforcement processes cannot be developed without using behavioural procedures which adequately measure reinforcement.

II. THE DETERMINANTS OF STIMULATION INITIATION

A. Rate-independent measures of reinforcement

Whereas criticisms of the validity of conventional methods of measuring self-stimulation (that is, continuous reinforcement [RF]) have been made repeatedly (De Witte and Bruyer, 1980; Valenstein, 1964; Liebman, 1983; Schiff, 1976), these procedures continue to be used at least as widely as ever. This reflects the tacit consensus that their alleged inadequacies do not substantially reduce the validity of CRF measures of brain stimulation reinforcement. The ease of implementing CRF and the vigour of the behaviour it produces obviously constitute powerful sources of reinforcement for the experimenter.

In the face of strong consensus a number of investigators have recognized potential methodological problems in conventional self-stimulation procedures. These problems have been, in general, associated with the use of rate-dependent measures of reinforcement (Valenstein, 1964; Liebman, 1983; Schiff, 1976). Numerous procedures have been developed to overcome the deficiencies of rate-dependent measures. These include: stimulation-time on; thresholds; autotitration; choice; latency and speed measures (for references see Liebman, 1983; Valenstein, 1964).

The great majority of these rate-independent, self-stimulation procedures use CRF. The possibility exists that these procedures have not addressed the central problem with conventional self-stimulation paradigms. It can be argued that there is nothing wrong with rate-dependent measures of reinforcement as long as the rates are not confounded by non-reinforcement-related performance factors. Perhaps the deficiency of conventional self-stimulation paradigms lies in their reliance on CRF and not on their use of rate-dependent measures. Or perhaps, as is widely believed, the above deficiencies are little more than minor flaws in what are fundamentally sound procedures. The nature and extent of the alleged deficiencies of CRF are largely unknown. Consequently, this potentially damning set of criticisms remains almost entirely speculative and is supported or refuted by almost no experimental data.

B. Reinforcement and forcement

The fundamental assumption underlying all self-stimulation research is that the initiation of brain stimulation indicates positive reinforcement. A corollary is that the vigour (rate or speed) of the initiation responding reflects the magnitude of positive reinforcement.

Reinforcing stimuli may also have "forcing" properties. Hypothalamic stimulation, in particular, directly elicits or forces skeletal, autonomic and endocrine responses as well as potentiating responsivity and altering sensorimotor integration in a variety of motor and sensory modalities (Ángyán, 1976; Sadowski, 1976). If the forcement produces performance changes incompatible with the instrumental response it may decrease response vigour. If the forcement produces performance changes compatible with the instrumental response it may increase response vigour. An obvious example of forcement-induced alterations in performance is the reduced response vigour produced by high stimulation intensities (Atrens, 1970). The data presented below indicate less obvious, but perhaps more serious, performance artifacts in a wide variety of other self-stimulation situations.

Since forcement is directly related to the temporal density of the brain stimulation, high stimulation density will be most likely to obscure the relation between response vigour and reinforcement. The highest stimulation density is produced by continuous reinforcement (CRF). Since the vast majority of self-stimulation research has been, and continues to be, conducted using CRF procedures the validity of these data in the measurement of reinforcement is questionable. The validity of CRF measures of brain stimulation reinforcement is widely assumed, yet it is supported by very little evidence.

C. Forcement and reinforcement density

We have recently directly approached the problem as to how the temporal density of brain stimulation affects the validity of measures of positive and negative reinforcement (Atrens *et al.*, 1983b). These experiments used a signalled discrete-trials shuttle-box procedure much like that of Sinden and Atrens (1983). By providing a long interval between small blocks of continuous reinforcement (CRF) it is possible to directly compare stimulation initiation (and termination) under low and high stimulation density. This paradigm provides data which may be analysed with correlational and factor analytic techniques to show the determinants of self-stimulation and how they are affected by stimulation density. The demonstration that self-stimulation under low and high stimulation density has the same determinants would constitute a strong vindication of the validity of CRF self-stimulation procedures in measuring reinforcement.

The demonstration that stimulation density changes the determinants of self-stimulation would constitute a strong indictment of the validity of CRF procedures in measuring brain stimulation reinforcement.

In the discrete-trials shuttle-box procedure, stimulation availability was signalled by a tone. The tone indicated that the rat could shuttle to initiate the stimulation, and then, as is usual in the shuttle-box under CRF, the rat could shuttle to terminate the stimulation. Three such CRF initiation-termination sequences constituted a block of trials after which the tone terminated and was presented again after a three minute interval. There were 10 blocks of CRF trials in each session and each of the seven rats was run 10 times.

The pattern of intercorrelations between the initiation and termination latencies within blocks of CRF trials is presented in Table 9.1. These data will be discussed in a later section of this chapter so for the moment all that need to be noted about them is that 14 of the 15 correlations were significant ($P < 0.01$). The correlation matrix was subject to a factor analysis with varimax rotation (Kaiser, 1958). A two factor solution emerged (eigenvalues > 1.0) with the two factors together accounting for 62.4% of the variance. The weighting of each of the variables in terms of the proportion of explained variance is presented in the component structure matrix in Table 9.2. Factor 1 has high loadings from all three initiation latencies. It may therefore be called the initiation factor. Factor 2 has high loadings from all three termination latencies. It may be called the termination factor.

Since the first initiation response in each block of trials (I_1) occurs at least three minutes after any preceding stimulation, it is least affected by forcement and should therefore have relatively high validity as a measure of positive reinforcement. Conversely, since the second and third initiations in each block of trials (I_2 and I_3) are both immediately preceded by brain stimulation they should be most affected by forcement and should therefore have relatively low-validity as measures of positive reinforcement. If the initiation factor represents the effect of positive reinforcement, I_1 should have the highest loading on this factor, whereas I_2 and I_3 should have much lower loadings. However, exactly the opposite pattern of loadings was found. The first initiation, I_1 had by far the lowest loading on the initiation factor, whereas the loadings of I_2 and I_3 were nearly twice as great.

This factor analysis shows that the most valid measure of positive reinforcement, I_1, is by far the least powerful determinant of CRF initiation. In contrast the least valid measure of positive reinforcement, I_3, is the most powerful determinant of CRF initiation. These data suggest that, under CRF, the initiation of lateral hypothalamic stimulation is primarily determined by forcement, not positive reinforcement. The use of changes in CRF responding for brain stimulation to make inferences about

TABLE 9.1: Intercorrelations between the three latencies to initiate (I_1, I_2, I_3) and the three latencies to terminate (T_1, T_2, T_3) within each block of trials. All of the correlation coefficients except for $I_1 - T_2$ were significantly ($P < 0.01$) different from zero.

	Correlation Coefficients				
	I_2	I_3	T_1	T_2	T_3
I_1	0.42	0.42	0.35	−0.03	−0.11
I_2		0.72	0.42	0.27	0.15
I_3			0.48	0.17	0.10
T_1				0.44	0.42
T_2					0.78

Adapted from Atrens *et al.*, 1983b.

TABLE 9.2: Proportion of the variance in the three initiation and termination latencies accounted for by each factor after factor analysis with varimax rotation on the correlation matrix in Table 9.1.

Latencies	Explained Variance	
	Factor 1	Factor 2
I_1	36%	2%
I_2	60%	0%
I_3	71%	1%
T_1	30%	17%
T_2	2%	74%
T_3	0%	82%

Adapted from Atrens *et al.*, 1983b.

positive reinforcement is clearly not justified. This criticism applies whether the response measure is rate, latency, speed, threshold, etc. The critical point is not the nature of the response measure, but the reinforcement schedule. If, as seems likely, this criticism applies to other instrumental responses, such as lever pressing, most self-stimulation research to date must be considered to be only peripherally relevant to the psychobiology of positive reinforcement. At the very least, these data constitute a strong indictment of the use of CRF in shuttle-box self-stimulation and such procedures are being used increasingly in psychopharmacology (for references see Liebman, 1983; Wauquier *et al.*, 1981).

It is important to stress that, whereas the use of intermittent reinforcement schedules may avoid the confounding influence of forcement, these schedules too may bring problems of their own (Sanger and Blackman, 1976). For example, on intermittent reinforcement schedules the behaviour may come under such strong schedule control that it does not adequately reflect changes in reinforcement strength produced by various experimental manipulations (Weiss, 1983). Schedule dominance is particularly evident with ratio schedules. Perhaps because intermittent reinforcement schedules are still so rarely used, this elementary principle of operant behaviour does not appear to have been incorporated into brain stimulation research.

The importance of schedule control in the evaluation of drug effects was clearly demonstrated by Dews (1955). He showed that the same dose of pentobarbital could significantly enhance fixed-ratio (FR) 50 responding, whereas it virtually eliminated fixed-interval (FI)-15 s responding. We have recently demonstrated the importance of schedule control in evaluating the effects of stimulation parameter changes on responding for reinforcing hypothalamic stimulation.

D. Pseudo-reinforcement

The nature and magnitude of forcement and its relation to positive reinforcement in determining stimulation initiation behaviour will likely vary widely in different areas of the brain. An extreme example of the confounding effects of forcement in evaluating reinforcement comes from our recent studies of self-stimulation of the nucleus accumbens (Jenkins *et al.*, 1983). Under continuous reinforcement (CRF) in the shuttle-box, rats with accumbens electrodes learn to self-stimulate just as vigorously as rats with hypothalamic electrodes. On the basis of their stabilized CRF performance one would have to conclude that stimulation of the nucleus accumbens is just as reinforcing as stimulation of the lateral hypothalamus. However, when switched to an intermittent reinforcement schedule, the accumbens rats stabilize at rates barely above those seen in extinction, whereas hypothalamic rats continue responding vigorously. Thus, intermittent reinforcement, by reducing forcement, almost completely eliminates accumbens self-stimulation, whereas it has relatively little effect on hypothalamic self-stimulation (Atrens, Jenkins and Jackson, in preparation). Accumbens self-stimulation is therefore primarily a phenomenon of forcement almost totally devoid of reinforcement.

Accumbens self-stimulation is an example of pseudo-reinforcement. It is more properly classified as a stimulation-induced stereotypy. Just as it is not reasonable to infer positive reinforcement from the repetitive performance of other stereotypies, repetitive, even vigorous shuttling or lever-pressing do not necessarily indicate positive reinforcement. Whereas there are numerous data suggesting that the rate of initiation may not indicate the magnitude of positive reinforcement, these are the first data which suggest that initiation may not even indicate that there is positive reinforcement at all. Although forcement is usually thought to produce performance deficits (Liebman, 1983), these data show how forcement can produce a strong performance facilitation. Pseudo-reinforcement is merely the extreme instance of the performance facilitation that invalidates virtually all CRF measures of positive reinforcement.

The insidious nature of the confounding due to forcement is further illustrated by the time course of changes in accumbens self-stimulation. Although the stabilized CRF shuttle-box initiation rates of accumbens and hypothalamic rats are nearly identical, the rates of acquisition of this behaviour are very different. Rats with hypothalamic electrodes typically show asymptotic initiation performance after only a few sessions, whereas rats with accumbens electrodes initially show little or no performance and they then take 20–30 daily sessions to stabilize their initiation rates. The extremely slow acquisition of the initiation of accumbens stimulation is paralleled by the gradual development of motor convulsive activity. These data suggest that the acquisition of accumbens self-stimulation reflects progressive changes in the motor control functions of the nucleus accumbens (Jenkins *et al.*, 1983).

Just as the progressive changes in accumbens function are acquired gradually, they also appear to extinguish gradually. This is indicated by the fact that when rats with accumbens electrodes are switched to intermittent reinforcement the initial decrement in their response rates is not much greater than that shown by rats with hypothalamic electrodes. However, when the rats are tested repeatedly until their fixed-interval (FI) performance becomes stabilized, any similarity between self-stimulation at the two sites vanishes. Hypothalamic self-stimulation on a FI-30 s initiation, FI-10 s termination schedule stabilizes at rates about 25%–35% of those produced by CRF. In contrast, the FI-30 s initiation rates of nucleus accumbens rats gradually decline to levels barely distinguishable from those seen in extinction. These data suggest that the extinction of the initiation stereotypy is as gradual as the acquisition.

All of these data show that orderly changes in self-stimulation can take place in the virtual absence of positive reinforcement. Orderly changes in self-stimulation in response to various experimental manipulations are widely held to indicate that the procedure is measuring positive reinforcement (for references see Liebman, 1983). This assumption is no longer tenable. Orderliness in changes in self-stimulation performance may simply reflect the lawful nature of the forcement processes which are so pervasive in CRF self-stimulation.

The deleterious effects of forcement on measuring positive reinforcement may be circumvented by employing a fixed-interval (FI) initiation schedule. Whereas numerous other intermittent reinforcement schedules also interpose delays between reinforcements (for references see Liebman, 1983), the variability of the interreinforcement intervals means that there is substantial local variability in forcement both within and between rats. The minimum interreinforcement intervals which will provide a valid measure of positive reinforcement remains to be determined. However, it is apparent that this critical interval will depend on a number of factors including electrode location and stimulation parameters.

Another way of increasing the intervals between reinforcements is to use a discrete trials procedure as opposed to free-operant procedure. The most commonly-used discrete trials paradigm is the runway procedure developed by Gallistel (for references see Gallistel *et al.*, 1981). However, the fact that, in this procedure, non-contingent brain stimulation is almost always given immediately before testing for positive reinforcement tends to vitiate the methodological refinement resulting from the use of long inter-reinforcement intervals. This procedure quite explicitly uses forcement as a prelude to measuring reinforcement. Perhaps this underlies the admission by these authors that their data are characterized by high variability and consequent refractoriness to statistical analysis (Gallistel *et al.*, 1981). Whereas Gallistel *et al.* (1982) refer to pre-stimulation as "priming" of the reward system, the motivationally neutral term forcement appears to be more appropriate.

III. THE DETERMINANTS OF STIMULATION TERMINATION

A. Reinforcement and forcement

The confounding influence of forcement on stimulation termination is even more serious than with initiation, since the termination takes place during the stimulation when the effects of forcement are presumably maximal. The extreme position would be that the termination is simply forced, and not reinforced at all. This would parallel the pseudo-reinforcement described above for stimulation initiation. The elicitation hypothesis of stimulation termination (Fibiger, 1978; Hu, 1971) has yet to be convincingly supported or refuted. Liebman (1983) maintains that the demonstration that certain drugs selectively affect termination shows that the termination is not simply elicited. This argument, which was largely developed by the writer (for references see Hunt *et al.*, 1981; Liebman, 1983), is not very strong since there is no reason why a drug should not act selectively on forcement.

Whether the termination of positively reinforcing stimulation is forced as opposed to being reinforced may be determined by examining the importance of the termination contingency on termination responding. This was done in seven rats that had been extensively trained on a fixed-interval

(FI)-30 s (initiate) FI-10 s (terminate) schedule in the shuttle box. After both the initiation and termination rates had fully stabilized, the rats were given a single 30 minute test run in which the termination contingency was removed. Under this condition, the stimulation terminated after 10 seconds independently of the rats' behaviour. This may be referred to as a fixed time 10 second schedule (FT-10 s). Under the response contingent termination condition (FI-10 s) the rats were invariably responding vigorously by the end of the 10 second period. This ensured that terminating the stimulation in a response-independent manner (FT-10 s) resulted in their receiving only fractionally less stimulation. Consequently, the amount of forcement in the two experimental conditions was nearly identical. This procedure provides a straightforward test of the relative merits of the forcement and reinforcement hypothesis of stimulation termination. If the termination is simply forced, the response contingency should not matter and the response rates under the FI-10 s and FT-10 s conditions should be nearly identical. However, if the responding is reinforced by the termination of the stimulation, removing the response contingency should produce a large reduction in responding.

Removing the termination contingency by changing the termination schedule from FI-10 s to FT-10 s produced a large reduction in "termination" responding (-59.2%, $t = 2.50$, d.f. $= 6$, $P < 0.025$). That the decreased responding produced by removing the response contingency did not represent a general disruption of performance is indicated by the fact that the concurrent FI-30 s initiation rates showed a small ($+14.3\%$), but non-significant, increase. Thus, the importance of the termination being contingent on responding shows that the termination responding is reinforced — it is not simply an elicited or forced response. We have also demonstrated the same relationship when the instrumental response is lever pressing.

The problem remains of accounting for the residual responding that occurs even when that responding is not effective in terminating the stimulation. Does the residual responding represent a residual elicitation component, or does it simply represent the gradual extinction of the learned termination response? This question was examined in a paradigm similar to that described above, except that the rat was given eight runs, with the termination contingency being removed on alternate days. If the residual responding simply represents an extinction process, repeated testing should progressively reduce the residual termination rates. Conversely, persistence of responding with repeated testing would suggest that the residual rates represent an elicitation process.

The first removal of the response termination contingency reduced responding by 47.8%, whereas the initiation responding was reduced by only 11.1%. The fourth removal of the response termination contingency reduced responding by 51.8%, whereas the initiation responding was reduced by only 6.0%. There was no indication of any progressive decrease in responding during successive removals of the response termination contingency. Moreover, the overall reduction in termination responding produced by removing the response termination contingency (56.0%) was almost identical to that seen in the seven rats above (59.2%), each of which was tested only once on the FT-10 s termination contingency.

The fact that alternating periods of response-contingent termination with periods of response-independent termination does not result in any extinction of the ineffective termination responding suggests that there is a significant element of elicitation in the termination responding.

B. Adaptation of positive reinforcement

The above experiments suggest that on a fixed-interval (FI)-10 s termination schedule, although there may be a significant element of forcement, the termination behaviour is primarily determined by reinforcement. This raises the question as to the nature of the reinforcement for stimulation termination. There are two clear alternative sources of reinforcement for the termination of positively reinforcing stimulation.

According to the adaptation of positive reinforcement hypothesis the termination of stimulation is positively reinforced by permitting more rapid reinitiation (Deutsch and Hawkins, 1972). Rapid reinitiation maximizes positive reinforcement by maximizing the time spent at shorter durations of stimulation where the positive reinforcement is presumably at a higher or unadapted level relative to that at longer durations of stimulation.

According to the negative reinforcement hypothesis, positively reinforcing stimulation, when prolonged, produces an aversive state whose termination is reinforcing (Liebman, 1983). According to this view, the termination of positively reinforcing stimulation is reinforced by a negative process analogous to that which reinforces the termination of electric foot shock.

Rather surprisingly, in spite of the importance and longstanding nature of this controversy (which is well detailed by Liebman, 1983) there are only a few experiments that have directly approached the problem (Deutsch and Hawkins, 1972; Hodos, 1964; Keesey, 1964). The results of these experiments tend to support the adaptation of positive reinforcement hypothesis.

Support for the negative reinforcement hypothesis (which is also well detailed by Liebman, 1983) is more indirect. This support consists of numerous reports of conditions under which the initiation and termination behaviour respond differentially to various experimental manipulations. The logic behind this is that, if the initiation and termination are both related to positive reinforcement, they should covary. Failures to covary have been interpreted as indicating that the initiation and termination are not both related to positive reinforcement (Liebman, 1983). By elimination one might conclude that the termination is determined by an independent factor, perhaps negative reinforcement or aversion.

The logic of using the failure of initiation and termination behaviour to covary as support for the negative reinforcement hypothesis is not compelling. These failures to covary are easily incorporated within the adaptation of positive reinforcement hypothesis. This only requires the assumption that magnitude of positive reinforcement and the rate at which the positive reinforcement adapts are independent. By making this assumption, the failures of the initiation and termination to covary are to be expected. They certainly do not constitute support for the negative reinforcement hypothesis of stimulation termination.

In contrast, Deutsch and Hawkins (1972) have provided apparently strong and direct support for the adaptation of positive reinforcement hypothesis of stimulation termination. They demonstrated that, after receiving enough stimulation to have produced the putative negative reinforcement or aversive process, rats chose to increase stimulation frequency rather than terminate it. These data are widely used to refute the development of negative reinforcement in longer trains of positively reinforcing stimulation and, by inference, to support the adaptation of positive reinforcement hypothesis. The analysis below shows that these data support neither hypothesis.

After forced stimulation in the start box of a T-maze, Deutsch and Hawkins (1972) gave four rats the choice of either terminating the stimulation or doubling its frequency for one second. The increase in stimulation frequency would likely exacerbate any stimulation-produced aversion. If this were the case the rat would be expected to terminate the stimulation rather than exacerbate an ongoing aversive process by doubling the stimulation frequency. However, doubling the stimulation frequency also enhances positive reinforcement. Further, the enhancement of positive reinforcement should be maximal within one second (Deutsch et al., 1976), whereas the putative aversiveness is thought to develop much more slowly (Shizgal and Matthews, 1977). Consequently, it is not surprising that under these conditions rats chose to increase the stimulation frequency. The choice of increasing stimulation frequency simply shows that 200 Hz stimulation is more positively reinforcing than 100 Hz stimulation. These data do not indicate adaptation of positive reinforcement nor do they contraindicate the development of negative reinforcement during long trains of hypothalamic stimulation. However, if the rats had chosen to terminate the stimulation rather than experience still more positively reinforcing stimulation, this would constitute strong evidence for the development of negative reinforcement. We have recently provided such evidence (Atrens et al., 1983b).

Our experiment was essentially a replication of that of Deutsch and Hawkins (1972), with an important procedural modification. After receiving five seconds of 50 Hz stimulation in the start box, the rats were given the choice of either a further five seconds of either no stimulation or five seconds of 100 Hz stimulation in the goal box. The duration of stimulation in the goal box was increased in order to allow enough time for the putative negative reinforcement to develop. Otherwise, as in Deutsch and Hawkins (1972), the choice could simply represent the effect of increasing positive reinforcement.

The results of the above experiment are summarized in Table 9.3. Rats with anterior hypothalamic electrodes consistently chose to terminate the stimulation rather than receive five seconds of still more positively reinforcing stimulation. In contrast, rats with posterior hypothalamic electrodes consistently chose to increase the stimulation frequency to 100 Hz (Atrens et al., 1983b). The data from the rats with anterior electrodes constitute the first direct demonstration of the development of negative reinforcement in longer trains of positively reinforcing stimulation.

Since the above T-maze paradigm does not provide data relevant to the adaptation of positive reinforcement, one may ask what data do. It is possible that the adaptation to prolonged stimulation which occurs in several sensory modalities (Kuffler and Nicholls, 1976) does not occur in the positive reinforcement system(s).

Evidence for the existence of adaptation of positive reinforcement may be found in the correlation data in Table 9.1. These data show that eight of the nine initiation–termination correlations were significantly ($P < 0.01$) different from zero, which suggests that initiation and termination have a common determinant. There appear to be two distinct possibilities for the common determinant of initiation and termination. One is forcement and the other is positive reinforcement. If the initiation–termination associations represented a common effect of forcement it would be expected that the correlation coefficients would be highest under conditions of highest forcement and lowest under conditions of lowest forcement. If forcement is the common determinant accounting for the initiation–termination intercorrelations, the correlation between I_3 and T_3 should be high and that between I_1 and T_1 should be low. However, exactly the opposite pattern of initiation–termination correlations within blocks of trials was found. The I_3–T_3 correlation coefficient was 0.10, whereas the I_1–T_1 correlation coefficient was 0.35. The difference between these two correlation coefficients is significant ($P < 0.01$, Fisher's r to z transformation).

TABLE 9.3: Summarized T-maze data for nine rats with anterior or posterior hypothalamic electrodes. UP indicates the trials on which the rats chose to increase the stimulation frequency from 100 Hz to 200 Hz. OFF indicates the trials on which the rats chose to terminate the stimulation.

Site of Electrode	UP	OFF
Anterior (n = 5)	22%	78%
Posterior (n = 4)	78%	22%

Adapted from Atrens et al., 1983b.

The most parsimonious explanation of the pattern of association between initiation and termination responding under continuous reinforcement (CRF) is that the termination reflects the adaptation of positive reinforcement that occurs during prolonged stimulation. Rapid termination permits rapid reinitiation and the renewal of a maximal, relatively unadapted, level of positive reinforcement. The determination of stimulation termination by adaptation of positive reinforcement under CRF is also supported by the factor analysis presented in Table 9.2. If, between successive stimulations, the recovery from adaptation of positive reinforcement is not complete, this factor should account for progressively more of the variance in termination within each block of trials. This speculation is verified by the increase in the explained variance in termination within blocks of CRF trials from 17.2% to 74.3% to 81.9%. However, since the first initiation in each CRF block is the most positive reinforcement related (least forced), and the third is the least positive reinforcement related (most forced), the initiation–termination correlations should decrease within blocks. The data in Table 9.1 confirm this, with the initiation–termination correlations within blocks decreasing from 0.35 to 0.10.

Within blocks of CRF trials, as the termination of stimulation becomes less related to magnitude of positive reinforcement, the factor analysis indicates that adaptation of positive reinforcement accounts for progressively more of the termination variance. These divergent patterns of association suggest that the magnitude of positive reinforcement, and the rate at which positive reinforcement adapts, are independent. The assumption of this independence was all that was needed to incorporate the failures of initiation and termination to covary, within an adaptation of positive reinforcement framework (see Section III, B).

Thus far, it appears that the adaptation of positive reinforcement can adequately account for the termination of stimulation under conditions of free-operant CRF (Atrens et al., 1983b). This means that this hypothesis can account for the vast majority of the stimulation termination data to date. However, the discrete trials T-maze data described above show that the termination of positively reinforcing stimulation may also indicate the development of negative reinforcement. The next section shows how negative reinforcement may be reflected in stimulation initiation.

C. Negative reinforcement

If long trains of positively reinforcing stimulation become negatively reinforcing, the net positive reinforcement value of longer trains should be less than that of shorter trains. On the other hand, if all that occurs during long stimulation trains is adaptation of positive reinforcement, the net positive reinforcement value of long trains should reach an asymptotic level, but it should not decline. Longer trains of stimulation should always be at least as positively reinforcing as shorter trains. Any decrease in positive reinforcement produced by increasing stimulation train duration indicates the development of negative reinforcement. Of course, this logic assumes that the initiation rates are measuring the positive reinforcement value of the stimulation. This requirement has been approximated in a few studies which have used intermittent reinforcement (Atrens et al., 1983b; Hodos, 1964; Keesey, 1964).

Keesey (1964) showed that the rate to initiate hypothalamic stimulation on a variable interval reinforcement schedule continued to increase at train lengths that were twice those that the rats self selected on CRF. However, since the longest trains used in that study were less than 10 seconds, it is possible that they were not long enough to permit negative reinforcement to develop. Hodos (1964) showed, in one rat, that intermittently reinforced response rates did not decline even at train lengths of 120 seconds. However, in the only other rat in that study with a hypothalamic electrode, the response rates began to decline at train lengths longer than five seconds.

We have recently conducted experiments similar to those of Hodos (1964) and Keesey (1964) in the shuttle box (Atrens et al., 1983b). These experiments measured the rates to initiate different length trains of stimulation on a fixed-interval (FI)-30 s or fixed ratio 3 initiation schedule. These data, which are adapted from those of Atrens et al. (1983b) are presented in Fig. 9.1. The positive reinforcement value of the stimulation reaches a peak at stimulation durations of 5–10 s. Longer stimulation durations (15–30 s) significantly ($P < 0.01$) reduce the positive reinforcing value of the stimulation. We have also shown that these same relationships are found when the instrumental response is lever pressing.

Thus the two paradigms that have provided the most direct evidence against the development of negative reinforcement in long trains of positively reinforcing brain stimulation actually provide the first unequivocal evidence for the development of negative reinforcement. The

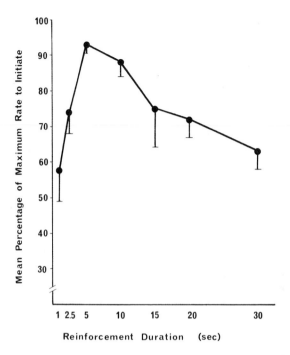

Fig. 9.1: The effect on intermittently reinforced initiation rates (FI 30 s or FR3) of reinforcement duration varying from 1–30 s. The T-bars indicate the standard error of the mean (N = 13). The initiation rates for 5 and 10 s were significantly ($P < 0.01$) greater than for any other reinforcement duration. Adapted from Atrens *et al.* (1983).

negative reinforcement is found at both anterior and posterior hypothalamic sites. Negative reinforcement, therefore, appears to be as general a property of lateral hypothalamic stimulation as is positive reinforcement. However, stimulation termination paradigms as used to date have not measured this fundamental property of hypothalamic stimulation. Consequently, its psychology, physiology and pharmacology remain to be explored.

D. Stimulation offset positive reinforcement

On a fixed-interval (FI)-30 s initiation, FI-10 s termination schedule the termination is not reinforced by the opportunity to reinitiate stimulation more rapidly, since the inter-reinforcement interval is an irreducible 30 seconds. Consequently, under these conditions the termination of stimulation is not explicable by the adaptation of positive reinforcement hypothesis. Further, negative reinforcement does not typically develop at posterior hypothalamic electrodes until the stimulation duration is from 15 to 30 seconds. High rates to terminate posterior hypothalamic stimulation occur under conditions where the termination is not reinforced through more rapid reinitiation and *before* the stimulation becomes negatively reinforcing.

The above considerations suggest that there may be something positively reinforcing about the offset of hypothalamic stimulation. Just as there are cells in the visual system that respond maximally to light onset and/or light offset (Kuffler and Nicholls, 1976) there may be cells mediating positive reinforcement that respond in an analogous manner. The existence of OFF positive reinforcement in addition to ON positive reinforcement would add a new dimension of complexity to self stimulation research. It would mean, for example, that the initiation of the short trains of stimulation that are typically used in self-stimulation research may be reinforced by both ON and OFF positive reinforcement. The dual sources of positive reinforcement for initiation may in part account for the observation that short trains of stimulation produce much more behaviour per unit of charge than do long trains. However, at the same time this analysis suggests that in typical self-stimulation experiments the effects of the two putative types of positive reinforcement are confounded. With longer trains of stimulation, the OFF positive reinforcement is sufficiently temporally remote from the initiation response so that the initiation primarily, if not exclusively, reflects ON positive reinforcement.

The existence of OFF positive reinforcement would also require a complete re-evaluation of "aversion" mapping in the brain. Pure termination, which is termination without initiation, is widely used as evidence that the stimulation is aversive. However, if OFF positive reinforcement existed independently of ON positive reinforcement, stimulation termination could simply indicate OFF positive reinforcement. Thus the inference of aversion or negative reinforcement would be incorrect. These data point to the great care that must be exercised in inferring hedonic processes such as reward and aversion from operant behaviour.

It should be added that at the present moment the existence of OFF positive reinforcement rests on very insubstantial foundations. Rather like sub-atomic particles, its existence is demanded by the failure of other explanations to account for the phenomena at hand. Until it is proven by more than default, it must remain as merely a titillating possibility. The reinforcing effect of termination other stimuli such as light and sound, neither of which would be considered to be aversive, has been demonstrated by Glow and Winefield (1982). They suggest that such behaviour is due to the intrinsically positively reinforcing nature of exerting environmental control.

IV. THE PSYCHOPHARMACOLOGY OF REINFORCEMENT

The preceding analysis suggests that there is little justification for using self-stimulation as a model for the hedonic processes of reward and aversion. Hedonic processes may well be involved in self-stimulation, but dissociating them from performance and reinforcement factors is not yet possible. More elementary dissocations of performance from the diverse sources of reinforcement in self-stimulation are difficult enough.

Since self-stimulation procedures as used to date have very rarely provided valid measures of reinforcement, the psychopharmacology of reinforcement remains to be elucidated. The following analysis is an attempt to develop some guidelines that will aid in avoiding some of the pitfalls that have characterized this type of research.

The first element in developing a psychopharmacology of reinforcement is a valid measure of reinforcement as opposed to the undifferentiated motor-motivational amalgam that is measured in most self-stimulation procedures. This issue is addressed in Section II of this chapter. However, even when responding accurately reflects reinforcement, drug-induced changes in responding could still reflect non-specific changes in perform- ance. For example, the rate to initiate stimulation on a fixed-interval (FI)-30 s schedule is minimally affected by forcement, consequently it is a good measure of reinforcement. Nevertheless, if this rate were changed by a drug the change could just as well represent a change in performance as in reinforcement. Initiation rates on a FI-30 s schedule are adequately protected from the forcing effects of the brain stimulation, but they are not protected from the forcing effects of drugs. The forcing effects of drugs are well documented by Spealman and Goldberg (1978). This is the heart of the problem with the pharmacology of reinforcement. Here the experimenter has to deal with two quite different sources of forcement, either one of which may invalidate the measure of reinforcement. The following sections consider a number of ways in which this problem of differentiating performance from reinforcement effects has been addressed.

A. Stimulation termination and performance deficits

The data concerning this approach have been discussed extensively by Liebman (1983). The present discussion will be largely confined to the rationale and validity of this approach in light of our recent work (Atrens *et al.*, 1982, 1983b; Sinden and Atrens, 1983; Jenkins *et al.*, 1983).

246 Dale M. Atrens

Allowing the rat to both initiate and termination brain stimulation gives the experimenter data on two concurrent operants. The initiation is commonly assumed to be a measure of positive reinforcement, whereas the termination is often assumed to be a measure of negative reinforcement (Liebman, 1983). Although earlier sections of this chapter question both of these assumptions, the following analysis will question the validity of these procedures even granting their dubious basic assumptions.

If a drug changes initiation performance without producing a comparable change in termination performance, it is assumed that the effect is not due to a general shift in performance. In this case the effect is said to be a selective effect on positive reinforcement. However, if the drug similarly alters both initiation and termination, a non-selective or general shift in performance remains a viable explanation of the effect (Liebman, 1983). It is questionable whether a selective change initiation indicates a selective effect on reinforcement. Instead, the selectivity could simply indicate the relative insensitivity of termination performance (Fibiger, 1978) and/or that the performance deficit was relatively inoperative during the stimulation (Sinden and Atrens, 1983). In either case, such selectivity is not adequate contraindication of a performance impairment since only gross performance deficits would be seen under all conditions.

Essentially the same logic applies to the use of changes in any operant to control for the specificity of drug effects on any other operant. This applies whether the alternate operant is reinforced by entirely different means such as food, water or escape from foot shock, or whether it is self-stimulation at another brain site. The same logic even applies if the alternate operant is self-stimulation at the same site but under different brain stimulation parameters. Differential effects of drugs on different operants merely reflect the diversity of the determinants of operant behaviour and their differential sensitivity to disruption.

B. Response thresholds and performance deficits

Wherever reinforcement strength is estimated by response vigour, reinforcement modulating effects of drugs are particularly likely to be obscured by performance changes (forcement) produced by the drugs. Numerous investigations have tried to circumvent this problem by estimating reinforcement strength by the amount of stimulation required to produce some performance criterion (for references see Liebman, 1983). These procedures are thought to produce a "threshold" value of the stimulation parameter(s) required to produce reinforcement. The absolute values of responding which are so prone to artifactual changes due to forcement are unimportant in threshold determinations. Threshold determinations depend on relative levels of responding. These are exemplified in the "trade-off" and "locus of rise" functions described by Gallistel *et al.* (1981).

One difficulty with reinforcement threshold determinations is that they are almost always made under conditions of free-operant continuous reinforcement (CRF). This means that the thresholds may just reflect the thresholds for forcement. There is little justification for using such forcement-prone measures to determine reinforcement. Even under discrete trials procedures such as that used by Gallistel *et al.* (1981), the use of pre-stimulation renders such data subject to the same criticism. Both the thresholds and locus of rise functions could well represent critical points for the development of forcement, not reinforcement.

There is another deficiency in the logic of threshold determinations which is not widely recognized. Even if the threshold reflected reinforcement and not forcement, changes in thresholds have an interpretive limitation. It appears to be assumed that the reinforcement threshold and the reinforcement strength are inversely correlated. Drugs which block reinforcement are assumed to raise thresholds, whereas drugs which enhance reinforcement are assumed to lower thresholds. This assumption appears to be neither psychometrically nor physiologically justified.

The limited usefulness of threshold measures to control for the specificity of drug effects is indicated by the strikingly conflicting findings using such procedures (Stein and Ray, 1960; Nazarro *et al.*, 1981; Schaefer and Michael, 1980; Zarevics and Setler, 1981). However, whether these inadequacies result from the use of thresholds *per se* and/or the use of CRF procedures to determine the thresholds remains to be determined.

The locus of rise variation on the threshold theme (for references see Gallistel *et al.*, 1981) produces data that are characterized by so much variability that statistical analysis is difficult. This has led to the peculiar state where the authors used the high inherent variability of their data to dismiss a statistically significant effect which detracted from their central thesis (Gallistel *et al.*, 1982).

C. Response patterning and performance deficits

Another way of differentiating between performance effects and a specific modulation of reinforcement is by comparing response patterns under different conditions. The logic behind this approach is that performance changes can be dissociated from reinforcement changes by the way that they effect response patterns. Here, as with threshold measures, absolute levels of responding are not important. These techniques have recently been used to clarify the nature of the inhibitory effects on self-stimulation of the dopamine receptor antagonist pimozide (for references see Sinden and Atrens, 1983).

There are numerous reports that pimozide inhibits self-stimulation, but since pimozide has marked sedative-ataxic effects it is not clear whether these data support the controversial "dopamine theory of reward" (Wise, 1982) as opposed to the well established dopamine theory of motor function (Hornykiewicz, 1975). Several investigators have attempted to resolve this controversy by highlighting the similar changes in patterns of responding produced by pimozide and extinction (Fouriezos and Wise, 1976; Gallistel et al., 1982; Wise, 1982). Central to this argument is the thesis that extinction and simple motor deficits produce different patterns of response changes.

Within an experimental session, extinction is characterized by a relatively high rate of responding early in the session followed by a roughly exponential decrease in responding as the session progresses. Pimozide has been reported to produce this same pattern of changes in responding (Fouriezos and Wise, 1976). This extinction-like pattern of response inhibition is said to indicate that pimozide, like extinction, induces a state of reinforcement blockade. In contrast, a simple performance deficit would be expected to uniformly inhibit self-stimulation across a test session. However, Fibiger (1978) has criticized this logic pointing out that the increased susceptibility to motor fatigue produced by pimozide would also result in an exponential decrease in responding across an experimental session. In this case, the similarity in effects of pimozide and extinction would be the fortuitous outcome of totally different processes. In other words, the across-session reduction in responding does not discriminate between motor and reinforcement deficits.

Sinden and Atrens (1983) addressed this problem with the signalled discrete trials shuttle-box procedure. This procedure allows the comparison of response patterns both across and within small blocks of well-spaced trials. Whereas extinction and pimozide produced roughly similar patterns of inhibition across blocks of trials, these data, like those of Fouriezos et al. (1978), do not rule out a fatigue explanation (Fibiger, 1978). However, the patterns of responding within blocks of trials permit a less equivocal interpretation.

Reducing stimulation frequency (that is, extinction) had relatively little inhibitory effect on the first initiation response within each block of trials, whereas it produced a large inhibition of the second and third initiation responses within each block. In contrast, pimozide preferentially inhibited the first initiation response within each block of trials, whereas it had relatively little effect on the second and third initiation responses with each block (Sinden and Atrens, 1983). This analysis of within blocks of trials effects shows that the inhibitory patterns produced by extinction and pimozide are almost exactly opposite. This difference suggests that pimozide does not inhibit self-stimulation by blocking positive reinforcement. Similarly, the relatively unimpaired performance in the later trials in each block throughout the entire experimental session suggests that pimozide does not inhibit self-stimulation by producing a simple motor deficit such as fatigue.

The selective inhibition of the first initiation response within each block of trials suggests that pimozide inhibits self-stimulation by inhibiting the ability to initiate motor responding. Akinesia produced by dopamine dysfunction is a well documented phenomenon (Hornykiewicz, 1975). The relatively unimpaired responding that follows the first initiation suggests that hypothalamic stimulation reverses the drug-induced akinesia. This is also in accord with reports that akinesia is partly reversible by a variety of activational influences (Schwab, 1972). Arousal induced reversal of akinesia may also account for the observation that the attenuation of self-stimulation produced by catecholamine synthesis inhibition is partly reversible by experimenter and brain stimulation-induced arousal (Roll, 1970). The fact that pimozide uniformly inhibits lever-press self-stimulation in the absence of additional activation (for references see Liebman, 1983; Wise, 1982), suggests that short stimulation trains by themselves do not provide sufficient arousal to reverse the pimozide-induced akinesia.

Stimulation-reversible akinesia shows how drug effects can interact with brain stimulation to produce complex behavioural disturbances. However, these behavioural disturbances should not be confused with changes in the reinforcing value of the stimulation. The inhibitory effects of pimozide on self-stimulation are explicable within a motor dysfunction framework. They are not relevant to a dopamine theory of reward except to illustrate the ease with which motor and motivational effects may be confused.

D. Rate dependency of drug effects

It is a common observation that the effects of certain drugs appear to interact with the rate of the operant behaviour used to evaluate the drug effect (for references see Liebman, 1983; Sanger and Blackman, 1976). In order for this to be a non-trivial observation these relations must not simply reflect floor or ceiling effects. Similarly, the non-triviality of this observation requires demonstrating rate dependency under conditions where reinforcement density is held constant. Failure to exercise this control simply reduces rate dependency to another case of confounding resulting from differential amounts of forcement. True rate dependency does not appear to have been demonstrated with brain stimulation reinforcement.

In the unlikely event that rate dependency of drug effects on brain stimulation reinforcement were to be demonstrated under rigorous conditions, its implications would be rather peculiar. It would suggest a qualitative change in the neurochemistry of reinforcement produced by the rate of the behaviour to obtain the reinforcement. At the moment the rate dependency hypothesis appears to be little more than an *ad hoc* attempt to account for the distressing variability in drug effects on self-stimulation. This variability appears to be due to a number of more easily demonstrable and more logical phenomena.

E. How should drugs modulate reinforcement?

Given a self-stimulation methodology that permits the differentiation of performance and reinforcement effects, it remains to be adequately specified how drugs would be expected to modulate self-stimulation. The prevailing view has been that pharmacologically enhancing activity in the reinforcement system will enhance self-stimulation, whereas pharmacologically inhibiting activity in the reinforcement system will inhibit self-stimulation. The logic of these assumptions has not been adequately scrutinized.

Neurotransmitter activity is most commonly enhanced by postsynaptic receptor agonists, presynaptic release enhancers, presynaptic reuptake inhibitors or inhibitors of enzymatic degradation. Neurotransmitter activity is most commonly inhibited by postsynaptic receptor antagonists, agonists of presynaptic inhibitory receptors, synthesis inhibitors and neurotoxins. These are by no means the only ways of modulating neurotransmitter activity. They are only some of the more common modes of action of drugs figuring prominently in self-stimulation research. Even setting aside the fundamental inadequacies of conventional measures of reinforcement, it is apparent that almost all drugs inhibit self-stimulation, whereas only a handful reliably enhance self-stimulation. The paradox is that although there are many ways of enhancing activity in the putative positive reinforcement system(s) most of these appear to inhibit self-stimulation. The resolution of this paradox has important implications.

Positive reinforcement of an operant response by brain stimulation may be neurochemically described as follows. The positive reinforcement is produced by the contingency of increased transmitter release on the instrumental response. The response produces the electrical stimulation which increases neurotransmitter release. It is some consequence (likely post-synaptic) of the neurotransmitter release which reinforces the response. The critical relation is the contingency of the reinforcement upon the response. If this contingency is broken and reinforcement does not occur in the proper temporal association with the response, the response would be expected to extinguish. The response reinforcement contingency is clearly broken by drugs which inhibit neurotransmitter activity in the positive reinforcement system(s). However, it is not as widely appreciated that the response reinforcement contingency is also usually broken by drugs which enhance neurotransmitter activity.

Postsynaptic receptor agonists, presynaptic reuptake inhibitors and inhibitors of enzymatic degradation all enhance neurotransmitter activity in a way that is relatively, if not totally, independent of presynaptic activity. In other words, they break the contingency of postsynaptic activity on the operant response. Under these circumstances, reduced responding is the expectable outcome of enhanced reinforcement activity. The analogy in food reinforcement would be the reduction in responding for food produced by providing response-independent food.

Enhanced responding is the expected outcome of enhancing positive reinforcement only when the positive reinforcement is contingent on that responding. This contingency appears to be maintained only by release enhancers or perhaps by drugs which increase postsynaptic receptor responsivity. Even if self-stimulation procedures were providing valid measures of positive reinforcement, most pharmacological manipulations would be expected to decrease self-stimulation. Just how one can differ-entiate between a reduction in reinforcement strength and an uncoupling of the response-reinforcement contingency remains to be determined.

However, there is an important qualification to the above analysis. It only applies to that population of neurons which directly mediates the reinforcement process. The excitability of this system could well be modulated through the tonic activity of other neurons. Changes in the activity of this latter population of neurons would not adversely effect the association between responding and activity in the neurons which directly mediate reinforcement. Consequently, if postsynaptic receptor agonists, presynaptic reuptake inhibitors or inhibitors of enzymatic degradation were shown to enhance reinforcement it would implicate the relevant neuro-transmitter(s) in the tonic excitation of reinforcement neurons. If these same drugs inhibited reinforcement, it would then be necessary to differen-tiate between an indirect tonic inhibitory role and a primary involvement by way of uncoupling the response–reinforcement contingency. This funda-mental distinction between the direct and indirect modulation of reinforce-ment represents another dimension of complexity in this area.

F. Drug self-administration and motivational homeostasis

Since electrical stimulation of the brain is transduced into a neuro-chemical message, it should be possible to bypass the electrical step and study reinforcement processes more directly by chemically stimulating the brain. If one is interested in the neurochemistry of reinforcement, why not start at the neurochemical level? As appealing as this logic is, implementing it is impeded by some simple physical constraints.

The minimum volume of an intracerebral injection is so large relative to the volume of the hypothalamus that more than a few closely-spaced microinjections would produce grossly unphysiological tissue displacement. This limitation essentially eliminates the possibility of using continuous reinforcement (CRF) free-operant self-stimulation. On the other hand, volume considerations do not constitute a serious limitation if the inter-reinforcement interval is long enough. As with electrical stimulation, the validity of the reinforcement measures provided by intracerebral drug self-administration procedures can be improved by the use of discrete trials or intermittent reinforcement. This interesting line of pursuit remains unexplored.

The most common chemical self-stimulation paradigm involves self-injection into the vascular system (for references see Spealman and Goldberg, 1978). This procedure is generally not significantly limited by volume considerations and it bears obvious resemblance to a prominent method of human drug abuse. Further, whereas the evidence for brain stimulation produced hedonia is weak (Sem-Jacobsen, 1976), there is no question that drugs have potent euphorigenic properties.

The syntax of drug self-stimulation is so different from that of electrical self-stimulation that one may question whether they are subserved by a common mechanism. For example, rats self-administering amphetamine show obvious hedonic regulation. Increasing the concentra-tion of the injection decreases response rate, whereas decreasing the concentration of the injection increases response rate (for references see Spealman and Goldberg, 1978). Rats self-administering drugs appear to regulate postsynaptic excitability. In the case of drugs which are euphori-genic this could be thought of as hedonic regulation.

In marked contrast, increasing brain stimulation current clearly increases response rate, whereas decreasing current decreases response rate. Rats self-administering electrical stimulation of the brain appear to show none of the regulatory changes in responding that characterize drug self-administration. This difference could indicate that positive reinforcement produced by electrical stimulation is quite unrelated to hedonic–euphoric experience. Alternatively, it could be argued that rats regulate drug self-administration because of the cumulative effects of the drugs, whereas the cumulative effects of electrical stimulation are far less. In this case the difference could be seen as a procedural artifact.

In fact, electrical stimulation of the hypothalamus can be shown to have long lasting and probably cumulative effects. We have recently demonstrated that even small amounts (15–30 s) of low level electrical stimulation of the hypothalamus can produce large and long lasting (15–45 min) changes in blood glucose, insulin, oxygen consumption and respiratory quotients. Daily test sessions produce changes in energy balance that may last for months (Atrens *et al.*, 1982; 1983a). These changes are not directly related to reinforcement processes, but they do show that the time scale of the effects of electrical stimulation of the hypothalamus is far longer than is generally appreciated. Consequently, such effects are likely to be cumulative. Further, the fact that hypothalamic stimulation produces such profound, even dangerous, physiological disturbances has important implications.

The autonomic endocrine and skeletal motor changes produced by hypothalamic stimulation are clearly counter-regulatory and, if they have any affective component, it is likely to be negative. These changes are inimicable to pleasure and euphoria. However, it could be argued that the state of pleasure or euphoria produced by the brain stimulation is so intense that mundane physiological regulatory considerations become secondary.

G. Taking the fun out of self-stimulation

Inferring a hedonic–affective (pleasure; reward; fun) basis for self-stimulation originally had no justification. A generation of research has provided very little additional support for this notion. That hypothalamic stimulation is positively reinforcing is now beyond dispute. That self-stimulation of the hypothalamus models hedonic–affective processes is more questionable than ever. Self-stimulation needs to be dehedonized.

Dissociating reinforcement processes from hedonic states has a number of advantages. First of all, it resolves the otherwise paradoxical self-induction of counterregulatory physiological responses by reinforcing brain stimulation. The strengthening of responding produced by hypothalamic stimulation may be viewed as being essentially devoid of pleasure. Consequently, the fact that the same stimulation has probably unpleasant consequences becomes much less of a problem. The mistake was in approaching the behaviour within a hedonic framework in the first place. Strength and persistence of behaviour may be unequivocal indicators of reinforcement. However, these same characteristics are orthogonal to the question as to whether the behaviour is pleasurable or hedonically motivated.

The anhedonic approach also simplifies the pharmacological analysis of self-stimulation. For example, most drugs used in self-stimulation research probably have very few pleasure-modulating or euphoriant properties. If self-stimulation is viewed from a hedonic framework it is difficult to see how such drugs could modulate self-stimulation. On the other hand, it is not difficult to see how affectively neutral drugs could modulate affectively neutral reinforcement processes.

If self-stimulation is not pleasure motivated, then its modulation by drugs which are not implicated in pleasure is not paradoxical. This also resolves the apparently paradoxical self-administration of drugs whose effects are, if anything, unpleasant. For example, there is little indication that tricyclic antidepressants, phenothiazines, dopamine receptor agonists or presynaptic α-adrenoreceptor agonists are pleasurable. This is reflected in the low abuse potential of such drugs. However, drugs from all of these classes will support self-administration behaviour (for references see Spealman and Goldberg, 1978).

Dehedonizing brain stimulation reinforcement means that self-stimulation is not likely to provide data relevant to the hedonic–affective psychopathologies towards which it has largely been directed. The gratuitous hedonizing of self-stimulation generated a host of iatrogenic problems which continue to dominate self-stimulation research without illuminating psychopathology.

Dehedonizing brain-stimulation reinforcement suggests a number of quite different psychopathologies to which self-stimulation research may well be very relevant. For example, a great many strong and persistent behaviours seem to be conspicuously devoid of pleasure, or at least whatever pleasure is involved in these behaviours appears to be clearly outweighed by a variety of aversive effects. Obsessive–compulsive, addictive and self-punitive behaviours have very little to do with pleasure. They certainly indicate powerful reinforcement processes, as does self-stimulation. However, the understanding of both of these classes of behaviour has been impeded, not furthered, by inappropriate hedonic speculation.

REFERENCES

Ángyán, L. Autonomic effects of self-stimulation. In A. Wauquier and E.T. Rolls (Eds.), *Brain Stimulation Reward*. New York: Elsevier, 1976: 461–466.

Atrens, D.M. Reinforcing and emotional consequences of electrical self-stimulation of the subcortical limbic forebrain. *Physiology and Behavior*, 1970, 5: 1461–1471.

Atrens, D.M., Williams, M.P., Brady, C.J. and Hunt, G.E. Energy balance and hypothalamic self-stimulation. *Behavioural Brain Research*, 1982, 5: 131-142.

Atrens, D.M., Marfaing-Jallat, P. and Le Magnen, J. Ethanol preference following hypothalamic stimulation: Relation to stimulation parameters and energy balance. *Pharmacology Biochemistry and Behavior*, 1983a, 19: 571-575.

Atrens, D.M., Sinden, J.D. and Hunt, G.E. Dissociating the determinants of self-stimulation. *Physiology and Behavior*, 1983b, 31: 787-799.

Bower, G.H. and Miller, N.E. Rewarding and punishing effects from stimulating the same place in the rat's brain. *Journal of Comparative and Physiological Psychology*, 1958, 51: 669-674.

Deutsch, J.A. and Hawkins, R.D. Adaptation as a cause of apparent aversiveness of prolonged rewarding brain stimulation. *Behavioral Biology*, 1972, 7: 285-290.

Deutsch, J.A., Roll, P.L. and Wetter, F. Choice between rewarding brain stimuli of differing length. *Behavioral Biology*, 1976, 18: 369-377.

De Witte, P. and Bruyer, R. Self-stimulation behaviour: Methods for evaluating intracranial reward and their relations with motivational states. *Physiological Psychology*, 1980, 8: 386-394.

Dews, P.B. Studies on behavior. I. Differential sensitivity to pentobarbital of pecking performance in pigeons depending on the schedule of reward. *Journal of Pharmacology and Experimental Therapeutics*, 1955, 113: 393-401.

Fibiger, H.C. Drugs and reinforcement mechanisms: A critical review of the catecholamine theory. *Annual Review of Pharmacology and Toxicology*, 1978, 18: 37-56.

Fouriezos, G., Hansson, P. and Wise, R.A. Neuroleptic-induced attenuation of brain stimulation reward in rats. *Journal of Comparative and Physiological Psychology*, 1978, 92: 661-671.

Fouriezos, G. and Wise, R.A. Pimozide-induced extinction of intracranial self-stimulation: Response patterns rule out motor or performance deficits. *Brain Research*, 1976, 103: 377-380.

Gallistel, C.R., Shizgal, P. and Yeomans, J.S. A portrait of the substrate for self-stimulation. *Psychological Review*, 1981, 88: 228-273.

Gallistel, C.R., Boytim, M., Gomita, Y. and Klebanoff, L. Does pimozide block the reinforcing effect of brain stimulation? *Pharmacology Biochemistry and Behavior*, 1982, 17: 769-781.

Glow, P.H. and Winefield, A.H. Effect of regular noncontingent sensory changes on responding for sensory change. *Journal of General Psychology*, 1982, 107: 121-137.

Hodos, W.H. Motivational properties of long durations of rewarding brain stimulation. *Journal of Comparative and Physiological Psychology*, 1964, 59: 219-224.

Hornykiewicz, O. Parkinsonianism induced by dopaminergic antagonists. In D.B. Calne, T.N. Chase and A. Barbeau (Eds.), *Advances in Neurology* (Vol. 9). New York: Raven Press, 1975: 155-164.

Hu, J.W. Activity change as the cause of apparent aversiveness during prolonged hypothalamus stimulation. *Science*, 1971, 172: 84-85.

Hunt, G.E., Atrens, D.M. and Johnson, G.F.S. The tetracyclic antidepressant mianserin: Evaluation of its blockade of presynaptic alpha-adrenoceptors in a self-stimulation model using clonidine. *European Journal of Pharmacology*, 1981, 70: 59-63.

Jenkins, O.F., Atrens, D.M. and Jackson, D.M. Self-stimulation of the nucleus accumbens and some comparisons with hypothalamic self-stimulation. *Pharmacology Biochemistry and Behavior*, 1983, 18: 585-591.

Kaiser, H.F. The varimax criterion for the analytic rotation in factor analysis. *Psychometrika*, 1958, 23: 187-200.

Keesey, R.E. Duration of stimulation and the reward properties of hypothalamic stimulation. *Journal of Comparative and Physiological Psychology*, 1964, 58: 201-207.

Kuffler, S.W. and Nicholls, J.G. *From Neuron to Brain.* Sunderland, Mass.: Sinauer, 1976.

Liebman, J.M. Discriminating between reward and performance: A critical review of intracranial self-stimulation methodology. *Neuroscience and Biobehavioral Reviews*, 1983, 7: 45-72.

Nazzaro, J.M., Seeger, T.F. and Gardner, E.L. Morphine differentially affects ventral tegmental and substantia nigra brain reward thresholds. *Pharmacology Biochemistry and Behavior*, 1981, 14: 325–331.

Olds, J. Hypothalamic substrates of reward. *Physiological Reviews*, 1962, 42: 554–604.

Olds, J. and Milner, P. Positive reinforcement produced by electrical stimulation of septal area and other regions of rat brain. *Journal of Comparative and Physiological Psychology*, 1954, 47: 419–427.

Olds, M.E. and Fobes, J.L. The central basis of motivation: Intracranial self-stimulation studies. *Annual Review of Psychology*, 1981, 32: 523–574.

Roll, S.K. Intracranial self-stimulation and wakefulness: Effects of manipulating ambient catecholamines. *Science*, 1970, 168: 1370–1372.

Rolls, E.T. The neurophysiological basis of brain stimulation reward. In A. Wauquier and E.T. Rolls (Eds.), *Brain Stimulation Reward*. New York: Elsevier, 1976: 65–87.

Sadowski, B. Physiological correlates of self-stimulation. In A. Wauquier and E.T. Rolls (Eds.), *Brain Stimulation Reward*. New York: Elsevier, 1976: 433–460.

Sanger, D.J. and Blackman, D.C. Rate-dependent effects of drugs: A review of the literature. *Pharmacology Biochemistry and Behavior*, 1976, 4: 73–83.

Schaefer, G.J. and Michael, R.P. Acute effects of neuroleptics on brain self-stimulation thresholds in rats. *Psychopharmacology*, 1980, 67: 9–15.

Schiff, B.B. Caudate lesions and self-stimulation: An argument for better behavioral methods in research on intracranial self-stimulation. In A. Wauquier and E.T. Rolls (Eds.), *Brain Stimulation Reward*. New York: Elsevier, 1976: 405–407.

Schwab, R.S. Akinesia paradoxica. *Electroencephalography and Clinical Neurophysiology*, 1972, suppl. 31: 87–96.

Sem-Jacobsen, C.W. Electrical stimulation and self-stimulation in man with chronic implanted electrodes: Interpretation and pitfalls of results. In A. Wauquier and E.T. Rolls (Eds.), *Brain Stimulation Reward*. New York: Elsevier, 1976: 505–520.

Shizgal, P. and Matthews, G. Electrical stimulation of the rat diencephalon: Differential effects of interrupted stimulation on on- and off-responding. *Brain Research*, 1977, 129: 319–333.

Sinden, J.D. and Atrens, D.M. Dopaminergic and noradrenergic inhibition of hypothalamic self-stimulation: Differentiation of reward and performance deficits. *European Journal of Pharmacology*, 1983, 86: 237–246.

Spealman, R.D. and Goldberg, S.R. Drug self-administration by laboratory animals: Control by schedules of reinforcement. *Annual Review of Pharmacology and Toxicology*, 1978, 18: 313–339.

Stein, L. and Ray, O.S. Brain stimulation reward "thresholds" self-determined in rat. *Psychopharmacologia*, 1960, 1: 251–256.

Valenstine, E.S. Problems of measurement and interpretation with reinforcing brain stimulation. *Psychological Review*, 1964, 71: 425–437.

Wauquier, A., Clincke, G. and Fransen, J. Brain reinforcement mechanisms: Alpha-adrenergic and dopaminergic agonists and antagonists. In H. Lal and S. Fielding (Eds.), *Psychopharmacology of Clonidine*. New York: A.R. Liss, 1981: 177–196.

Weiss, B. Specifying the nonspecific. In G. Zbinden, V. Cuomo, G. Racagni and B. Weiss (Eds.), *Application of behavioral pharmacology in toxicology*. New York: Raven Press, 1983: 71–86.

Wise, R.A. Neuroleptics and operant behavior. The anhedonia hypothesis. *Behavioral Brain Sciences*, 1982, 5: 39–53.

Zarevics, P. and Setler, P.E. Simultaneous rate-independent and rate-dependent assessment of intracranial self-stimulation: Evidence for the direct involvement of dopamine in brain reinforcement mechanisms. *Brain Research*, 1979, 169: 499–512.

10
ANIMAL MODELS OF MEMORY DISORDERS

DAVID H. OVERSTREET AND ROGER W. RUSSELL

I. INTRODUCTION

This chapter focuses on the potential usefulness of animal models for understanding memory disorders in humans. For three of the major conditions associated with the latter (global amnesias, Korsakoff's disease, and Alzheimer's disease), there is growing evidence for differences in both the brain areas involved in and the behavioural features of the disorders (for example, Corkin, 1982). However, until recently there has been comparatively little work on the possibility of developing animal models for these conditions. This is particularly so for Alzheimer's disease, which will receive special attention in the discussion to follow.

Memory disorders occur with sufficient frequency to be significant social problems, as well as constituting major handicaps for those who suffer from them. For example, epidemiological studies suggest that Alzheimer's disease affects more elderly people than any other brain disease, with estimates of from 4% to 15% of the population over 65 affected (Coyle *et al.*, 1983). The need to provide personal attention for such persons places heavy demands upon public health services. Considerable research is now underway to identify underlying causes and potential treatments for those affected. Included are studies of neurochemical abnormalities and the characteristics of various neurotransmitter systems (for example, receptors) in post-mortem brain samples, of ways to intervene physiologically to improve memory function (or at least to retard its loss),

ANIMAL MODELS IN PSYCHOPATHOLOGY
ISBN 0 12 114180 2

of behavioural and electrophysiological markers with which to predict the prognosis and to monitor the course of the disorder, and of differential diagnosis of memory impairment from other disorders (for example, depressive illnesses).

Despite the broad range of these investigations, research methods are limited by restrictions on the use of human subjects. Investigators are dependent upon the "spontaneous" development of the memory disorder whether retrospective or prospective studies are involved. The advantages of the logic of experimental methods, in which independent variables are manipulated systematically while dependent variables are being measured and proper controls exercised, cannot be realized. The advantage of using animal models has been well documented by the successes of the biomedical sciences over many years. Clearly it is desirable that such models be developed for use in the study of memory disorders.

II. CHARACTERISTICS OF MODELS

Before evaluating the evidence for and against the various animal models, a discussion of which characteristics such models should have is important. In considering animal models of mania, Robbins and Sahakian (1980) proposed the following three characteristics: (i) the animal model should mimic the behavioural features of the disorder; (ii) there should be a similarity in the aetiology of the condition in the animal model and in the human condition; and (iii) drugs which are known to counteract the symptoms in humans should also alleviate the behavioural pathology in the animal model.

It is difficult to apply the last of these characteristics to animal models of memory disorders because the therapy of these conditions is still in its infancy. For example, there are virtually no therapeutically effective drugs in the treatment of the global amnesias or Alzheimer's disease. Nevertheless, a potential benefit of animal models is their use to devise behavioural and/or pharmacological strategies that will alleviate the memory disorders. If such strategies could be found, then tests of their effectiveness in alleviating memory disorders in humans could be attempted.

Applying the first characteristic will often involve considerable difficulty. For example, it has been suggested the primate models of global amnesia only became possible when investigators realized the extreme richness of memory capacities of their subjects and devised more sophisticated approaches to assess these capacities (Mishkin *et al.*, 1982). Similarly, these characteristics of the memory failure in Alzheimer's disease patients (for example, Fuld, 1982; Weingartner *et al.*, 1982) are still being evaluated and it is unlikely that it will be possible to simulate exactly Alzheimer's disease type memory disorders in infrahuman models. However, it must be emphasized that models are not intended to be perfect representations. Their utility lies in our ability to look more closely at the functional relationship between anatomy and behaviour in them and gain new insights which can be applied to the human condition (see Chapter 1).

Applying the second characteristic to animal models of memory disturbance is rather straightforward for global amnesia and Korsakoff's disease because of the clear aetiology; however, it would be particularly difficult for Alzheimer's disease because of the uncertainties about its aetiology. As an alternative, it is proposed that animal models could attempt to reproduce, in whole or in part, the neuroanatomical and/or neurochemical abnormalities that have been reported to occur in the human conditions. Again, this approach has its limitations because of the difficulties in exactly reproducing the changes that have been observed in (for example) Alzheimer's disease (Coyle *et al.*, 1983). Nevertheless, the utility of the approach should once again be emphasized. It is possible to produce more selective alterations in neuroanatomy or neurochemistry in the animal model; therefore, the involvement of these selected regions or systems in the behavioural pathology (that is, memory disorders) can be more conclusively determined. It is important to know whether a selected neurochemical change is associated with the behavioural disturbance, because of the therapeutic implications. This point will be expanded in a later section.

In sum, then, it is proposed that animal models of memory disorders should exhibit at least the following two features: (i) a memory disorder that is similar in some respects to that observed in the human condition; and (ii) neuroanatomical and/or neurochemical disturbances that mimic those observed in the human condition. In addition, it is proposed that a third feature might be incorporated as further studies are conducted: effective treatments of the memory disturbances in humans, which may have arisen through chance, may be applied to the animal models in a systematic way. The outcome of such studies could lead to a more rational and effective therapy of the memory disorders in humans.

III. THE NATURE OF MEMORY

Within the general conceptual framework of the biobehavioural sciences, "memory" is a theoretical construct. Memory is never measured directly, but in terms of the overt behaviours of living organisms — in terms of what form past learning can be recalled or recognized, or in terms of how much saving is incurred during relearning as a consequence of the prior learning. Closer examination suggests that "information input" to an organism is transduced by sense organs into nerve impulses in afferent nerves and is carried to the central nervous system (CNS) where it is "stored" until it may be "read out" or "retrieved" later to affect behaviour. The latter effect provides evidence of "memory". Malfunction occurring at the input, storage or retrieval stages in this series of events can be expected to impair memory.

What malfunctions may occur? Attempts to answer this question begin with descriptions of living organisms in terms of four basic properties: behavioural; biochemical; electrophysiological; and morphological. The state of an organism at any one time is some function of interactions among all these properties. From the earliest interests in the nature of interactions involved in memory it has been assumed that a period of "consolidation" follows the input of information (Mueller and Pilzecker, 1900). Hypotheses have been advanced as to the nature of events (neurochemical, electrophysiological, and morphological) occurring during this period which result in storage of the information for future retrieval. Several models of the temporal stages involved in memory consolidation have been proposed and some have implicated such biochemical mechanisms as hyperpolarization associated with potassium conductance changes, the sodium pump, and protein synthesis (Gibbs and Ng, 1979). Other studies using animal models have demonstrated that retrieval of memories may be affected by neurochemical changes even when information input and storage have not been impaired (for example, Russell and Macri, 1978).

Because of the complexity and richness of memory processes in humans, there is some concern about the quality of animal models. In other words, certain species of animal may provide more reasonable models than others. As indicated previously, it was impossible to mimic the features of global amnesia in rodents and the attempts to develop a primate model of global amnesia were fraught with difficulties (Mishkin *et al.*, 1982).

IV. GLOBAL AMNESIAS

Although severe memory disturbance is seen in individuals with damage to either hippocampal–temporal lobe regions or the midline diencephalic regions, and both conditions are commonly referred to as global amnesias, we would like to confine our discussion here to the first condition. The second condition will be considered later under Korsakoff's disease. Global amnesia refers to the fact that the memory disturbance of the individual is widespread and includes all modalities (both verbal and non-verbal memory capacities are severely affected). Recent work by Squire and others has suggested differences in the memory disturbance in these two groups of individuals. If training is sufficiently prolonged so that all individuals do in fact acquire the task, then those individuals with midline diencephalic lesions show a normal "forgetting" curve, while those with the bitemporal lesions have a more rapid rate of forgetting (Squire and Zola-Morgan, 1983). Most of the animal work has centred around reproducing the behavioural deficit by lesions of various regions of the temporal lobe and underlying structures. This work has recently been reviewed (Mishkin *et al.*, 1982; Squire and Zola-Morgan, 1983); consequently, only a few brief comments will be made here.

Fig. 10.1 illustrates the relationship between some of the important structures within the temporal lobes which have been implicated in the bitemporal amnesic syndrome. In many of the earlier surgical cases, the amygdala, temporal stem, and hippocampus have all been removed. Consequently, it has not been possible to establish conclusively which of these three areas is related to the memory disturbance from the clinical data. Many of the earlier studies with non-human primates failed to provide any data which clarified this situation. As indicated previously, one reason for this failure was the lack of recognition of the richness of memory processes in non-human primates (Mishkin *et al.*, 1982). However, recent studies have been more successful and it has been proposed by Squire and Zola-Morgan (1983) that the data for humans and for non-human primates can be compared. Their conclusions will be briefly summarized below.

Several recent studies have provided evidence against the involvement of the temporal stem in the memory disturbance associated with global amnesia. In two studies, monkeys with hippocampal lesions without accompanying damage to the temporal stem exhibited severe impairments of memory (Moss *et al.*, 1982; Mahut *et al.*, 1982). In a third study, it was found that lesions of the temporal stem without concomitant damage to the hippocampus did not cause any discernible impairment of memory (Zola-Morgan *et al.*, 1981). However, lesions of the temporal stem did result in an impairment of visual discrimination performance, confirming an earlier report (Horel and Misantone, 1976). Thus, while damage to the temporal stem may produce a visual information processing deficit, it does not produce global amnesia.

There is still some uncertainty about the brain structures involved in the memory disturbance. At present, it cannot be conclusively stated whether the amnesia depends upon damage to the hippocampus or upon damage to both the hippocampus and the amygdala. In an extensive survey of the relevant literature (Squire and Zola-Morgan, 1983), only two direct comparisons were found, between monkeys with hippocampal lesions, and those with combined hippocampal–amygdala lesions in which key

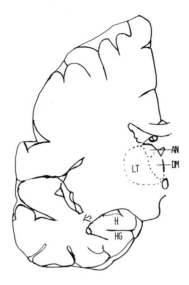

Fig. 10.1: Frontal Section through a primate brain to show the relationship between the temporal stem (TS) and the hippocampus (H) and hippocampal gyrus (HG). Other structures are the lateral thalamus (LT), anterior nucleus of the thalamus (AN) and the dorso-medial nucleus of the thalamus (DM). (Redrawn from Squire and Zola-Morgan, 1983).

behavioural tasks were used: the combined lesion group was more impaired in only one of the three tasks. Moreover, it was pointed out that, in most studies which compared the two conditions, the anterior third of the hippocampus was spared in the monkeys with hippocampal lesions, but was damaged in monkeys with combined lesions. Thus, it is still uncertain whether only damage to the hippocampus or damage to both the hippo- campus and the amygdala is responsible for the amnesia.

A final important conclusion by Squire and Zola-Morgan (1983) relates to the behavioural tasks used. It has recently been established that some forms of learning and memory, such as motor learning and cognitive-skill learning, are spared in human global amnesic patients (Squire, 1982). It was suggested by Squire and Zola-Morgan (1983) that visual discrimination tasks in monkeys are similar to motor learning in humans and should not be sensitive to hippocampal lesions. Such a conclusion is consistent with all of the negative findings in the literature. They make the valuable suggestion of the tasks in monkeys that should be sensitive to hippocampal lesions: the concurrent task; the matching-to-sample task; the spatial tasks (see Squire and Zola-Morgan, 1983, for a fuller description of these tasks). Thus, there is now some agreement about the type of behavioural tasks that should result in amnesia in monkeys after damage to particular anatomical regions. Such tasks will undoubtedly be used in future studies to elucidate the relative involvement of the amygdala and hippocampus in the bitemporal amnesic syndrome and may also be employed in studies to model the diencephalic syndrome, which appears to be relatively unexplored as yet.

V. KORSAKOFF'S DISEASE

Although Korsakoff's disease is associated with the abuse of alcohol, the evidence indicates that the brain pathology associated with this disease is not the consequence of the direct effects of alcohol; rather, the degenerative brain changes have been attributed to a deficiency of thiamine (Blass and Gibson, 1979a; Victor *et al.*, 1971). Therefore, in this section the extensive literature on ethanol intake in animals will not be considered. The reader is referred to a number of recent reviews (for example, Chapter 2; Eriksson *et al.*, 1980). Korsakoff's disease is one of the most frequently studied syndromes of human amnesia, as indicated by a summary of its neuropsychological aspects by Butters and Cermak (1980). In spite of the extensive investigations in humans, there appear to have been relatively few attempts to develop a primate model of the syndrome. On the other hand, there has been considerable work on metabolic encephalopathies, particularly those produced by thiamine deficiency, and it is this literature that is most relevant to the purposes of the present discussion.

The main neuropathological changes in Korsakoff's disease are degeneration of neurons in the diencephalic regions, in particular, the dorsomedial nucleus of the thalamus and the mammillary bodies of the hypothalamus (Victor *et al.*, 1971). In some cases there is also some damage to the cerebral cortex and the cerebellum, while damage to the hippocampus is usually infrequent (Table 10.1). Because this pattern of damage is different than that seen in the bitemporal syndrome of global amnesias, it is now generally believed that Korsakoff's syndrome represents a separate form of amnesia related to damage to the diencephalic structures. The recent demonstration that an individual, who had suffered from severe anterograde amnesia since a fencing accident in 1960, had a lesion in the left dorsal thalamic region (Squire and Moore, 1979) is further evidence for there being an identifiable amnesic syndrome related to damage to this region. Even more recent behavioural tests have shown that persons with bitemporal lobe damage forget at a more rapid rate than do the diencephalic group, or normal individuals (Squire and Zola-Morgan, 1983). Thus, it is now clear that there are at least two distinct forms of amnesia in humans, and for each of these animal models must be sought.

TABLE 10.1: Involvement of various brain regions in Korsakoff's disease

Region	No. of Cases Examined	No. of Cases Involved	
Hypothalamic Nuclei			
Medial Mammillary	47	47	(100)%
Dorsal area	32	23	(71.9)%
Thalamic Nuclei			
Medial Dorsal	43	38	(88.4)%
Medial Pulvinar	20	17	(85.0)%
Lateral Dorsal	25	17	(68.0)%
Submedius/Medial Ventral	26	15	(57.7)%
Parafascicular	34	17	(50.0)%
Regions other than Diencephalon or Brain Stem			
Cerebral Cortex	51	29	(56.9)%
Cerebellum	27	15	(55.5)%
Hippocampus	22	8	(36.4)%
Fornix	22	5	(22.7)%

Adapted from Victor *et al.*, 1971.

It has been pointed out by earlier investigators that pathological changes closely resembling those of Korsakoff's disease could be induced in animals raised on thiamine-deficient diets. However, there is still some uncertainty about the pathophysiological basis of Korsakoff's disease, because thiamine deficiency is not seen in all individuals with the symptoms (Blass and Gibson, 1979a). Nevertheless, studying the pathological changes induced by thiamine deficiency in animals is a reasonable start in searching for animal models that will provide more conclusive clues to the pathophysiology of Korsakoff's disease. What, then, have studies of the thiamine-deficient animals revealed about Korsakoff's syndrome? This topic has recently been reviewed by Blass (1981). The reader is also referred to the series of papers in the *Annals of the New York Academy of Sciences* (for example, Gibson *et al.*, 1982; Plaitakis et al., 1982).

Models of thiamine deficiency have been reported for rats (Gubler, 1961), mice (Seltzer and McDougal, 1974), cats (Jubb *et al.*, 1956) and monkeys (Rinehart *et al.*, 1949). The deficiency can be achieved by feeding the experimental animals commercially available diets which contain all necessary nutrients except thiamine or by treating them with the centrally acting thiamine antagonist, pyrithiamine. Early studies indicated that the abnormal lesions in the thiamine-deficient animals were similar to those generally reported in Korsakoff's disease (Robertson *et al.*, 1968). More recent studies have concentrated on the neurochemical and behavioural changes associated with thiamine deficiency.

Blass and colleagues have recently attempted to establish a role for the cholinergic system in the behavioural abnormalities associated with thiamine deficiency. They developed and standardized a string test (Barclay *et al.*, 1981a) for the rapid and reproducible testing of rats. In this test a rat is placed in the middle of an elevated taut string and its ability to traverse the string is scored according to the criteria in Table 10.2. Treatment with thiamine-deficient diets and pyrithiamine resulted in deficient performance on the string test.

On the other hand, rats treated with oxythiamine, a peripherally acting thiamine antagonist, did not show any deficits on the test. They also demonstrated an impaired synthesis of acetylcholine (ACh) in these rats and reported that physostigmine, an acetylcholinesterase (AChE) inhibitor, and arecoline, a direct muscarinic agonist, restored string test performance in the thiamine-deficient rats (Barclay *et al.*, 1981b). This work has recently been reviewed by Gibson *et al.*, 1982:400, who concluded: "Several lines of reasoning implicate the cholinergic system in the pathophysiology of thiamine deficiency. *In vitro* and *in vivo* acetylcholine synthesis as well as synaptic transmission are decreased in severe thiamine deficiency. Pharmacological manipulation of the tight-rope test and open-field staring behavior demonstrate the presence of a cholinergic lesion in early stages of thiamine deficiency. The importance of this lesion and its treatment with cholinergic drugs in other metabolic encephalopathies require further investigation, as does the precise molecular mechanism by which thiamine deficiency produces it".

These recent observations of the possible involvement of the cholinergic system in thiamine deficiency may help to account for many of the early reports of the behavioural deficits in thiamine-deficient animals. Although these early studies often suffered from lack of controls, Munn (1950) concluded that: "It is clearly established that deficiency in vitamin B complex retards the learning process in maze and conditioned-response situations". However, later studies indicated that these learning impairments may have been the consequence of motor impairments because they only occurred if the peripheral neuropathies already existed (Knopfelmacher *et al.*, 1956; Khairy *et al.*, 1957). These workers also showed that perseverations of behaviour did precede the neuropathies. Behavioural deficits in the string test have been detected long before the animals exhibited weight loss (Barclay *et al.*, 1981a,b; Gibson *et al.*, 1982). Nevertheless, it is particularly important to conduct other behavioural tests on thiamine-deficient rats in order to determine the generality of the deficits; other cholinergically mediated behaviours may be affected.

Another series of studies by Plaitakis and colleagues has suggested a role for serotonin in the pathophysiology of thiamine-deficient rats (Plaitakis *et al.*, 1978). In their most recent work on the topic, they reported an increased turnover of serotonin in several brain regions, particularly in the cerebellum (Plaitakis *et al.*, 1982). They also noted alterations in aspartate and in cyclic guanosine monophosphate in the cerebellum, but the changes in acetylcholine (ACh) were not as marked as those reported by Gibson *et al.* (1982). The conclusion that serotonin abnormalities, by themselves or coupled with cholinergic malfunctions, are key changes in thiamine deficiency must await confirmation by other investigators.

Despite these recent studies of rats with thiamine deficiency, there have been virtually no studies of post-mortem neurochemical changes in Korsakoff's disease (Blass, personal communication). Consequently, it is not possible to validate the cholinergic hypothesis of Blass's group or the serotonergic hypothesis of Plaitakis's group. Certainly, post-mortem neurochemical observations are necessary in Korsakoff's disease patients to resolve this issue. It is possible that both groups could be right, because, as indicated previously, there is often cerebellar damage in Korsakoff's disease as well as the more commonly reported diencephalic lesions (Table 10.1).

In summary, there is considerable evidence that thiamine deficiency is at least partly responsible for the pathophysiological changes in Korsakoff's disease. Recent studies of thiamine-deficient rats implicate the cholinergic and serotonergic systems in some of the behavioural deficits associated with thiamine deficiency. Further work must be conducted to determine if the neurochemical pathology of Korsakoff's disease patients will resemble the pathology of rats with thiamine deficiency. It may also be fruitful to conduct clinical trials on the usefulness of cholinergic agonists in treating the memory disturbances of Korsakoff's disease patients.

VI. ALZHEIMER'S DISEASE

There is now considerable interest in the syndrome known variously as presenile dementia, Alzheimer's disease, or senile dementia of the Alzheimer type (SDAT). It has been estimated that from 4% to 15% of the population above the age of 65 suffers from dementia, a severe impairment of cognitive functions. The present cost of nursing home care for such patients in the United States has been estimated to exceed US $6 billion per year (Coyle *et al.*, 1983). Thus, it is likely that the economic and social consequences of SDAT will far outweigh those of the global amnesias. Development of an ameliorative or preventive treatment for SDAT would therefore have a much greater impact. The aetiology of SDAT has not been clearly established; however, there is some evidence for a familial form, which may be inherited by means of a dominant gene (Corkin *et al.*, 1982). Since the early discovery of severe deficits in choline acetyltransferase (CAT) activity in brains from SDAT patients examined after death (Perry *et al.*, 1977), there has been an increased interest in what has become known

TABLE 10.2: Criteria for string test scoring

Scoring	
1 point	for each paw the rat keeps on the twine for at least 5 sec.
1 point	if the rat keeps its tail on the twine for at least 5 sec.
3 points	if the rat travels along the twine for at least 5 sec.
2 points	if the rat reaches one of the vertical poles in less than 25 sec.
−3 points	if the rat falls in 0–15 sec.
−2 points	if the rat falls in 16–30 sec.
−1 point	if the rat falls in 31–60 sec.
	Minimum score = −3
	Maximum score = 10

The testing apparatus consisted of a piece of twine 50 cm long tied tightly between two vertical poles and suspended over a landing pad. The rat was held by the tail and suspended over the twine near its midpoint until it fell off the string, traversed the string completely, or until one minute elapsed (from Barclay et al., 1981a).

as the cholinergic hypothesis of senile dementia (for example, Bartus et al., 1982). Although there is now evidence for other neurochemical deficits in the brains from SDAT patients (for example, Davies et al., 1982; Rosser et al., 1982; Winblad et al., 1982), there is still considerable interest in the cholinergic hypothesis, as witnessed by a recent paper proposing that SDAT may be a disorder of cortical cholinergic innervation (Coyle et al., 1983). Consequently, the present discussion will focus on potential animal models of SDAT by emphasizing the cholinergic system. For other potential animal models the reader is referred to Finch (1982) and Pepeu et al. (1980).

A. The cholinergic system(s)

Fig. 10.2 illustrates the main features of the cholinergic synapse. Acetylcholine (ACh) is synthesized from the precursors acetyl-coenzyme A (CoA) and choline in the presence of the enzyme, CAT. Although choline is actively transported into cholinergic neurons and may normally be the rate-limiting step in ACh biosynthesis, there is also evidence that acetyl-CoA may contribute, because conditions which limit its availability (such as reductions in carbohydrate metabolism) will lead to a reduction in ACh synthesis (Blass and Gibson, 1979b). Also, although CAT is not usually rate-limiting, it is still specific for cholinergic neurons and its activity has been widely used as a marker of the integrity of cholinergic neurons. Acetylcholinesterase (AChE) hydrolyses ACh into choline and acetate; its distribution is wider than that of cholinergic neurons and it is generally regarded as a rather poor marker of cholinergic innervation. Receptors for ACh, particularly those of the muscarinic type (mAChR), are generally

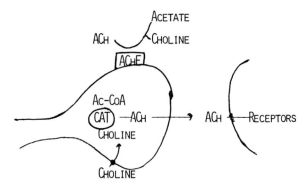

Fig. 10.2: A Typical Cholinergic Synapse in Schematic form. Acetylcholine (ACh) is synthesized from choline and acetyl-coenzyme A (Ac-CoA) by the enzyme, choline acetyl-transferase (CAT). The action of ACh is rapidly terminated by the enzyme, acetylcholinesterase (AChE), which is located on the surface of cholinergic neurons as well as neurons receiving cholinergic innervation. (Adapted from Coyle *et al.*, 1983.)

found in high concentrations in the same brain regions where CAT activity is high (Yamamura and Snyder, 1974). Thus, mAChR binding is generally regarded as a good marker of cholinoceptive neurons (which are sensitive to ACh) and CAT activity as a good marker of cholinergic neurons (which release ACh). In post-mortem studies of senile dementia of the Alzheimer type (SDAT) patients, the most common findings are a decrease in CAT and AChE activities and little or no change in mAChR binding (Bartus *et al.*, 1982). These deficits in CAT activity are regarded as signs of deterioration of cholinergic neurons.

Many recent studies emphasize three important cholinergic systems: the striatal; the septohippocampal; and the cortical. It is generally believed that all of the striatal cholinergic innervation is intrinsic, with both cell bodies and axon terminals located within the striatum. On the other hand, until recently all of the cholinergic innervation to the hippocampus was believed to be extrinsic, with the cell bodies in the septum and the terminals in the hippocampus. However, Swanson (1982) has pointed out that not all of the septo-hippocampal neurons are cholinergic and a recent communication (Arst *et al.*, 1983) provides evidence for possible intrinsic cholinergic neurons in the hippocampus. Work by Coyle and colleagues has suggested that the cortical cholinergic innervation is about 30% intrinsic and about 70% extrinsic, the cell bodies being located in the nucleus basalis of Maynert and the nucleus of the diagonal band of Broca (Coyle *et al.*, 1983).

It is generally recognized that the cholinergic systems are involved in many behavioural phenomena (Karczmar, 1977). In recent years its involvement in behavioural plasticity (for example, learning and tolerance) has received considerable attention (Overstreet, 1984). As indicated previously, there is now general agreement that there are large deficits in cholinergic enzymes in brains from SDAT patients and it has been suggested that these deficits are responsible for the memory disturbances seen in individuals with SDAT. What evidence is there for memory disturbances in animals with altered cholinergic function?

B. Cholinergic antagonists

Both humans and non-human primates suffer memory disturbance when treated with cholinergic antagonists such as scopolamine (Bartus, 1978; Drachman, 1977; Drachman et al., 1980). These memory deficits may be similar to those seen in older animals or individuals with senile dementia of the Alzheimer type (SDAT). Consequently, it has been proposed that animals treated with muscarinic antagonists could serve as useful animal models of dementia (Pepeu et al., 1980). However, there have been relatively few attempts to explore such models in any depth. It is important to note that physostigmine, but not adrenergic stimulants, counteracted the memory deficits induced by scopolamine in both animals and humans (Bartus, 1978; Drachman, 1977). There is also some recent evidence of a therapeutic potential of physostigmine in SDAT (Davis et al., 1982). However, choline has also been recently reported to counteract the memory impairment produced by scopolamine in humans (Mohs et al., 1981) but it is generally without much effect in the treatment of SDAT (Corkin, 1981).

Overall, the use of antagonist-treated animals as models of SDAT will provide only limited information because they produce only a temporary functional deficit in the cholinergic system, as distinct from the permanent deficits in SDAT. Thus, while it may be possible to find the best conditions for counteracting scopolamine-induced memory deficits by treatment with cholinergic agonists, this information may be of little value in devising suitable treatments for SDAT in humans. It would seem that animal models which involve more permanent deficits in cholinergic function would be more appropriate.

C. Aging

There is now considerable evidence that aged animals exhibit deficits in cholinergic markers. This evidence has been extensively reviewed by Bartus and colleagues (Bartus, 1982; Bartus et al., 1982) and only a few pertinent points will be made here. The memory deficits in aged mice can be reduced by placing them on diets enriched in choline or exacerbated by placing them on diets deficient in choline (Bartus *et al.*, 1980b). However, in other species acute choline may have little effect by itself, but may have a profound effect when combined with piracetam, a drug which increases cerebral oxidation (Bartus *et al.*, 1981). In aged primates, neither choline nor physostigmine leads to consistent improvements in memory, whereas the direct muscarinic agonist, arecoline, leads to a dose-related improvement (Bartus *et al.*, 1980a). Thus, there is evidence from aged animals that administration of cholinergic agonists can lead to an improvement of memory. The data from various studies in humans with senile dementia of the Alzheimer type (SDAT) have not been very encouraging to date. However, there has not yet been a thorough investigation of direct agonists (Corkin, 1981; Bartus *et al.*, 1982; Christie, 1982).

It is possible that aged animals may be more suitable as models of aged humans, rather than as models of SDAT. It is well recognized that there are age-related changes in other neurochemical systems (Finch, 1982), as well as those documented for the cholinergic system (Bartus *et al.*, 1982). Therefore, it is not possible at this time to conclude that the memory dysfunction is solely the consequence of the dysfunction of the cholinergic system (Kubanis and Zornetzer, 1981). There is also increasing doubt about whether the "cholinergic hypothesis" can completely account for the memory disturbance seen in SDAT patients (Corkin *et al.*, 1982). In order to test the cholinergic hypothesis more conclusively in animal models, other experimental approaches are necessary.

D. Neurotoxins to cell bodies

One approach used recently is the administration of the excitotoxic amino acids, kainic acid and ibotenic acid, into the cell bodies of origin of the cortical cholinergic projections (Coyle *et al.*, 1983). These studies have provided extensive information about the distribution of cholinergic neurons and have led to neuropathological studies in humans which have confirmed the significant deficit in the cortical cholinergic projections in senile dementia of the Alzheimer type (SDAT) (Price *et al.*, 1982; Coyle *et al.*, 1983). However, further studies of the behavioural consequences of these manipulations in a range of infrahuman animal species are urgently needed. The development of potential therapeutic agents for SDAT may rest with further exploration of this animal model and the demonstration that memory disturbance does result from destruction of the cortical cholinergic pathways.

It has been frequently reported that septal lesions result in learning and memory deficits (McCleary, 1961). However, almost all of these studies have used electrolytic or radio frequency techniques to produce the lesions and other behavioural consequences of these lesions (for example, hyper-activity and increased reactivity — Russell and Macri, 1979), have been reported. It would be very important to know whether lesions in the medial septum produced by either or both the excitotoxic amino acids, kainic acid and ibotenic acid, produce disturbances of memory. It is well established that hippocampal as well as cortical cholinergic systems are severely disturbed in SDAT patients (Corkin *et al.*, 1982), and the association of the hippocampus with memory in animals and humans has a much longer history than does the cortical cholinergic projection. In fact, it may be that the deficit in the cortical cholinergic pathways is in part responsible for the greater deficits seen in SDAT patients compared to patients with global amnesia (Corkin, 1982). To mimic SDAT completely, it may be necessary to lesion both the cortical and the septohippocampal cholinergic pathways.

In sum, excitotoxic lesions of cholinergic cell bodies projecting to the cortex and/or hippocampus may provide a useful animal model of (at least) the cholinergic deficits in SDAT patients. There are insufficient data available at present to evaluate the utility of such a model.

E. Specific cholinergic neurotoxins

Another experimental approach of considerable interest is the develop-ment of neurotoxins that are specific to the cholinergic system, analogous to 6-hydroxydopamine for the catecholamines and 5,7-dihydroxytrypta-mine for the indoleamines (Fisher and Hanin, 1980). Among the more promising compounds are acetylcholine mustard and certain derivatives. Early work by Clement and colleagues pointed to the inhibition of choline transport as the mode of action of these compounds (Clement *et al.*, 1974; Clement and Colhoun, 1975a,b). More recent studies by Hanin and colleagues have focused on a particular analogue, ethylcholine mustard aziridinium ion (AF64A), and the early findings are promising (Mantione *et al.*, 1981; Fisher *et al.*, 1982). These studies have been reviewed (Hanin *et al.*, 1982), but they deserve to be considered in some detail because of their potential significance in the development of animal models of senile dementia of the Alzheimer type (SDAT).

As illustrated in Fig. 10.3, AF64A is similar in structure to choline. It is generally prepared from the ethylcholine mustard analogue, AF64, and Fisher *et al.* (1982) have detailed the means of synthesis. It was selected for

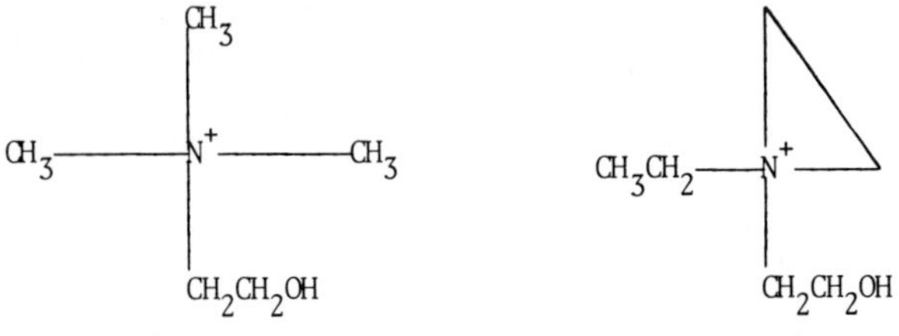

Fig. 10.3: Chemical structures of choline and ethylcholine mustard aziridinium (AF64A). (From Fisher *et al.*, 1982.)

study because of its similarity to choline and the presence of the cytotoxic aziridinium moiety in the molecule. Intracerebroventricular (icv) injections of AF64A (65 nmol) in mice produce significant decreases in acetylcholine (ACh) levels, high affinity choline transport and CAT activity in the cerebral cortex, hippocampus and striatum that last for at least seven days after the injection (Fisher *et al.*, 1982). Interestingly, there are no significant changes in muscarinic type acetylcholine receptor (mAChR) binding in any of the three regions examined (Fisher *et al.*, 1982) and preliminary reports indicate no changes in other neurochemical systems (Mantione *et al.*, 1983). Thus, AF64A may be "a unique presynaptic cholinergic chemical neurotoxin that induces in mice a state of long-term reduced cholinergic activity" (Fisher *et al.*, 1982:145).

However, there were differences among the regional cholinergic systems in the effects of AF64A. For example, the ACh levels in the striatum were decreased only marginally (28%), even though high affinity choline transport was dramatically decreased (80%). On the other hand, both ACh levels (45%) and high affinity choline transport (80%) were dramatically decreased in the hippocampus. It was also observed that the reduction in ACh levels persisted in the hippocampus until at least 21 days after the icv injection of AF64A, but recovery was seen in the cortex and the striatum (Fisher *et al.*, 1982). These findings suggest that the different cholinergic systems have a differential vulnerability to icv injected AF64A, with the hippocampus being the most susceptible.

The most recent work from this group of investigators was a communication in which long-term learning and memory impairments were reported in rats following icv injections of AF64A into rats (Walsh *et al.*, 1983). Specifically, they noted a reduced rate of habituation of motor activity 14, 21 and 28 days after the injection, markedly impaired passive avoidance retention 35 days after the injection and impaired radial-arm maze performance 60–90 days after the injection. Thus, long-term reduction of cholinergic activity in the hippocampus induced by AF64A was accompanied by long-term deficits in learning and memory. Further studies with this compound should produce other valuable results. One important direction that such work could take is to attempt to counteract or overcome the memory deficits in AF64A-treated animals by the administration of cholinergic agonists.

The finding of a neurotoxin selective at presynaptic cholinergic terminals may even provide some clues as to the aetiology of senile dementia of the Alzheimer type (SDAT). It is possible that an endogenous AF64A-like toxin is formed in some individuals, leading to the progressive degeneration of cholinergic nerve terminals. There is some evidence (Price *et al.*, 1982) that the characteristic senile plaques seen in SDAT may consist of degenerating cholinergic terminals; however, no-one, as far as we are aware, has previously suggested that the formation of an endogenous cholinergic neurotoxin may be the causative agent in this degenerative process. Detailed histopathological studies of the brain of AF64A-treated animals are needed to see if the evolution of senile plaques occurs. It would indeed be an exciting discovery if it could be demonstrated that AF64A mimicked an endogenous process that occurred in SDAT patients because it might open the way for the development of preventive rather than just ameliorative therapies.

F. Choline acetyltransferase antibodies

Another possible means of altering cholinergic neurotransmission would be the administration of antibodies to the synthesizing enzyme for actylcholine (ACh), choline acetyltransferase (CAT). However, progress in this area has been hampered by the extreme difficulties investigators have found in developing specific antibodies to this enzyme (Levey *et al.*, 1983). There is still much work to be done in this area before CAT antibodies can be used to attempt to disrupt the cholinergic system *in vivo*. For example, if relatively pure and specific antibodies to CAT were demonstrated, it would be necessary to determine whether central administration of such antibodies would produce an irreversible degeneration of cholinergic terminals. Also, although CAT is a reliable marker for cholinergic neurons, it is not a rate-limiting step in ACh synthesis; consequently large amounts of the antibodies may have to be injected to produce a significant alteration in cholinergic function. In general, the effects of inhibitors of CAT activity have not been very dramatic and such drugs are not regarded as useful tools for manipulation of the cholinergic system *in vivo*. Nevertheless, it could be important to continue work in this direction, because it may turn out that antibodies to CAT may be a causal factor in the pathogenesis of SDAT. The hypothesis that cholinergic nerve terminals degenerate because of the formation of antibodies to CAT has just as much merit as the suggestion of the formation of an endogenous cholinergic neurotoxin. In the search for preventive treatments for SDAT no promising directions should be curtailed.

VII. CONCLUSIONS AND FURTHER DIRECTIONS

This chapter has discussed some of the literature related to the development of animals models of memory disturbance. No attempt has been made to provide a comprehensive review and additional readings have been cited in some sections. Because of the speculative vein in which we have deliberately approached our task, conclusions reached should be treated with caution. It is hoped they will stimulate further thinking about mechanisms underlying memory disorders and about how they may be studied using animal models. There is an impressive correspondence in the three areas examined in this chapter: the bitemporal global amnesias; Korsakoff's disease; and senile dementia of the Alzheimer type (SDAT). We suggest that a unifying link in these three conditions could be the cholinergic system. First, the hippocampus and amygdala, structures implicated in the bitemporal amnesic syndrome, are known to contain cholineric innervation. Second, the areas damaged in Korsakoff's disease also contain cholinergic neurons and some behavioural deficits in thiamine-deficient animals can be overcome by treatment with cholinergic agonists (Gibson *et al.*, 1982). Third, there is considerable evidence for the involvement of cortical and hippocampal cholinergic systems in SDAT (Bartus *et al.*, 1982; Coyle *et al.*, 1983). The differences in the behavioural features among the three syndromes (Squire and Zola-Morgan, 1983; Corkin, 1982) may be related, at least in part, to the involvement of separate cholinergic systems. Although it is unlikely that the "cholinergic hypothesis" will be able to provide a complete account of the three syndromes, it is presently an heuristic hypothesis worthy of attention. In closing, we would like to consider briefly some of the potential directions this research could take.

A completely undeveloped area in the primate models of global amnesia is the neurochemical consequences of the lesions. The extent to which acetylcholine (ACh) and other neurotransmitters are decreased in these models would be important new information, as could studies on the neurochemical pathology in Korsakoff's disease and global amnesias. Further study with animal models of cholinergic hypofunction induced by injection of excitotoxic amino acids in cell body regions and of AF64A and/or antibodies into terminal regions should be carried out. Finally the possibility of restoring memory functions in animals, which have suffered a lesion, by transplanting fetal brain tissue (Dunnett *et al.*, 1982) requires further exploration. Through such studies, new hypotheses about the aetiologies of the disorders, particularly SDAT, may arise and these could lead eventually to preventive treatments. In addition, however, these models may lead to the development of rational pharmacotherapeutic strategies.

ACKNOWLEDGEMENTS

We wish to thank Larry Squire, Israel Hanan and John Blass for sending us prepublication copies of their work. Completion of this chapter was aided by a grant from the Flinders University Research Budget.

REFERENCES

Arst, D.S., Berger, T.W., Fisher, A. and Hanin, I. AF64A reduces acetylcholinesterase (AChE) staining, and uncovers AChE-positive cell bodies in rat hippocampus, *in vivo*. *Federation Proceedings*, 1983: 42: 657.

Barclay, L.L., Gibson, G.E. and Blass, J.P. The string test: An early behavioral change in thiamine deficiency. *Pharmacology Biochemistry and Behavior*, 1981a, 14: 153–157.

Barclay, L.L., Gibson, G.E. and Blass, J.P. Impairment of behavior and acetylcholine metabolism in thiamine deficiency. *Journal of Pharmacology and Experimental Therapeutics*, 1981b, 217: 537–543.

Bartus, R.T. Evidence for a direct cholinergic involvement in the scopolamine-induced amnesia in monkeys: Effects of concurrent administration of physostigmine and methylphenidate with scopolamine. *Pharmacology, Biochemistry and Behavior*, 1978, 9: 833–836.

Bartus, R.T. Effects of cholinergic agents on learning and memory in animal models of aging. In S. Corkin *et al.* (Eds.), *Alzheimer's Disease: A Report of Progress in Research*. New York: Raven Press, 1982: 271–280.

Bartus, R.T., Dean, R.L. and Beer, B. Memory deficits in aged cebus monkeys and facilitation with central cholinomimetics. *Neurobiology of Aging*, 1980a, 1: 145–152.

Bartus, R.T., Dean, R.L., Goas, J.A. and Lippa, A.S. Age-related changes in passive avoidance retention: Modulation with dietary choline. *Science*, 1980b, 209: 301–303.

Bartus, R.T., Dean, R.L., Sherman, K.A., Friedman, E. and Beer, B. Profound effects of combining choline and piracetam on memory enhancement and cholinergic function in aged rats. *Neurobiology of Aging*, 1981, 2: 105–111.

Bartus, R.T., Dean, R.L., Beer, B. and Lippa, A.S. The cholinergic hypothesis of geriatric memory dysfunction. *Science*, 1982, 217: 408–417.

Blass, J.P. Thiamine and the Wernicke-Korsakoff syndrome. In M.H. Briggs (Ed.), *Vitamins in Human Biology and Medicine*. Miami: CRC Press, 1981: 107–135.

Blass, J.P. and Gison, G.E. Genetic factors in Wernicke-Korsakoff syndrome. *Alcoholism: Clinical and Experimental Research*, 1979a, 3: 126–134.

Blass, J.P. and Gibson, G.E. Carbohydrates and acetylcholine synthesis: Implications for cognitive disorders. In K.L. Davis and P.A. Berger (Eds.), *Brain Acetylcholine and Neurophychiatric Disease*. New York: Plenum Press, 1979b: 215–236.

Butters, N. and Cermak, L.S. *Alcoholic Korsakoff's Syndrome: An Information Processing*

Approach to Amnesia. New York: Academic Press, 1980.

Christie, J.E. Physostigmine and arecoline infusions in Alzheimer's Disease. In S. Corkin *et al.* (Eds.), *Alzheimer's Disease: A Report of Progress in Research.* New York: Raven Press, 1982: 413–420.

Clement, D.G., Hirst, M. and Colhoun, E.H. Comparative toxicity of acetylcholine mustard (methyl-2-acetoxyethyl-2'-chlorolthylamine) in the mouse and American cockroach. *Agricultural and Food Chemistry,* 1974, 22: 873–876.

Clement, J.G. and Colhoun, E.H. Presynaptic effect of the aziridinium ion of acetylcholine mustard (methyl-2-acetoxyethyl-2'-chlorolthylamine) on the phrenic nerve-rat diaphragm preparation. *Canadian Journal of Physiology and Pharmacology,* 1975a, 53: 264–272.

Clement, J.G. and Colhoun, E.H. Inhibition of choline transport into human erythrocytes by choline mustard aziridinium ion. *Canadian Journal of Physiology and Pharmacology,* 1975b, 53: 1089–1093.

Corkin, S. Acetylcholine, aging and Alzheimer disease: Implications for treatment. *Trends in Neurosciences,* 1981, 4: 287–290.

Corkin, S. Some relationships between global amnesias and the memory impairments in Alzheimer's disease. In S. Corkin *et al.* (Eds.), *Alzheimer's Disease: A Report of Progress in Research.* New York: Raven Press, 1982: 149–164.

Corkin, S., Davis, K.L., Growdon, J.H., Usdin, E. and Wurtman, R.J. *Alzheimer's Disease: A Report of Progress in Research.* New York: Raven Press, 1982.

Coyle, J.T., Price, D.L. and DeLong, M.R. Alzheimer's disease: A disorder of cortical cholinergic innervation. *Science,* 1983, 219: 1184–1190.

Davies, P., Katz, D.A. and Crystal, H.A. Choline acetyltransferase, somatostatin and substance P in selected cases of Alzheimer's Disease. In S. Corkin *et al.* (Eds.), *Alzheimer's Disease: A Report of Progress in Research.* New York: Raven Press, 1982: 9–14.

Davis, K.L., Mohs, R.C., Davis, B.C., Levy, M.I., Horvath, T.B., Rosenberg, G.S., Ross, A., Rothpearl, A. and Rosen, W. Cholinergic treatment in Alzheimer's disease: Implications for future research. In S. Corkin *et al.* (Eds.), *Alzheimer's Disease: A Report of Progress in Research.* New York: Raven Press, 1982: 483–494.

Drachman, D.A. Memory and cognitive function in man: Does the cholinergic system have a specific role? *Neurology,* 1977, 27: 783–790.

Drachman, D.A., Noffsinger, P.,Sahakian, B.J., Kurdzill, S. and fleming, P. Aging, memory and the cholinergic system: A study of dichotic listening. *Neurobiology of Aging,* 1980, 1: 39–43.

Dunnett, S.B., Low, W.C., Iversen, S.D., Stenevi, U. and Bjorklund, A. Septal transplants restore maze learning in rats with fornix-fimbria lesions. *Brain Research,* 1982, 251: 335–348.

Eriksson, K., Sinclair, J.D. and Kiianmaa, K. *Animals Models in Alcohol Research.* London: Academic Press, 1980.

Finch, C.E. Rodent models for aging processes in the human brain. In S. Corkin *et al.* (Eds.), *Alzheimer's Disease: A Report of Progress in Research.* New York: Raven Press, 1982: 249–258.

Fisher, A. and Hanin, I. Minireview: Choline analogs as potential tools in developing selective animal models of central cholinergic hypo-function. *Life Sciences,* 1980, 27: 1615–1634.

Fisher, A., Mantione, C.R., Abraham, D.J. and Hanin, I. Long-term central cholinergic hypofunction induced in mice by ethylcholine aziridinium ion (AF64A) *in vivo. Journal of Pharmacology and Experimental Therapeutics,* 1982, 222: 140–145.

Fuld, P.A. Behavioural signs of cholinergic deficiency in Alzheimer dementia. In S. Corkin *et al.* (Eds.), *Alzheimer's Disease: A Report of Progress in Research.* New York: Raven Press, 1982: 193–196.

Gibbs, M.E. and Ng, K.T. Behavioural stages in memory formation. *Neuroscience Letters,* 1979, 13: 279–283.

Gibson, G., Barclay, L. and Blass, J. The role of the cholinergic system in thiamine deficiency. *Annals of the New York Academy of Sciences,* 1982, 378: 382–403.

Gubler, C.J. Studies on the physiological functions of thiamine. 1. The Effects of thiamine deficiency and thiamine antagonists on the oxidation of α-keto acids by rat tissues. *Journal of Biological Chemistry*, 1961, 236: 2113-3120.

Hanin, I., Mantione, C.R. and Fisher, A. AF64A-induced neurotoxicity: A potential animal model in Alzheimer's Disease. In S. Corkin *et al.* (Eds.), *Alzheimer's Disease: A Report of Progress in Research.* New York: Raven Press, 1982: 267-270.

Horel, J.A. and Misantone, L.J. Visual discrimination impaired by cutting temporal lobe connections. *Science*, 1976, 193: 336-338.

Jubb, K.V., Saunders, L.Z. and Coates, H.V. Thiamine deficiency encephalopathy in rats. *Journal of Comparative Pathology*, 1956, 66: 217-225.

Karczmar, A.G. Exploitable aspects of central cholinergic function particularly with respect to EEG, motor, analgesic and mental function. In D.J. Jenden (Ed.), *Cholinergic Mechanisms and Psychopharmacology.* New York: Plenum Press, 1977: 679-708.

Khairy, M., Russell, R.W. and Yudkin, J. Some effects of thiamine deficiency and reduced caloric intake on avoidance training and on reactions to conflict. *Quarterly Journal of Experimental Psychology*, 1957, 9: 190-205.

Knopfelmacher, R., Khairy, M., Russell, R.W. and Yudkin, J. Some effects of thiamine deficiency and reduced caloric intake on "behavior under stress" and on learning. *Quarterly Journal of Experimental Psychology*, 1956, 8: 54-65.

Kubanis, P. and Zornetzer, S.F. Age-related behavioral and neurobiological changes: A review with an emphasis on memory. *Behavioral and Neural Biology*, 1981, 31: 115-172.

Levey, A.I., Armstrong, D.M., Atweh, S.F. and Wainer, B.H. Monoclonal antibodies to choline acetyltransferase: Production, specificity, and immunohistochemistry. *The Journal of Neuroscience*, 1983, 3: 1-9.

McCleary, R.A. Response specificity in the behavioural effects of limbic system lesions in the rat. *Journal of Comparative and Physiological Psychology*, 1961, 54: 605-613.

Mahut, H., Zola-Morgan, S. and Moss, M. Hippocampal resections impair associative learning and recognition memory in the monkey. *Journal of Neuroscience*, 1982, 2: 1214-1229.

Mantione, C.R., Fisher, A. and Hanin, I. The AF64A-treated mouse: Possible model for central cholinergic hypofunction. *Science*, 1981, 213: 579-580.

Mishkin, M., Spiegler, B.J., Saunders, R.C. and Malamut, B.L. An animal model of global amnesia. In S. Corkin *et al.* (Eds.), *Alzheimer's Disease: A Report of Press in Research.* New York: Raven Press, 1982: 235-247.

Mohs, R.C., Davis, K.L. and Levy, M.J. Partial reversal of anticholinergic amnesia by choline chloride. *Life Sciences*, 1981, 29: 1317-1323.

Moss, M., Mahut, H. and Zola-Morgan, S. Concurrent discrimination learning of monkeys after hippocampal, enterorhinal, or formix lesions. *Journal of Neuroscience*, 1981, 1: 227-240.

Mueller, G.E. and Pilzecker, A. Experimentelle beitrage zur lehre vom Gedachtniss. *Zietschrift für Psychologie*, 1900, 1: 1-288.

Munn, N.L. *Handbook of Psychological Research on the Rat.* Boston: Houghton-Mifflin, 1950.

Overstreet, D.H. Behavioural plasticity and the cholinergic system. *Progress in Neuropsychopharmacology and Biological Psychiatry*, 1984, 8: 133-151.

Pepeu, G., Gori, G. and Bartolini, L. Pharmacologic and therapeutic perspective on dementia: An experimental approach. In L. Amaducci, A.N. Davison and P. Antuono (Eds.), *Aging of the Brain and Dementia.* New York: Raven Press, 1980: 271-274.

Perry, E.K., Perry, E.H., Blessed, G. and Tomlinson, B.E. Necropsy evidence of central cholinergic deficits in senile dementia. *Lancet*, 1977, 1: 189.

Plaitakis, A., Nicklas, W. and Berl, S. Thiamine deficiency: Selective impairment of the cerebellar serotonergic system. *Neurology*, 1978, 28: 691-698.

Plaitakis, A., Hwang, E.C., Van Woert, M.H., Szilagy, P.I.A. and Berl, S. Effect of thiamine deficiency on brain neurotransmitter systems. *Annals of the New York Academy of Sciences*, 1982, 378: 367-381.

Price, D.L., Whitehouse, P.J., Struble, R.G., Clark, A.W., Coyle, J.T., DeLong, M.R. and Hedreen, J.C. Basal forebrain cholinergic systems in Alzheimer's disease and related dementia. *Neuroscience Commentaries*, 1982, 1: 84–92.

Rinehart, J.F., Friedman, M. and Greenberg, L.D. Effects of experimental thiamine deficiency on the nervous system of the rhesus monkey. *Archives of Pathology*, 1949, 48: 129–139.

Robbins, T.W. and Sahakian, B.J. Animal models of mania. In R.H. Belmaker and H.M. van praag (Eds.), *Mania: An Evolving Concept*. Lancaster: MTP Press, 1980: 143–216.

Robertson, D.M., Wasan, S.M. and Skinner, D.B. Ultrastructural features of early brain stem lesions of thiamine-deficient rats. *American Journal of Pathology*, 1968, 52: 1081–1098.

Rossor, M.N., Emson, P.C., Iversen, L.L., Mountjoy, L.Q., Roth, M., Fahrenburg, J. and Rihfeld, J.F. Neuropeptides and neurotransmitters in cerebral cortex in Alzheimer's Disease. In S. Corkin et al.(Eds.), *A Report of Progress in Research*.

Russell, R.W. and Macri, J. Central cholinergic involvement in behavioral hyper-reactivity. *Pharmacology, Biochemistry and Behavior*, 1979, 10: 43–48.

Seltzer, J.L. and McDougal, D.B. Temporal changes of regional carboxylase levels in thiamine-depleted mouse brain. *American Journal of Physiology*, 1974, 227: 714–178.

Squire, L.R. The neurophysiology of human memory. *Annual Review of Neuroscience*, 1982, 5: 241–273.

Squire, L.R. and Moore, R.Y. Dorsal thalamic lesion in a noted case of chronic memory dysfunction. *Annals of Neurology*, 1979, 6: 503–506.

Squire, L.R. and Zola-Morgan, S. The neurology of memory: The case for correspondence between the findings for man and non-human primate. In J.A. Deutsch (Ed.), *The Physiological Basis of Memory*, 2nd Ed. New York: Academic Press, 1983: 199–268.

Swanson, L.W. The anatomy of the septo-hippocampal pathway. In S. Corkin et al. (Eds.), *Alzheimer's Disease: A Report of Progress in Research*. New York: Raven Press, 1982: 207–212.

Victor, M., Adams, R.D. and Collins, G.H. *The Wernicke-Korsakoff Syndrome*. Philadelphia: F.A. Davis, 1971.

Walsh, T.J., Tilson, H.H., Fisher, A. and Hanin, I. AF64A, a selective cholinergic neurotoxin, produces long-term learning and memory impairments. *Federation Proceedings*, 1983, 42: 755.

Weingarten, H., Kaye, W., Smallberg, S., Cohen, R., Ebert, M.H., Gillin, J.C. and Gold, P. Determinants of memory failures in dementia. In S. Corkin et al. (Eds.), *Alzheimer's Disease: A Report of Progress in Research*. New York: Raven Press, 1982: 171–176.

Winbld, B., Adolfsson, R., Carlsson, A. and Gottfries, C.-G. Biogenic amines in brains of patients with Alzheimer's Disease. In S. Corkin et al. (Eds.), *Alzeheimer's Disease: A Report of Progress in Research*. New York: Raven Press, 1982: 25–33.

Yamamura, H.I. and Snyder, S.H. Muscarinic cholinergic binding in rat brain. *Proceedings of the National Academy of Sciences of the United States*, 1974, 71: 1725–1729.

Zola-Morgan, S., Squire, L.R. and Mishkin, M. The anatomy of amnesia: Amygdala-hippocampus vs. temporal stem. *Society of Neuroscience Abstract*, 1981, 7: 236.

11
BEHAVIOURAL TERATOLOGY:
FETAL ALCOHOL EXPOSURE AND HYPERACTIVITY

NIGEL W. BOND

I. INTRODUCTION

This chapter is an examination of the role that animal models can play in
the field of behavioural teratology. This discipline has emerged out of the
realization that, while morphological indicators of birth trauma are
important, they are unlikely to be as sensitive as behavioural indicators
(Coyle *et al.*, 1976; Joffe, 1969; Vorhees and Butcher, 1982). There are
many sources available detailing the theoretical background to and
techniques employed in this area and it is not my intention to rework such
material in any great detail. Rather, I wish to show, using the example of
work into the effects of fetal alcohol exposure, how an understanding of
an animal's development and the relationship of this development to
ecological factors can be exploited as a means of enhancing our understanding of an important human problem, and, tangentially, of normal
development as well. However, before we begin the latter examination, it
is as well to look briefly at the concepts and techniques employed in
behavioural teratology.

II. BEHAVIOURAL TERATOLOGY:
CONCEPTS AND TECHNIQUES

Behavioural anomalies arising from prenatal influences (behavioural
teratogenesis) are likely to result from insults to the central nervous system,

ANIMAL MODELS IN PSYCHOPATHOLOGY
ISBN 0 12 114180 2

which is acknowledged to be the most vulnerable of the body organs. This brief examination of behavioural teratology is restricted to drugs, although it is acknowledged that a wide variety of environmental insults can influence early development (Gottlieb, 1978). Further, since this chapter is concerned with the fetal alcohol syndrome (FAS), where possible, the examples chosen will be taken from this literature. There are several excellent reviews of behavioural teratology available and the interested reader is referred to these for further details (Coyle *et al.*, 1976; Joffe, 1969; Vorhees and Butcher, 1982).

It is now accepted that the placenta does not provide complete protection against harmful substances found in maternal blood. Typically, it acts as a slow filter; larger molecules and those that are not lipid soluble take longer to cross. Some compounds do appear to be prevented from crossing and others are taken up preferentially, but the above holds for most compounds (Snell, 1982). Alcohol, given its low molecular weight and lipid solubility, has been shown to readily cross the placenta and is distributed in the amniotic fluid, liver, pancreas, kidney, lung, thymus, heart and brain of the fetus (Ho *et al.*, 1971). This ubiquity results from its distribution in total body water. In the case of the rat, the fetus lacks alcohol dehydrogenase and cannot metabolize the alcohol (Holmes and Masters, 1978). Thus, the fetus may in fact be exposed to levels higher than those found in the mother. Further, since the placenta may contain enzymes for the biotransformation of such "xenobiotic" compounds, toxic intermediate products, for example, acetaldehyde, may be generated and passed to the fetus.

In humans, alcohol is typically taken recreationally and is consumed orally. In rare cases, it may be administered intravenously as part of medical treatment. It is important that animal models mimic the oral presentation of alcohol, since different routes of administration are associated with differences in absorption, metabolism and excretion. Different authors have used a variety of ways of exposing dams to alcohol including: presenting it in the drinking water, straight or sweetened; presenting it as part of a total liquid diet; intubating it; or injecting it intravenously or intraperitoneally. None of these techniques is perfect. For example, intubation is stressful, intraperitoneal injection can lead to placental bleeding, and presenting alcohol in the drinking water leads to a reduction in fluid consumption and can result in a decrease in food consumption. I prefer to use the liquid diet technique pair-feeding a control group a similar diet with sucrose substituted for the alcohol; that is, the same empty kilojoules are provided without the presumably toxic effects of the alcohol. However, as Abel (1980) has noted, alcohol has effects upon the absorption of nutrients and even this technique cannot be regarded as perfect. Suffice it to say that a multiplicity of techniques producing congruent data are to be preferred (this is further elaborated in Chapter 1).

The dose of the drug administered is a factor of prime importance. As with any drug, the effects of *in utero* exposure are likely to be dose-dependent. At low doses, it may have no physical and/or behavioural effects. At high doses gross physical abnormality and death may ensue. Between these dose levels, doses may produce behavioural teratogenicity without overt evidence of physical malformations. Drugs can have a variety of influences upon normal cellular development including effects upon mutation, interference with meiosis, alterations of nucleic acid function, deficiencies in precursor, enzyme and substrate availability, enzyme inhibition, osmotic balance and cell membrane characteristics (Wilson, 1977). This list indicates the profound effect that early drug exposure can have upon the developing organism (Snell, 1982).

The duration of drug administration is important in two ways. First, the longer a drug is administered, the greater the build-up of the drug and its metabolites, which may themselves have teratogenic effects. For example, alcohol is metabolized to acetaldehyde utilizing the enzyme, alcohol dehydrogenase. Acetaldehyde is then metabolized to acetic acid utilizing the enzyme, aldehyde dehydrogenase. This latter enzyme is also lacking in the fetal rat (Holmes and Masters, 1978). There is considerable controversy as to whether it is alcohol or acetaldehyde that is the causative agent in the FAS, and, recently, it has been shown that acetic acid may be a behavioural teratogen (Barrett and Livesey, 1982). The second factor related to the duration of administration is the developmental stage of the organism at the time of administration. It is accepted in teratology that an organ is more vulnerable to insult at a time of growth and change. This means that teratogenic effects are likely to be seen if the drug is administered during the period of organogenesis, which lasts for approximately six to 19 days after conception in the rat. In mammals the central nervous system (CNS) has the longest period of development. Indeed, in rodents the central nervous system shows substantial development after birth. At the same time the blood–brain barrier is poorly developed in the fetus, meaning that compounds may have a greater effect on the fetal brain than in the adult.

As with the administration of a drug to an adult, we are likely to see individual and species differences in teratogenic susceptibility to the drug. Examples can be found in the animal work into the FAS. For example, Chernoff (1977) found that skeletal anomalies and soft tissue malformations occurred at lower blood alcohol levels in CBA mice than C3H mice. Similarly, Webster *et al.* (1980) found inbred C57 mice more susceptible than outbred QS strain mice. Such differences may be explained by the fact that during the course of development, genes are being switched on and off rapidly. If a compound interferes with the production of RNA at any point, it may prevent the development of a particular gene product and thus damage the fetus. Even within strains there is a variability and Riley *et al.* (1979) have noted that in rats this variability is reduced with higher doses of alcohol as presumably more litters and more individuals in a litter are affected. The finding of individual differences in susceptability may be related to the fact that, in mammals which produce multiple young, there are often differences in the rate of development of littermates. Given that the effects of a drug are determined by the developmental stage of the fetus, after a single exposure to a teratogen we can expect to find unaffected, malformed and dead fetuses.

The factors outlined above refer, in the main, to *prenatal influences*. However, it is recognized in teratology that there are also likely to be *postnatal factors* operating to influence the outcome of administration of a drug. A drug administered during the prenatal period may influence not only fetal development, but also maternal functioning. If the effect on the dam is long-term, then this may influence the way that she mothers her young and/or, it may affect lactation performance. Indeed, if the drug has a long half-life, there is also the possibility of the drug being passed into the neonate via the mothers milk and thus having a postnatal action. All of these factors may influence the outcome of a study and confound any conclusion as to the teratogenic effect of a drug. There are a variety of ways that one can overcome these problems. If the sole interest is whether a compound is teratogenic or not, all offspring, treated and control, can be fostered to other control dams, following the removal of the latter's litter. If there is interest as to whether effects may be maternally mediated, one can employ a fostering/cross-fostering design. In this case, some treated and control offspring remain with their biological mother, others are transferred to mothers within the same group; for example, pups of one treated dam are transferred to another treated dam (fostering), and pups of treated dams are transferred to control dams and vice versa (cross-fostering). Such a design enables one to determine whether there are prenatal or postnatal effects of a drug and their interactions. There is some controversy as to whether one should always control for postnatal influences. As the reader will have realized these are expensive and time-consuming designs. My personal view is that where a drug has been tested for postnatal influences and none have been found, it is appropriate to dispense with them (a view shared with Vorhees and Butcher, 1982).

Finally, it is taken for granted that the environment of treated and control dams and their offspring are as alike as possible, both before and after weaning. Within this context, one problem that can arise is litter size. Most investigators attempt to cull litters down to a uniform size across treatments. However, a decision must be made as to which offspring should be culled from a treated litter (Abel, 1980). As noted above, some pups will be more affected than others. I have taken the conservative view that the healthiest looking pups should always be chosen, on the grounds that any overt physical damage is likely to affect the behaviour of the pup yet be a trivial finding. (I am reminded of Peter Dews's comment (Dews, 1958) that diarrhoea is likely to have a more profound influence on the performance of an animal than most psychoactive drugs.) Further, if there is differential mortality as a result of the treatment, keeping the healthiest pups is likely to lead to greater survival in treated litters.

III. FETAL ALCOHOL SYNDROME

The consumption of alcohol during pregnancy has been viewed with suspicion since antiquity. Thus, one finds statements warning against imbibing in the writings of Aristotle, and both Carthaginians and Spartans prohibited the use of alcohol by newly married couples to prevent conception during intoxication (Warner and Rosett, 1975). Hogarth's lithographs depicting the "gin epidemic" in England in the early 1700s provide graphic illustration of children with the facial characteristics that are now used to define a syndrome associated with fetal alcohol exposure. Sullivan, working in a prison in Liverpool, England, reported an increased number of spontaneous abortions and stillbirths in women who were chronic alcoholics and an increased frequency of epilepsy in the surviving offspring (Sullivan, 1899). However, it was not until 1973 and a report by Jones *et al.* in *The Lancet* that the occurrence of a syndrome associated with fetal alcohol exposure was generally accepted.

The report by Jones *et al.* (1973) described a syndrome observed in eight children of alcoholic mothers. Briefly, this consisted of intrauterine growth retardation, facial dysmorphology, a variety of somatic malformations and mental retardation. The facial anomalies are particularly distinct. The crown is small (probably due to microcephaly), as are the eye sockets (due to microphthalmia). The position of the ears is often not symmetrical. The nasal bridge is flattened, the philtrum is long and the upper lip (vermilion) is extremely narrow, leading to what has been described as a "fish mouth" (Finnegan, 1981). Cleft palate is also observed. In addition, cardiac, genital, and urinary tract malformations and various joint anomalies have also been reported in numerous cases. Following the Jones *et al.* report, clinical descriptions of children displaying the fetal alcohol syndrome (FAS) have emanated from many countries (*Neurobehavioral Toxicology and Teratology*, volume 3, number 2, 1981).

The characteristics described above allow for a neonatal diagnosis of FAS. However, just as disturbing are the CNS sequelae of the syndrome, including developmental and intellectual retardation. Examination of a variety of clinical cases indicates that the vast majority of children diagnosed as FAS on the basis of physical malformations exhibit mental retardation (Abel, 1981). Indeed, there appears to be a correlation between the severity of the physical defects and the degree of intellectual retardation (Majewski, 1981; Streissguth *et al.*, 1978). Thus far, the FAS has only been reported in the offspring of women who are chronic alcoholics. Estimates of its frequency range between two and three per 1000 births. However, the incidence is much greater if the population is restricted to alcoholic women, where it rises to approximately 25 in 1000 births (Abel, 1981).

The adverse effects of alcohol are not restricted to the FAS and it is now recognized that there are a range of what might be termed fetal alcohol effects (FAE) encompassing spontaneous abortion, stillbirth and postnatal growth retardation to a variety of behavioural difficulties including poor, fine and gross motor development, sleep disorders and hyperactivity (Streissguth *et al.*, 1980). As might be expected, the incidence of such effects is much greater than that for the FAS ranging from approximately two per 1000 to 90 per 1000 births. Again, alcoholic women are at much greater risk; the incidence of FAE amongst them ranges from 78 per 1000 to 690 per 1000 (cf. Abel, 1981).

Importantly, it is possible to observe effects of fetal alcohol exposure in the absence of observable physical malformation (Landesman-Dwyer *et al.*, 1981; Majewski *et al.*, 1976). This latter finding fits with classical teratological theory which suggests that any teratogen will have a range of dose-response effects. Below the range of teratogenic and fetolethal doses is a range of doses which are associated with developmental functional disorders, that is, behavioural effects, possibly based upon CNS abnormalities, as noted previously (see Section II). The two major behavioural problems associated with fetal alcohol exposure appear to be mental retardation and hyperactivity. The former is ubiquitous, as noted above. Since it is the latter symptom and its physiological underpinnings that are the focus of this chapter, it is worth examining reports of its occurrence in more detail.

IV. FETAL ALCOHOL EXPOSURE AND HYPERACTIVITY

Lemoine *et al.* (1968) report observing hyperactivity in fetal alcohol syndrome (FAS) children, describing them as, "too lively, and ceaselessly agitated''. Dehaene *et al.* (1977) reported that newborn offspring of chronic alcoholic mothers were very active, agitated, tremulous, slept little and were easily awakened. This hyperactivity lasted for several months but eventually attenuated. Hanson *et al.* (1976) reported "tremulousness, hyperactivity, and irritability''. Further, they found that these symptoms may persist for years.

In a comparison of heavy drinkers, moderate drinkers and abstainers, Ouellette and Rosett (1976) found that the number of children displaying hypotonia and jitteriness was directly related to increases in maternal alcohol intake. Sander *et al.* (1977) examined state-regulation in neonates and observed more frequent startles and more extended body movements in the children of a group of women classified as heavy drinkers. The children of a group similarly classified, but who had reduced their consumption during pregnancy, did not show such alterations.

Streissguth *et al.* (1978) provide a more detailed case-study report of 20 patients diagnosed as suffering from FAS. Mental retardation was present in most children and, as noted previously, appeared to be related to the degree of physical dysmorphogenesis. Streissguth *et al.* note that: "Many of these children were hyperactive during their preschool years, often described by caretakers as 'always on the go' and 'never sits still'. A few were so excessively hyperactive that it was difficult to keep their attention during the intellectual examination. Many with less severe hyperactivity were distractable, had short attention spans, and could best be described as 'fidgety' ''. Despite the hyperactivity and the mental retardation, none of the children was reported as having severe behaviour problems, or of being "rebellious", "antisocial" or "psychotic". Indeed, Streissguth *et al.* (1978) note that such children are so co-operative and friendly that they may appear less retarded than they actually are.

Shaywitz *et al.* (1980) have suggested that the list of symptoms associated with the FAS should be expanded to include hyperactivity and learning difficulties. They base this suggestion upon the examination of 15 children born to mothers who had consumed excessive amounts of alcohol during pregnancy. None of the children was intellectually retarded; their IQ scores fell in the range of 82–113, with a mean of 98.2. Despite this all of them displayed early experience of school failure. All but one was described as hyperactive and a number had received or were currently receiving stimulant medication. A similar finding was reported by Iosub *et al.* (1981). Of their sample of 61 patients, hyperactivity was present in 74% and was sufficiently severe in 50% of the children to require drug therapy.

The studies described above contain a mixture of retrospective and prospective designs, some reporting case-studies and some group comparisons. However, in all of them the children described are generally badly affected, coming from mothers who were chronically alcoholic and who continued to drink heavily during pregnancy. A more recent study suggests that the dosage of alcohol required to produce identifiable changes may be quite moderate. Landesman-Dwyer *et al.* (1981) have found that the offspring of women who consumed a mean of 12.8 mL (0.45 oz) absolute alcohol per day were less attentive, less compliant with parental commands and more fidgety. The parents of these children were clearly non-alcoholic and the home-environments were highly stimulating. Despite this, a symptom associated with the FAS was observed (see also Davis *et al.*, 1982). This finding highlights the fact that alcohol, like other teratogens, will produce a range of effects depending upon the dose (Section II).

Individually, there are methodological problems with the majority of the studies described in this section. Nevertheless, there is such consistency in them that I think we can conclude that hyperactivity is one of the behavioural sequelae of fetal alcohol exposure. The importance of this fact has been noted by Shaywitz *et al.* (1980) who have indicated that fetal alcohol exposure may be one of a number of factors leading to the hyper-active child syndrome or minimal brain dysfunction (Rapoport and Ferguson, 1981). That the hyperactivity can be associated with learning difficulties in the absence of retardation (Shaywitz *et al.*, 1980) and wanes as the child gets older (Dehaene *et al.*, 1977; Hanson *et al.*, 1976) provides a further correspondence with this disorder. Hyperactivity is not regarded as abnormal *per se*, since children in general are hyperactive at about 18–20 months of age (Gesell and Ilg, 1943). The problem arises because the hyper-activity is developmentally inappropriate. The fact that hyperactivity is a problem only in older children suggests that it is due to a delay in normal development. This suggestion is further supported by the finding that the hyperactivity commonly disappears with age (Wender, 1971). The possi-bility that *in utero* alcohol exposure leads to developmental delays is one that can be investigated in animals. This fact and the finding that there is some correspondence between the effects reported here and the results of such studies has enabled us to examine the putative mechanisms underlying this symptom (Section VI).

V. CONFOUNDING FACTORS IN HUMAN STUDIES OF THE FETAL ALCOHOL SYNDROME

A large number of clinical reports and both retrospective and prospec-tive studies focusing upon the fetal alcohol syndrome (FAS) have now been published (*Neurobehavioral Toxicology and Teratology*, volume 3, number 2, 1981). While these studies have established that alcohol consumption is in some way related to the FAS and fetal alcohol effects (FAE), a number of confounding factors have impeded precise delineation of the exact role played by alcohol. A brief examination of some of these factors is worthwhile in establishing the utility of infrahuman animal models in determining the teratogenic potential of alcohol and, more importantly, elucidating the mechanism(s) by which it has such effects.

The most obvious factors associated with alcohol consumption are malnutrition and maternal ill-health. A woman who drinks heavily consumes a considerable proportion of her daily kilojoules as alcohol. Since these are "empty" kilojoules containing no vitamins and minerals, the female alcoholic is likely to be malnourished. Even if she compensates by taking supplements, chronic alcohol consumption is known to impair gastrointestinal absorption and metabolism of nutrients (Olson, 1973). Therefore it is possible that the effects of fetal alcohol exposure are secondary to the malnutrition that may accompany such exposure.

Abel (1981) has noted that, in addition to the above, the alcoholic woman is likely to experience more difficulties during parturition and it may be these that are the cause of FAE, in particular. For example, he notes that breech births are far more common in alcoholic women than in the general population and breech birth has been implicated in mental retardation (Manzke, 1978) and hyperactivity (Fianu and Joelsson, 1979).

As noted previously, the FAS has only been observed in the offspring of women who are chronic alcoholics (Abel, 1981). Such women are likely to have experienced a variety of health problems related to their alcoholism and these may be important in the aetiology of the FAS. For example, of the eight mothers described by Jones et al. (1973), five had cirrhosis of the liver and two experienced delirium tremens during the relevant pregnancy. On the basis of this and other findings, Majewski (1981) has suggested that fetal alcohol exposure per se is not sufficient to cause FAS. Only if it is linked with chronic alcoholism is the FAS a likely outcome. This suggests that some impairment associated with maternal alcoholism is the key factor. (Majewski suggests that this factor is impaired acetaldehyde metabolism.) Clearly, it is difficult to separate such possibilities in the alcoholic.

It is also true that the woman who consumes one drug to excess is likely to abuse others. This has certainly been the case in the cohorts of alcoholic women who have been examined in some of the more ambitious studies of the FAS (Alpert et al., 1981; Kuzma and Kissinger, 1981; Sokol et al., 1981; Streissguth et al., 1981). Again, it is difficult to find a sufficient cohort of women whose addiction is exclusive to alcohol. The importance of this factor is highlighted by studies indicating that the effects of alcohol on the fetus appear to be synergized by smoking (Martin et al., 1977).

Paternal alcoholism and genetic factors are also likely to be confounded in human studies. Very little research has been done on the possibility that the defects seen in the FAS might be due to paternal alcoholism even though sperm samples from alcoholic men have been shown to be abnormal. In commenting upon this possibility, Abel (1982a) noted that, of 38 cases of FAS where the father's status was reported, 26 were themselves alcoholic! Clearly, this is a factor that must be taken into account.

Certain subsets of alcoholism have been shown to be inherited both in men (Goodwin *et al.*, 1973) and in women (Bohman *et al.*, 1981). Similarly, some of the putative effects of fetal alcohol exposure have been shown to be associated with alcoholism in the parent. Thus, there is a high incidence of alcoholism in the parents of hyperactive children (Cantwell, 1972; Goodwin *et al.*, 1975; Morrison and Stewart, 1971, 1973). Further, hyper-activity in childhood seems to be associated with adult alcoholism (Tarter *et al.*, 1977; Wood *et al.*, 1983). On the basis of these results, one can ask whether it is hyperactivity which predisposes to alcoholism, or is it prenatal alcohol exposure which predisposes to both alcoholism and hyperactivity (Bond and Di Giusto, 1976)?

The factors outlined above illustrate some of the difficulties that have to be faced when one is trying to interpret the human findings in this area. To ascertain whether fetal alcohol exposure is teratogenic in the absence of these confounding factors, it is appropriate to turn to studies on infra-human animals. Of course, such studies cannot establish that alcohol is teratogenic in humans, but, given the overwhelming evidence that alcohol is implicated in such effects, findings from animal experimentation reinforce our confidence in such evidence (see Chapter 1). Further, animal studies enable us to examine the mechanisms by which alcohol might have its deleterious effects.

VI. ANIMAL STUDIES OF FETAL ALCOHOL EXPOSURE

The number of studies conducted in this area appears to be growing exponentially. Rather than attempt an exhaustive review of extant studies, I propose to indicate those areas where animal studies have complemented the symptoms observed in human cases of FAS (Sections III and IV).

A large number of studies have sought to produce physical malforma-tions, spontaneous abortions and still-births in a variety of animal species exposed to alcohol *in utero*. Attempts have been successful in certain strains of mouse (Chernoff, 1977; Randall *et al.*, 1977), chick (Sandor, 1968), miniature swine (Tumbleson *et al.*, 1981), beagle dog (Ellis and Pick, 1976), lamb (Potter, 1980), domestic cat (Himwich *et al.*, 1977) and the rat (Bond, 1982; Lochry *et al.*, 1980; Weiner *et al.*, 1981). Work is currently in progress employing *Macaca fascicularis* and *Macaca mulatta* to ascertain the effects of fetal alcohol exposure in infrahuman primates (Altshuler and Shippenberg, 1981; Jacobson *et al.*, 1980). It is impossible to determine a threshold dose from such studies, but it is clear that, when other factors are controlled, alcohol is a teratogen (Section IV).

Prenatal and postnatal growth retardation following alcohol treatment have been observed in a variety of species (Abel, 1979a; Lochry *et al.*, 1980; Weiner *et al.*, 1981). In addition, various other developmental effects have been observed, including delays in vaginal opening (Boggan *et al.*, 1979, Tittmar, 1977), myelination (Druse and Hofteig, 1977), body composition (Abel and Greizerstein, 1979), immunoreactivity (Monjan and Mandell, 1980), neuronal and organ development (Hammer and Scheibel, 1981; Sorette *et al.*, 1980). Similarly, delays in the development of various physical landmarks, such as eye-opening (Lee *et al.*, 1980; Martin *et al.*, 1979), and reflexes, such as negative geotaxis and surface righting (Demers and Kirouac, 1978; Fish *et al.*, 1981; Gallo and Weinberg, 1982; Lee *et al.*, 1980) have been found.

A number of studies have reported changes in biochemical function in a variety of organs accompanying fetal alcohol exposure. These include alterations (typically reductions) in catecholamine levels in the brain, liver and adrenals (Lau *et al.*, 1976; Rawat and Kumar, 1977) and reductions in serotonin levels in the brain (Krsiak *et al.*, 1977). There are also reports of alterations of protein, DNA and RNA content in the brain, heart, liver and kidney of affected offspring (Henderson and Schenker, 1977; Rawat, 1975, 1976, 1979). At a gross level, postnatal alcohol exposure leads to impaired brain growth in neonates (Diaz and Samson, 1980). Further, fetal alcohol exposure has been shown to reduce the number of pyramidal neurons in the dorsal hippocampus (Barnes and Walker, 1981), and to alter the organization of mossy fibres in the temporal region of the hippocampus in the rat (West *et al.*, 1981; West and Hodges-Savola, 1983). More recently, Abel *et al.* (1983) observed significant reductions and alterations in dendritic structure in the hippocampus correlated with impairments on a shuttle avoidance task. These findings have suggested that some of the effects of fetal alcohol exposure may be due to associated zinc deficiencies brought about by such exposure. The hippocampus contains the highest levels of zinc in the central nervous system and zinc deficiencies are known to cause abnormal development (Bliss *et al.*, 1974; Buell *et al.*, 1977). Given that alcohol reduces placental zinc transport, it is a prime suspect in the changes described above (Ghishan *et al.*, 1982).

There are two outstanding behavioural sequelae of prenatal alcohol exposure in animals, just as there are in people, these being the effects on activity and learning ability (Bond 1981a). A more detailed discussion of the effects of *in utero* alcohol exposure on activity will be attempted later (Section VII), as will studies elucidating the putative behavioural mechanisms involved in this effect. As such, this section will examine the effects on learning ability. These effects are ubiquitous. Virtually every learning paradigm investigated, appetitive and aversive, has provided evidence of the deleterious effects of early alcohol exposure. Shuttlebox avoidance learning is impaired (Abel, 1979b; Bond, 1981b; Bond and DiGiusto, 1977, 1978; Shaywitz *et al.*, 1979) as is T-maze shock escape (Anandam and Stern, 1980; Riley *et al.*, 1979), passive avoidance (Abel, 1982b; Riley *et al.*, 1979) and taste aversion learning (Riley *et al.*, 1979). Interestingly, performance on various Sidman avoidance schedules is enhanced (Riley *et al.*, 1982). A variety of appetitive tasks are also affected including discrimination learning (Lee *et al.*, 1980; Linakis and Cunningham, 1980; Means *et al.*, 1981; Phillips and Stainbrook, 1976), reversal learning of such tasks (Anadam and Stern, 1980; Riley *et al.*, 1979; Lee *et al.*, 1980) and operant tasks including both fixed-ratio and differential reinforcement of low rates of responding (DRL) schedules (Driscoll *et al.*, 1980; Martin *et al.*, 1977; Riley *et al.*, 1980). Retention of such tasks is also compromised (Lochry and Riley, 1980).

The variety of the effects described above testifies to the ubiquitous nature of early ethanol exposure and provides empirical support for the view, based upon the human studies (Sections III and IV), that alcohol acts as a teratogen when confounding factors are controlled.

VII. FETAL ALCOHOL EXPOSURE AND HYPERACTIVITY IN ANIMALS

A. The evidence

Examination of a variety of human studies indicates that early alcohol exposure is associated with hyperactivity (Section IV). In 1981, I published an extensive review of the work examining the effects of prenatal alcohol exposure on hyperactivity in rodents (Bond, 1981a). To summarize the conclusions of that review, the extant data indicated that: "If rats are exposed to doses of alcohol greater than 6–7 g kg^{-1} per day, and are tested prior to 70 days of age, they exhibit an increase in activity in comparison with control offspring". This conclusion held whether the measure of activity was the open-field, running-wheel, jiggle-cage or latency to step down from a platform. Further (and somewhat surprisingly) it seemed to hold over studies that had exposed the dam to alcohol from as few as five days (Caul *et al.*, 1979) to as many as 23 (Bond and DiGiusto, 1976). The common element was that all studies exposed the dam at some time during the period of organogenesis (approximately from the sixth to the 19th day of gestation). This finding was not due to any confounding influence such as malnutrition, nor was it due to maternal influences since studies which controlled these factors reported results similar to those that did not.

Studies completed since that review have borne out its general conclusion. Abel (1982b) exposed rats to liquid diets from the fifth to the 20th day of gestation. The offspring of a group which consumed 5.9 g kg^{-1} of alcohol did not differ in activity from controls at any age. In contrast the offspring of dams who consumed 11.6 g kg^{-1} differed from controls in displaying increased activity from the 13th through to the 26th day after birth.

Anandam *et al.* (1980) exposed dams to 8 g kg^{-1} of alcohol per day from the sixth to the 21st day of gestation via intubation. Offspring were tested for acoustic startle in a small chamber at 35 days of age. While there were no differences in body movement, alcohol exposed offspring displayed an increase in acoustic startle in comparison with controls. Interestingly, they showed the same rate of decline in the startle response as controls, indicating that they did not differ in habituation.

Chen and Smith (1979) gave dams alcohol in saccharin sweetened drinking water from the seven to the 21st day of gestation. The dose consumed cannot be determined from their paper. Offspring were tested for their activity in an open-field at approximately 175 days of age. There were no differences between alcohol treated and control offspring.

Fernandez *et al.* (1983) exposed rats to a liquid diet containing alcohol for four weeks prior to mating and for the first 20 days of gestation. The dams drank approximately 12 g kg^{-1} (my analysis of their figures). Offspring were tested for five minutes in an open-field on each of two days when 63 and 64 days of age. On both days, alcohol treated offspring were significantly more active than controls. In a later study, Fernandez *et al.* (1983) intubated rats with 8 g kg^{-1} from the 10th to the 14th day of gestation and then fostered and cross-fostered appropriate litters at birth. When tested in an open-field for five minutes on each of two days when either 31 and 32 or 53 and 54 days of age, alcohol treated offspring were significantly more active than controls, irrespective of rearing condition.

Da Silva *et al.* (1980) gave dams alcohol in sweetened drinking water seven days prior to mating and throughout gestation. Dams consumed 7.9 g kg^{-1} if the solution was 10% alcohol and 13.3 g kg^{-1} if it was 20%. In contrast to previous findings, they found no differences in activity in an open-field when offspring were tested at 60 days of age. It is possible that the "70 day" criterion is an outer limit, as we shall see later (Section VIII, A).

Riley *et al.* (1979) fed dams a liquid diet from the fifth to the 20th day of gestation. One group drank 6.7 g kg^{-1} and another drank 13.8 g kg^{-1}. Offspring were tested in a head-dipping apparatus at 18 days of age or in a nose-poking apparatus at 29 or 34 days of age. Alcohol treated offspring exhibited dose related increases in both head-dipping and nose-poking at all ages tested.

Finally, Ulug and Riley (1983) exposed rats to a liquid diet containing ethanol from the sixth to the 20th day of gestation. The dams consumed a mean of 13.6 g kg^{-1} of alcohol per day. The pups were tested in an open-field for three consecutive days at 19 days of age. Pups exposed to alcohol *in utero* were significantly more active than controls on all three days.

The results obtained from animal research appear to be, at the very least, analogous to those observed in affected children. Thus, alcohol exposure *in utero* leads to hyperactivity in affected offspring and this hyperactivity disappears as they get older. As with the human studies, this suggests that the hyperactivity is due to a delay in the development of a normal process.

B. The hypothesis

The finding that prenatal alcohol exposure leads to increased activity in treated offspring and that this overactivity disappears at about 60–70 days of age, poses two questions. First, we can ask why the overactivity occurs in the first place, and, second, why does it disappear with age?

The most likely explanation of these two findings is that prenatal alcohol exposure leads to a delay in the development of response inhibition in treated offspring. This hypothesis was first put forward by Riley and his coworkers in a series of papers, some of which have been mentioned previously. Riley's theory would suggest that alcohol treated offspring should have difficulty in inhibiting a prepotent response. Thus, he and his co-workers have demonstrated that alcohol treated offspring have difficulty in acquiring a passive avoidance response or a taste-aversion (Riley *et al.*, 1979). They are less likely to show spontaneous alternation and make more errors to criterion in learning a T-maze reversal task (Riley *et al.*, 1979). Having acquired a response they are also more resistant to extinction (Riley *et al.*, 1980). All of these tasks require that the animal withhold a response to display efficient performance. Treated offspring also evidence increased nose-poking and head-dipping (Riley *et al.*, 1979) indicative of an inability to habituate to a novel situation. Further, all of these effects were dose-related in that the more alcohol the dam had consumed, the greater the deficit in response inhibition. These findings indicate that treated offspring are deficient in the ability to inhibit a response. This proposition can account for the finding of enhanced activity in such offspring. As Riley *et al.* (1979) have suggested, such animals would be expected to be more active than controls initially and a further increase in activity might be expected when other inhibitory influences wane, for example, fear. Just such an outcome was reported by Bond and DiGiusto (1976).

The fact that the activity of alcohol treated offspring returns to normal levels at around 60–70 days of age suggests that the deficiency in response inhibition is a retardation of a normal developmental process. For example, during the course of normal development, the young rodent passes through a period where it displays extreme hyperactivity if it is isolated from the rest of the litter (Campbell and Mabry, 1972). The age of peak activity in rats is approximately 16 days and in mice it is 13 days (Campbell *et al.*, 1969; Nagy *et al.*, 1975). This isolation-induced hyperactivity is associated with the earlier maturation of adrenergic–excitatory areas located in the brainstem as compared with cholinergic–inhibitory areas located in the forebrain (Campbell *et al.*, 1969).

In support of the above, in the rat, catecholamine-containing cell bodies located in the brainstem are nearly mature at birth, although the axons are not yet fully grown. In contrast, cholinergic neurones in the cortex grow slowly from birth to the 10th day, then quickly from the 10th to the 28th day (Coyle and Yamamura, 1976; Mabry and Campbell, 1977). Campbell and his coworkers have also examined these propositions pharmacologically. They demonstrated that amphetamine, which is a sympathomimetic agent causing release of catecholamines from nerve terminals and preventing their reuptake, enhances activity in rats from 10 days of age (the earliest that they tested). In contrast, the anticholinergic drug, scopolamine, which acts by blocking the receptor, did not increase activity until about 20 days of age and was not fully effective until 25 days of age (Campbell *et al.*, 1969). Similarly, the cholinomimetic drug, pilocarpine, did not decrease amphetamine-induced activity and scopolamine did not enhance such activity until 20–25 days of age (Fibiger *et al.*, 1970). Further, both reserpine, which disrupts the storage of catecholamines, and α-methyl-p-tyrosine which inhibits tyrosine hydroxylase, the rate-limiting enzyme in catecholamine synthesis, depressed activity in 15-day-old rat pups, the age of greatest activity. This depression of activity was reversed if the animals were treated with L-dopa, the precursor of dopamine and noradrenaline (Campbell and Mabry, 1973).

If *in utero* alcohol exposure retards the development of a cholinergic inhibitory system, then the peak of isolation-induced activity should remain in evidence longer in the alcohol treated offspring since the development of their inhibitory system is being retarded in comparison with control offspring. This hypothesis is shown in Fig. 11.1. The fact that *in utero* alcohol exposure interferes with the development of the hippocampus is of great interest in this regard since the hippocampus has been posited as the structure modulating response inhibition and contains one of three major cholinergic systems in the CNS.* In addition, many of the deficits displayed by animals exposed to alcohol *in utero* are similar to those exhibited by animals that have had the hippocampus removed (Altman *et al.*, 1973).

VIII. RATIONALE OF PRESENT RESEARCH PROGRAMME

A. Background

Isolation-induced hyperactivity would appear to provide an excellent "marker" for the development of the excitatory and inhibitory neuro-transmitter systems. However, it is subject to a number of environmental influences which suggest that the development of such systems is not as straightforward as first thought. For example, the hyperactivity is attenuated by the presence of siblings and/or an adult rat, indicating that it is only observed when the pup is isolated (Randall and Campbell, 1976; Teacher *et al.*, 1981). Similarly, Campbell and Raskin (1978) have found that if the isolated rat pup is tested in the presence of shavings from its home case, then it fails to show enhanced activity. Further, they observed that if the pup is separated and placed in an environment of 33°C (thermoneutrality) again the pup does not show an increase in activity unless it has been isolated for several hours (Bronstein *et al.*, 1978). A possible explanation for the effect of home-cage shavings is that, at this age of the pup, the dam is secreting a substance in her faeces named "caecotrophe" (Leon, 1974), whose function appears to be to attract pups back to the nest at a time when they are becoming increasingly mobile but are still quite vulnerable (Leon, 1979). The effect of environmental temperature would appear to indicate that an important factor in observing isolation-induced hyperactivity is that the pup be under thermal stress.

All of the experiments to be reported employed Wistar rats. Timed pregnant dams were housed individually in plastic-bottomed wire-topped cages and fed on a liquid diet containing ethanol (alcohol group), pair-fed a similar diet with sucrose substituted for ethanol (sucrose group) or fed laboratory chow *ad libitum* (chow group) from the sixth to the 19th day of

* For further elaboration of this topic, see Overstreet and Russell (Chapter 10).

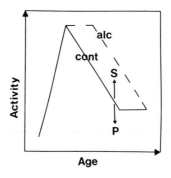

Fig. 11.1: Hypothetical effects of prenatal alcohol exposure on the ontogeny of the cholinergic inhibitory system as indexed by activity. The arrows indicate the inferred effects of scopolamine (see Section VIII, B.) and physostigmine (see Section VIII, C.).

gestation. At all other times the dams were fed chow and water. At birth, litters were culled to four male and four female pups where possible. The activity of the pups was examined by placing them on their own in a series of small wire cages (24 cm long; 14.5 cm wide; 18 cm high) situated in sound-attentuating chambers with clear perspex lids. The behaviour of the pups was recorded on a time-lapse video recorder by television camera located directly above the chambers. Activity was scored as a movement of all four paws across the shorter axis of the cage (Campbell and Raskin, 1978). Pups were tested on either the 10th, 16th, 22nd or 28th day of age.

The characteristics of the dams and their litters utilized in the various experiments are shown in Table 11.1. There were no differences between the dams in weight on the first day of gestation, but they did differ in weight gain from the sixth to the 19th days, with the chow group gaining most weight and the alcohol group being intermediate between the chow and sucrose groups. The alcohol group evidenced a significantly longer gestation period in accord with numerous other studies (Abel, 1979; Bond, 1982; Henderson and Schenker, 1977; Lochry *et al.*, 1980; Martin *et al.*, 1977; Weiner *et al.*, 1981). During the last 24 hours the alcohol group consumed 11.1 g kg^{-1} of alcohol. There were no differences in litter size, mean little-weight at birth or numbers of litters with observed dead at birth. Pups from the three groups did not differ in weight at any of the ages tested.

The initial experiments were designed to examine the ontogeny of isolation-induced activity in alcohol treated and control rat pups, to determine if the alcohol treated pups would remain hyperactive at a later age than control pups. Further, they examined the effects of home-cage shavings and environmental temperature on such activity to determine whether such factors would discriminate between alcohol treated and control pups. (Both home-cage shavings and the temperature of the test

TABLE 11.1: Characteristics of the dams and their litters

Characteristics	Alcohol group (n = 87)	Sucrose group (n = 79)	Chow group (n = 82)
Body weight of dams (g) Day 1 (gestation)	284.2	273.0	276.3
Weight gain (g) Days 6–19	60.1	49.7	78.8
Length of gestation (days)	24.0	23.6	23.3
Litter size (n)	10.6	11.0	10.7
Number of litters with observed dead at birth	33	37	23
Weight of pups at birth (g)	5.7	5.6	5.8
Weights at 10 days	19.9	19.0	21.3
Weights at 16 days	32.1	32.0	33.7
Weights at 22 days	50.1	51.5	47.0
Weights at 28 days	69.9	74.6	75.4

chamber influenced the activity of the 16-day-old pups, replicating Campbell and Raskin [1978]. However, in neither case were the alcohol treated pups differentially affected by the environmental changes. As a result, all subsequent experiments tested the animals in the presence of clean shavings and at an environmental temperature of 23°C, conditions that produced the greatest activity in 16-day-old pups.)

Of most interest is the activity of the three groups at the different ages and this is summarized in Fig. 11.2. Alcohol treated pups were more active than either set of control pups at both the 16th and 22nd days of age. Differences between the three groups had disappeared by the 28th day of age. These findings pose a problem for the hypothesis that *in utero* alcohol exposure leads to a deficit in response inhibition. Such an hypothesis is in accord with the finding that the alcohol treated pups were more active at the 22nd day of age, because the cholinergic inhibitory system is presumed to be functional in control animals at this time (Russell, 1982). However, it cannot account for the finding that alcohol treated pups were more active at the 16th day of age, since the cholinergic system is believed to be non-functional at this age in control pups. It is true that there is some evidence that a serotonergic system is involved in the inhibition of activity at around 15 days of age (Mabry and Campbell, 1974) although the influence of such a system has been shown to be transient (Lucot and Seiden, 1982). Similarly, there is evidence that γ-aminobutyric acid (GABA) plays an important role in modulating behavioural arousal (Murphy *et al.*, 1979). However, much of the data relating to the effects of *in utero* alcohol exposure on response inhibition (see Section VII, B) is quite consistent with the view that treated offspring are overaroused, rather than lacking in response inhibition (alternatively, a combination of the two hypotheses might account for the behavioural changes observed). One obvious way to

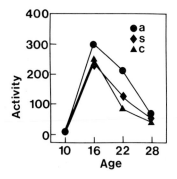

Fig. 11.2: Activity over the six hour test period of the alcohol, sucrose and chow groups at 10, 16, 22 and 28 days of age. (These data are taken from the experiment examining the influence of home-cage shavings on activity and illustrate the activity of the groups exposed to clean shavings.)

distinguish between these possibilities would be to examine such things as steady-state levels, metabolism and rate of turnover of the various neurotransmitters in discrete areas of the brain. Some work has been done on this problem, but at present the findings are too fragmentary and contradictory to be of much use in deciding between the alternatives described above. As a result, we decided to examine these possibilities by pharmacological means following the lead of Campbell *et al.* (1969). Specifically, to examine the possible involvement of the cholinergic system, animals were administered either scopolamine or physostigmine. In both cases, the pups were placed in the activity cages for 30 minutes, removed and injected with a dose of one of the two drugs and then returned to the activity cages for a further 120 minutes. In all experiments pups were tested at either the 10th, 16th, 22nd or 28th day of age. (The pups displayed little activity at the 10th day and these data are not reported here. Suffice it to say that neither drug had any effect on activity at this age, as would be predicted.)

B. Effects of scopolamine on activity

Scopolamine blocks the effects of acetylcholine at the receptor (Cooper *et al.*, 1978). If the cholinergic system affected is functioning to bring about behavioural inhibition, then administration of scopolamine will interfere with this function. In the present case, an inactive animal will become active (Harris, 1961; Meyers and Domino, 1964). Male and female pups from the alcohol, sucrose and chow groups received one of four doses of scopolamine hydrobromide (placebo, 0.5, 1.0 or 4.0 mg kg^{-1} given intraperitoneally). The activity of the various groups at each age and dose is shown in

Fig. 11.3. A total of 424 pups was employed and each data point in Fig. 11.3 represents at least 10 subjects. The left panel indicates the activity of the three groups at 16 days of age. Comparisons of the groups receiving no dosage (placebo) demonstrate again that alcohol treated pups are more active than control pups at this age. Scopolamine had no effect on the activity of either the sucrose or the chow pups suggesting that their cholinergic inhibitory system was non-functional at this time. In contrast, the high level of activity observed in the 16-day-old alcohol treated pups was completely abolished. This "paradoxical" response has been reported in normal 13–14-day-old rat pups (Blozovski and Blozovski, 1973; Fibiger *et al.*, 1970; Murphy and Nagy, 1976; Smith *et al.*, 1979) although the reason for its occurrence is unclear. However, it does suggest that the alcohol treated pups were more immature neurochemically than the control pups.

The activity of the various groups at the 22nd day is indicated in the middle panel. As previously noted, alcohol treated pups were more active at this age than controls (compare with the groups receiving no dosage). The activity of the control pups was increased in a dose-related fashion following the administration of the scopolamine indicating that they now possessed a functional cholinergic inhibitory system (Campbell *et al.*, 1969; Fibiger *et al.*, 1970; Murphy and Nagy, 1976). In comparison, the activity of the alcohol treated pups was unaffected by any dose of scopolamine; all groups continued to display high levels of activity. Of particular interest is the fact that the increases in activity observed in the control pups reached similar levels to those displayed by the alcohol treated pups, which lends credence to the view that the difference between the alcohol treated and control pups was a functioning cholinergic inhibitory system.

The activity of the three groups at 28 days of age is indicated in the right panel. There were no differences between the three groups in activity at this age (compare with the groups receiving no dosage) in accord with our earlier findings. Further, all three groups evidenced dose-related increases in activity following the administration of scopolamine, replicating previous studies (Campbell *et al.*, 1969; Fibiger *et al.*, 1970; Murphy and Nagy, 1976).

The present findings provide firm evidence that the overactivity observed in 22-day-old alcohol treated offspring is due to a retardation in the development of a cholinergic inhibitory system which is presumed to become functional at around 20 days of age in normal pups. At 22 days of age, control pups were much less active than they had been at 16 days of age and evidenced increased activity when the anticholinergic, scopolamine, was administered. In contrast, alcohol treated pups were still very active at this age and were unaffected by scopolamine. That the differences in

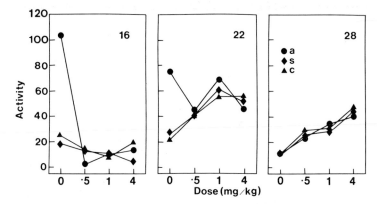

Fig. 11.3: Activity of the alcohol, sucrose and chow groups over the two hour period following the injection of scopolamine. The left panel shows the activity of the 16 day groups; the middle panel the 22 day old groups; and the right panel the 28 day old groups.

activity are due to a delay in the development of a putative inhibitory system is suggested by the finding that the alcohol treated pups did not differ from controls in activity at 28 days of age and evidenced similar dose-related increases in activity following the administration of scopolamine.

As in previous studies, alcohol treated pups were found to be more active than control pups at 16 days of age. Further, they displayed decreases in activity following the administration of scopolamine in contrast to control pups who showed no change in activity. While the "paradoxical" response to scopolamine may be taken as further evidence of the immaturity of the cholinergic system in the alcohol treated pups, the initial difference in activity must be due to other factors.

C. Effects of physostigmine on activity

Physostigmine is an anticholinesterase, enhancing cholinergic functioning by inhibiting the enzyme, acetylcholinesterase, which functions to break down acetylcholine in the synaptic cleft (Cooper *et al.*, 1978). In the present case, this means that an active animal should become less active (Adams, 1973; Frances and Jacob, 1971). [The story is somewhat more complicated than this. At the same time, there is likely to be less synthesis and/or release of acetylcholine from the synapse. This results from the action of the excess acetylcholine in the presynaptic cleft on autoreceptors on the presynaptic membrane whose function it is to modulate the release of acetylcholine. For a summary, see Jenden (1979, 1980) and Russell

(1982)]. Male and female pups from the alcohol, sucrose and chow groups were administered one of four doses of physostigmine (placebo, 0.05, 0.1 or 0.4 mg kg^{-1} administered intraperitoneally). The activity of the various groups is shown in Fig. 11.4. A total of 453 pups were employed and each data point in Fig. 11.4 represents at least 10 subjects. (Physostigmine is metabolized relatively rapidly. Therefore, one might expect that a short test period would be more appropriate.While this may be so, we found that the shorter the test period, the greater the variability in the data. As such, the data reported here are from the total 120 minute period.) The left panel indicates the activity of the three groups at 16 days of age. It is clear that the alcohol treated offspring were more active than control pups. However, all three groups showed no change in activity following administration of the physostigmine. Activity at 22 days of age is shown in the middle panel. Again, the alcohol treated pups were more active than controls. Further, while the administration of physostigmine had no influence on the activity of the alcohol treated pups, it led to dose-related decreases in activity in control pups. As illustrated in the right panel, the three groups did not differ in activity at 28 days of age and all three showed dose-related decreases in activity following the administration of the physostigmine.

The present data are in accord with that obtained following the administration of scopolamine. While control pups displayed evidence of inhibitory control at 22 days of age and reacted to the administration of the anticholinesterase, physostigmine, by reducing their activity, the alcohol treated offspring were still relatively active at this age and were unaffected by the drug. At 28 days all pups displayed reductions in activity following the administration of the physostigimine. Again these data suggest that the differences in activity at 22 days of age are due to a delay in the development of an inhibitory system in the alcohol treated pups.

D. A summary of the pharmacological data

The present data demonstrate quite conclusively that alcohol treated rat pups are more active than control pups, but that this hyperactivity disappears with age. This was demonstrated in the preliminary studies determining the effects of environmental influences such as presence of home-cage shavings and temperature of the test chamber. Further, it was replicated in each of the pharmacological studies. I had previously noted that the hyperactivity disappears at around 60–70 days of age (Bond, 1981a). The reader may be surprised to find it disappearing at 28 days in the present studies. One obvious difference that may account for this discrepancy is that previous studies have examined activity over very short

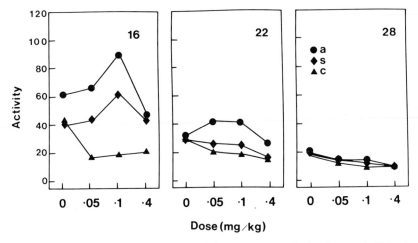

Fig. 11.4: Activity of the alcohol, sucrose and chow groups over the two hour period following the injection of physostigmine. The left panel shows the 16 day old groups; the middle panel the 22 day old groups and the right panel the 28 day old groups.

periods; that is, minutes, rather than the hours of observation employed in the present study. It may be that subtle differences between groups get obscured when one examines activity over a much longer time period. If so it suggests that the effects we did observe are robust indeed.

It should be noted that these findings are not due to nutritional factors. The energy intake of the dams in the alcohol group was similar to, if not greater than, that of the sucrose group. Similarly, the offspring from the alcohol group did not differ in weight from the two control groups at any age. Clearly, the hyperactivity observed at 16 and 22 days of age was not due to the alcohol offspring being lighter (Michaelson *et al.*, 1977). This latter finding is important because it suggests that the differences observed here are not due to a general developmental lag. Such a lag is observed in malnourished offspring who exhibit delays in physical markers such as eye-opening, reflexive markers and in the age at which the peak activity associated with isolation is observed (Nagy, 1979). Nagy reported that malnourished mice exhibited a three to four day delay in the attainment of peak activity, but, interestingly, the form of the curve was the same as in control offspring suggesting that both the excitatory systems and inhibitory systems were equally retarded in their development. This does not appear to be the case with *in utero* alcohol exposure. Careful pilot work established that the strain of rats that we employed in the present study reach their peak activity at 16 days of age, the age examined here. Thus the enhanced activity observed in the alcohol treated offspring is an increase over and above that observed during normal ontogeny. This suggests that while more than one neurotransmitter system may be delayed in its development by *in utero* alcohol exposure, it is clearly the case that they are likely to be retarded to different degrees.

The pharmacological data indicate that the alcohol treated pups were different from the control pups at both 16 and 22 days of age. Administration of the anticholinergic, scopolamine, abolished the hyperactivity observed in 16-day-old alcohol treated offspring. While the mechanism of this effect is unclear, it has been taken as a sign of the immaturity of the cholinergic system (Smith *et al.*, 1979, 1982). At 22 days of age control animals displayed dose-related increases in activity following administration of scopolamine. In contrast, the high levels of activity in the alcohol treated animals were unaffected at this age. All groups displayed the "adult" pattern of increased activity following administration of scopolamine at 28 days of age. The effects of the anticholinesterase, physostigmine, mirrored those of scopolamine. No group was affected at 16 days of age. At 22 days of age, the control groups showed dose-related decreases in activity while the alcohol treated animals were unaffected at any dose. At 28 days all three groups showed decreases in activity. These data indicate that, in part, the hyperactivity observed in alcohol treated offspring is due to a delay in the development of a cholinergic inhibitory system.

At this point it would be appropriate to examine the data on steady-state levels, metabolism and release of acetylcholine, and the enzymic systems involved in its synthesis and hydrolysis. However, there is a complete paucity of data relating to the effects of prenatal alcohol exposure on any aspect of acetylcholine, despite the fact that chronic alcohol exposure has a profound influence on steady-state levels in adults (Feldstein, 1971). Undoubtedly, this state of affairs will change and such data will be invaluable. The pharmacological data reported here appear clear-cut, but it must be remembered that drugs are rarely specific in their effects and may affect other systems in addition to their primary targets (Hingtgen and Aprison, 1976). For example, we have yet to examine the effects of the quaternary compounds to determine that the changes in activity we have observed, following administration of scopolamine and physostigmine, are due to central rather than peripheral action. Further, it must be recognized that the approach taken in the present studies is somewhat simplistic. It is clearly the case that a number of neurotransmitter systems are involved in the control of activity. In addition to the putative cholinergic system examined here, we have already mentioned the possible roles played by dopamine, norepinephrine, γ-aminobutyric acid (GABA) and serotonin, and there are others. It is also the case that some systems may play a secondary role, influencing activity by modulating the functioning of a primary system. Finally, it should be remembered that, while I have discussed "a cholinergic inhibitory" system, there are clearly several cholinergic systems, developing at different rates and controlling different aspects of behaviour. For example, in the medulla, acetylcholine receptors reach near-adult levels by 10 days of age (in the rat). In contrast, striatal levels increase from about eight days of age to adulthood (Coyle and Yamamura, 1976). Similarly, the effects of scopolamine are not only dependent upon the animal's age (as illustrated here), but also upon the particular behaviour being investigated (Bauer, 1982). Thus, Bauer observed that while scopolamine increased locomotor activity at 21 days of age, it did not increase rearing until 35 days. The cholinergic system has also been implicated in memorial processing and this system appears to develop even more slowly, attaining adult levels at around 90 days of age (see Chapter 10). While this plethora of systems may appear to complicate things, they also make the present findings all the more intriguing. If prenatal alcohol exposure affects the development of various cholinergic systems, as it appears to affect the putative inhibitory system examined here, this suggests a mechanism that may underlie the mental retardation and learning difficulties observed in affected human children.

IX. CONCLUSIONS

This chapter has concerned itself with one concomitant of fetal alcohol exposure, hyperactivity. The empirical studies have demonstrated that this hyperactivity is not a byproduct of an alteration in the rat pup's sensitivity to its environment. The activity of alcohol treated pups was affected by home-cage shavings and environmental temperature in a fashion similar to that observed in control pups. As suggested previously, the increased activity is age-dependent, disappearing at 28 days of age in the present study. Of most importance is the finding that, in part, this increased activity is due to a delay in the functional development of a cholinergic inhibitory system. These findings support the views of a number of different groups (Abel, 1981; Bond, 1981a; Riley et al., 1979). The utility of the pharmacological approach employed here is that it suggests a number of fruitful avenues of research dealing with the way a variety of different neurotransmitter systems may be implicated in the hyperactivity associated with in utero alcohol exposure. For example, we are currently examining the roles played by dopamine and norepinephrine in the enhanced activity observed at 16 and 22 days of age in alcohol treated offspring. Further, such investigations need not be restricted to activity. Pharmacological investigations of the development of learning and memory processes have been successfully performed in the area of malnutrition (Nagy, 1979).

In the present chapter, I have taken it for granted that the hyperactivity observed in infrahuman animals following *in utero* alcohol exposure is at least analogous to that observed in human children so affected. However, as noted in Chapter 1, such an hypothesis deserves to be tested empirically. The investigations reported here suggest that prenatal alcohol exposure may lead to a delay in the development of a cholinergic inhibitory system. To establish that this is at least one mechanism underlying the hyperactivity seen in children, we need to investigate this hypothesis in humans. At present such work can only be pursued with great difficulty. Invasive techniques are clearly inappropriate, and yet the hypotheses derived from the animal work described here are very specific. We are not suggesting (at least until we find otherwise) that the effects of alcohol upon cholinergic neurotransmission are ubiquitous. We are suggesting that they may well be restricted to a delay in the development of such a system in the hippocampus. The problem is how to measure this development with any specificity when acetylcholine is so ubiquitous (for example, acetylcholine is the neurotransmitter found at the neuromuscular junction). As a result, there would have to be massive differences between alcohol treated children and control children to enable one to detect differences in the levels of neurotransmitter functioning, even under normal circumstances. One way of overcoming this is to subject the child to a pharmacological intervention similar to those described here. For example, Shekim *et al.* (1982) have demonstrated that differences between hyperactive and normal children in urinary levels of 3-methoxy-4-hydroxyphenylglycol (MHPG) and homovanillic acid (HVA), indicators of dopaminergic activity, only appeared when the two groups were challenged with *d*-amphetamine, an effective treatment for many hyperactive children.

Assuming that we find a delay in the development of the cholinergic neurotransmitter systems in children exposed to alcohol *in utero*, we are still left with two important questions to answer. First, we need to know in what way the ontogeny of the neurotransmitter systems is altered to bring about the delay in development. Goldberg and Silbergeld (1977) indicate some of the possible mechanisms underlying hyperactivity, which are appropriate here. Suffice it to say that their outline indicates that the search for the mechanism will be no easy task. At the same time we shall need to address a second, related question, and that concerns the factors associated with alcohol abuse that lead to the altered ontogeny and consequently the developmental delay; for example, is it alcohol or acetaldehyde that is the culprit? An excellent summary of the evidence bearing on this question can be found in Pratt (1980).

If the previous paragraph seems to pose some complicated questions, we should remember the benefits to be gained from research such as that reported here. It not only tells us something that may be of great benefit in increasing our understanding of a pressing human problem; in doing so it enhances our understanding of normal development. We cannot ask much more from an animal model.

ACKNOWLEDGEMENTS

The work described in this chapter was supported by Grant No. 401019 from the National Health and Medical Research Council and a Macquarie University Research Grant. Thanks are due to Ron Claasens and Wayne McTegg for their valuable technical assistance, and David Overstreet, Roger Russell and Len Storlein for their comments upon earlier versions of this chapter.

REFERENCES

Abel, E.L. Effects of ethanol exposure during different gestation periods on maternal weight gain and intrauterine growth retardation in the rat. *Neurobehavioral Toxicology*, 1979a, 1: 145-151.

Abel, E.L. Prenatal effects of alcohol on adult learning in rats. *Pharmacology, Biochemistry and Behavior*, 1979b, 10: 239-243.

Abel, E.L. Fetal alcohol syndrome: Behavioral teratogenesis. *Psychological Bulletin*, 1980, 87: 29-50.

Abel, E.L. Behavioral teratology of alcohol. *Psychological Bulletin*, 1981, 90: 564-581.

Abel, E.L. Characteristics of mothers of fetal alcohol syndrome children. *Neurobehavioral Toxicology and Teratology*, 1982a, 4: 3-4.

Abel, E.L. *In utero* alcohol exposure and developmental delay of response inhibition. *Alcoholism: Clinical and Experimental Research*, 1982b, 6: 369-376.

Abel, E.L. and Greizerstein, H.B. Ethanol-induced prenatal growth deficiency: Changes in fetal body composition. *Journal of Pharmacology and Experimental Therapeutics*, 1979, 211: 668-671.

Abel, E.L., Jacobson, S. and Sherwin, B.T. *In utero* alcohol exposure: Functional and structural brain damage. *Neurobehavioural Toxicology and Teratology*, 1983, 5: 363-366.

Adams, P.M. The effects of cholinolytic drugs and cholinesterase blockade on deprivation-based activity and appetitive behavior. *Neuropharmacology*, 1973, 12: 825-833.

Alpert, J.J., Day, N., Dooling, E., Hingson, R., Oppenheimer, E., Rosett, H.L., Weiner, L. and Zuckerman, B. Maternal alcohol consumption and newborn assessment: Methodology of the Boston City Hospital prospective study. *Neurobehavioral Toxicology and Teratology*, 1981, 3: 195-201.

Altman, J., Brunner, R.L. and Bayer, S.A. The hippocampus and behavioral maturation. *Behavioral Biology*, 1973, 8: 557-596.

Altshuler, H.L. and Shippenberg, T.S. A subhuman primate model for fetal alcohol syndrome research. *Neurobehavioral Toxicology and Teratology*, 1981, 3: 121-126.

Anandam, N., Felegi, W. and Stern, J.M. *In utero* alcohol heightens juvenile reactivity. *Pharmacology, Biochemistry and Behavior*, 1980, 13: 531-535.

Anandam, N. and Stern, J.M. Alcohol *in utero*: Effects on preweanling appetitive learning. *Neurobehavioral Toxicology*, 1980, 2: 199-205.

Barnes, D.E. and Walker, D.W. Prenatal ethanol exposure permanently reduces the number of pyramidal neurons in rat hippocampus. *Developmental Brain Research*, 1981, 1: 3-24.

Barrett, J. and Livesey, P.J. The acetic acid component of lead acetate: Its effect on rat weight and activity. *Neurobehavioral Toxicology and Teratology*, 1982, 4: 105-108.

Bauer, R.H. Age-dependent effects of scopolamine on avoidance, locomotor activity, and rearing. *Behavioral Brain Research*, 1982, 5: 261-279.

Bliss, T.V.P., Chung, S.-H. and Stirling, R.V. Structural and functional development of the mossy fibre system in the hippocampus of the postnatal rat. *Journal of Physiology*, 1974, 239: 92-93.

Blozovski, D. and Blozovski, M. Effets de l'atropine sur l'exploration l'apprentissage et l'activite electrocorticale chez le rat au cours du developpement. *Psychopharmacologia*, 1973, 33: 39-52.

Boggan, W.D., Randall, C.L. and Dodds, H.M. Delayed sexual maturation in female C57BL/6J mice prenatally exposed to alcohol. *Research Communications in Chemical Pathology and Pharmacology*, 1979, 23: 117-125.

Bohman, M., Sigvardsson, S. and Cloninger, C.R. Maternal inheritance of alcohol abuse. *Archives of General Psychiatry*, 1981, 38: 965-969.

Bond, N.W. Prenatal alcohol exposure in rodents: A review of its effects on offspring activity and learning ability. *Australian Journal of Psychology*, 1981a, 33: 331-344.

Bond, N.W. Effects of prenatal ethanol exposure on avoidance conditioning in high- and low-avoider rat strains. *Psychopharmacology*, 1981b, 74: 77-81.

Bond, N.W. Prenatal exposure to ethanol: Association between increased gestational length and offspring mortality. *Neurobehavioral Toxicology and Teratology*, 1982, 4: 501-503.

Bond, N.W. and DiGiusto, E.L. Effects of prenatal alcohol consumption on open-field behaviour and alcohol preference in rats. *Psychopharmacology*, 1976, 46: 163-165.

Bond, N.W. and DiGiusto, E.L. Effects of prenatal alcohol consumption on shock avoidance learning in rats. *Psychological Reports*, 1977, 41: 1269-1270.

Bond, N.W. and DiGiusto, E.L. Avoidance conditioning and Hebb-Williams maze performance in rats treated prenatally with alcohol. *Psychopharmacology*, 1978, 58: 69-71.

Bronstein, P.M., Marcus, M. and Hirsch, S.M. The ontogeny of locomotion in rats: The influence of ambient temperature. *Bulletin of the Psychonomic Society*, 1978, 12: 39-42.

Buell, S.J., Fosmire, G.J., Ollerich, D.A. and Sandstead, H.H. Effects of postnatal zinc deficiency on cerebellar and hippocampal development in the rat. *Experimental Neurology*, 1977, 55: 199-210.

Campbell, B.A., Lytle, L.D. and Fibiger, H.C. Ontogeny of adrenergic arousal and cholinergic inhibitory mechanisms in the rat. *Science*, 1969, 166: 637-638.

Campbell, B.A. and Mabry, P.D. Ontogeny of behavioral arousal: A comparative study. *Journal of Comparative and Physiological Psychology*, 1972, 81: 371-379.

Campbell, B.A. and Mabry, P.D. The role of catecholamines in behavioral arousal during ontogenesis. *Psychopharmacologia*, 1973, 31: 253-264.

Campbell, B.A. and Raskin, L.A. Ontogeny of behavioral arousal: The role of environmental stimuli. *Journal of Comparative and Physiological Psychology*, 1978, 92: 176-184.

Cantwell, D.P. Psychiatric illness in the families of hyperactive children. *Archives of General Psychiatry*, 1972, 27: 414-417.

Caul, W.F., Osborne, G.L., Fernandez, K. and Henderson, G.I. Open-field and avoidance performance as a function of prenatal ethanol treatment. *Addictive Behaviors*, 1979, 4: 311-322.

Chen, J.J. and Smith, E.R. Effect of perinatal alcohol on sexual differentiation and open-field behavior in rats. *Hormones and Behavior*, 1979, 13: 219-231.

Chernoff, G.F. The fetal alcohol syndrome in mice: An animal model. *Teratology*, 1977, 15: 223-230.

Cooper, J.R., Bloom, F.E. and Roth, R.H. *The Biochemical Basis of Pharmacology*. New York: Oxford University Press, 1978.

Coyle, I., Wayner, M.J. and Singer, G. Behavioral teratogenesis: A critical evaluation. *Pharmacology, Biochemistry and Behavior*, 1976, 4: 191-200.

Coyle, J.T. and Yamamura, H.I. Neurochemical aspects of the ontogenesis of cholinergic neurons in the rat brain. *Brain Research*, 1976, 118: 429–440.

Crawford, I.L. and O'Connor, J.D. Zinc in maturing rat brain: Hippocampal concentration and localization. *Journal of Neurochemistry*, 1972, 19: 1451–1458.

Da Silva, V.A., Ribeiro, M.J. and Masur, J. Developmental, behavioral, and pharmacological characteristics of rat offspring from mothers receiving ethanol during gestation and lactation. *Developmental Psychobiology*, 1980, 13: 653–660.

Davis, P.J., Partridge, J.W. and Storrs, C.N. Alcohol consumption in pregnancy: How much is safe? *Archives of Diseased Children*, 1982, 57: 940–943.

Dehaene, P.H., Smaille-Villette, C.H., Smaille, P.-P., Crepin, G., Walbaum, R., Deroubzis, P. and Blanc-Garin, A.P. Le syndrome d'alcoholisme foetal dans le nord de la France. *Nouvelle Presse Medicale*, 1977, 23: 145–158.

Demers, M. and Kirouac, G. Prenatal effects of ethanol on the behavioral development of the rat. *Physiological Psychology*, 1978, 6: 517–520.

Dews, P. *Federation Proceedings*, 1958, 17: 1024–1030.

Diaz, J. and Samson, H.H. Impaired brain growth in neonatal rats exposed to ethanol. *Science*, 1980, 208: 751–753.

Driscoll, C.D., Chen, J.-S. and Riley, E.P. Operant DRL performance in rats following prenatal alcohol exposure. *Neurobehavioral Toxicology*, 1980, 2: 207–211.

Druse, M.J. and Hofteig, J.H. The effect of chronic maternal alcohol consumption on the development of central nervous system myelin subfractions in rat offspring. *Drug and Alcohol Dependence*, 1977, 2: 421–429.

Ellis, F.W. and Pick, J.R. An animal model of the fetal alcohol syndrome in beagles. *Alcoholism: Clinical and Experimental Research*, 1980, 4: 123–134.

Feldstein, A. Effect of ethanol on neurohumoral amine metabolism. In B. Kissin and H. Begleiter (Eds.), *The Biology of Alcoholism, Vol. 1: Biochemistry*. New York: Plenum, 1971: 127–159.

Fernandez, K., Caul, W.F., Haenlein, M. and Vorhees, C.V. Effects of prenatal alcohol on homing behavior, maternal responding and open-field activity in rats. *Neurobehavioral Toxicology and Teratology*, 1983, 5: 351–356.

Fernandez, K., Caul, W.F., Osborne, G.L. and Henderson, G.I. Effects of chronic alcohol exposure on offspring activity in rats. *Neurobehavioral Toxicology and Teratology*, 1983, 5: 135–137.

Fianu, S. and Joelsson, I. Minimal brain dysfunction in children born in breech position. *Acta Obstetricia et Gynecologica Scandinavica*, 1979, 58: 295–299.

Fibiger, H.C., Lytle, L.D. and Campbell, B.A. Cholinergic modulation of adrenergic arousal in the developing rat. *Journal of Comparative and Physiological Psychology*, 1970, 72: 384–389.

Finnegan, L.P. The effects of narcotics and alcohol on pregnancy and the newborn. *Annals of the New York Academy of Sciences*, 1981, 362: 136–157.

Fish, B.S., Rank, S.A., Wilson, J.R. and Collins, A.C. Viability and sensorimotor development of mice exposed to prenatal short-term ethanol. *Pharmacology, Biochemistry and Behavior*, 1981, 14: 57–65.

Frances, H. and Jacob, J. Comparison of the effect of cholinergic and anticholinergic substances on the cerebral content of acetylcholine and the motility of mice. *Psychopharmacologia*, 1971, 21: 338–352.

Gallo, P.V. and Weinberg, J.E. Neuromotor development and response inhibition following prenatal ethanol exposure. *Neurobehavioral Toxicology and Teratology*, 1982, 4: 505–513.

Gesell, A. and Ilg, F. *Infant and Child in the Culture of Today*. New York: Harper and Row, 1943.

Ghishan, F.K., Patwardhan, R. and Greene, H.L. Fetal alcohol syndrome: Inhibition of zinc transport as a potential mechanism for fetal growth retardation in the rat. *Journal of Laboratory and Clinical Medicine*, 1982, 100: 45–52.

Goldberg, A.M. and Silbergeld, E.K. Animal models of hyperactivity. In I. Hanin and E.

Usdin (Eds.), *Animal Models in Psychiatry and Neurology.* New York: Pergamon, 1977.

Goodwin, D.W., Schulsinger, F., Hermansen, L., Gaze, S.R. and Winokur, G. Alcoholism and the hyperactive child syndrome. *Journal of Nervous and Mental Disorders*, 1975, 160: 349-353.

Gottlieb, G. *Early Influences.* New York: Academic Press, 1978.

Hammer, J.P., Jr, and Scheibel, A.B. Morphologic evidence for a delay of neuronal maturation in fetal alcohol exposure. *Experimental Neurology*, 1981, 74: 587-596.

Hanson, J.W., Jones, K.L. and Smith, D.W. Fetal alcohol syndrome: Experience with 41 patients. *Journal of the American Medical Association*, 1976, 235: 1458-1460.

Harris, L.S. A pharmacological demonstration of cholinergic mechanisms in the central nervous system. *Biochemical Pharmacology*, 1961, 8: 92.

Henderson, G.I. and Schenker, S. The effects of maternal alcohol consumption on the viability and visceral development of the newborn rat. *Research Communications in Chemical Pathology and Pharmacology*, 1977, 16: 365-367.

Himwich, W.A., Hall, J.S. and MacArthur, W.F. Maternal alcohol and neonatal health. *Biological Psychiatry*, 1977, 12: 495-505.

Hingtgen, J.N. and Aprison, M.H. Behavioral and environmental aspects of the cholinergic system. In A.M. Goldberg and I. Hanin (Eds.), *Biology of Cholinergic Function.* New York: Raven Press, 1976: 515-566.

Ho, B.T., Fritchie, G.E. Idanpaan-Heikkila, J.E. and McIsaac, W.M. Placental transfer of 14-C ethanol. *American Journal of Obstetrics and Gynecology*, 1971, 110: 426-428.

Holmes, R.S. and Masters, C.J. Genetic control and ontogeny of microbody enzymes: A review. *Biochemical Genetics*, 1978, 16: 171-190.

Iosub, S., Fuchs, M., Bingol, N. and Gromisch, D.S. Fetal alcohol syndrome revisited. *Pediatrics*, 1981, 68: 475-479.

Jacobson, S., Sehgal, P., Bronson, R., Door, B. and Burnap, J. Comparisons between an oral and an intravenous method to demonstrate the *in utero* effects of ethanol in the monkey. *Neurobehavioral Toxicology*, 1980, 2: 253-258.

Jenden, D.J. An overview of choline and acetylcholine metabolism in relation to the therapeutic uses of choline. In A. Barbeau, J.H. Growdon and R.J. Wurtman (Eds.), *Nutrition and the Brain.* New York: Raven Press, 1979: 13-24.

Jenden, D.J. Regulation of acetylcholine synthesis and release. In R.W. Yamamura, E. Olsen and E. Usdin (Eds.), *Psychopharmacology and Biochemistry of Neurotransmitter Receptors.* New York: Elsevier, 1980: 3-15.

Joffe, J.M. *Prenatal Determinants of Behaviour.* Oxford: Pergamon, 1969.

Jones, K.L.,Smith, D.W., Ulleland, C.N. and Streissguth, A.P. Pattern of malformation in offspring of chronic alcoholic mothers. *Lancet*, 1973, 1: 1267-1271.

Krsiak, M., Elis, J., Poschlova, N. and Masek, K. Increased aggressiveness and lower brain serotonin levels in offspring of mice given alcohol during gestation. *Journal of Studies on Alcohol*, 1977, 38: 1696-1704.

Kuzma, J.W. and Kissinger, D.G. Patterns of alcohol and cigarette use in pregnancy. *Neurobehavioral Toxicology and Teratology*, 1981, 3: 211-221.

Landesman-Dwyer, S., Ragozin, A.S. and Little, R.E. Behavioral correlates of prenatal alcohol exposure: A four-year follow-up study. *Neurobehavioral Toxicology and Teratology*, 1981, 3: 187-193.

Lau, C., Thadani, P.V., Schanberg, S.M. and Slotkin, T.A. Effects of maternal ethanol ingestion on development of adrenal catecholamines and dopamine B-hydroxylase in the offspring. *Neuropharmacology*, 1976, 15: 505-507.

Lee, M.H., Haddad, R. and Rabe, A. Developmental impairments in the progeny of rats consuming ethanol during pregnancy. *Neurobehavioral Toxicology*, 1980, 2: 189-198.

Lemoine, P., Harousseau, H., Borteryu, J.-P. and Meneut, J.-C. Les enfants de parents alcooliques: Anomalies observées a propos de 127 cas. *Quest Medicale*, 1968, 21: 476-482.

Leon, M. Maternal pheromone. *Physiology and Behavior*, 1974, 13: 441-453.

Leon, M. Mother–young reunions. In J.M. Sprague and A.M. Epstein (Eds.), *Progress in*

Psychobiology and Physiological Psychology, Vol. 8. New York: Academic Press, 1979: 301–334.

Linakis, J.G. and Cunningham, C.L. The effects of embryonic exposure to alcohol on learning and inhibition in chicks. *Neurobehavioral Toxicology*, 1980, 2: 243–251.

Lochry, E.A. and Riley, E.P. Retention of passive avoidance and T-maze escape in rats exposed to alcohol prenatally. *Neurobehavioral Toxicology*, 1980, 2: 107–115.

Lochry, E.A., Shapiro, N.R. and Riley E.P. Growth deficits in rats exposed to alcohol *in utero*. *Journal of Studies on Alcohol*, 1980, 41: 1031–1039.

Lucot, J.B. and Seiden, L.S. Effects of neonatal administration of 5,7-dihydroxytryptamine on locomotor activity. *Psychopharmacology*, 1982, 77: 114–116.

Mabry, P.D. and Campbell, B.A. Ontogeny of serotonergic inhibition of catecholamine-induced behavioral arousal. *Journal of Comparative and Physiological Psychology*, 1974, 86: 193–201.

Mabry, P.D. and Campbell, B.A. Developmental psychopharmacology. In L.L. Iversen, S.D. Iversen and S.H. Snyder (Eds.), *Handbook of Psychopharmacology: Principles of Behavioral Pharmacology*, Vol. 7. New York: Plenum Press, 1977: 393–444.

Majewski, F. Alcohol embryopathy: Some facts and speculations about pathogenesis. *Neurobehavioral Toxicology and Teratology*, 1981, 3: 129–144.

Majewski, F.J., Beirich, H., Loser, H., Michaelis, R., Leiber, B. and Bettecken, F. Zür Klinik und Pathogenses der Alkoholembryopathie (Bericht uber 68 Patienten). *Münchener Medizinische Wochenschrift*, 1976, 118: 1635–1642.

Manzke, H. Morbidity among infants born in breech position. *Journal of Perinatal Medicine*, 1978, 6: 127–140.

Martin, J.C., Martin, D.C., Lund, C.A. and Streissguth, A.P. Maternal alcohol ingestion and cigarette smoking and their effects on newborn conditioning. *Alcoholism: Clinical and Experimental Research*, 1977, 1: 243–247.

Martin, J.C., Martin, D.C, Sigman, G. and Radow, B. Offspring survival, development, and operant performance following maternal ethanol consumption. *Developmental Psychobiology*, 1977, 10: 435–446.

Means, L.W., Adams, J.M. and Gray, S.L. The effects of fetal ethanol exposure on adult discrimination reversal in rats. *IRCS Medical Science*, 1981, 9: 1092.

Meyers, B. and Domino, E.F. The effect of cholinergic blocking drugs on spontaneous alternation in rats. *Archives Internationale de Pharmacodynamie et de Therapie*, 1964, 150: 525–529.

Michaelson, I.A., Bornschtein, R.L., Loch, R.K. and Rafales, L.S. Minimal brain dysfunction hyperkinesis: Significance of nutritional status in animal models of hyperactivity. In I. Hanin and E. Usdin (Eds.), *Animal Models in Psychiatry and Neurology*. New York: Pergamon, 1977.

Monjan, A.A. and Mandell, W. Fetal alcohol immunity: Depression of mitogen-induced lymphocyte blastogenesis. *Neurobehavioural Toxicology*, 1980, 2: 213–216.

Morrison, J.R. and Stewart, M.A. A family study of the hyperactive child syndrome. *Biological Psychiatry*, 1971, 3: 189–195.

Morrison, J.R. and Stewart, M.A. The psychiatric status of the legal families of adopted hyperactive children. *Archives of General Psychiatry*, 1973, 28: 888–891.

Murphy, J.M., Meeker, R.B., Porada, K.J. and Nagy, Z.M. GABA-mediated behavioral inhibition during ontogeny in the mouse. *Psychopharmacology*, 1979, 64: 237–242.

Murphy, J.M. and Nagy, Z.M. Emerging cholinergic mechanisms and ontogeny of response inhibition in the mouse. *Pharmacology, Biochemistry and Behavior*, 1976, 5: 449–456.

Nagy, Z.M. Effects of early undernutrition on brain and behavior of developing mice. In M.E. Hahn, C. Jensen and B.C. Dudek (Eds.), *Development and Evolution of Brain Size: Behavioral Implications*. New York: Academic Press, 1979: 321–345.

Nagy, Z.M., Murphy, J.M. and Ray, D. Development of behavioral arousal and inhibition in the Swiss-Webster mouse. *Bulletin of the Psychonomic Society*, 1975, 7: 185–192.

Neurobehavioral Toxicology and Teratology, 1981, 3, Whole of Number 2.

Olson, R.E. Nutrition and alcoholism. in R.S. Goodhart and M.E. Shils (Eds.), *Modern

Nutrition in Health and Medicine. Philadelphia: Lea and Fibiger, 1973: 143–166.

Ouellette, E.M. and Rosett, H.L. A pilot prospective study of the fetal alcohol syndrome at the Boston City Hospital. Part II: The infants. *Annals of the New York Academy of Sciences,* 1976, 273: 123–129.

Phillips, D.S. and Stainbrook, G.L. Effects of early alcohol exposure on adult learning ability and taste preferences. *Physiological Psychology,* 1976, 4: 473–475.

Potter, B. Teratogenic studies in sheep. Paper presented at "The effect of alcohol on mammalian development" seminar. Royal Alexandra Hospital for Children, Sydney, 1980.

Pratt, O.E. The fetal alcohol syndrome: Transport of nutrients and transfer of alcohol and acetaldehyde from mother to fetus. In M. Sandler (Ed.), *Psychopharmacology of Alcohol.* New York: Raven Press, 1980: 229–256.

Randall, C.L., Taylor, W.J. and Walker, D.W. Ethanol-induced malformations in mice. *Alcoholism: Clinical and Experimental Research,* 1977, 1: 219–224.

Randall, P.K. and Campbell, B.A. Ontogeny of behavioral arousal in rats: Effects of maternal and sibling presence. *Journal of Comparative and Physiological Psychology,* 1976, 90: 453–459.

Rapoport, J.L. and Ferguson, H.B. Biological validation of the hyperkinetic syndrome. *Developmental Medicine and Child Neurology,* 1981, 23: 667–682.

Rawat, A.K. Ribosomal protein synthesis in the fetal and neonatal rat brain as influenced by maternal ethanol consumption. *Research Communications in Chemical Pathology and Pharmacology,* 1975, 12: 723–732.

Rawat, A.K. Effect of maternal ethanol consumption on foetal and neonatal hepatic protein synthesis. *Biochemistry Journal,* 1976, 160: 653–661.

Rawat, A.K. Derangement in cardiac protein metabolism in fetal alcohol syndrome. *Research Communications in Chemical Pathology and Pharmacology,* 1979, 25: 365–375.

Rawat, A.K. and Kumar, S. Effects of maternal ethanol consumption on the metabolism of dopamine in rat fetus and neonates. *Research Communications in Psychology, Psychiatry and Behavior,* 1977, 2: 117–129.

Riley, E.P., Lochry, E.A. and Shapiro, N.R. Lack of response inhibition in rats prenatally exposed to alcohol. *Psychopharmacology,* 1979, 62: 47–52.

Riley, E.P., Lochry, E.A., Shapiro, N.R. and Baldwin, J. Response perseveration in rats exposed to alcohol prenatally. *Pharmacology, Biochemistry and Behavior,* 1979, 10: 255–259.

Riley, E.P., Lochry, E.A., Shapiro, N.R. and Broida, J.P. Fixed-ratio performance and subsequent extinction in rats prenatally exposed to ethanol. *Physiological Psychology,* 1979, 8: 47–50.

Riley, E.P., Plonsky, M. and Rosellini, R.A. Acquisition of an unsignalled avoidance task in rats exposed to alcohol prenatally. *Neurobehavioral Toxicology and Teratology,* 1982, 4: 525–530.

Riley, E.P., Shapiro, N.R. and Lochry, E.A. Nose-poking and head-dipping behaviors in rats prenatally exposed to alcohol. *Pharmacology, Biochemistry and Behavior,* 1979, 11: 513–519.

Russell, R.W. Cholinergic system in behavior: The search for mechanisms of action. *Annual Review of Pharmacology and Toxicology,* 1982, 22: 435–463.

Sander, L.W., Snyder, P.A., Rosett, H.L., Lee, A., Gould, J.B. and Ouellette, E.M. Effects of alcohol intake during pregnancy on newborn state regulation: A progress report. *Alcoholism: Clinical and Experimental Research,* 1977, 1: 233–241.

Sandor, S. The influence of aethyl-alcohol on the developing chick embryo: II. *Revue Roumaine d'Embryologie et de Cytologie,* 1968, 5: 167–171.

Shaywitz, B.A., Griffieth, G.G. and Warshaw, J.B. Hyperactivity and cognitive deficits in developing rat pups born to alcoholic mothers: An experimental model of the expanded fetal alcohol syndrom (EFAS). *Neurobehavioral Toxicology,* 1979: 1: 113–122.

Shaywitz, S.E., Cohen, D.J. and Shaywitz, B.A. Behavior and learning difficulties in children of normal intelligence born to alcoholic mothers. *Journal of Pediatrics,* 1980, 96: 978–982.

Shekim, W.O., Dekirmenjian, H., Javaid, J., Bylund, D.B. and Davis, J.B. Dopamine-norepinephrine interaction in hyperactive boys treated with d-amphetamine. *Journal of Pediatrics*, 1982, 100: 830–834.

Smith, G.J., Spear, L.P. and Spear, N.E. Ontogeny of cholinergic mediated behaviors in the rat. *Journal of Comparative and Physiological Psychology*, 1979, 93: 636–647.

Smith, G.J., Spear, L.P. and Spear, N.E. Detection of cholinergic mediation of behavior in 7-, 9-, and 12-day old rat pups. *Pharmacology, Biochemistry and Behavior*, 1982, 16: 805–809.

Snell, K. *Developmental Toxicology*. London: Croom Helm, 1982.

Sokol, R.J., Miller, S.I., Debanne, S., Golden, N., Collins, G., Kaplan, J. and Martier, S. The Cleveland NIAAA alcohol-in-pregnancy study: The first year. *Neurobehavioral Toxicology and Teratology*, 1981, 3: 203–209.

Sorette, M.P., Maggio, C.A., Starpoli, A., Boissevain, A. and Greenwood, M.R.C. Maternal ethanol intake affects rat organ development despite adequate nutrition. *Neurobehavioral Toxicology*, 1980, 2: 181–188.

Streissguth, A.P., Herman, C.S. and Smith, D.W. Intelligence, behavior and dysmorphogenesis in the fetal alcohol syndrome: A report on 20 patients. *Journal of Pediatrics*, 1978, 92: 363–367.

Streissguth, A.P., Landesman-Dwyer, S., Martin, J.C. and Smith, D.W. Teratogenic effects of alcohol in humans and animals. *Science*, 1980, 209: 353–361.

Streissguth, A.P., Martin, D.C., Martin, J.C. and Barr, H.M. The Seattle longitudinal prospective study on alcohol and pregnancy. *Neurobehavioral Toxicology and Teratology*, 1981, 3: 223–233.

Sullivan, W.C. A note on the influence of maternal inebriety on the offspring. *Journal of Mental Science*, 1899, 45: 489–503.

Tarter, R.E., McBride, H., Buonpane, N. and Schneider, D.U. Differentiation of alcoholics: Childhood history of minimal brain dysfunction, family history, and drinking pattern. *Archives of General Psychiatry*, 1977, 34: 761–768.

Teicher, M.H., Shaywitz, B.A., Kootz, H.L. and Cohen, D.J. Differential effects of maternal and sibling presence on hyperactivity of 6-hydroxydopamine-treated developing pups. *Journal of Comparative and Physiological Psychology*, 1981, 95: 134–145.

Tittmar, H.-G. Some effects of ethanol, presented during the prenatal period, on the development of rats. *British Journal of Alcohol and Alcoholism*, 1977, 12: 71–83.

Tumbleson, M.E., Dexter, J.D. and Middleton, C.C. Voluntary ethanol consumption by female offspring from alcoholic and control Sinclair (S-1) miniature dams. *Progress in Biochemical Pharmacology*, 1981, 18: 179–189.

Ulug, S. and Riley, E.P. The effect of methylphenidate on overactivity in rats prenatally exposed to alcohol. *Neurobehavioral Toxicology and Teratology*, 1983, 5: 35–39.

Vorhees, C.V. and Butcher, R.E. Behavioural teratogenicity. In K. Snell (Ed.), *Developmental Toxicology*. London: Croom Helm, 1982: 247–298.

Warner, R. and Rosett, H.L. The effects of drinking on offspring: An Historical survey of the American and British literature. *Journal of Studies on Alcohol*, 1975, 36: 1395–1420.

Webster, W.S., Walsh, D.A., Lipson, A.M. and McEwen, S.E. Teratogenesis after acute alcohol exposure in inbred and outbred mice. *Neurobehavioral Toxicology*, 1980, 2: 227–234.

Weiner, S.G., Shoemaker, W.J., Koda, L.Y. and Bloom, F.E. Interaction of ethanol and nutrition during gestation: Influence on maternal and offspring development in the rat. *Journal of Pharmacology and Experimental Therapeutics*, 1981, 216: 572–579.

Wender, P. *Minimal Brain Dysfunction in Children*. New York: Wiley, 1971.

West, J.R., Hodges, C.A. and Black, A.C., Jr. Prenatal exposure to ethanol alters the organization of hippocampal mossy fibers in rats. *Science*, 1981, 211: 957–959.

West, J.R. and Hodges-Savola, C.A. Permanent hippocampal mossy fiber hyperdevelopment following prenatal ethanol exposure. *Neurobehavioral Toxicology and Teratology*, 1983, 5: 139–150.

Wood, D., Wender, P.H. and Reimherr, F.W. The prevalence of attention deficit disorder, residual type, or minimal brain dysfunction, in a population of male alcoholic patients. *American Journal of Psychiatry*, 1983, 140: 95–98.

INDEX

Jungle fowl, 166, 183

Korsakoff's disease, 257, 259, 260, 263, 264, 266, 274

Language, 15
Lateral geniculate nucleus, 71
Lateral hypothalamus, 62, 162, 263, 194–199, 232, 243
Lead, 44, 45
Learning
  animal models of, 1
  deficits, 37, 38, 49, 198, 265, 271–273, 285, 286, 303
  process, 31, 38, 45, 219, 237, 259, 260, 262, 268, 290, 304
Limbic forebrain, 47
Limbic system, 101, 110–112, 131
Lithium, 11, 167
  carbonate, 11
  urate, 11
Liver, 280, 289
Luxuskonsumption, 148, 170

Mammillary bodies, 263
Mania, 11, 40, 101, 179, 229
Manic-depressive, 11, 41, 101, 179, 229
Maprotiline, 123
Mechanist model, 2, 5, 6, 8, 18
Medial forebrain bundle, 6
Melatonin, 221
Memory, 4, 31, 46, 257–262, 269–275, 303, 304
Mental retardation, 283–285
Mercury, 38, 44–46
Metabolic rate, 148–154, 158, 160, 161, 168–171, 184, 187, 188, 190, 195, 197, 280
Methadone, 216
Methylmercury, 38, 46
4-Methyl valeric acid, 84, 85, 92
α-Methyl-p-tyrosine, 293
MHPG, 199, 304
Mianserin, 100, 110, 119, 122, 124, 167
Mice, 38, 51, 60, 90, 135, 155, 157, 160, 164, 200, 264, 269, 272, 281, 288, 293
Miniature swine, 289
Mitral cell, 61–65, 71, 76, 83, 84
  degeneration patterns, 66–70, 72, 75–86, 88–95
  electrophysiology, 90–93
  identification of, 70

measurement, 74, 82, 85, 87
  recovery, 90
Monkey, 64
Monosodium glutamate, 164, 165
Myasthenia gravis, 40
Myocardial necrosis, 131, 136, 138, 140, 141

Naloxone, 217, 219
Neurobehavioural toxicology, 23–34, 38–53
Neurotoxins, 270, 271, 273, 274
Nicotine, 214, 221
Nomifensine, 110
Nonreinforcement, 38
Non-shivering thermogenesis, 148–150, 154, 158, 169, 170
Noradrenaline/norepinephrine, 6, 45, 100–102, 111–115, 118, 122–125, 131, 136, 137, 158, 168, 197, 202, 217, 293, 302, 303
Nucleus accumbens septum, 219–221, 223, 234

Obese (ob/ob) mouse, 151–154
Obesity, 130, 147–171
  diet-induced, 147, 148, 153, 155, 158–161, 192
  lesion-induced, 148, 151, 161
Obsessive-compulsive, 179, 254
Octopus, 184, 186
Odorant/odour, 59–66, 72, 78, 79, 81, 164
Odour exposure, 59, 60, 66, 69–77, 79, 81–95
Oestrus, 201
Olfactory
  adaptation, 90–93
  bulb, 61–69, 72, 74, 76, 79, 82, 84–94, 103, 110, 113, 115
  bulbectomy, 99, 101–123
  epithelium, 60–62, 65, 66, 76
  receptors, 69, 70, 76, 90, 93
Operant response, 38, 45, 213–215, 219, 234, 241, 246–252, 290
Org 6582, 114, 117–121
Organophosphate anticholinesterases, 39–41
Oxythiamine, 265

Pain, 43
Pancreas, 151, 163, 165
Parkinson's disease, 198
Penguin, 184
  Adelie, 183, 187–189
  Emperor, 183, 187

4 5 6 7 8 9 0 1 2 3
A B C D E F G H I J